Helck

4

Story and Art by
Nanaki Nanao

Contents

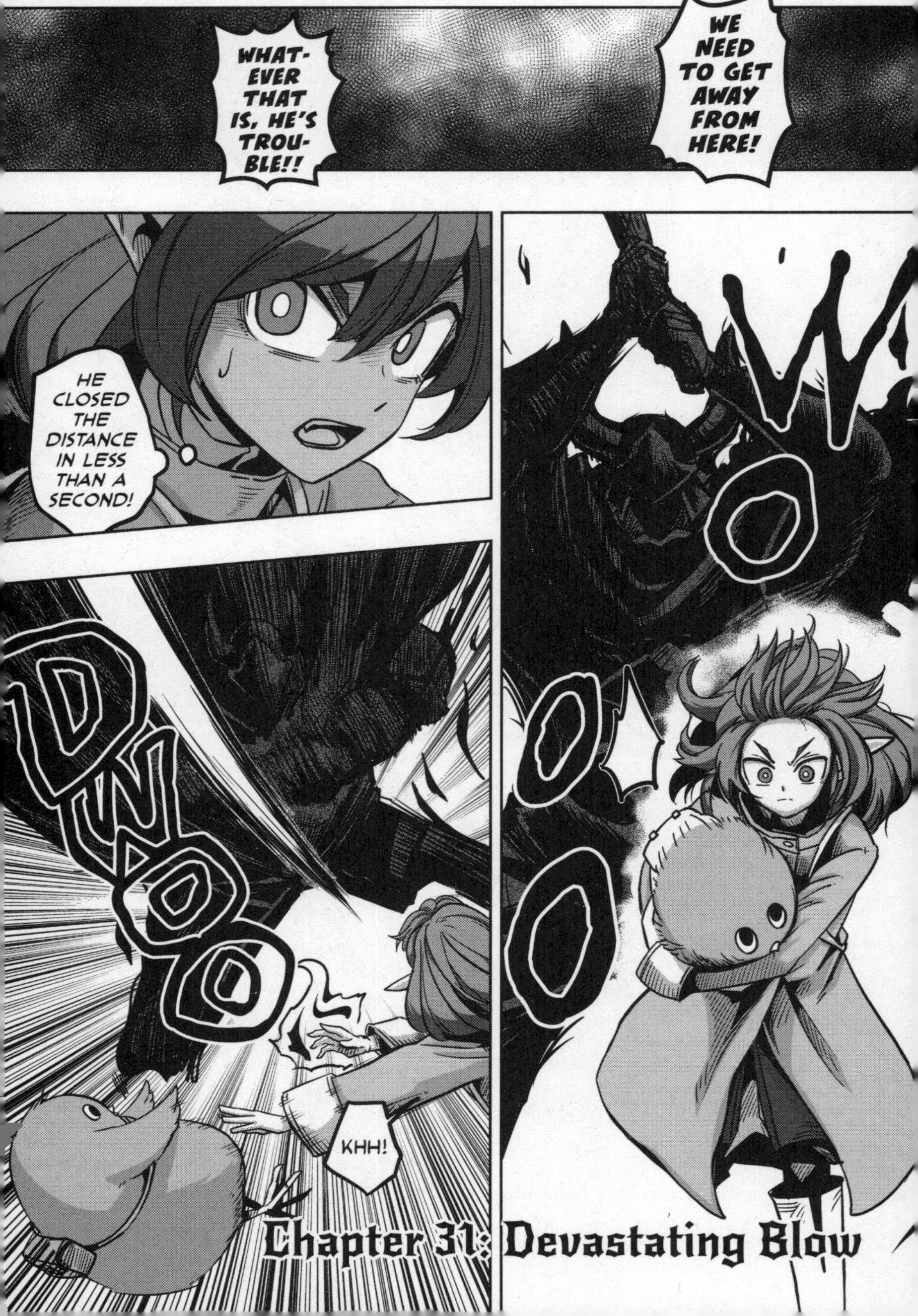
WE NEED TO GET AWAY FROM HERE!
WHAT-EVER THAT IS, HE'S TROUBLE!!
HE CLOSED THE DISTANCE IN LESS THAN A SECOND!
KHH!

Chapter 31: Devastating Blow

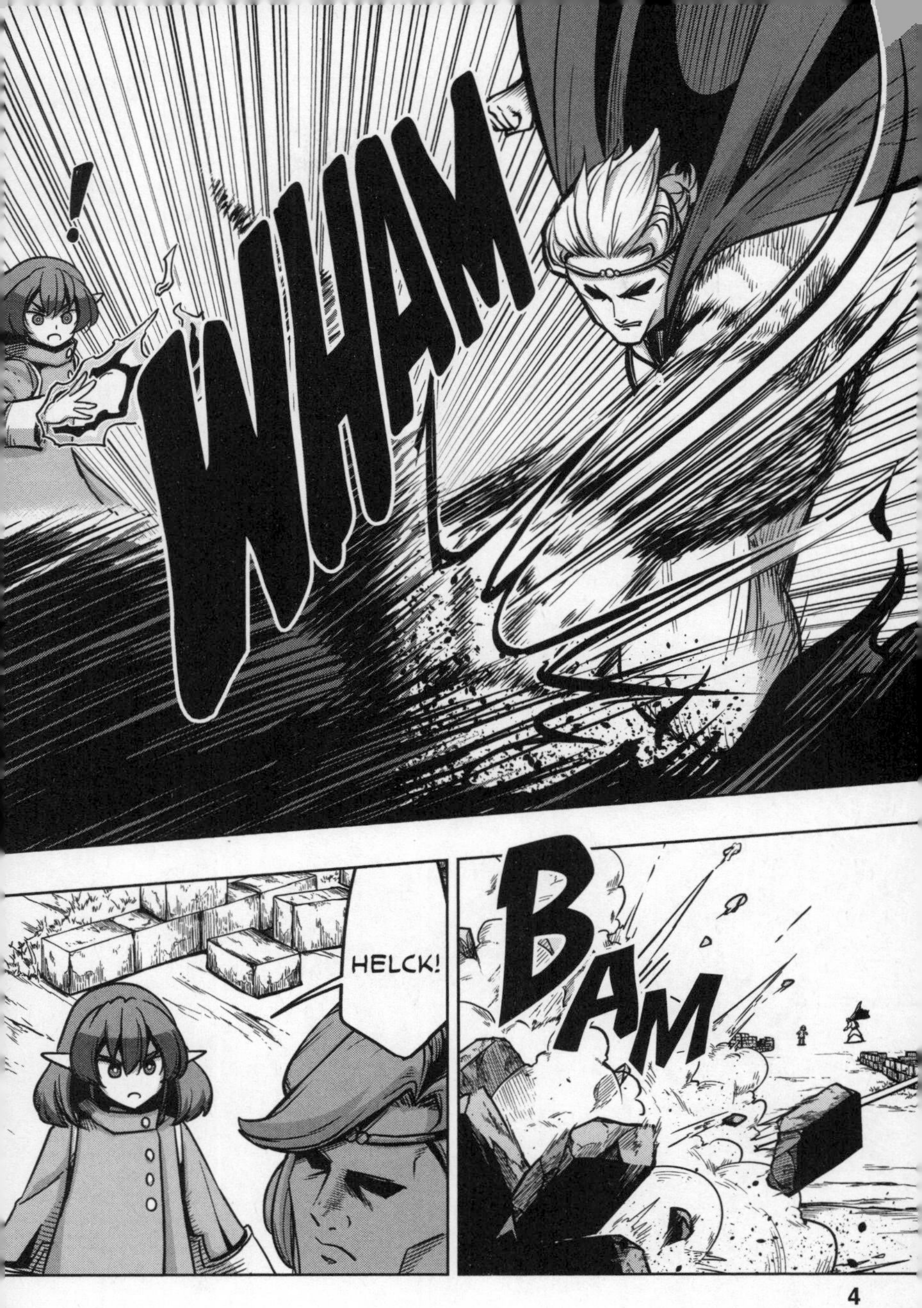
WHAM
!
BAM
HELCK!

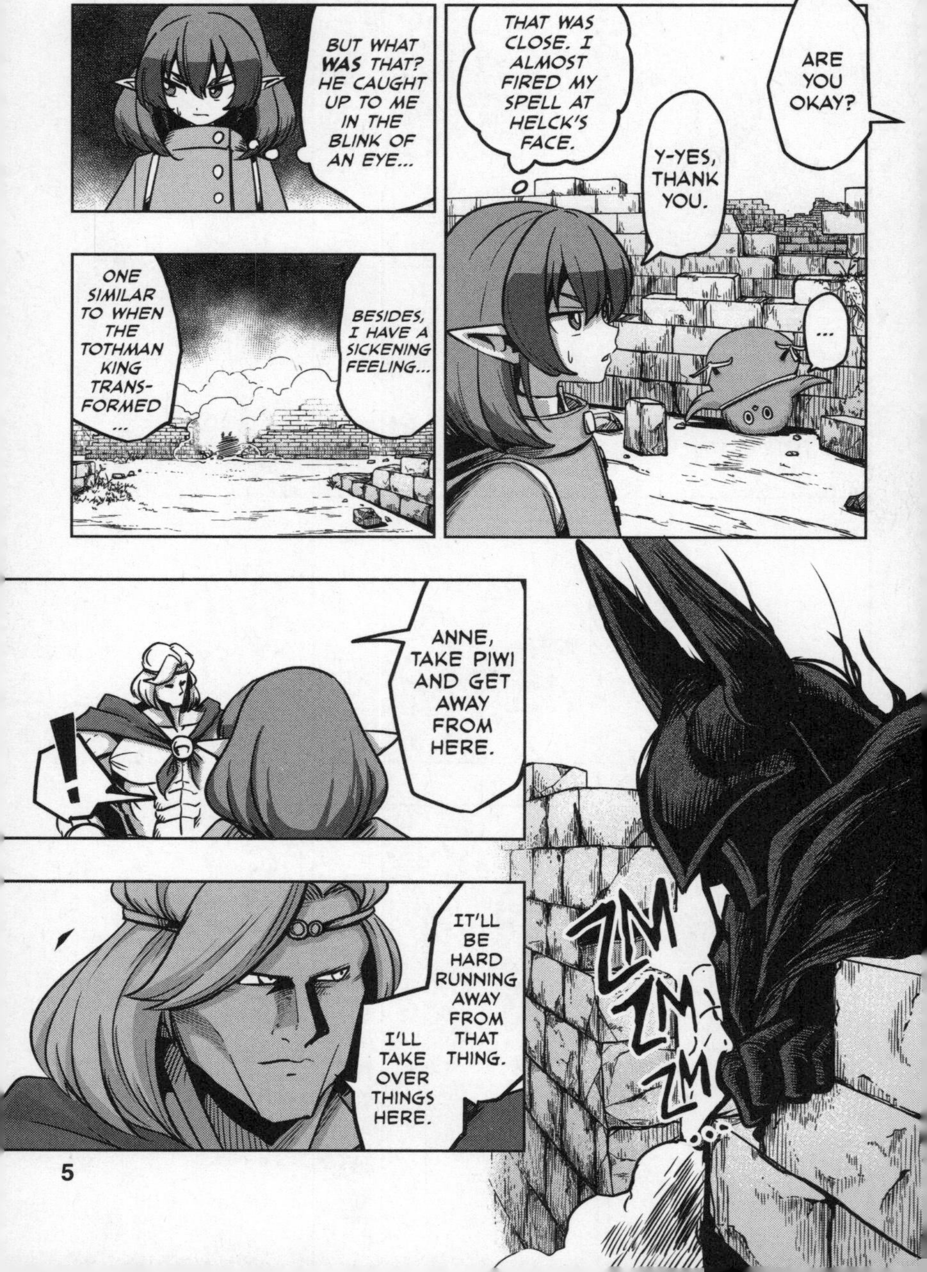
ARE YOU OKAY?
Y-YES, THANK YOU.
THAT WAS CLOSE. I ALMOST FIRED MY SPELL AT HELCK'S FACE.
...
BUT WHAT WAS THAT? HE CAUGHT UP TO ME IN THE BLINK OF AN EYE...
BESIDES, I HAVE A SICKENING FEELING...
ONE SIMILAR TO WHEN THE TOTHMAN KING TRANS-FORMED...
ZM ZM ZM ZM
ANNE, TAKE PIWI AND GET AWAY FROM HERE.
!
IT'LL BE HARD RUNNING AWAY FROM THAT THING.
I'LL TAKE OVER THINGS HERE.

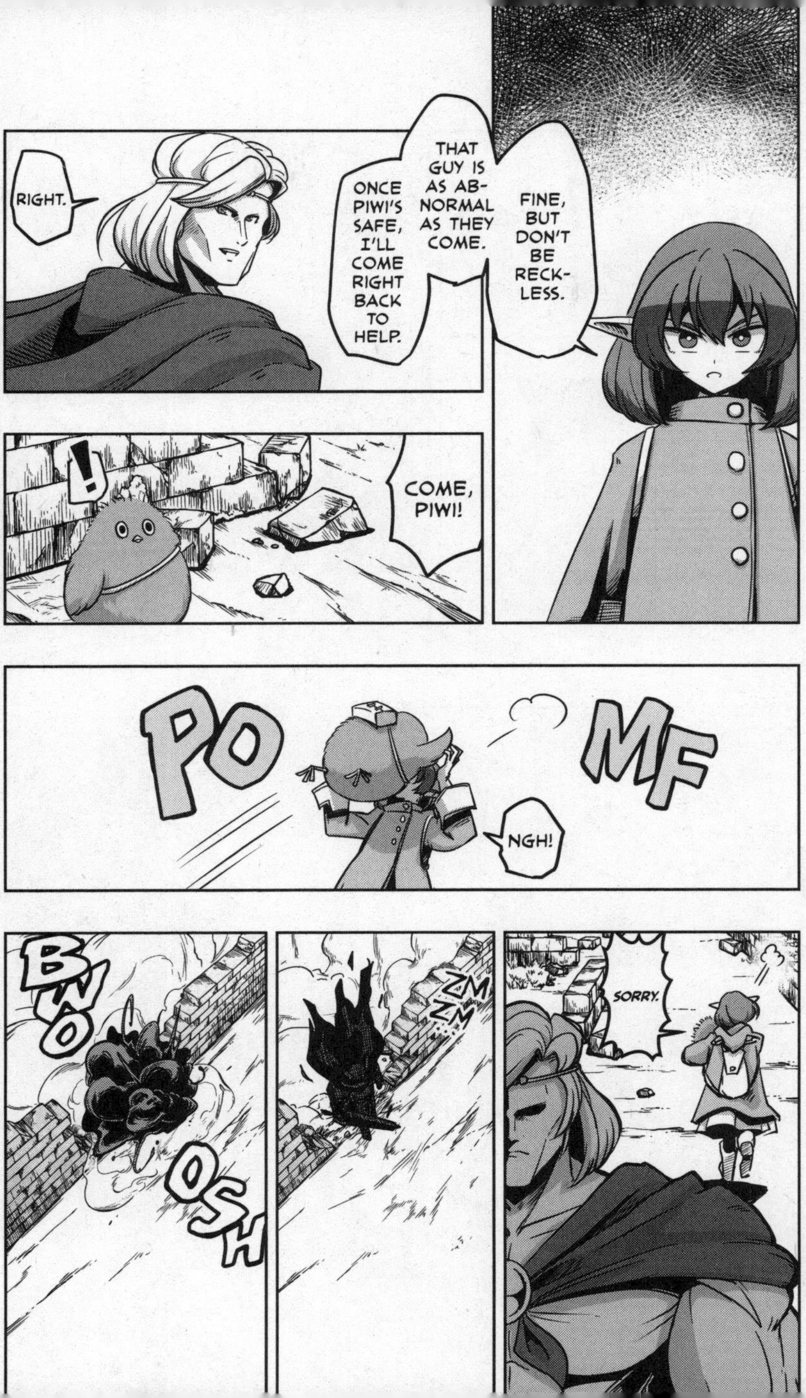
FINE, BUT DON'T BE RECK-LESS.
THAT GUY IS AS AB-NORMAL AS THEY COME.
ONCE PIWI'S SAFE, I'LL COME RIGHT BACK TO HELP.
RIGHT.
!
COME, PIWI!
POMF
NGH!
SORRY.
ZM ZM
BWOOSH

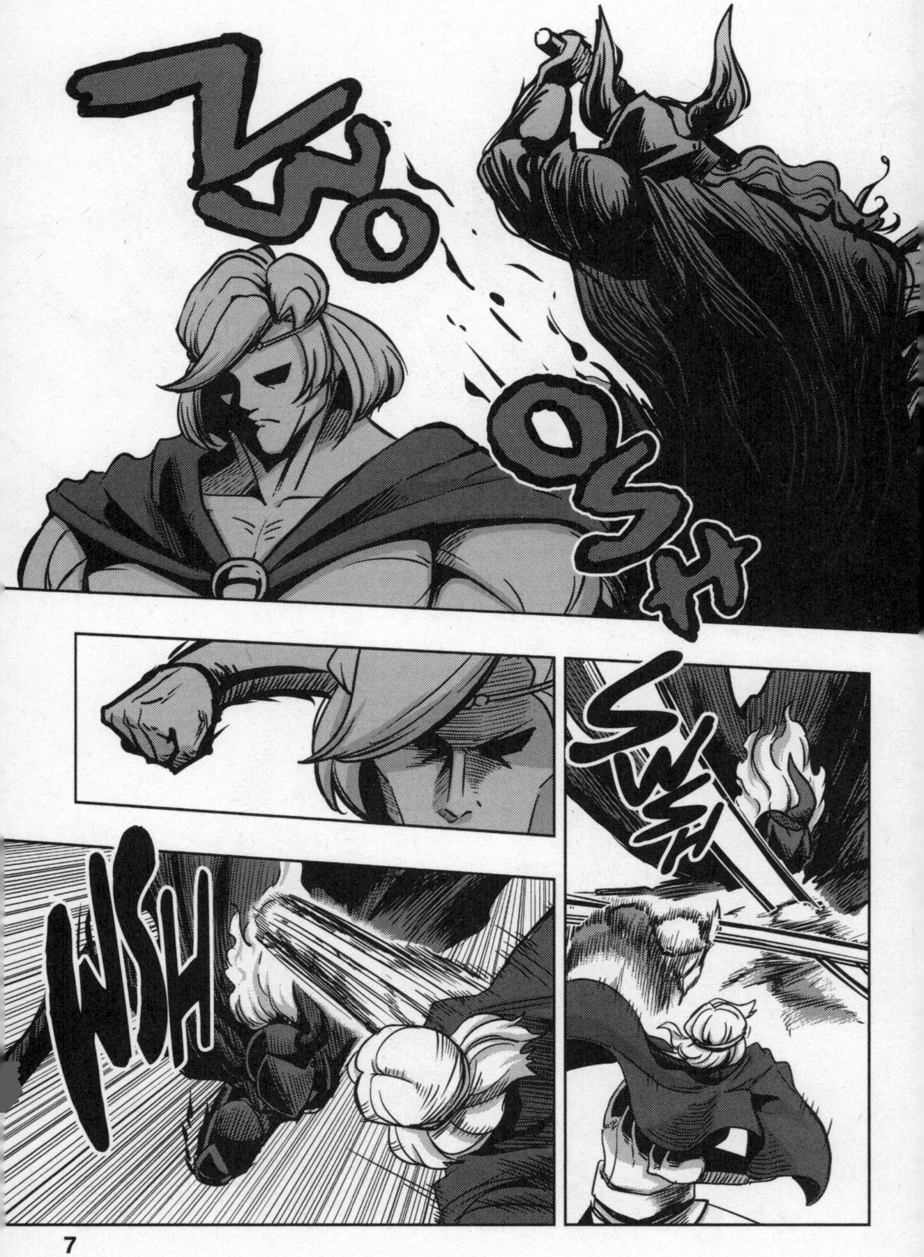
ZWOOSH
SWSH
WSH

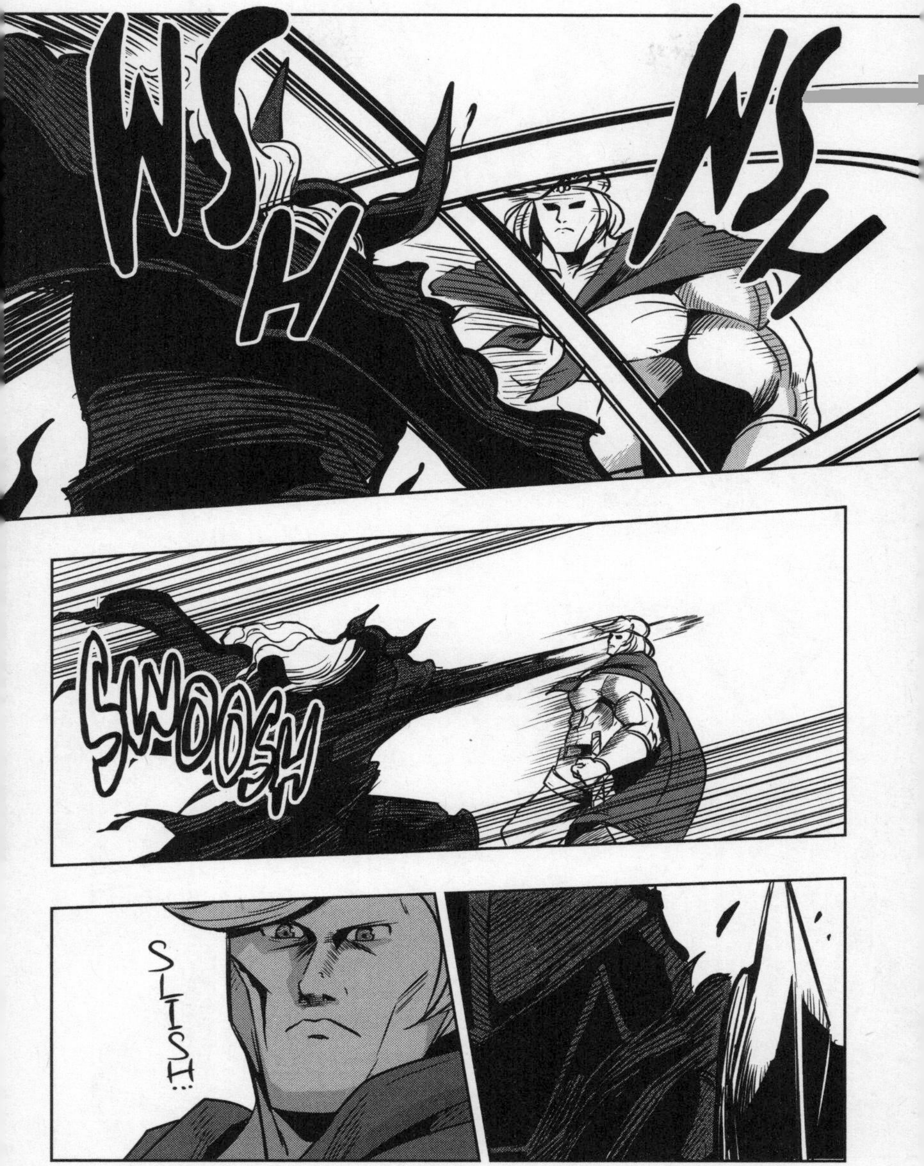
WSH
WSH
SWOOSH
SLISH..

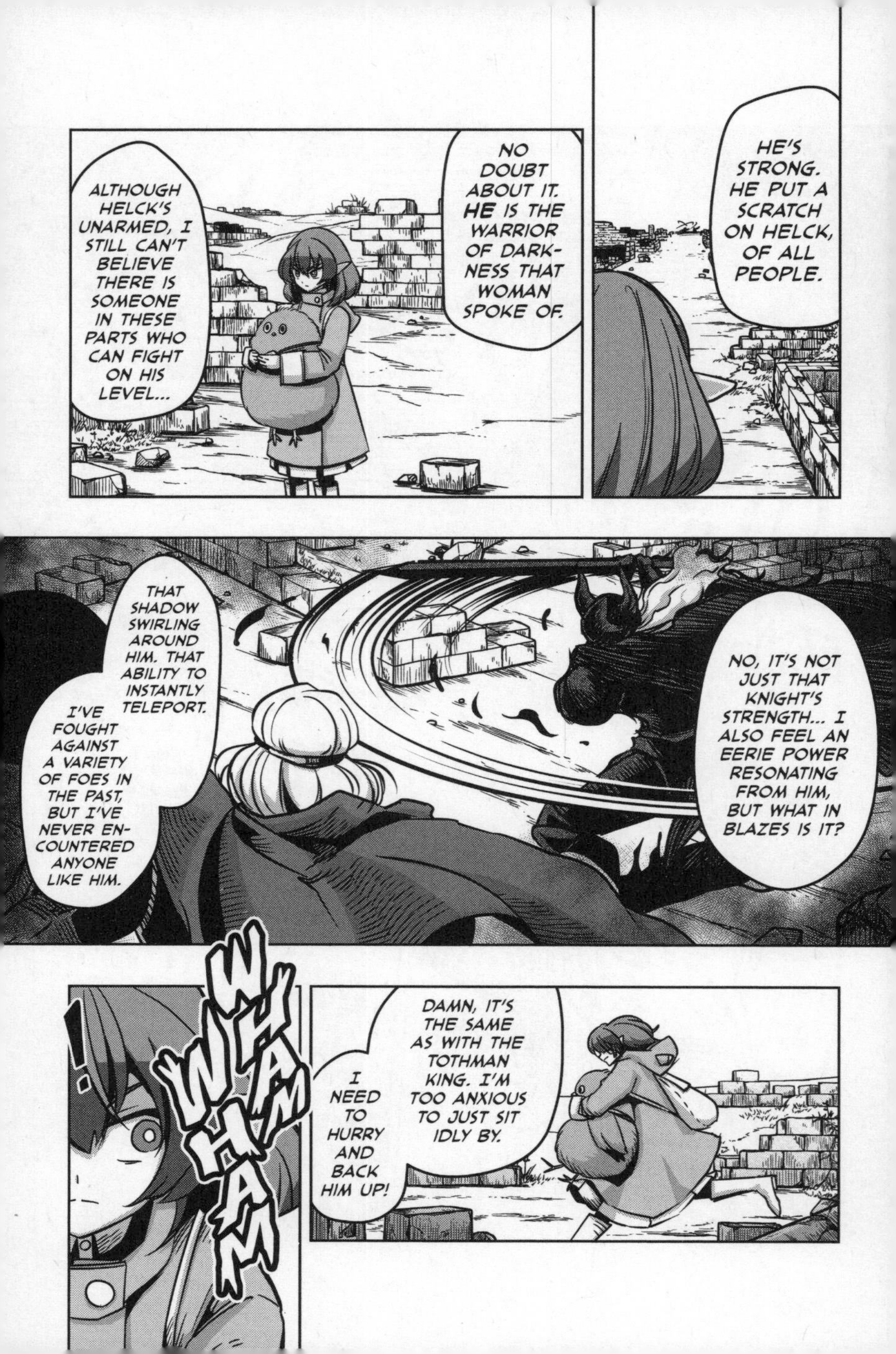
HE'S STRONG. HE PUT A SCRATCH ON HELCK, OF ALL PEOPLE.
NO DOUBT ABOUT IT. **HE** IS THE WARRIOR OF DARKNESS THAT WOMAN SPOKE OF.
ALTHOUGH HELCK'S UNARMED, I STILL CAN'T BELIEVE THERE IS SOMEONE IN THESE PARTS WHO CAN FIGHT ON HIS LEVEL...
NO, IT'S NOT JUST THAT KNIGHT'S STRENGTH... I ALSO FEEL AN EERIE POWER RESONATING FROM HIM, BUT WHAT IN BLAZES IS IT?
THAT SHADOW SWIRLING AROUND HIM. THAT ABILITY TO INSTANTLY TELEPORT.
I'VE FOUGHT AGAINST A VARIETY OF FOES IN THE PAST, BUT I'VE NEVER ENCOUNTERED ANYONE LIKE HIM.
DAMN, IT'S THE SAME AS WITH THE TOTHMAN KING. I'M TOO ANXIOUS TO JUST SIT IDLY BY.
I NEED TO HURRY AND BACK HIM UP!
!
WHAM WHAM

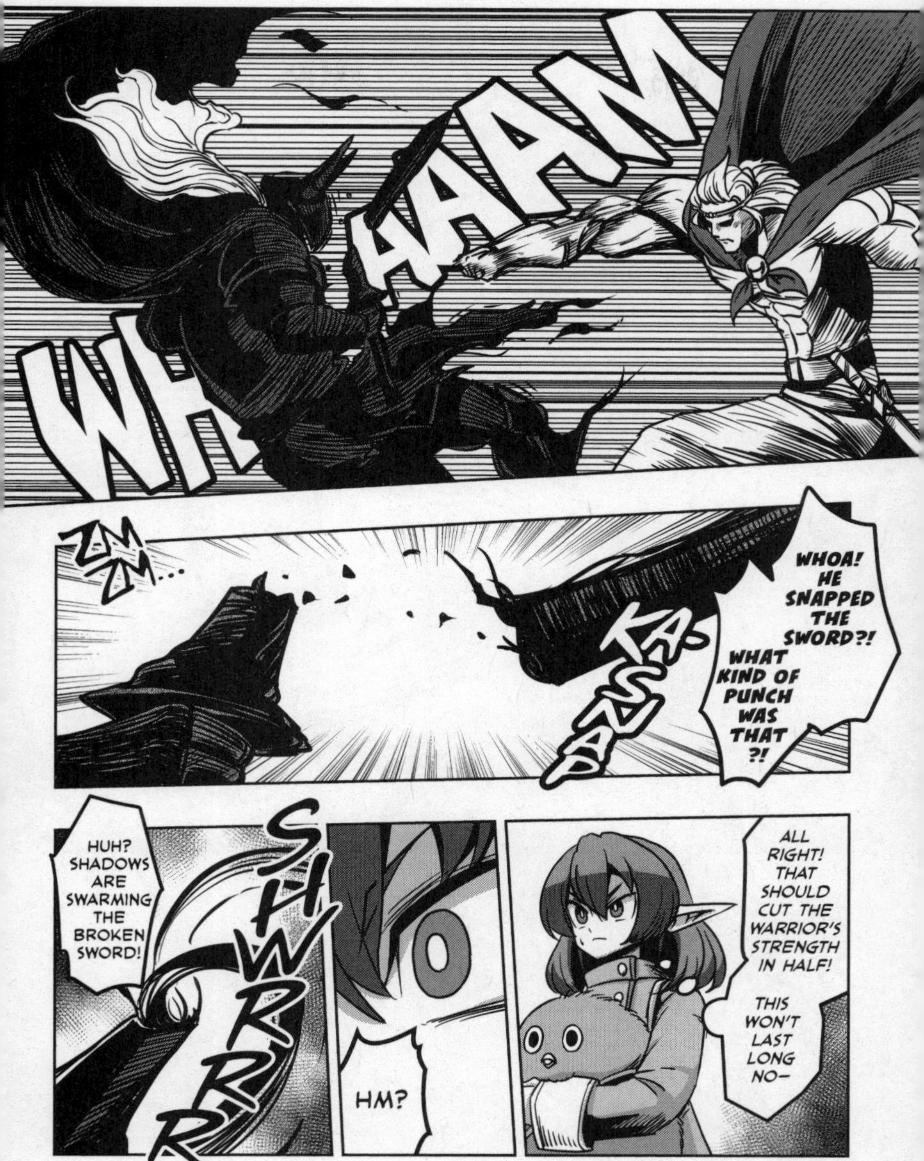
WHAAM
WHOA! HE SNAPPED THE SWORD?!
WHAT KIND OF PUNCH WAS THAT?!
KASNAP
ZM ZM...
ALL RIGHT! THAT SHOULD CUT THE WARRIOR'S STRENGTH IN HALF!
THIS WON'T LAST LONG NO—
HM?
SHWRRRR
HUH? SHADOWS ARE SWARMING THE BROKEN SWORD!

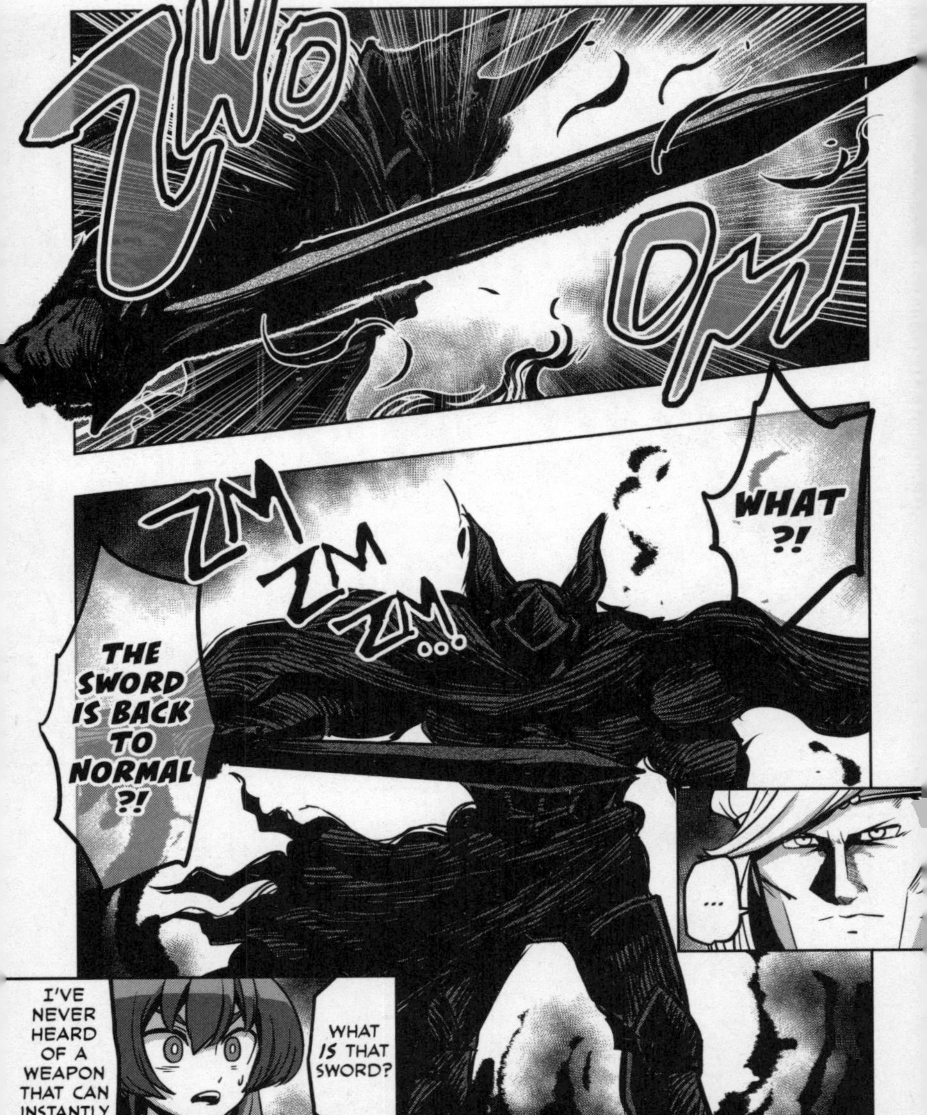
ZWOOM!
WHAT?!
ZM ZM ZM ZM!!
THE SWORD IS BACK TO NORMAL?!
...
WHAT *IS* THAT SWORD?
I'VE NEVER HEARD OF A WEAPON THAT CAN INSTANTLY REPAIR ITSELF.

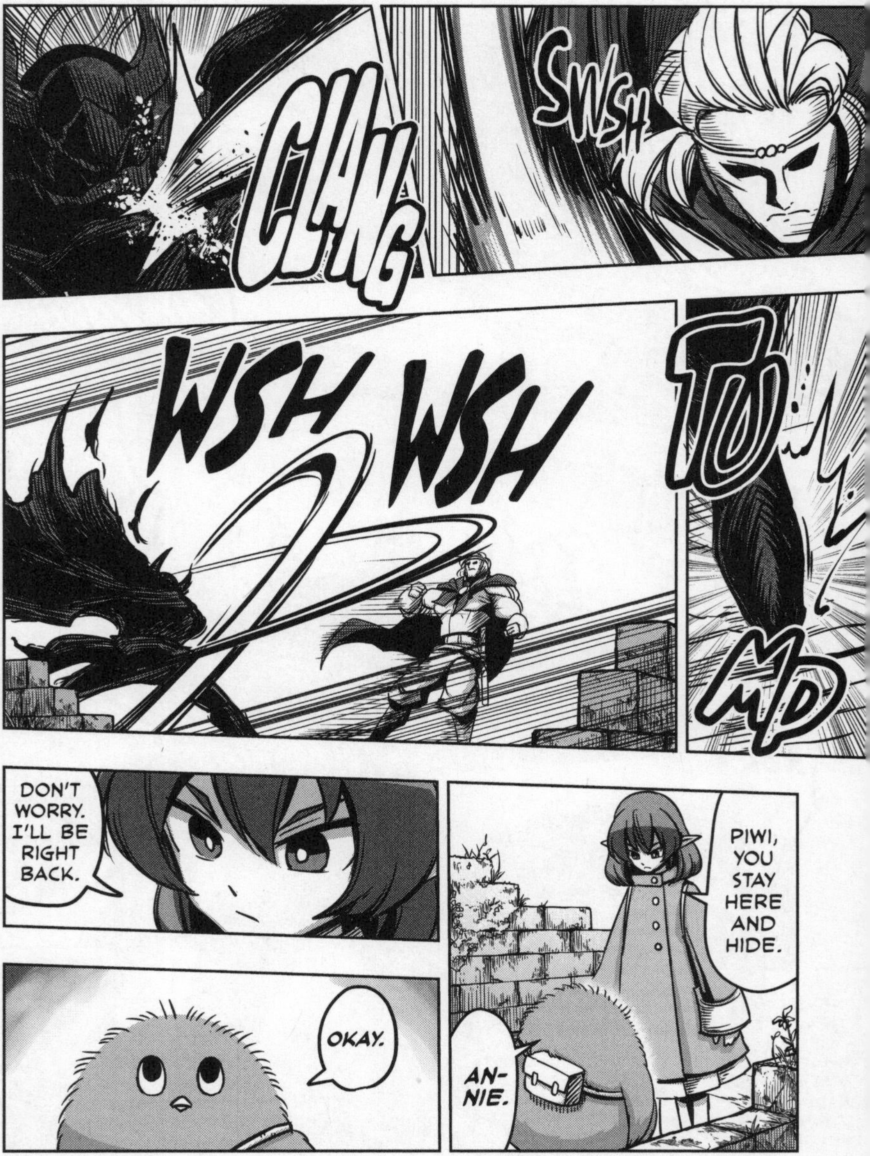

SWISH
CLANG
TUMP
WSH WSH
PIWI, YOU STAY HERE AND HIDE.
AN-NIE.
DON'T WORRY. I'LL BE RIGHT BACK.
OKAY.

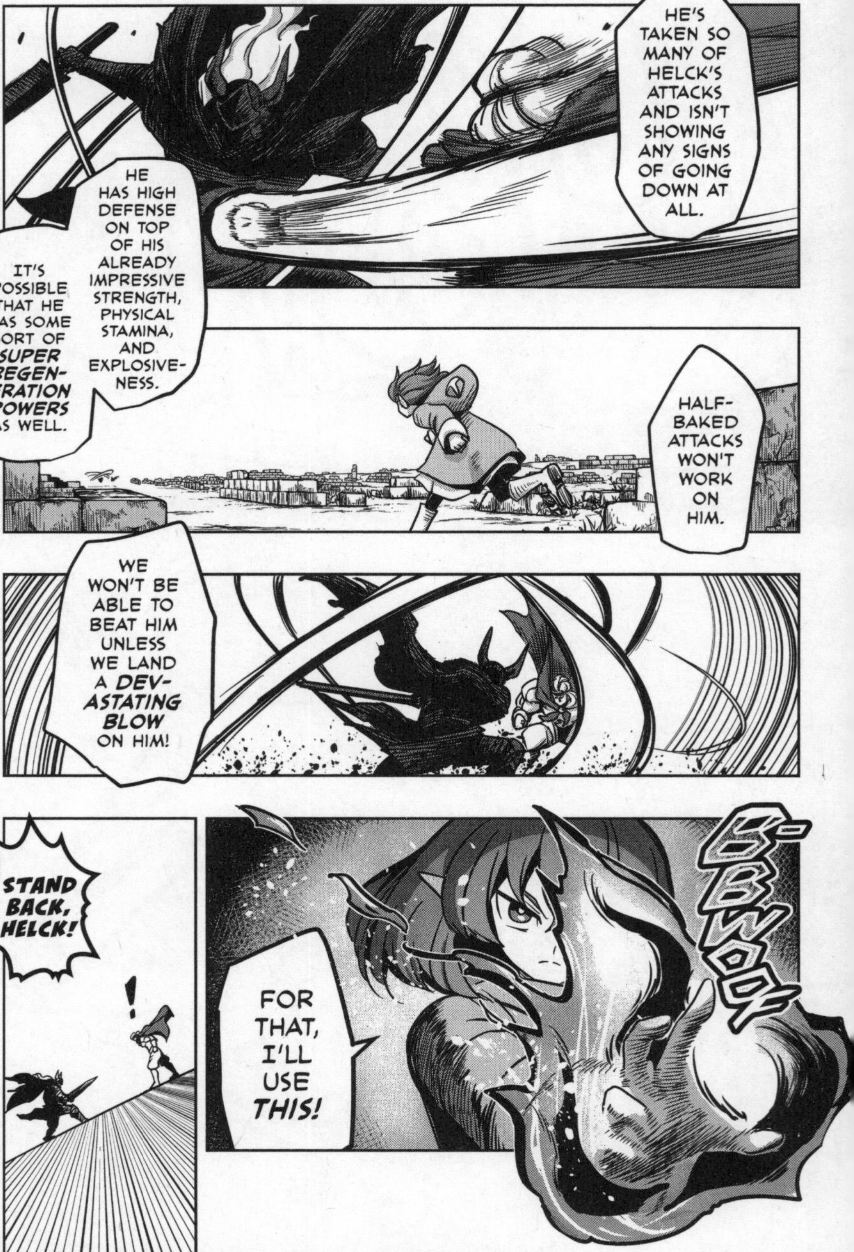
HE'S TAKEN SO MANY OF HELCK'S ATTACKS AND ISN'T SHOWING ANY SIGNS OF GOING DOWN AT ALL.
HE HAS HIGH DEFENSE ON TOP OF HIS ALREADY IMPRESSIVE STRENGTH, PHYSICAL STAMINA, AND EXPLOSIVE-NESS.
IT'S POSSIBLE THAT HE HAS SOME SORT OF SUPER REGEN-ERATION POWERS AS WELL.
HALF-BAKED ATTACKS WON'T WORK ON HIM.
WE WON'T BE ABLE TO BEAT HIM UNLESS WE LAND A DEV-ASTATING BLOW ON HIM!
FOR THAT, I'LL USE THIS!
STAND BACK, HELCK!
!

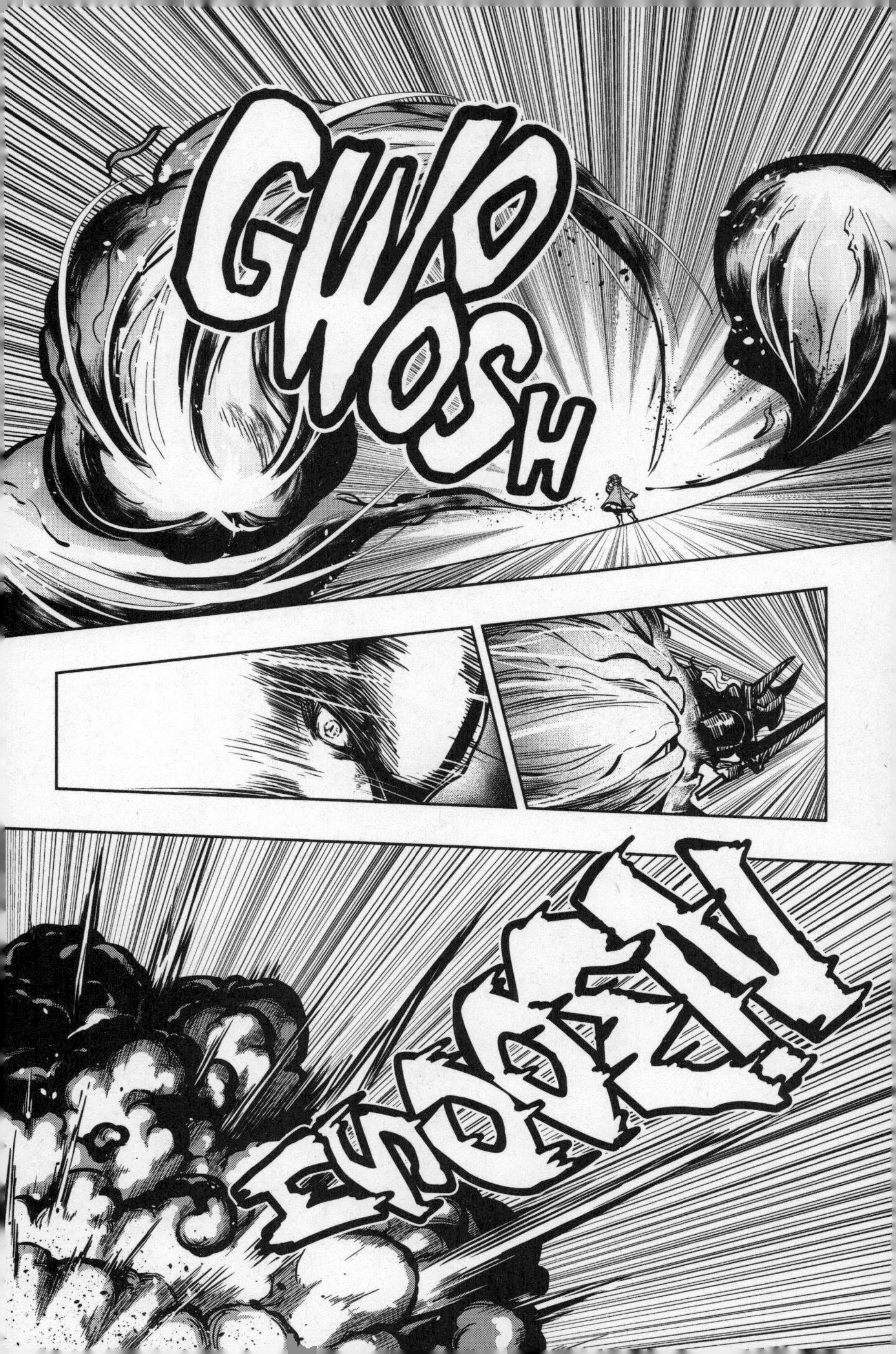

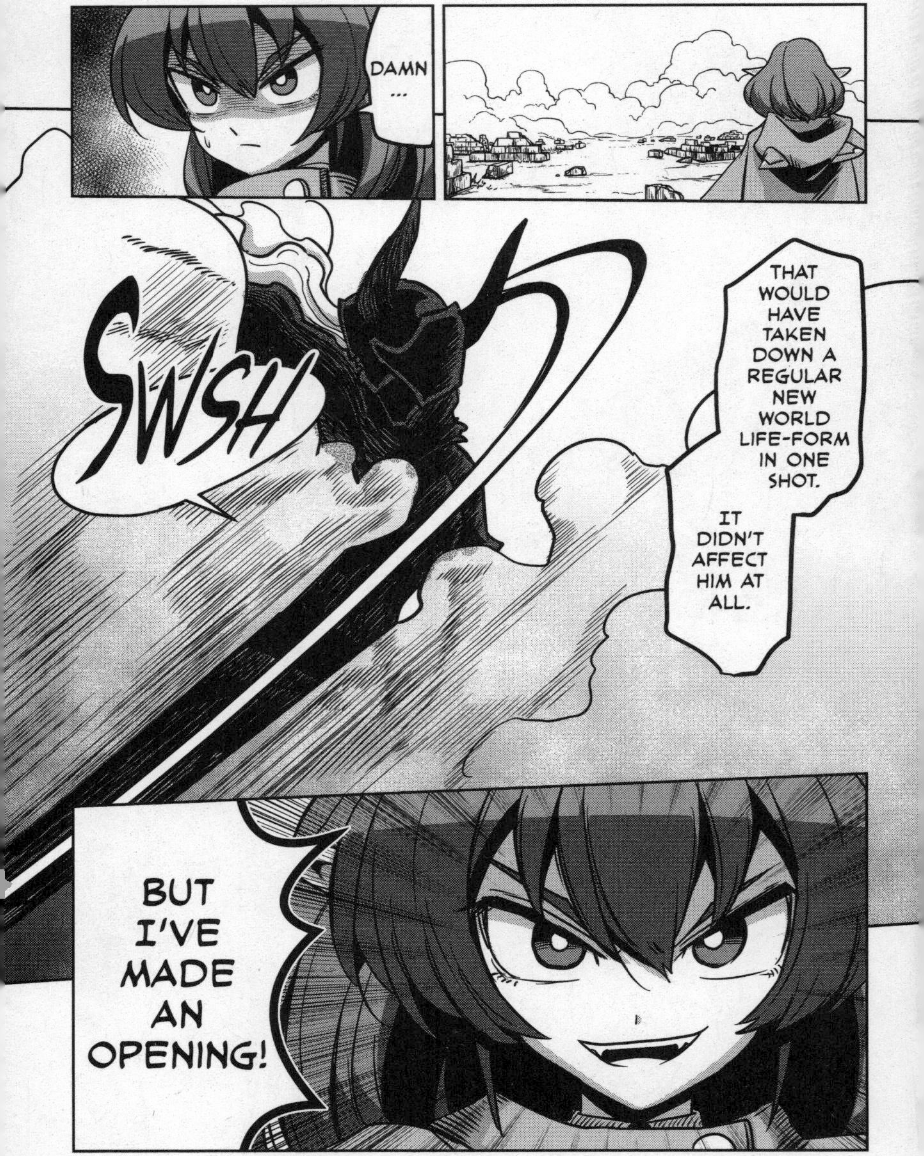
DAMN ...
THAT WOULD HAVE TAKEN DOWN A REGULAR NEW WORLD LIFE-FORM IN ONE SHOT.
IT DIDN'T AFFECT HIM AT ALL.
SWSH
BUT I'VE MADE AN OPENING!

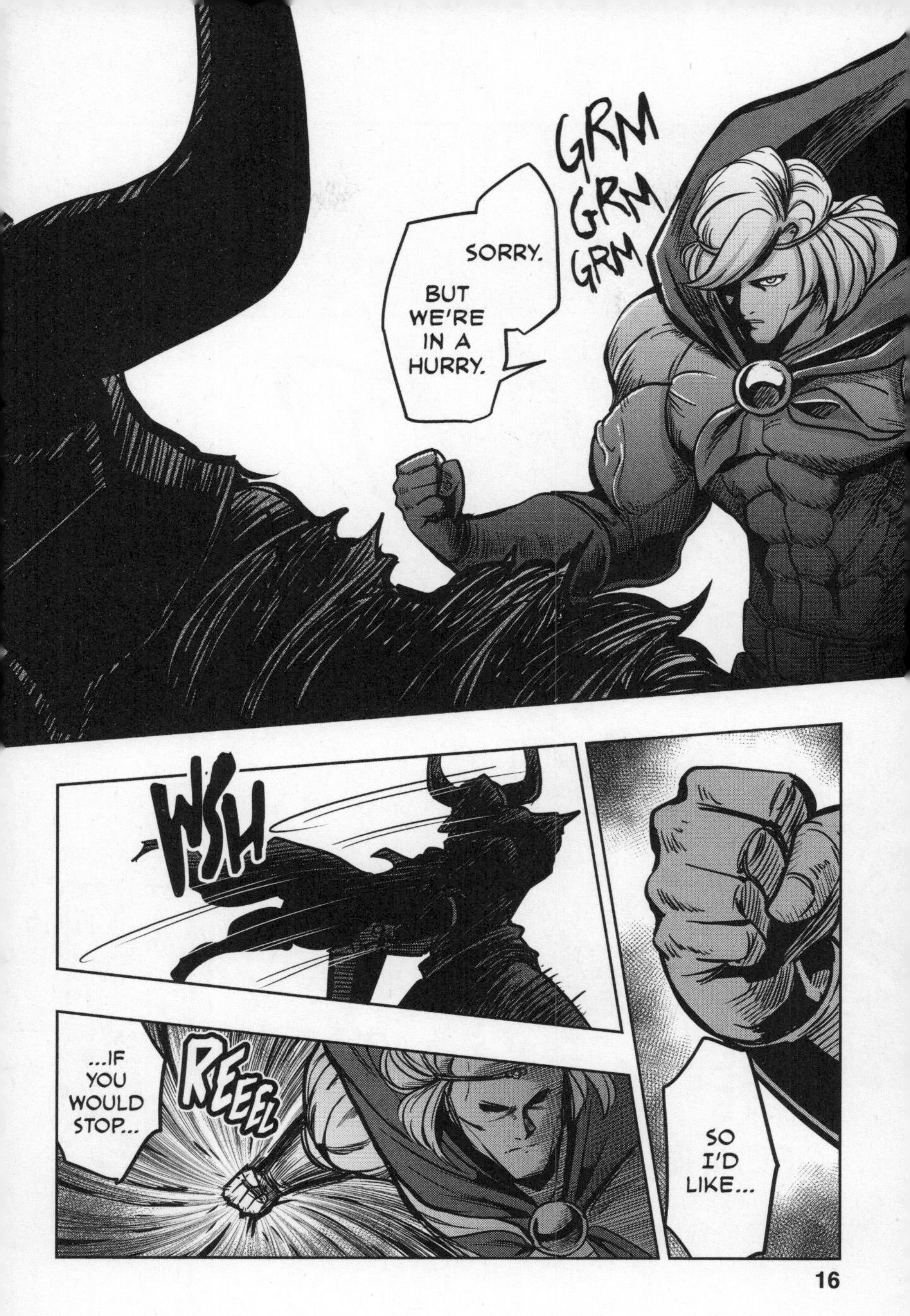
GRM GRM GRM
SORRY.
BUT WE'RE IN A HURRY.
SO I'D LIKE...
WSH
REEEL
...IF YOU WOULD STOP...

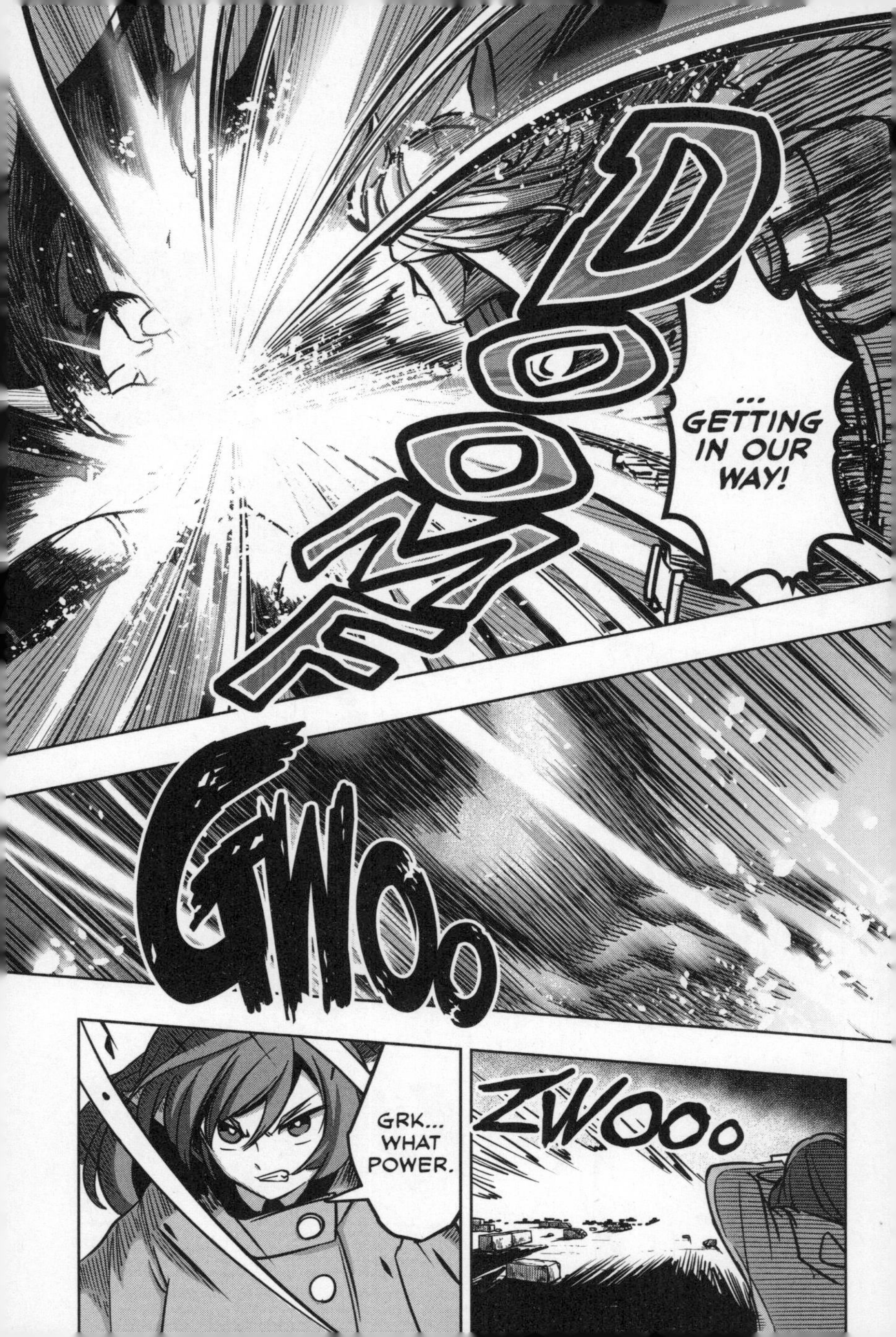
DOOM
...GETTING IN OUR WAY!
GWOO
ZWOOO
GRK... WHAT POWER.

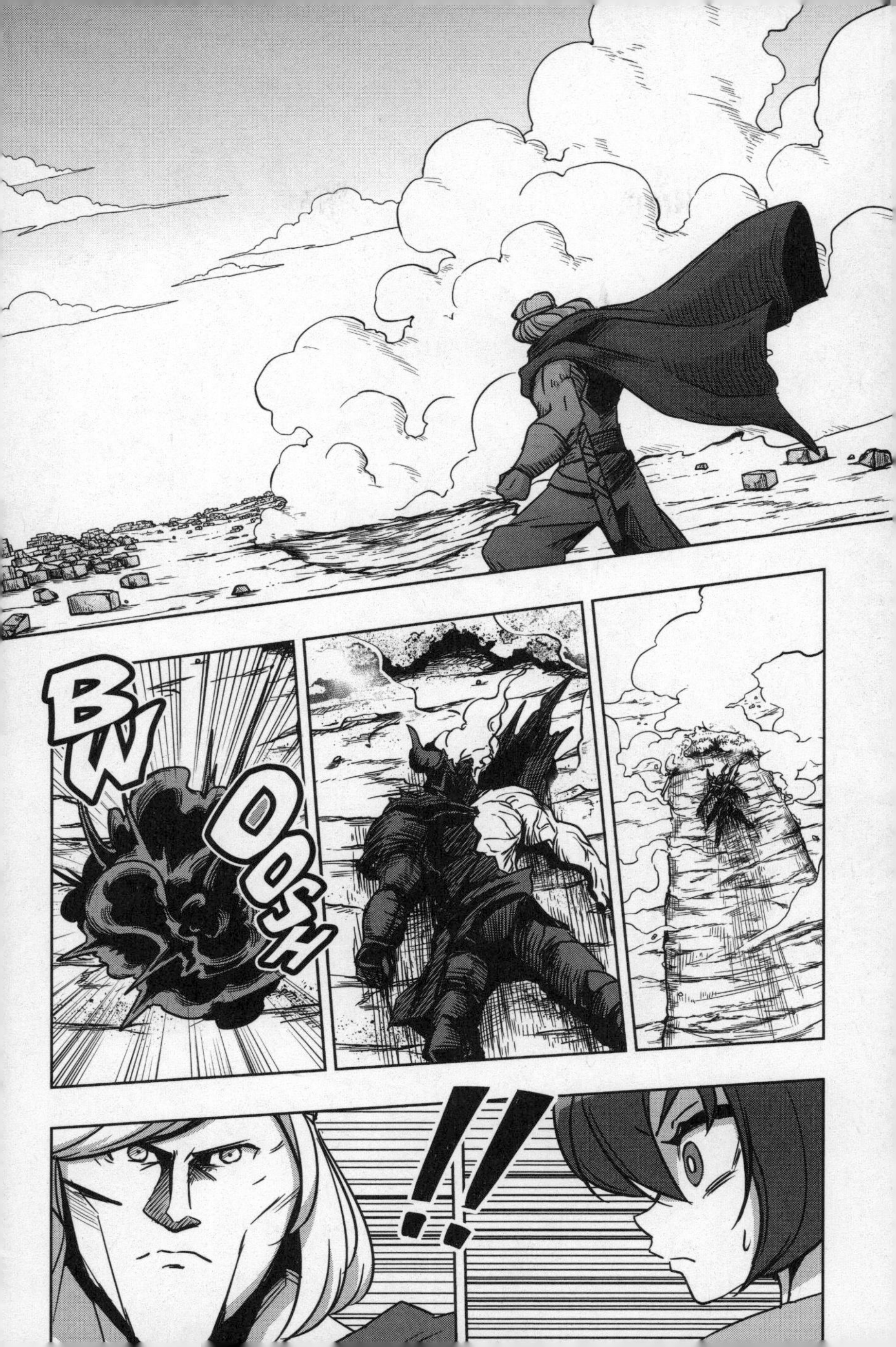
BWOOSH
!!

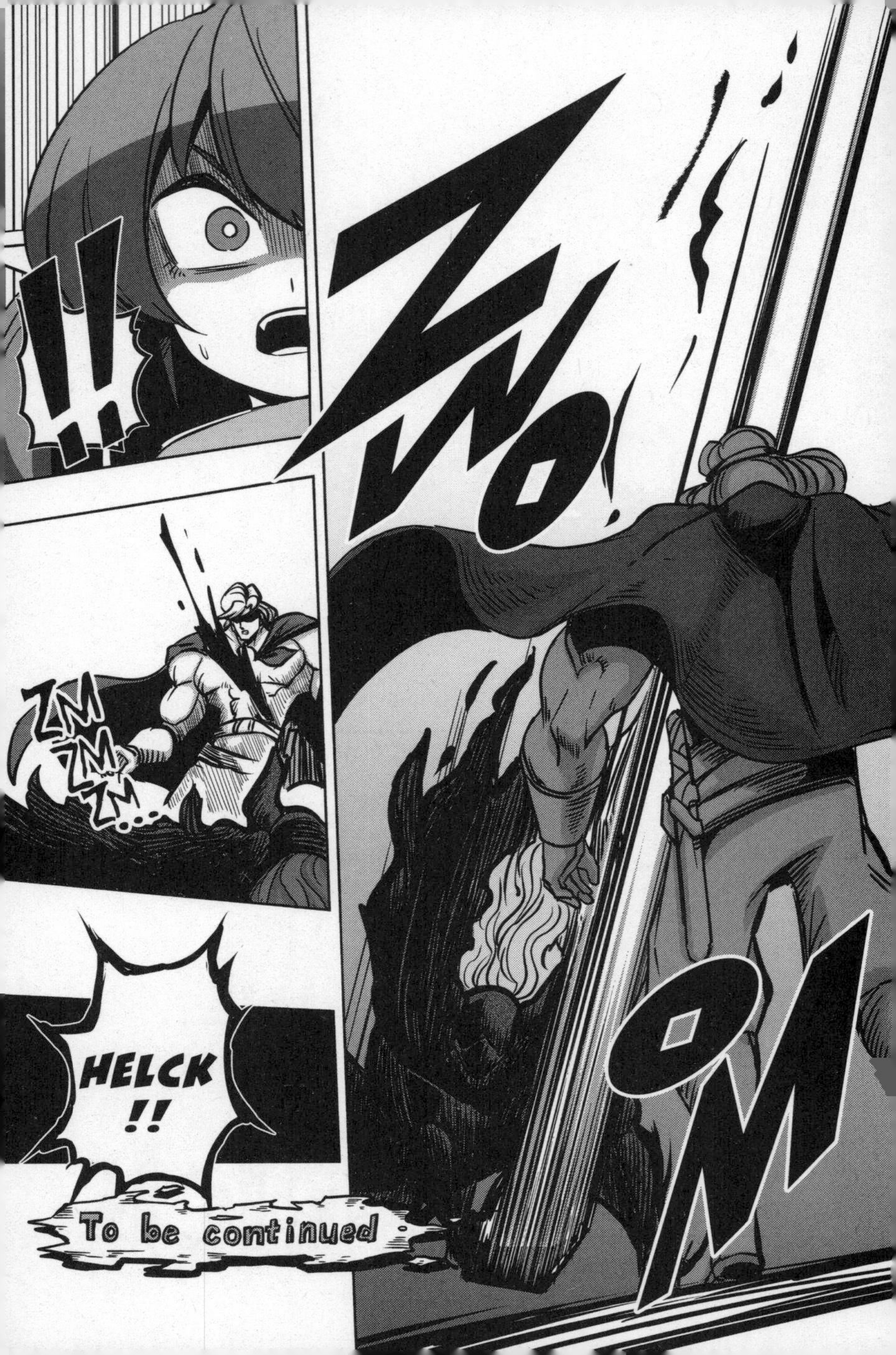
ZWO!
OM
!!
ZM ZM ZM...
HELCK !!
To be continued

Helck

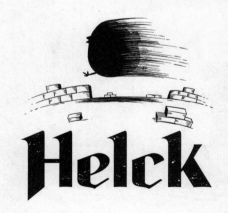

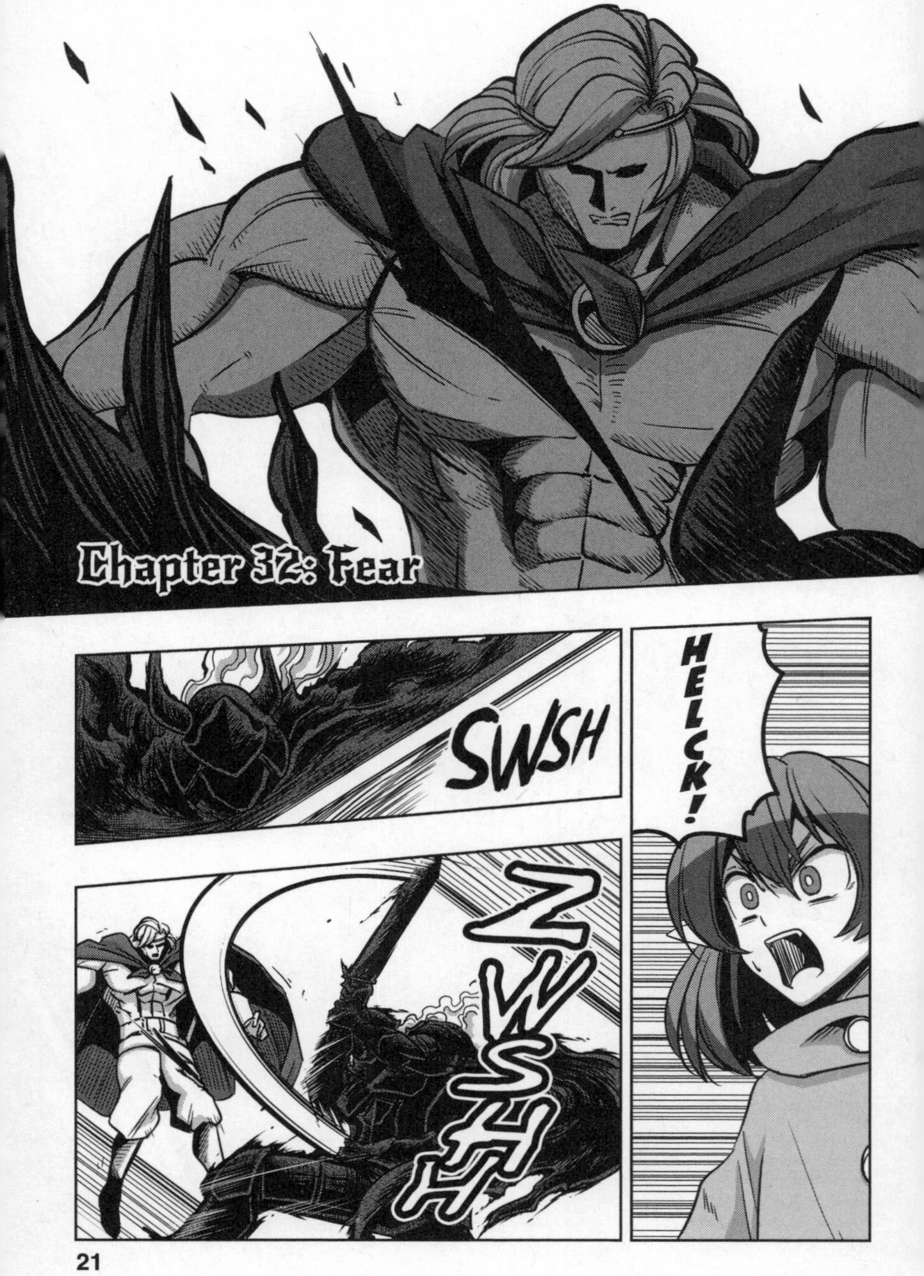
Chapter 32: Fear
HELCK!
SWSH
ZWSHH

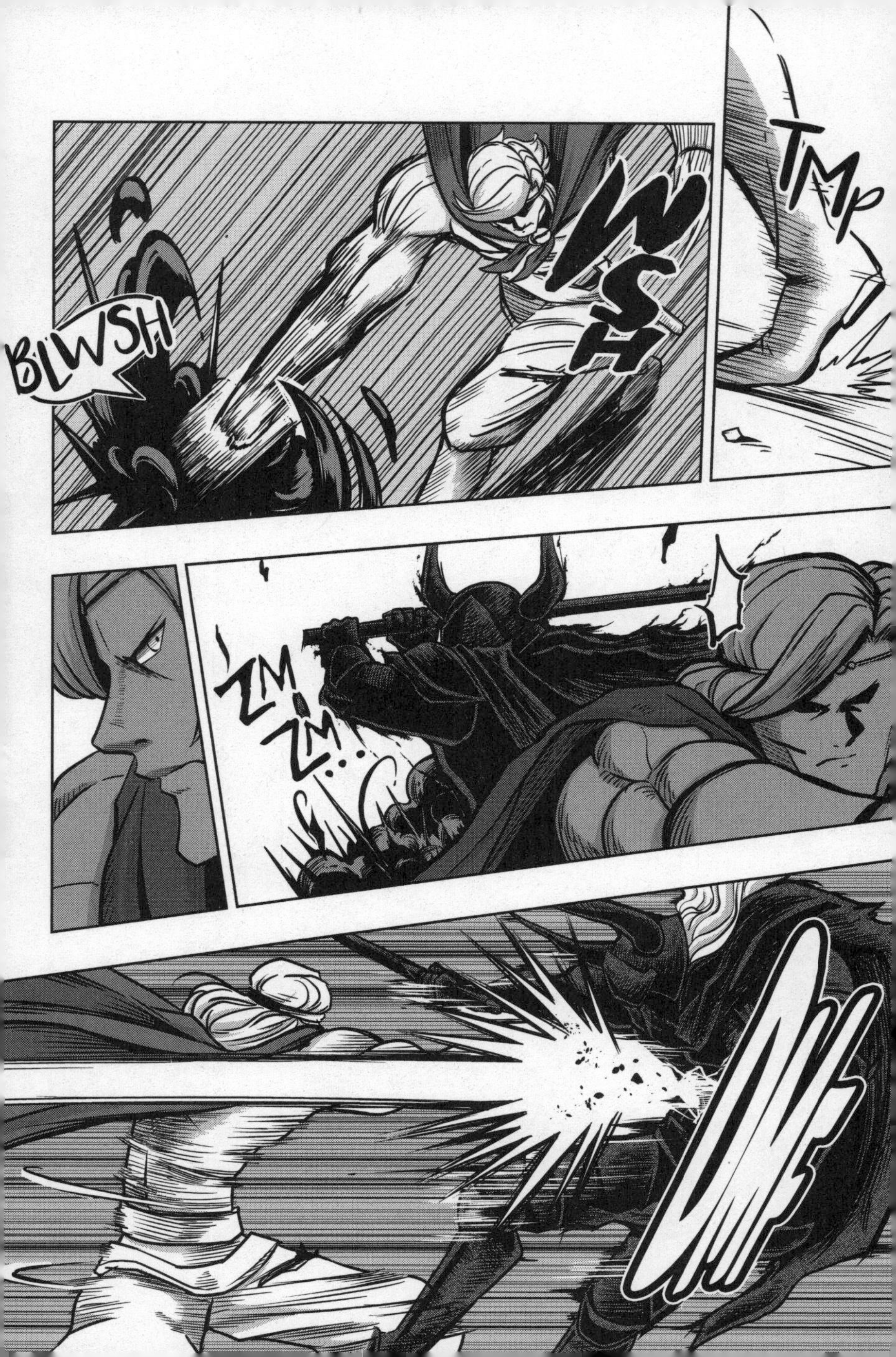
TMP
WSH
BLWSH
ZM ZM ZM...

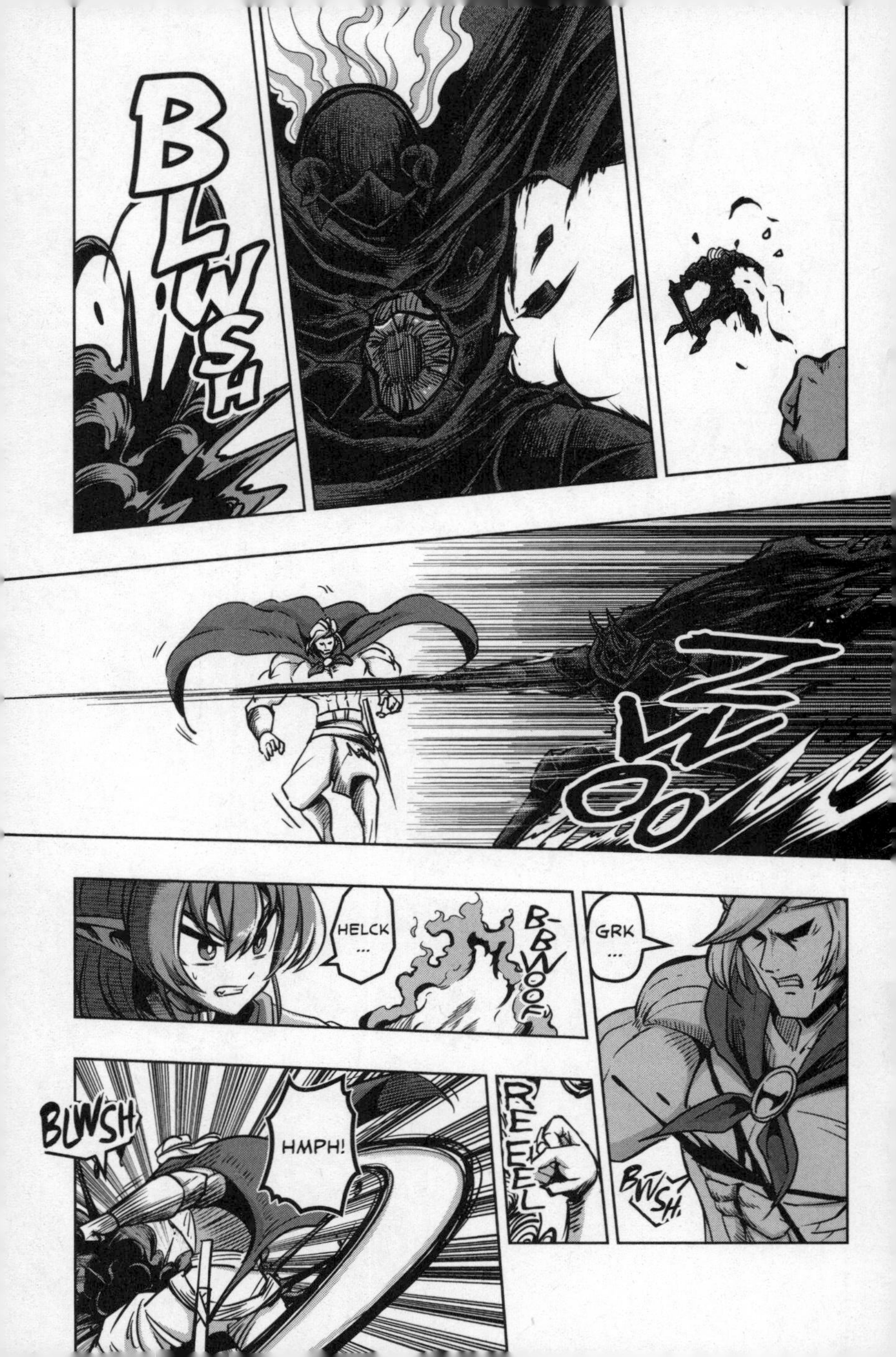
BLWSH
ZWOO
GRK ...
BWSH
B-BWOOF
HELCK ...
REEEEL
HMPH!
BLWSH

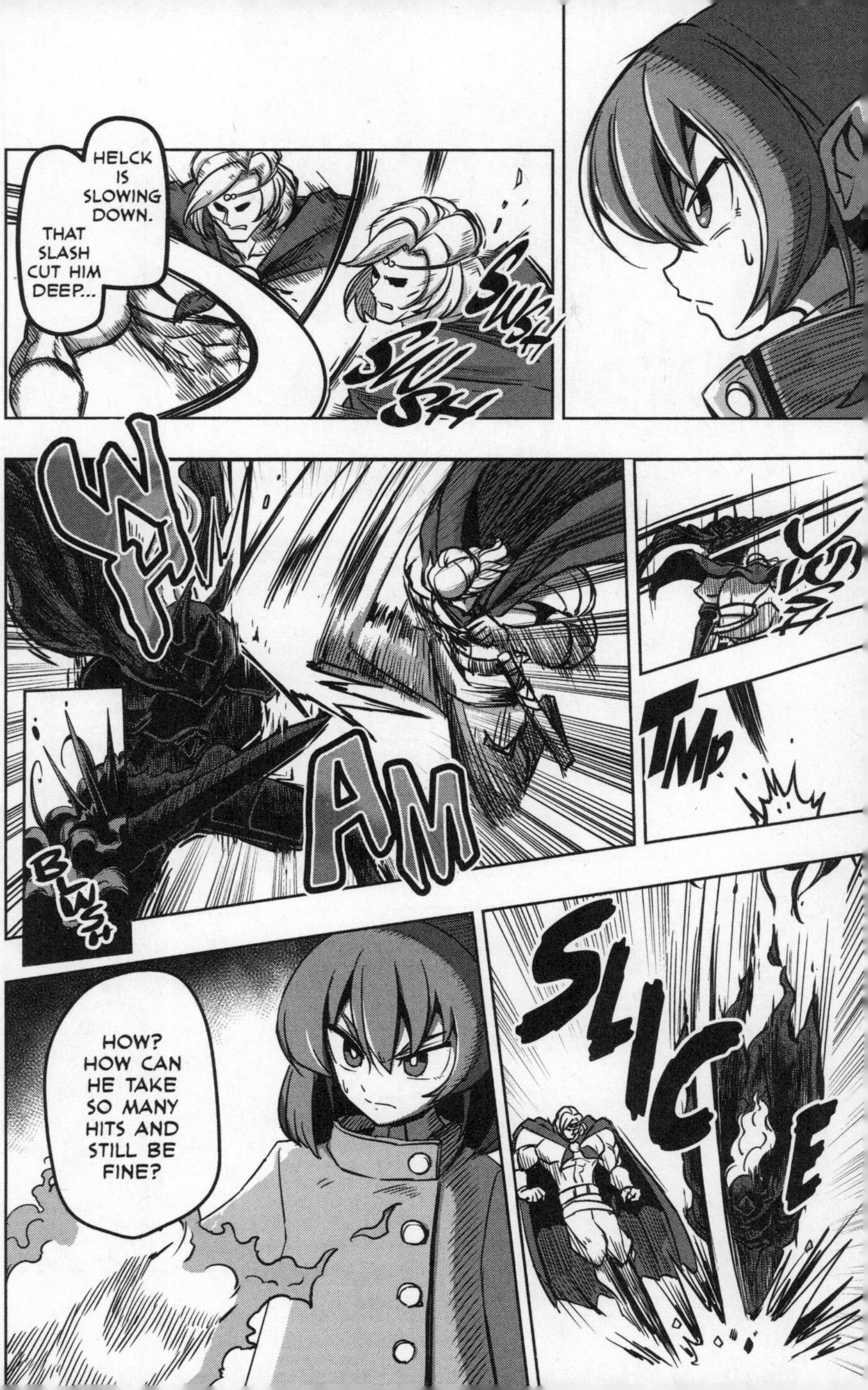
HELCK IS SLOWING DOWN. THAT SLASH CUT HIM DEEP...
SLISH!
WHAM
TMP
SLICE
HOW? HOW CAN HE TAKE SO MANY HITS AND STILL BE FINE?

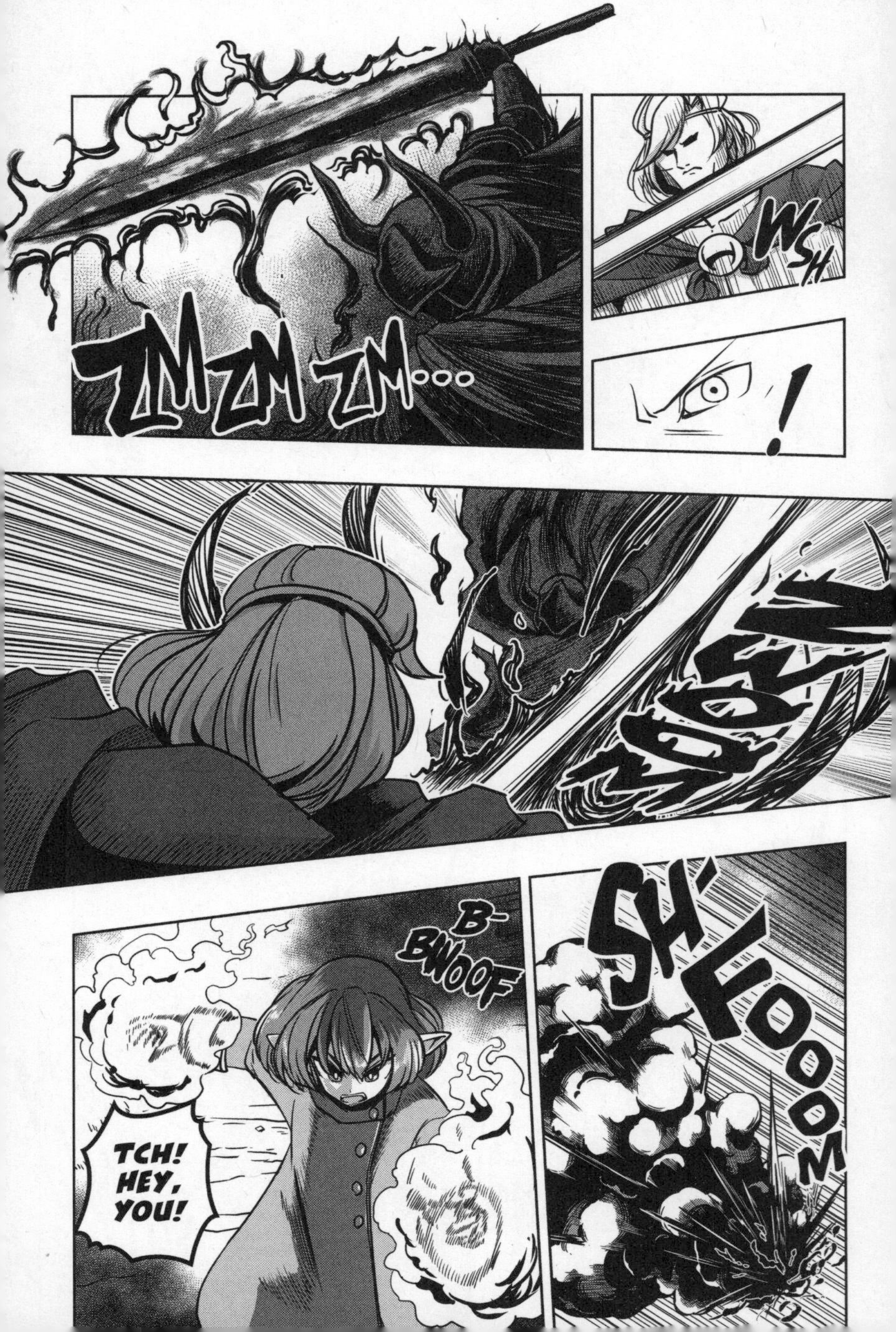
WSH
!
ZM ZM ZM...
SH'FOOOM
B-BWOOF
TCH! HEY, YOU!

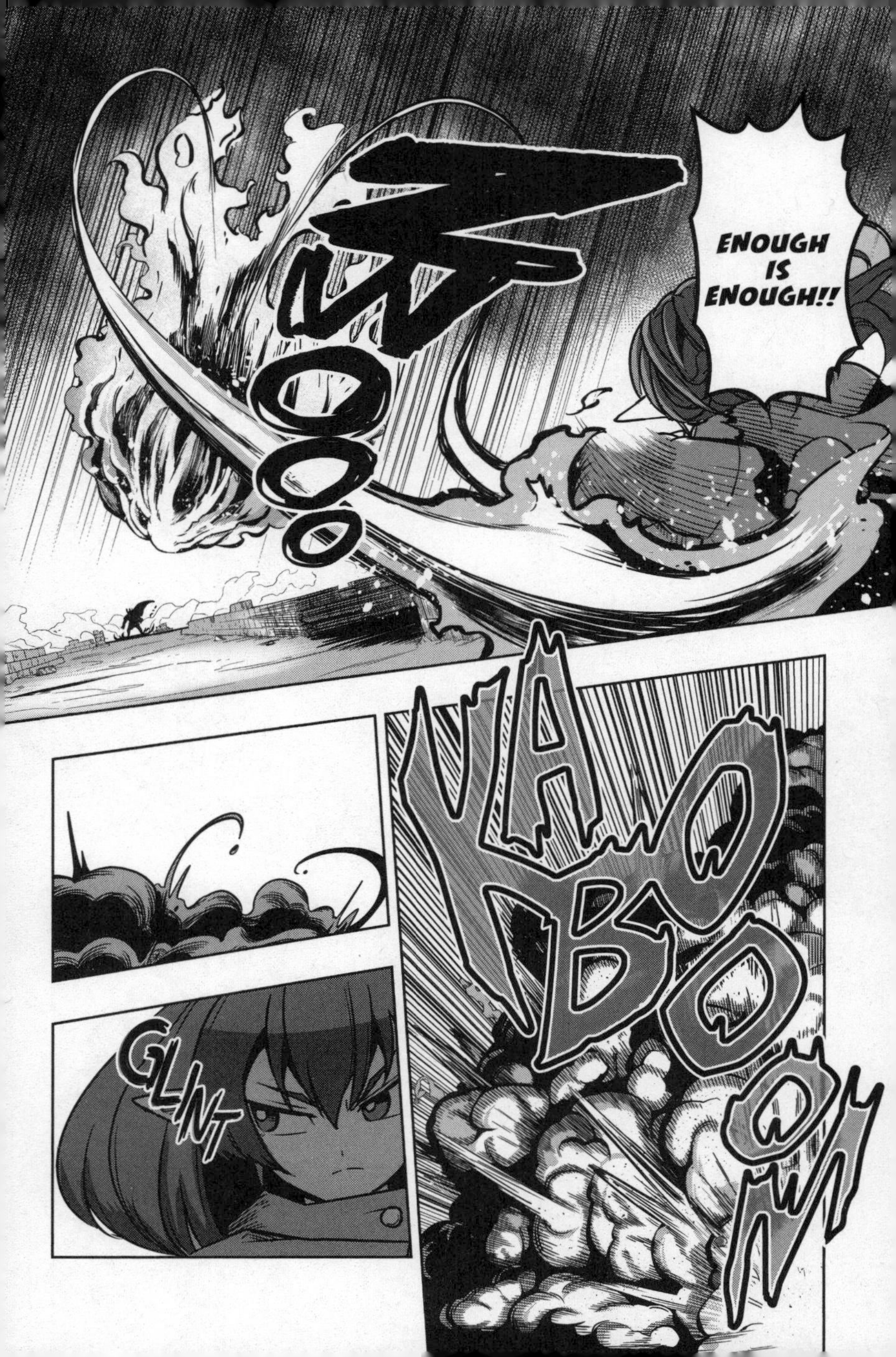
ENOUGH IS ENOUGH!!
KABOOM
GLINT

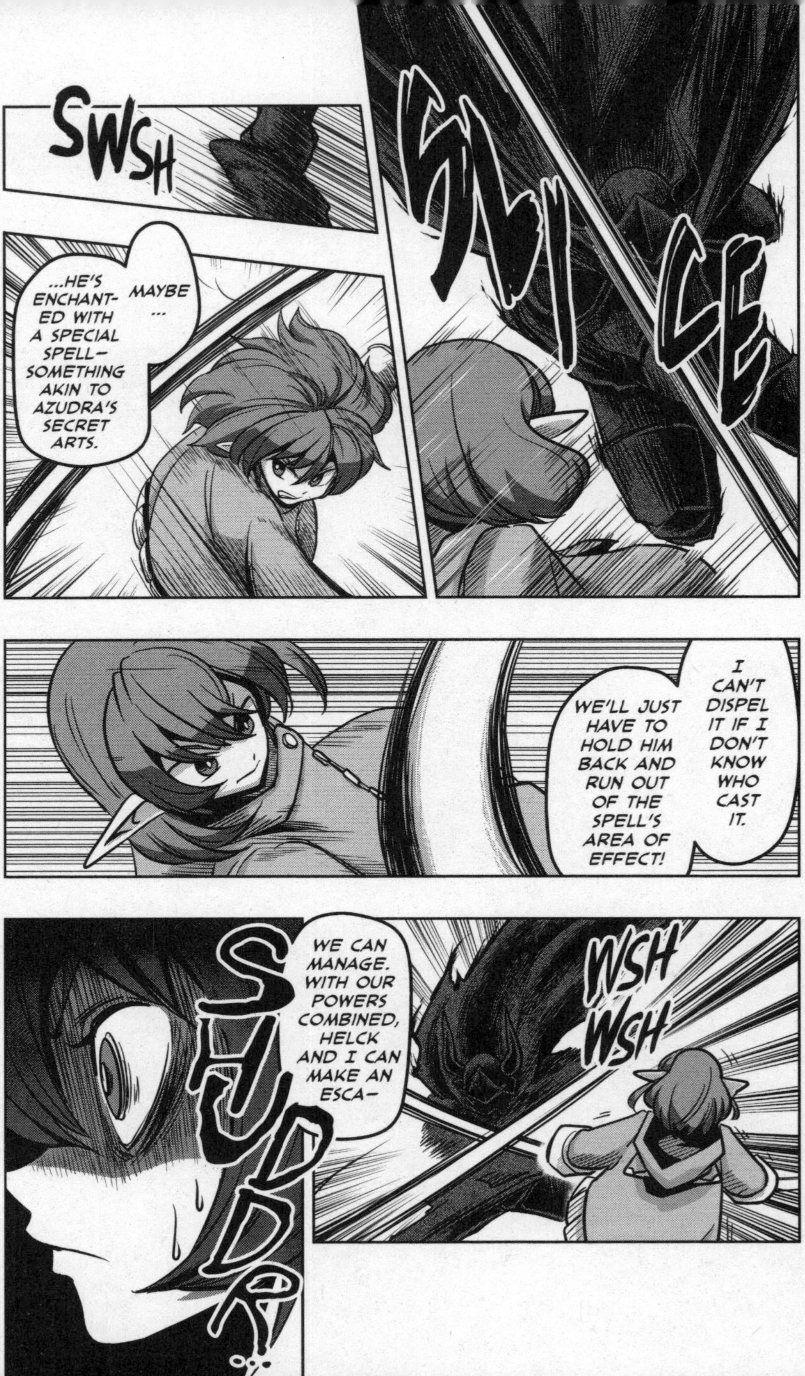
SLICE
SWSH
MAYBE ...
...HE'S ENCHANTED WITH A SPECIAL SPELL—SOMETHING AKIN TO AZUDRA'S SECRET ARTS.
I CAN'T DISPEL IT IF I DON'T KNOW WHO CAST IT.
WE'LL JUST HAVE TO HOLD HIM BACK AND RUN OUT OF THE SPELL'S AREA OF EFFECT!
WSH WSH
WE CAN MANAGE. WITH OUR POWERS COMBINED, HELCK AND I CAN MAKE AN ESCA—
SHUDDR...!

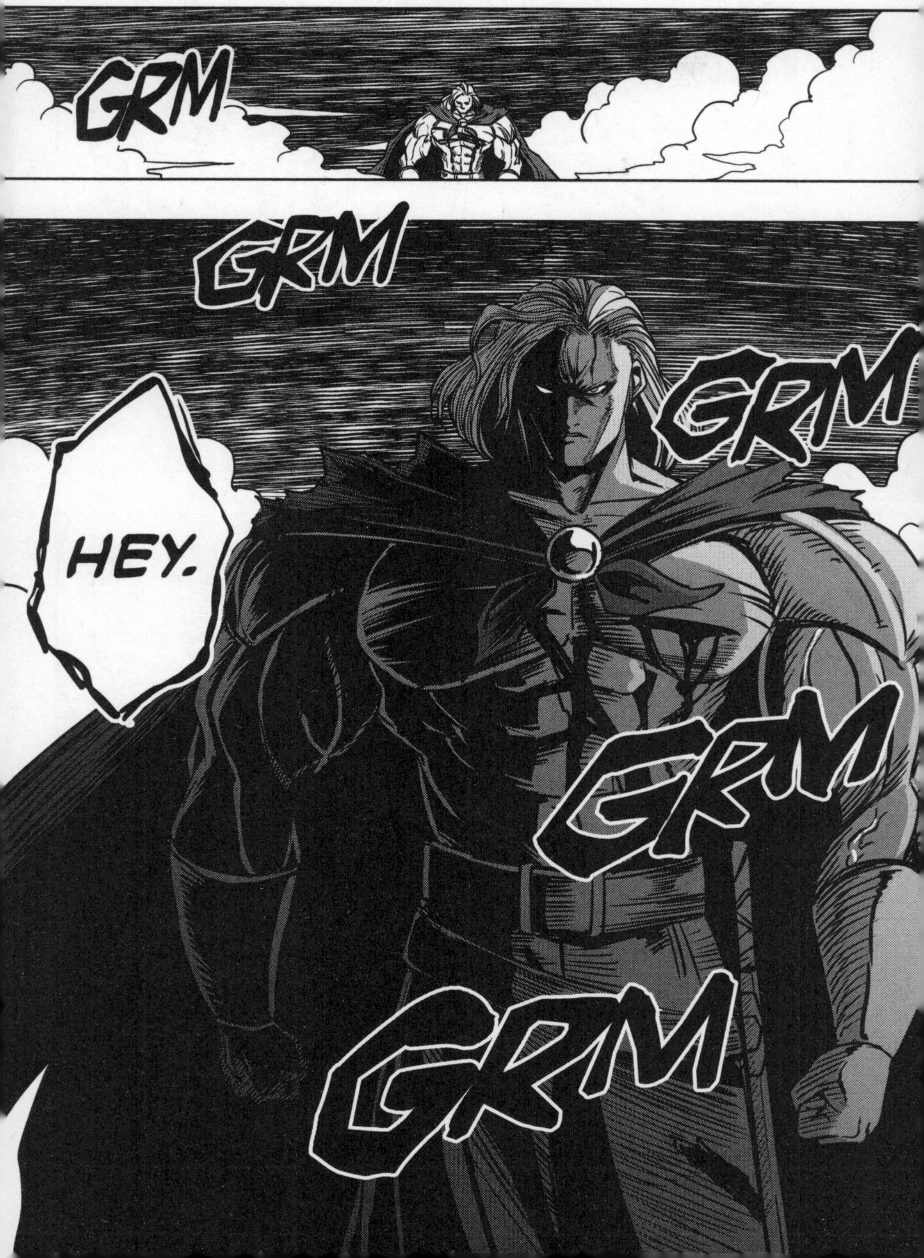
GRM
GRM
GRM
HEY.
GRM
GRM

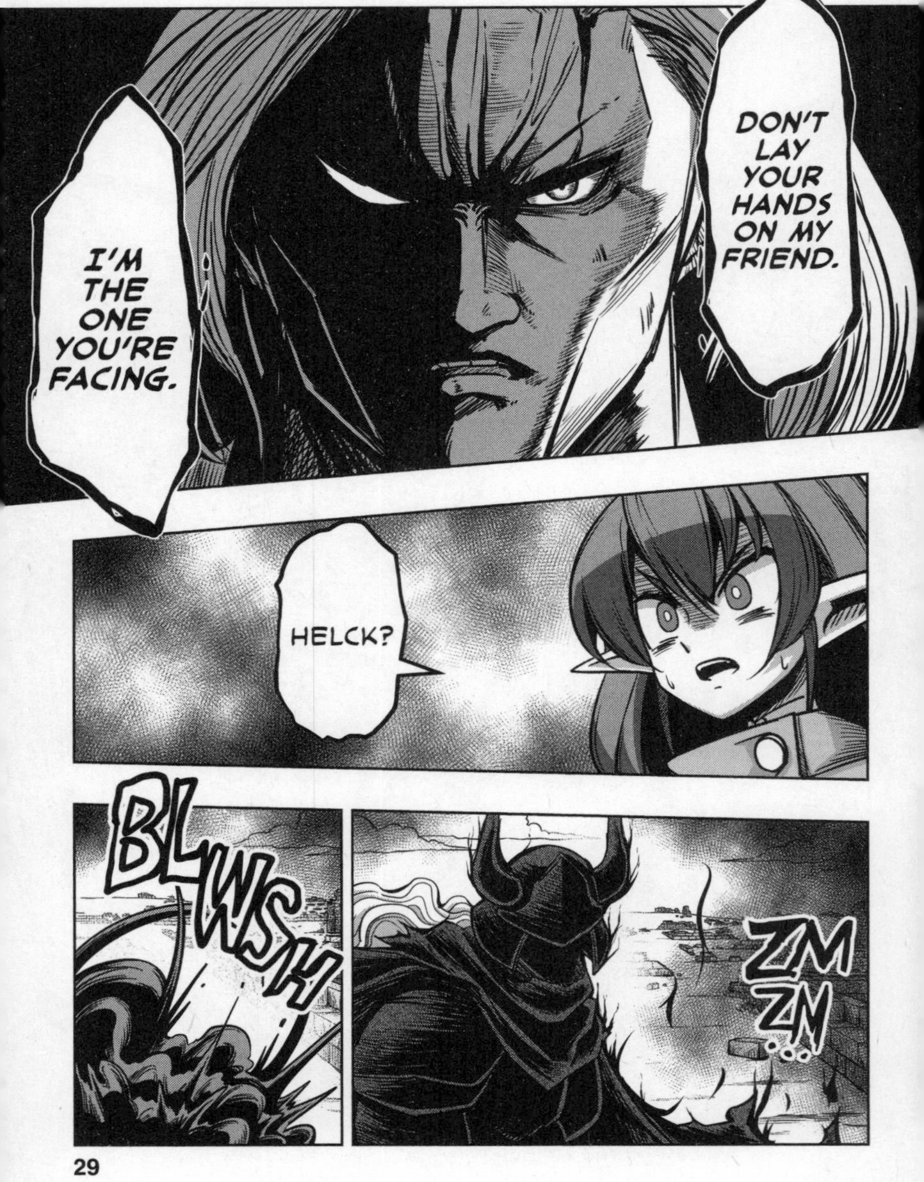

DON'T LAY YOUR HANDS ON MY FRIEND.
I'M THE ONE YOU'RE FACING.
HELCK?
ZM ZM...
BLWSH

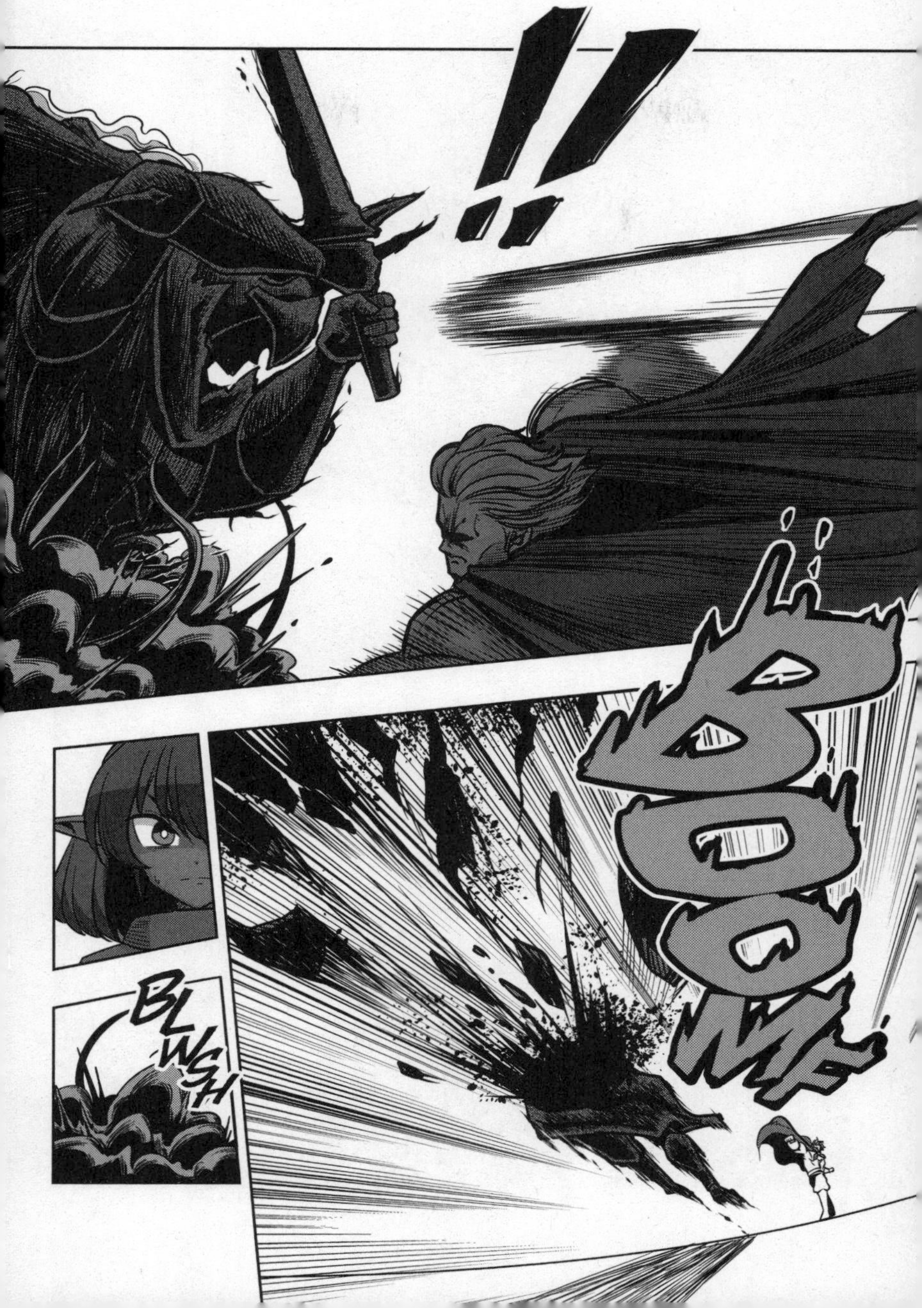
!!
BOOM
BLWSH

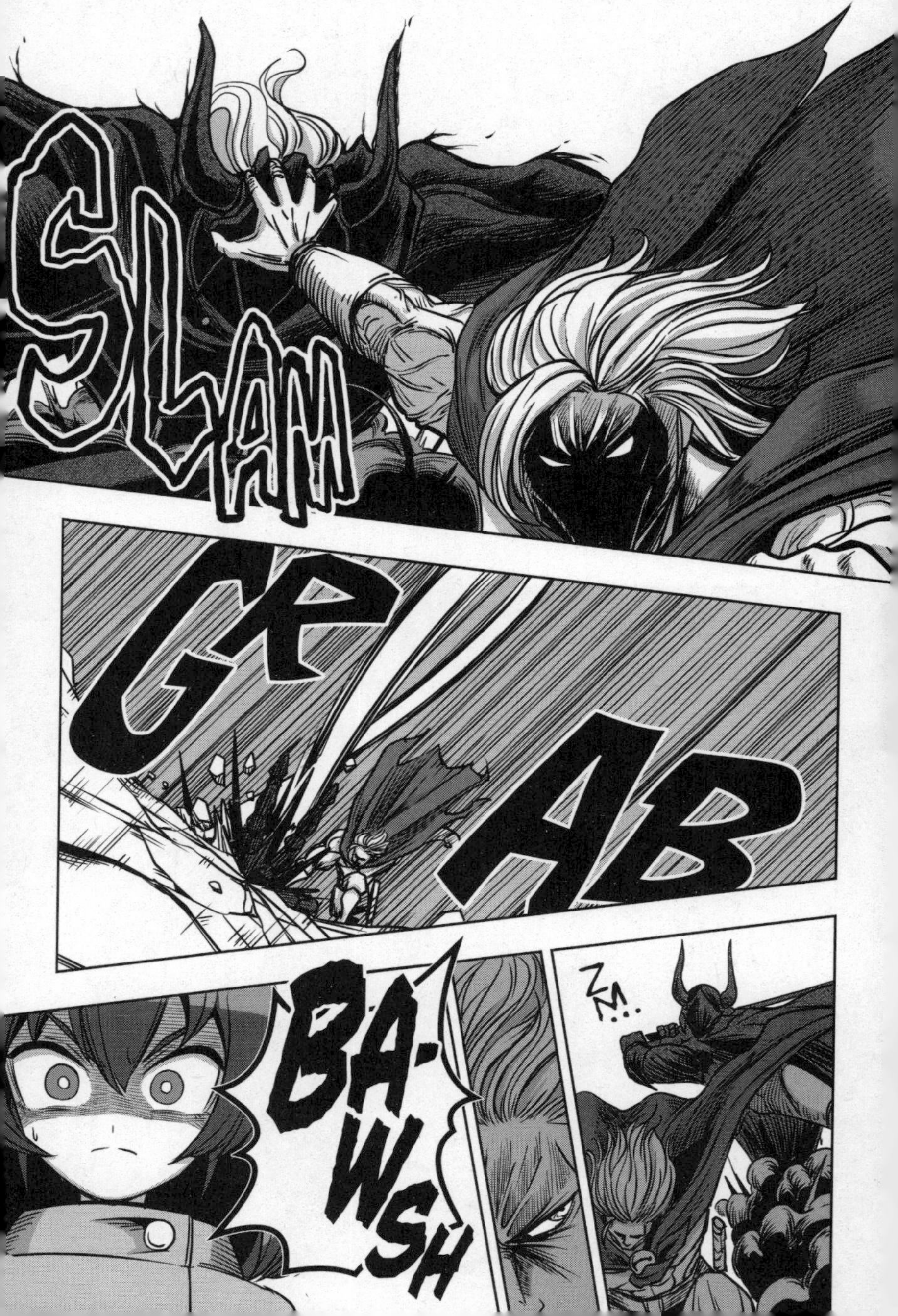
SLAM
GRAB
ZM...
BA-WSH

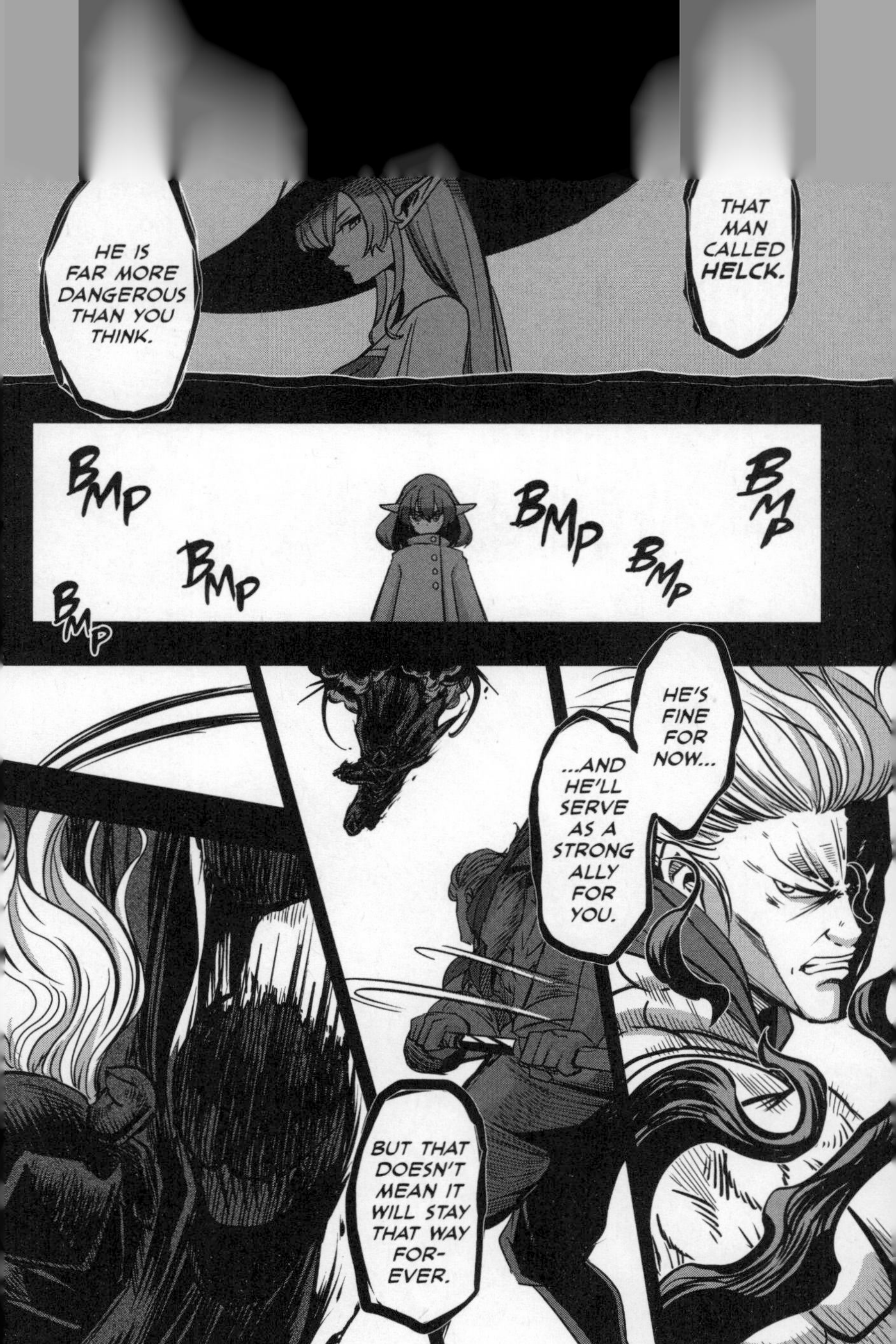
THAT MAN CALLED HELCK.
HE IS FAR MORE DANGEROUS THAN YOU THINK.
BMP
BMP
BMP
BMP
BMP
BMP
HE'S FINE FOR NOW...
...AND HE'LL SERVE AS A STRONG ALLY FOR YOU.
BUT THAT DOESN'T MEAN IT WILL STAY THAT WAY FOR-EVER.

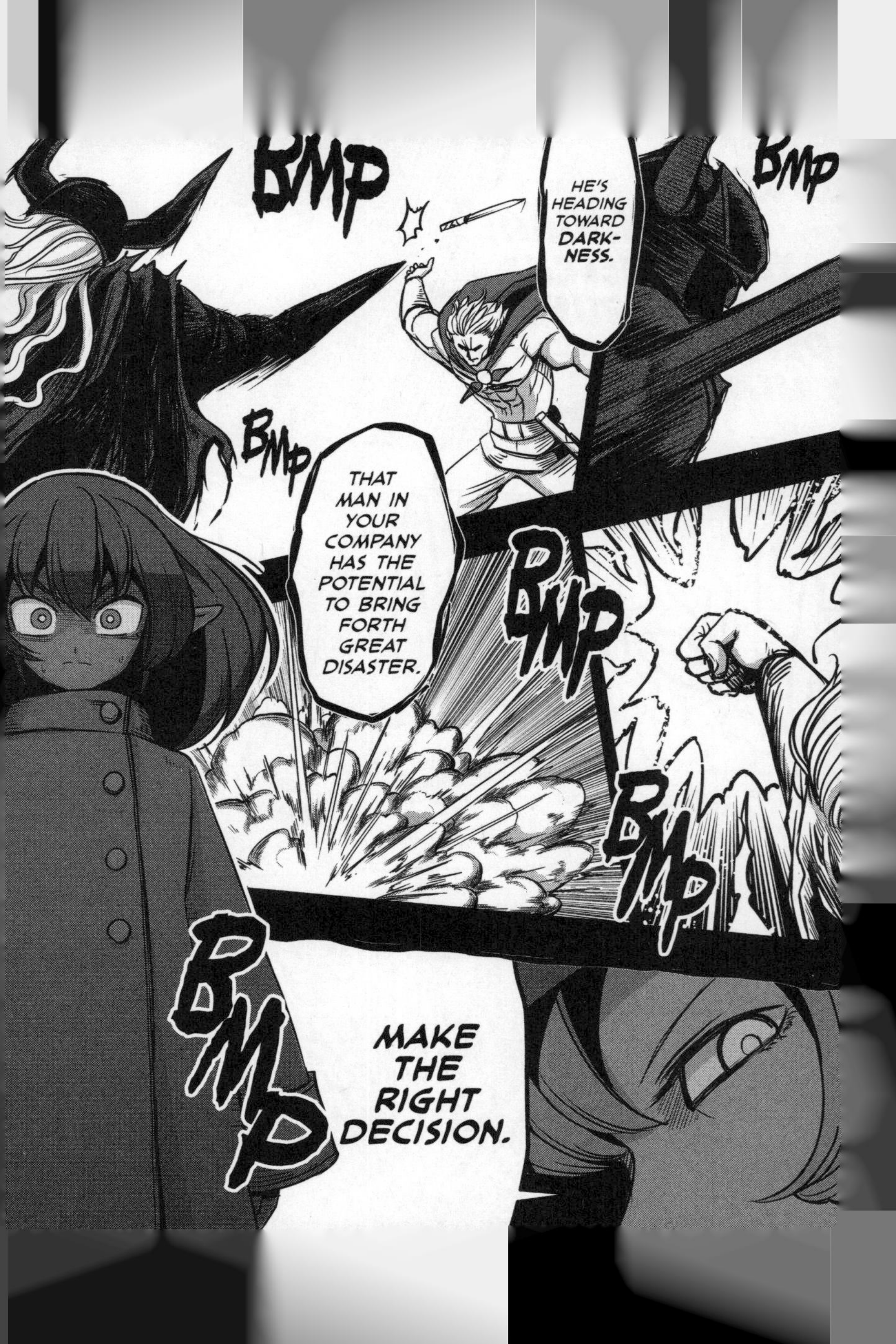
BMP
HE'S HEADING TOWARD DARK-NESS.
BMP
BMP
BMP
BMP
THAT MAN IN YOUR COMPANY HAS THE POTENTIAL TO BRING FORTH GREAT DISASTER.
MAKE THE RIGHT DECISION.
BMP

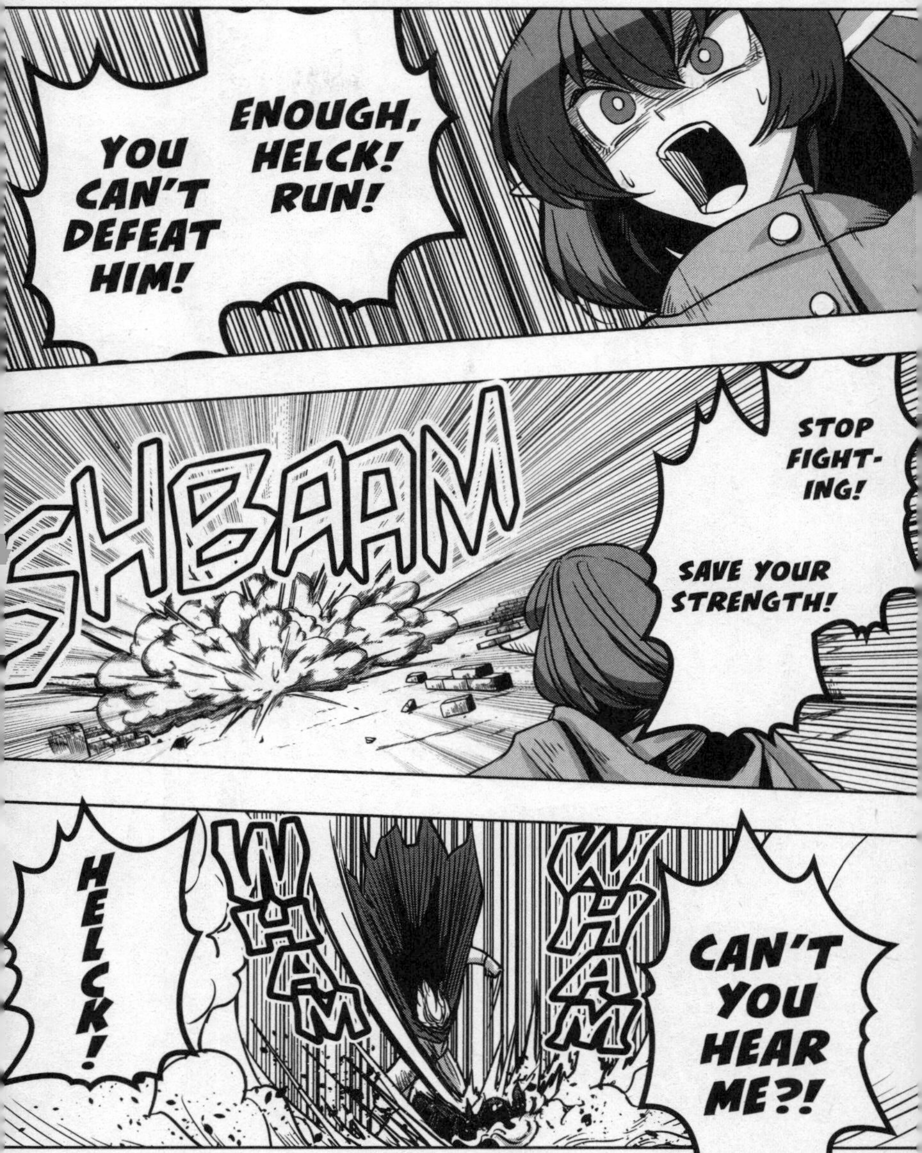
ENOUGH, HELCK! RUN!
YOU CAN'T DEFEAT HIM!
STOP FIGHT-ING!
SAVE YOUR STRENGTH!
SHBAAM
CAN'T YOU HEAR ME?!
WHAM
WHAM
HELCK!

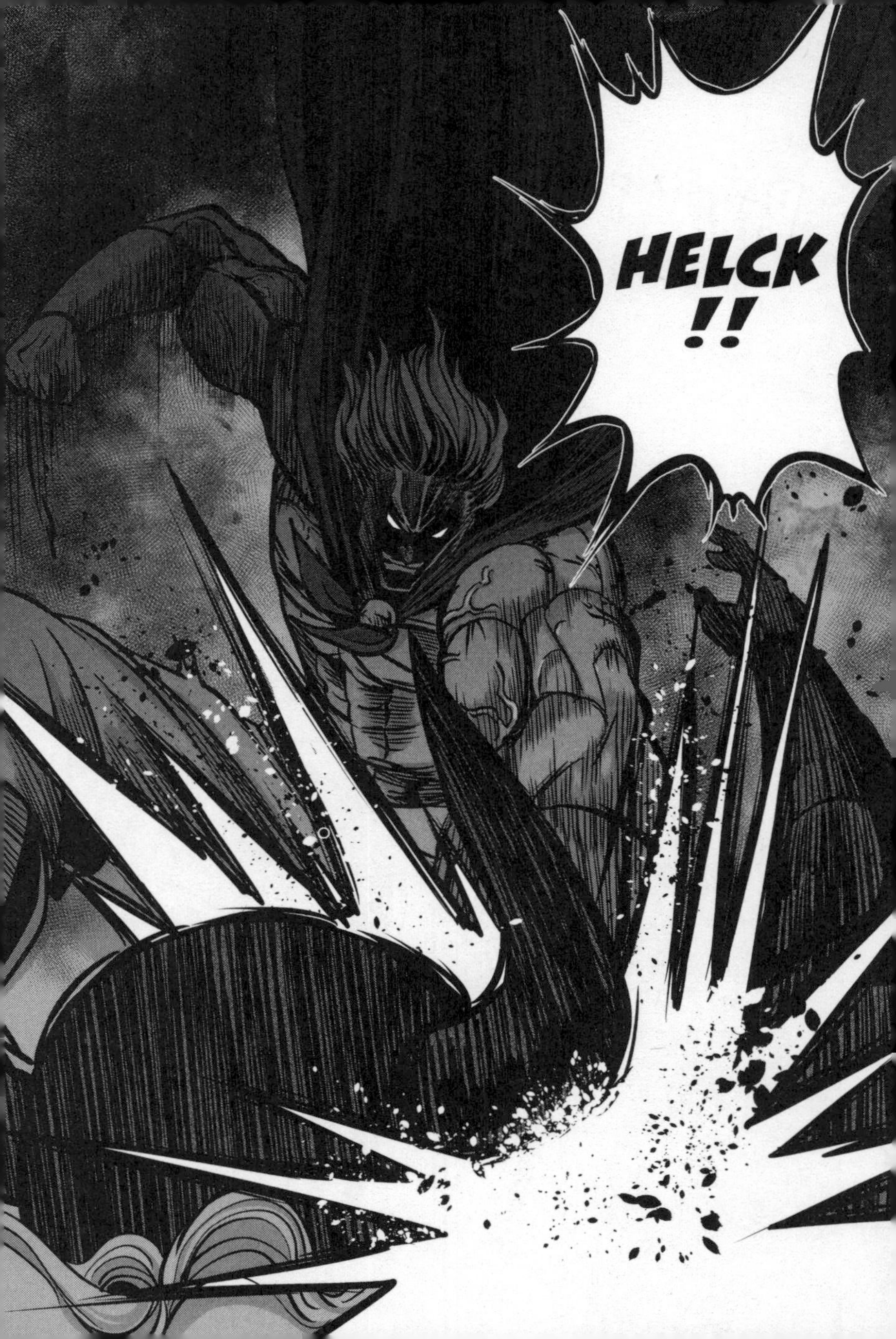
HELCK !!

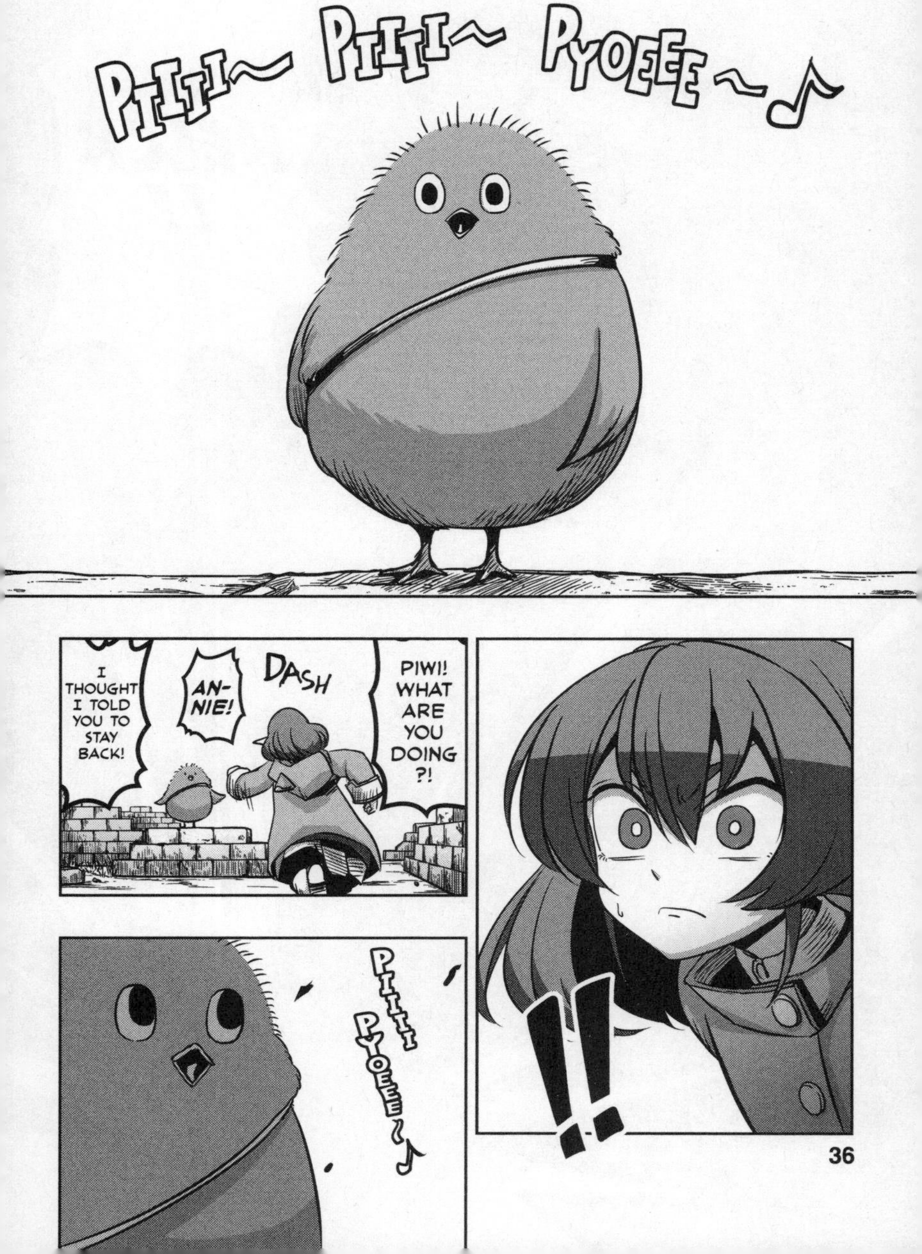
PIIII~ PIIII~ PYOEEE~♪
!!
PIWI! WHAT ARE YOU DOING?!
DASH
AN-NIE!
I THOUGHT I TOLD YOU TO STAY BACK!
PIIIII
PYOEEE~♪

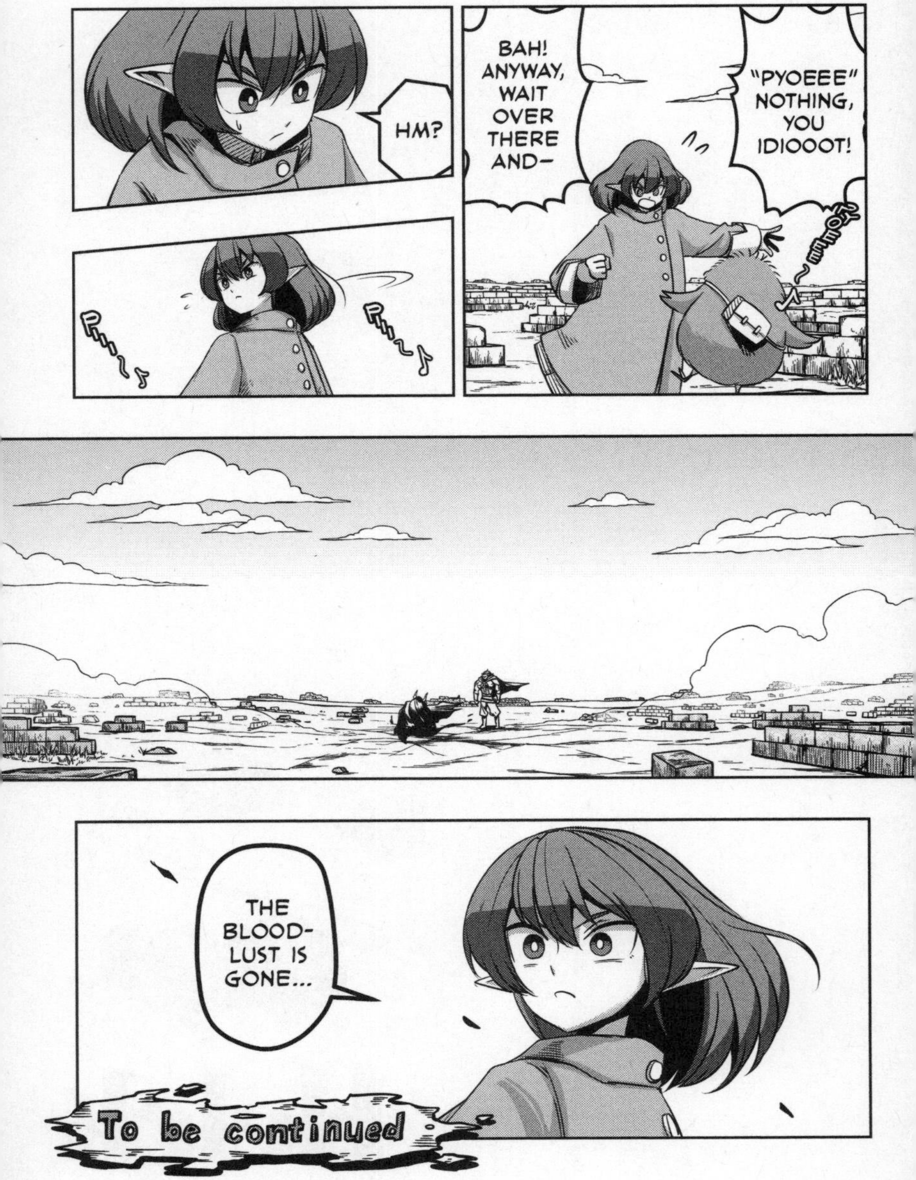

BAH! ANYWAY, WAIT OVER THERE AND—
"PYOEEE" NOTHING, YOU IDIOOOT!
HM?
Piii~♪
Piii~♪
THE BLOOD-LUST IS GONE...
To be continued

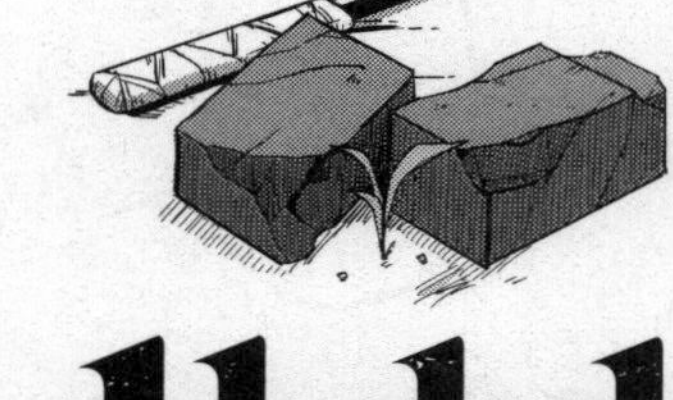

Helck

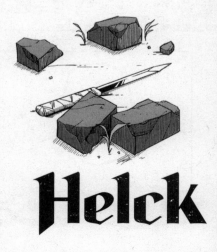

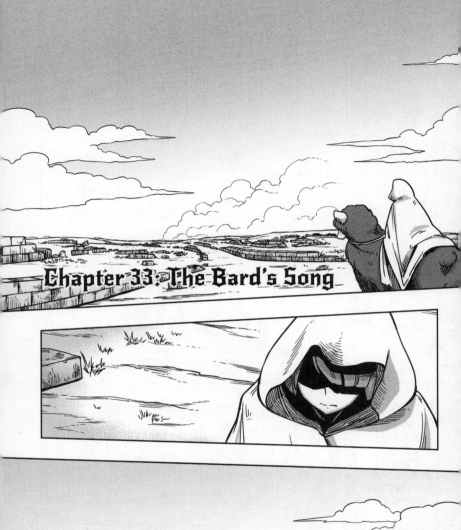

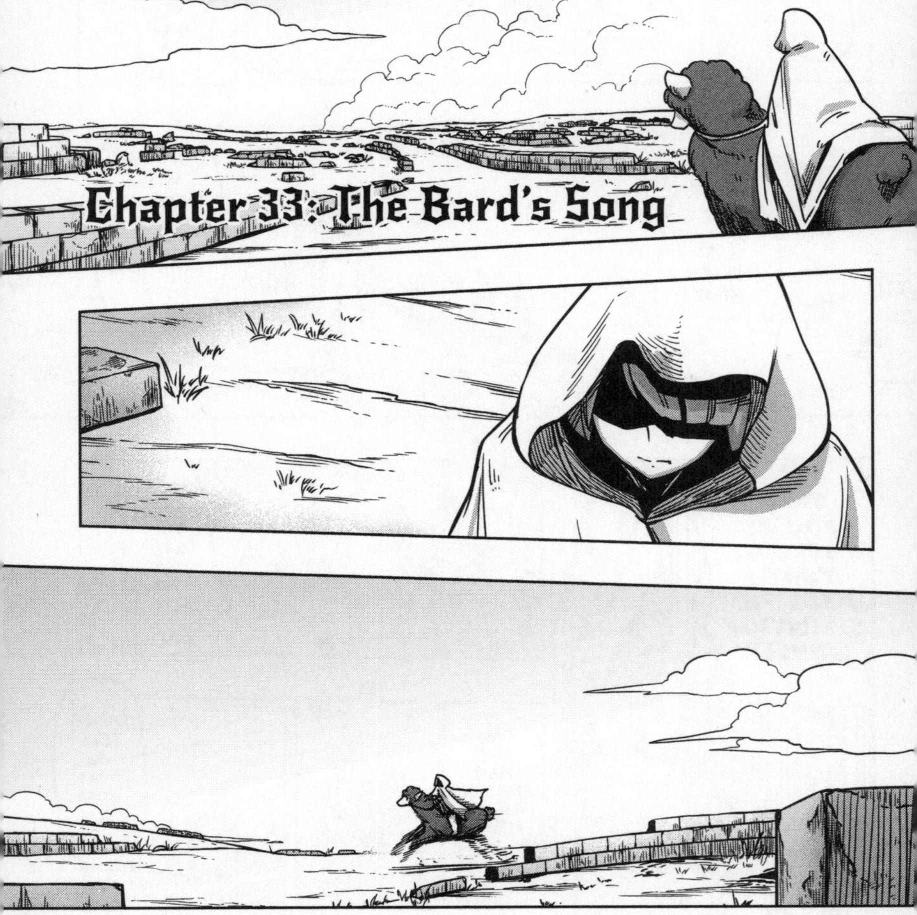
Chapter 33: The Bard's Song

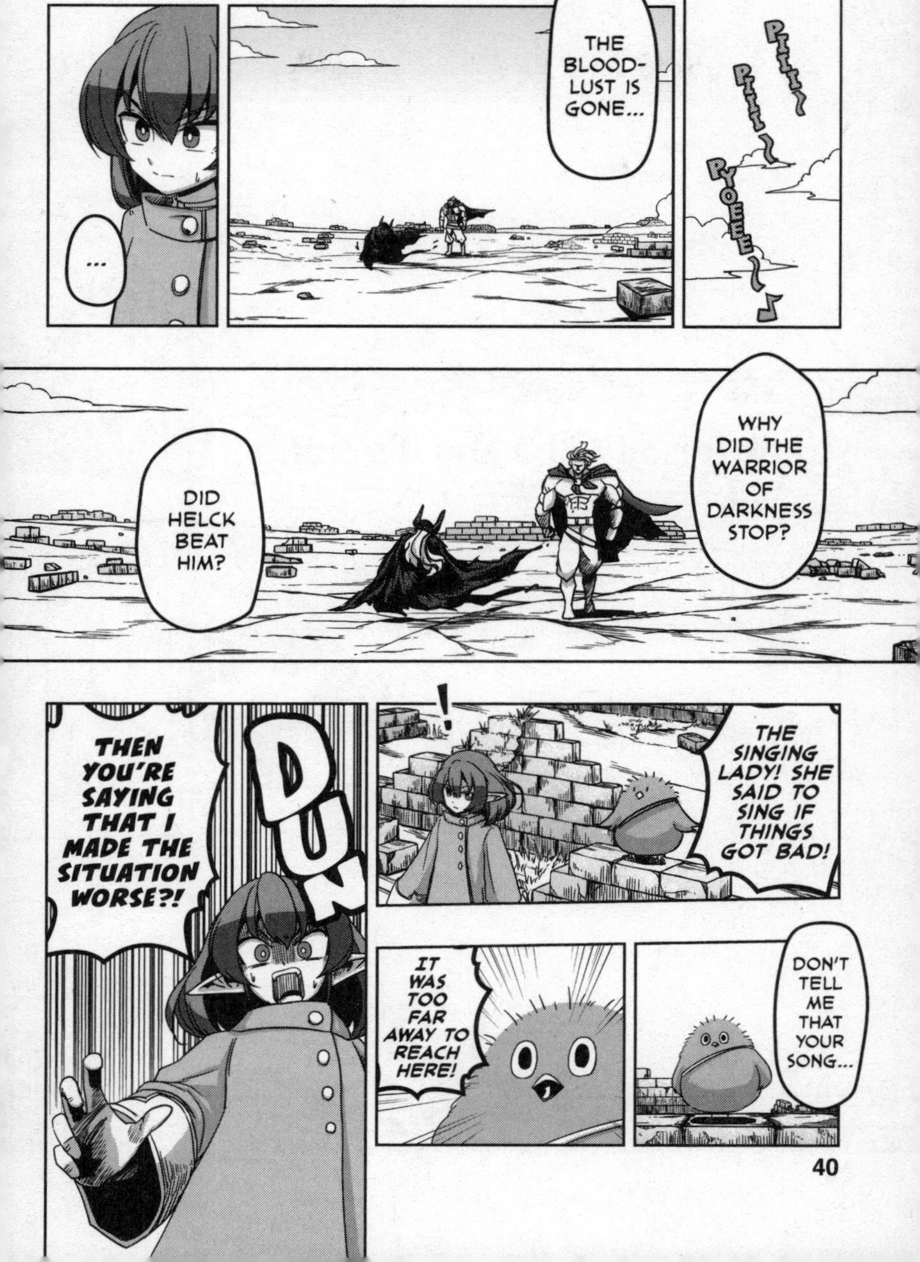
PIII~
PIII~
PYOEEE~♪
THE BLOOD-LUST IS GONE...
...
WHY DID THE WARRIOR OF DARKNESS STOP?
DID HELCK BEAT HIM?
!
THE SINGING LADY! SHE SAID TO SING IF THINGS GOT BAD!
DON'T TELL ME THAT YOUR SONG...
IT WAS TOO FAR AWAY TO REACH HERE!
DUN
THEN YOU'RE SAYING THAT I MADE THE SITUATION WORSE?!

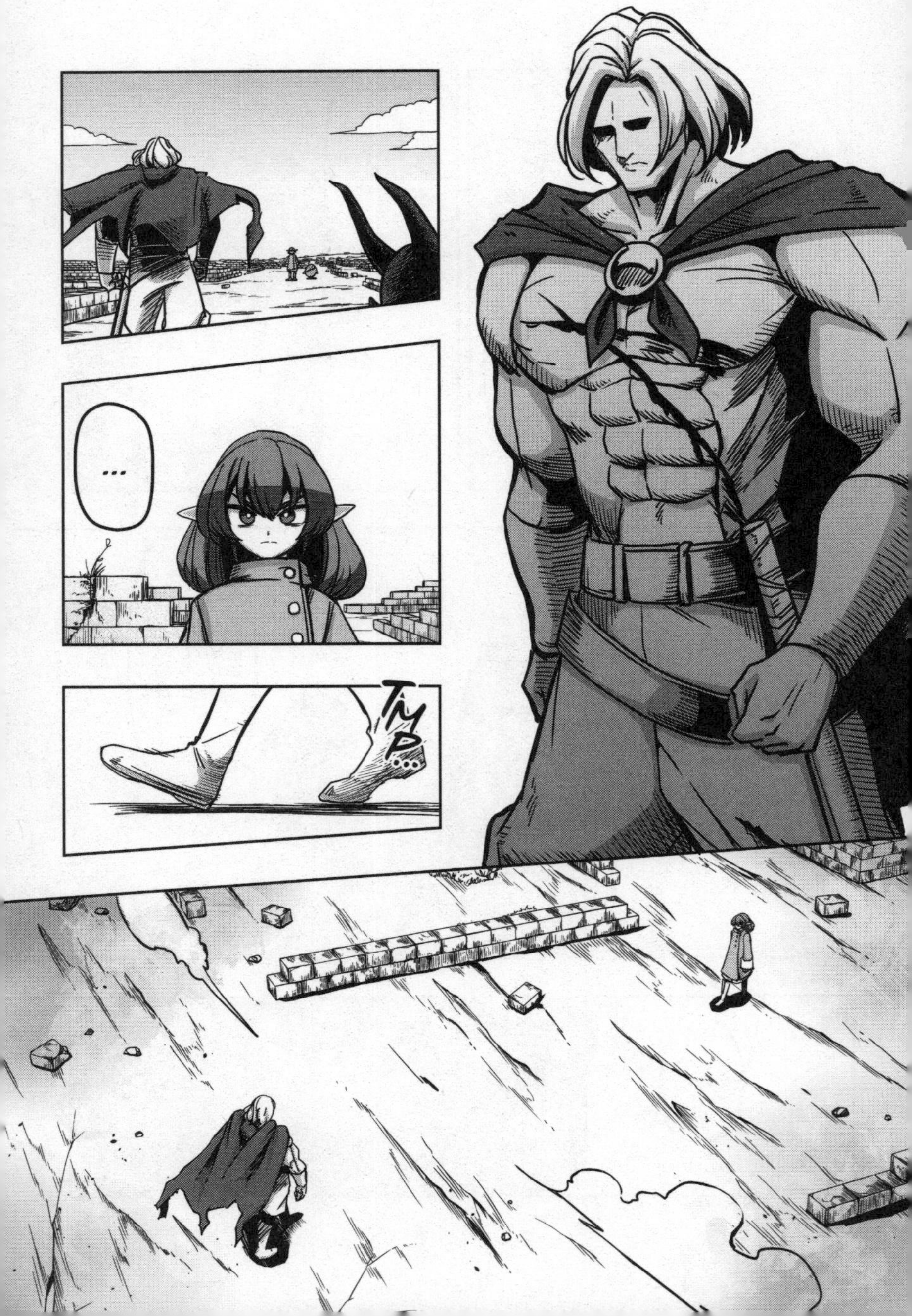
...
TMP...

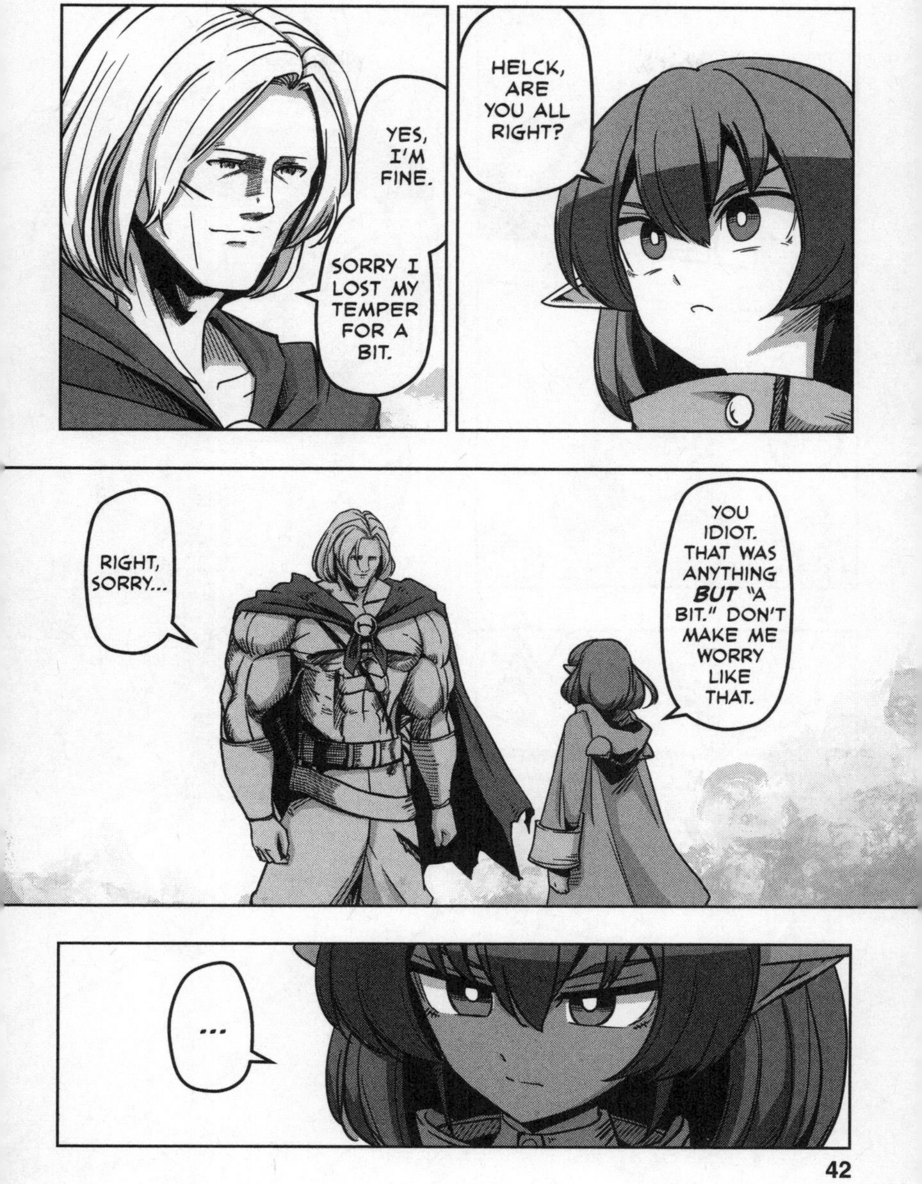
HELCK, ARE YOU ALL RIGHT?
YES, I'M FINE.
SORRY I LOST MY TEMPER FOR A BIT.
YOU IDIOT. THAT WAS ANYTHING **BUT** "A BIT." DON'T MAKE ME WORRY LIKE THAT.
RIGHT, SORRY...
...

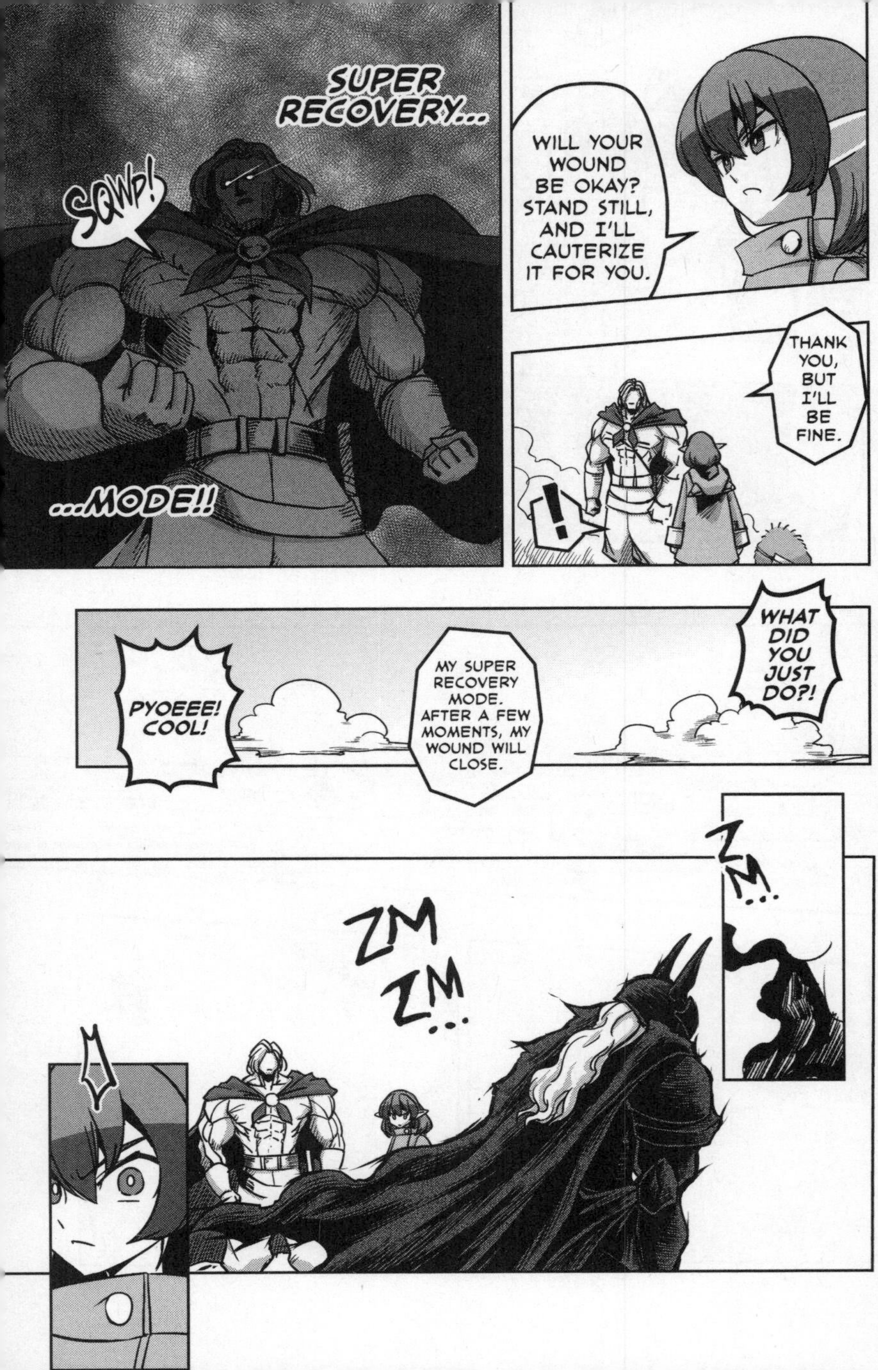
WILL YOUR WOUND BE OKAY? STAND STILL, AND I'LL CAUTERIZE IT FOR YOU.
THANK YOU, BUT I'LL BE FINE.
!
SUPER RECOVERY...
SQWP!
...MODE!!
WHAT DID YOU JUST DO?!
MY SUPER RECOVERY MODE. AFTER A FEW MOMENTS, MY WOUND WILL CLOSE.
PYOEEE! COOL!
ZM...
ZM ZM...

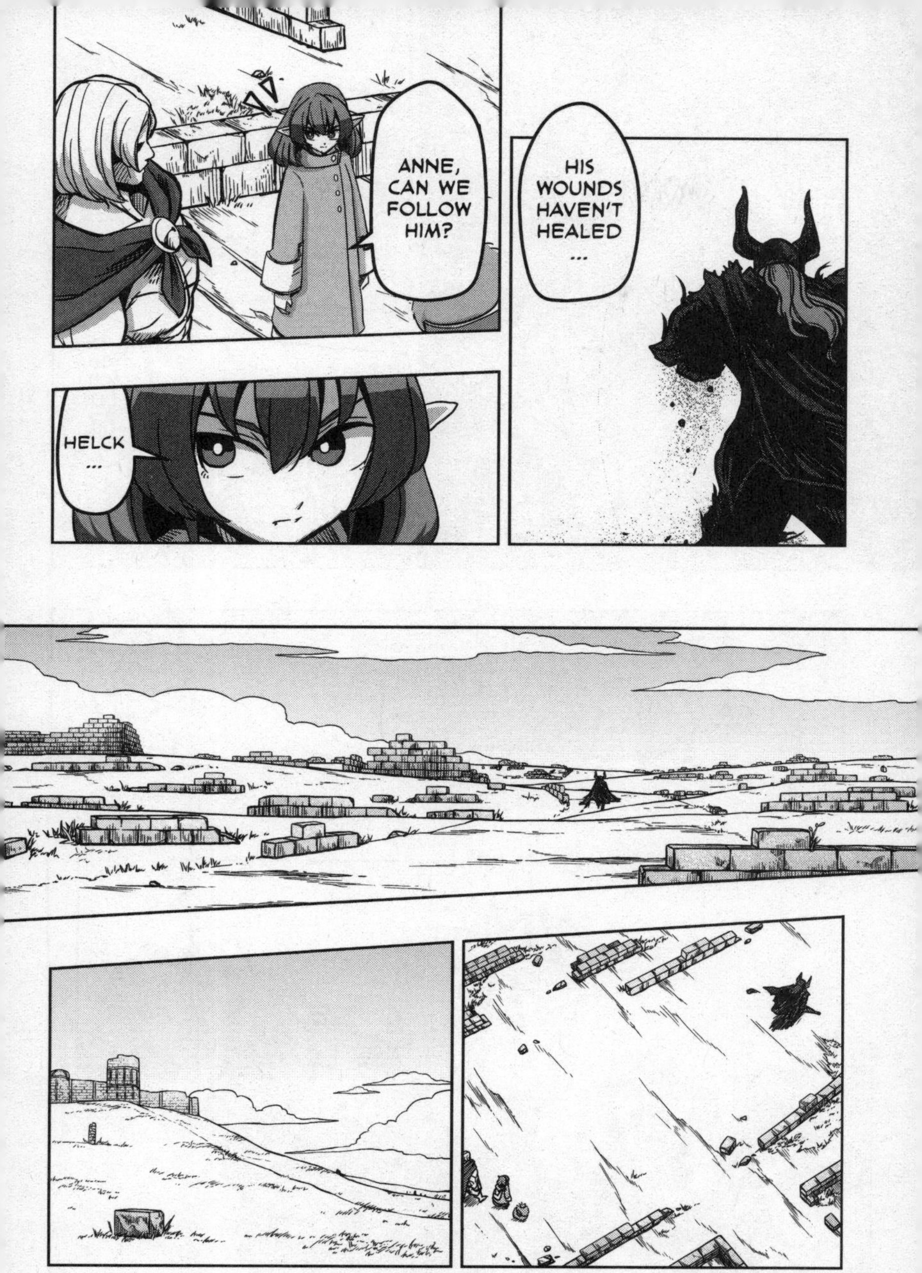
HIS WOUNDS HAVEN'T HEALED ...
ANNE, CAN WE FOLLOW HIM?
HELCK ...

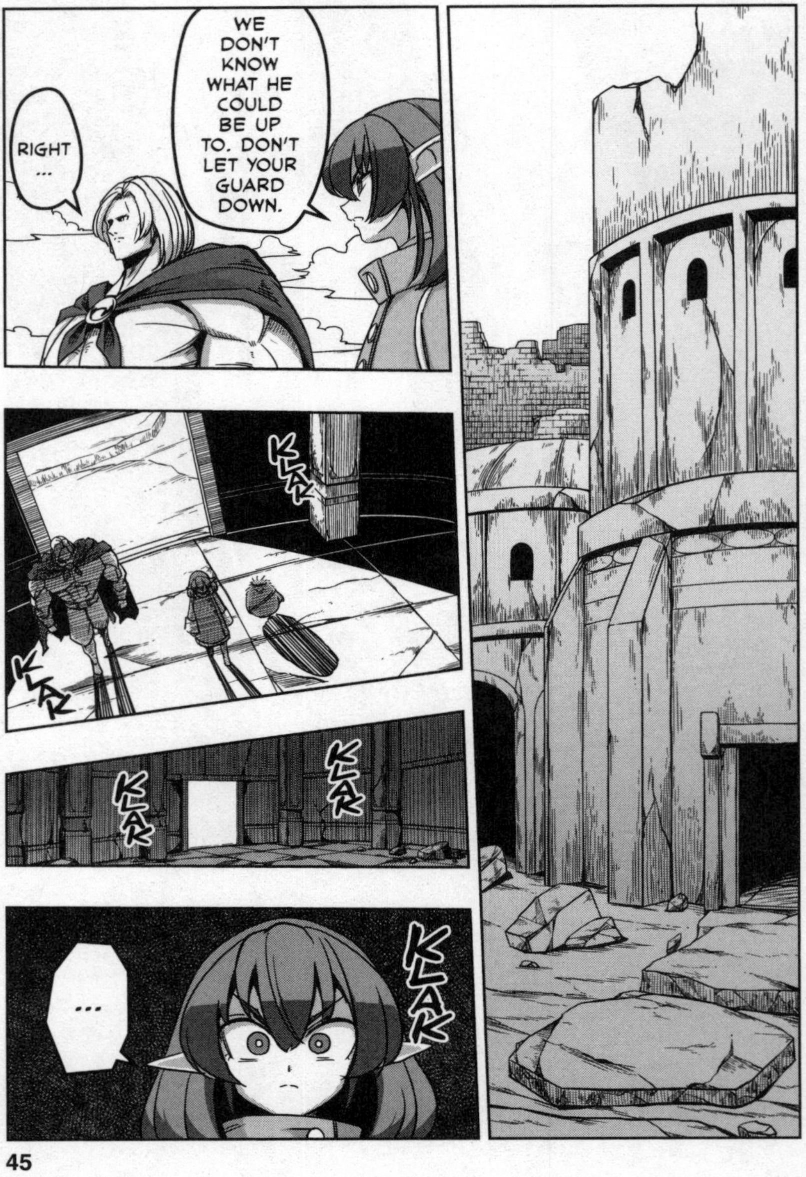
WE DON'T KNOW WHAT HE COULD BE UP TO. DON'T LET YOUR GUARD DOWN.
RIGHT ...
KLAK
KLAK
KLAK
KLAK
KLAK
...

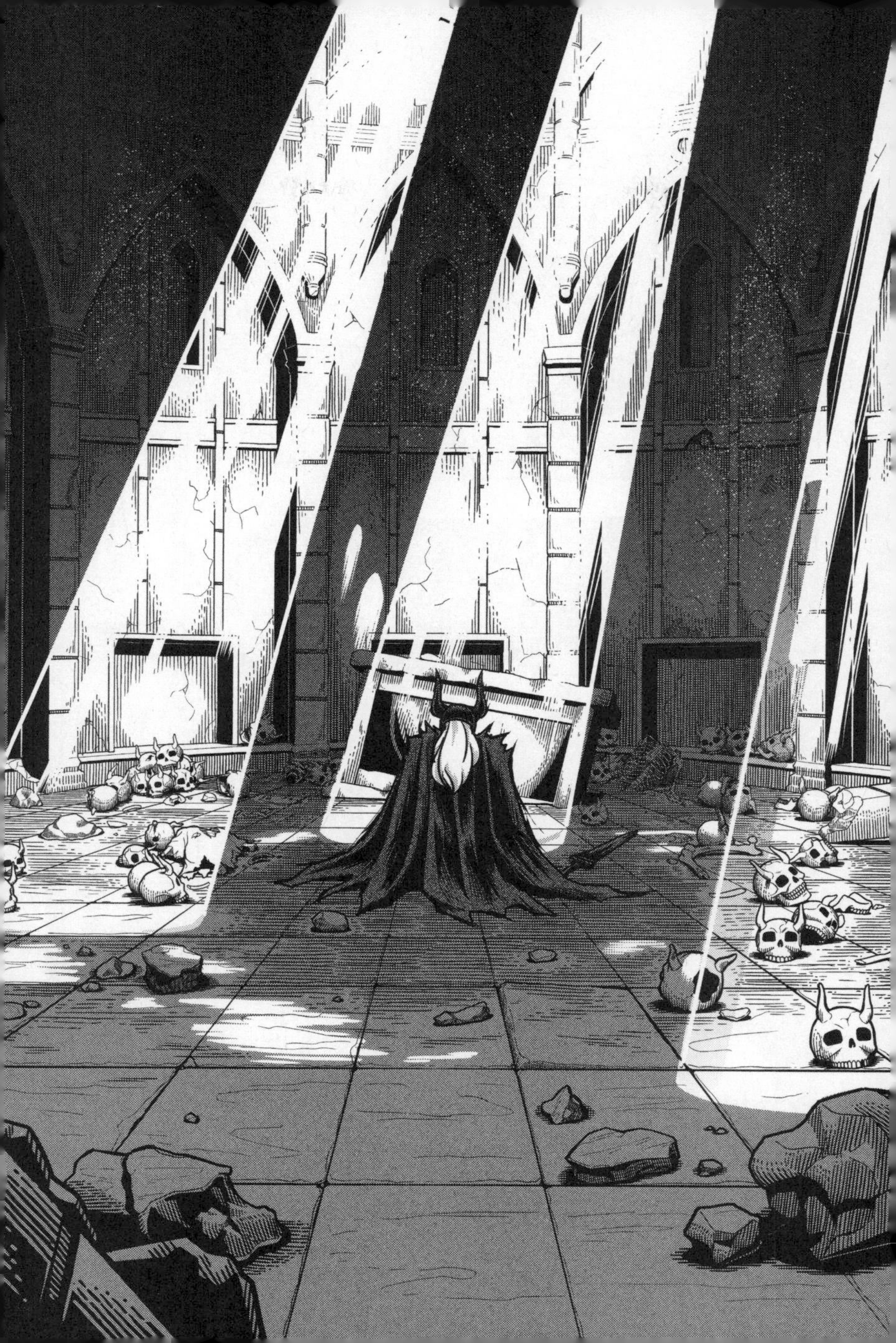

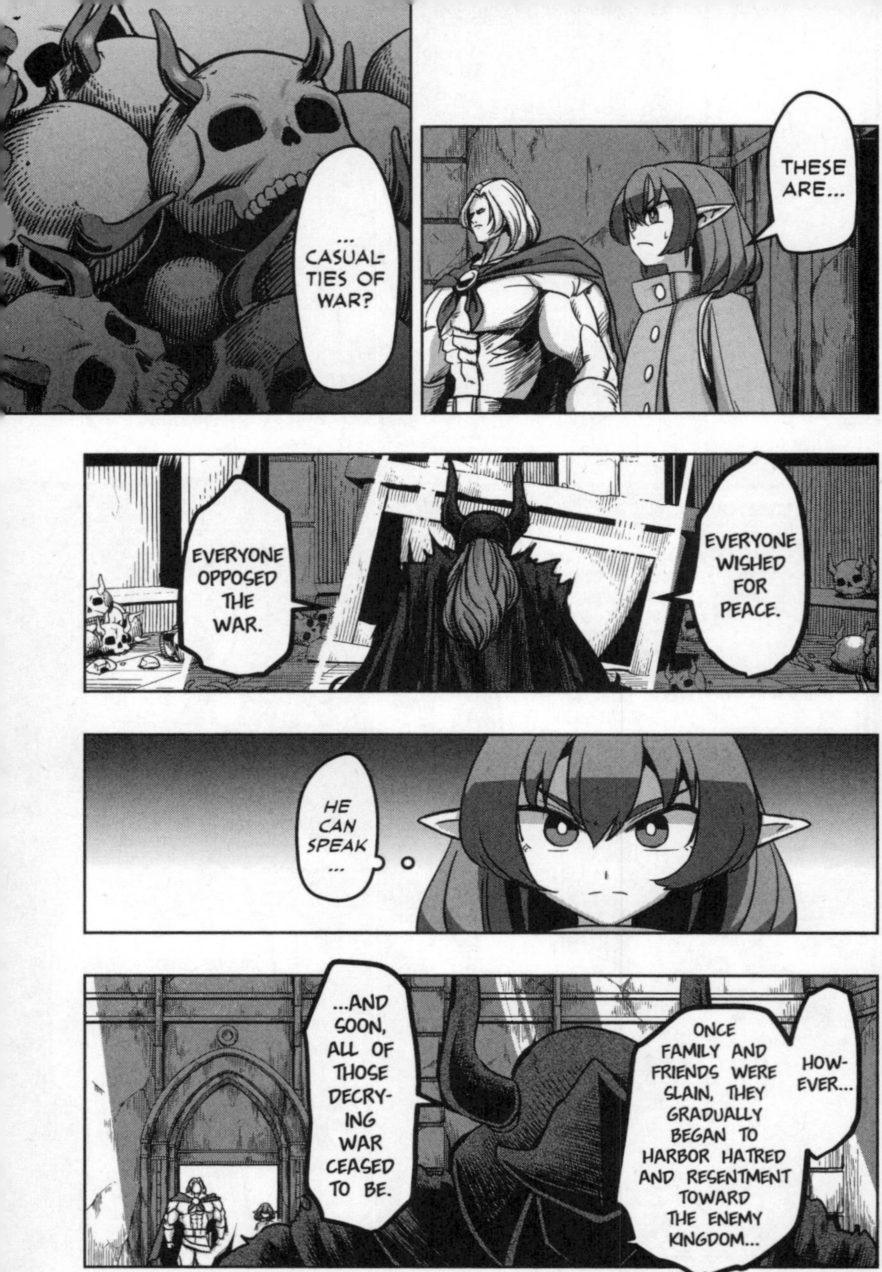
THESE ARE...
...CASUAL-TIES OF WAR?
EVERYONE WISHED FOR PEACE.
EVERYONE OPPOSED THE WAR.
HE CAN SPEAK...
HOW-EVER...
ONCE FAMILY AND FRIENDS WERE SLAIN, THEY GRADUALLY BEGAN TO HARBOR HATRED AND RESENTMENT TOWARD THE ENEMY KINGDOM...
...AND SOON, ALL OF THOSE DECRY-ING WAR CEASED TO BE.

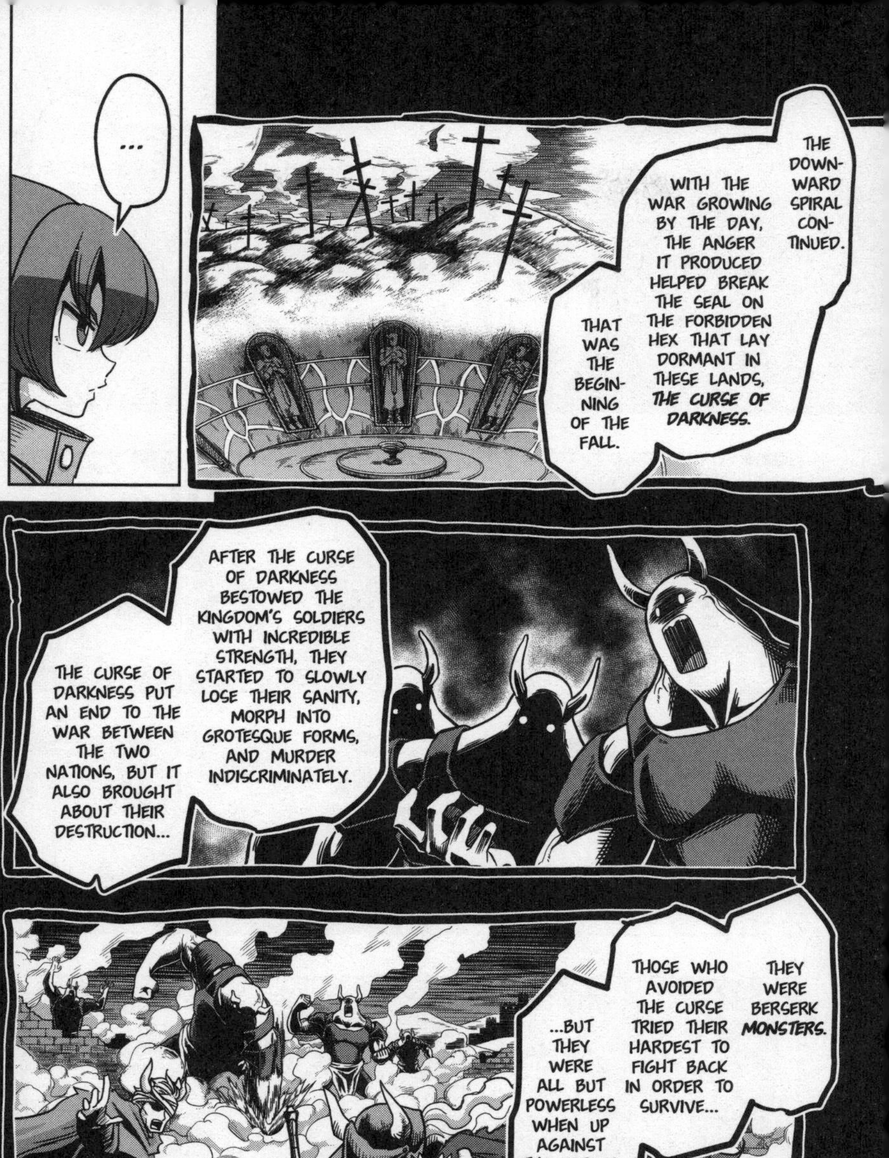
THE DOWNWARD SPIRAL CONTINUED.
WITH THE WAR GROWING BY THE DAY, THE ANGER IT PRODUCED HELPED BREAK THE SEAL ON THE FORBIDDEN HEX THAT LAY DORMANT IN THESE LANDS, *THE CURSE OF DARKNESS.*
THAT WAS THE BEGINNING OF THE FALL.
...
AFTER THE CURSE OF DARKNESS BESTOWED THE KINGDOM'S SOLDIERS WITH INCREDIBLE STRENGTH, THEY STARTED TO SLOWLY LOSE THEIR SANITY, MORPH INTO GROTESQUE FORMS, AND MURDER INDISCRIMINATELY.
THE CURSE OF DARKNESS PUT AN END TO THE WAR BETWEEN THE TWO NATIONS, BUT IT ALSO BROUGHT ABOUT THEIR DESTRUCTION...
THEY WERE BERSERK *MONSTERS.*
THOSE WHO AVOIDED THE CURSE TRIED THEIR HARDEST TO FIGHT BACK IN ORDER TO SURVIVE...
...BUT THEY WERE ALL BUT POWERLESS WHEN UP AGAINST THE FORCES OF DARKNESS.

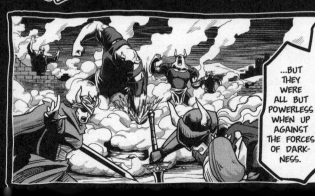

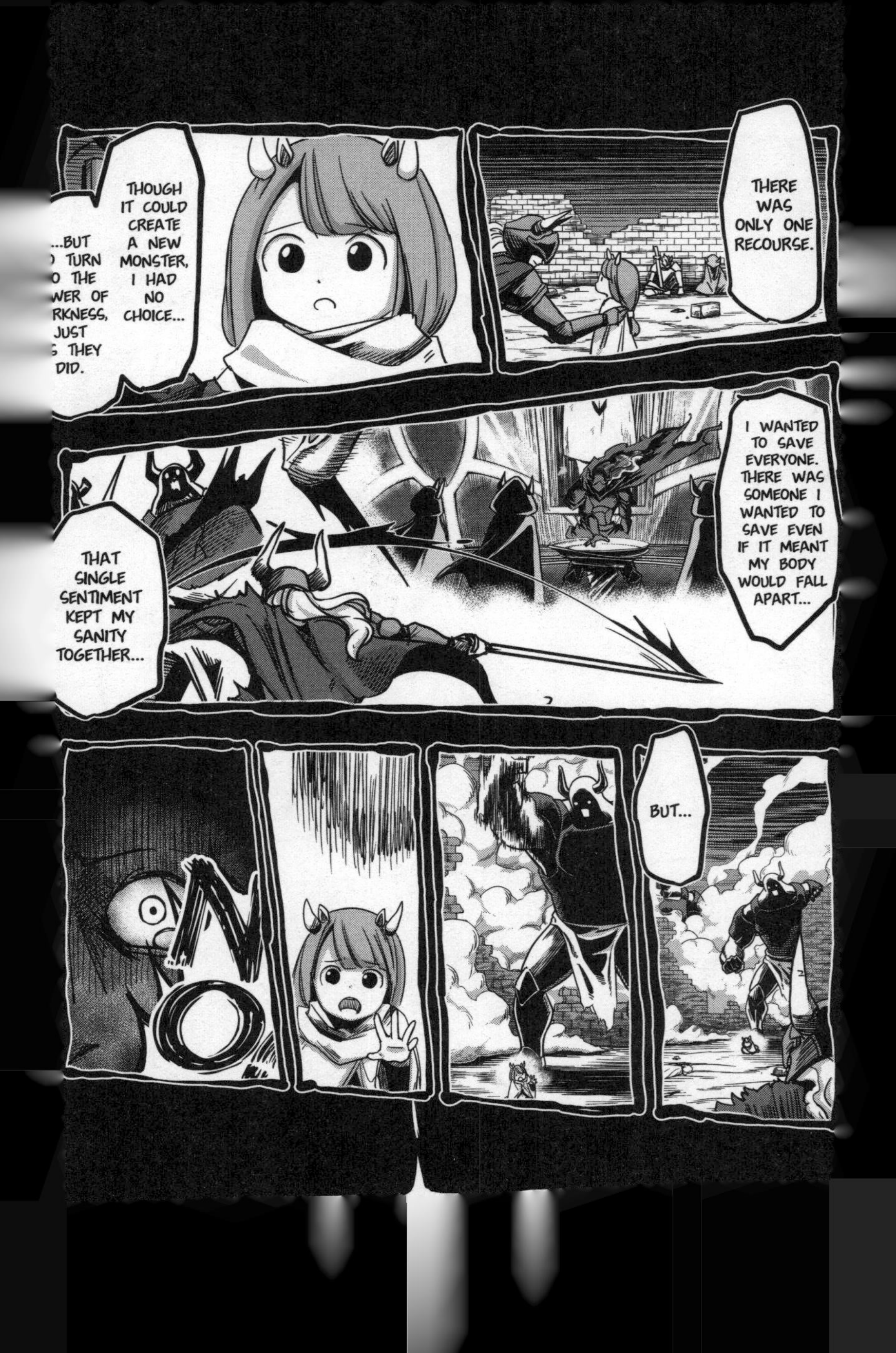

THERE WAS ONLY ONE RECOURSE.
THOUGH IT COULD CREATE A NEW MONSTER, I HAD NO CHOICE...
...BUT TURN THE WER OF RKNESS, JUST THEY DID.
I WANTED TO SAVE EVERYONE. THERE WAS SOMEONE I WANTED TO SAVE EVEN IF IT MEANT MY BODY WOULD FALL APART...
THAT SINGLE SENTIMENT KEPT MY SANITY TOGETHER...
BUT...
NO

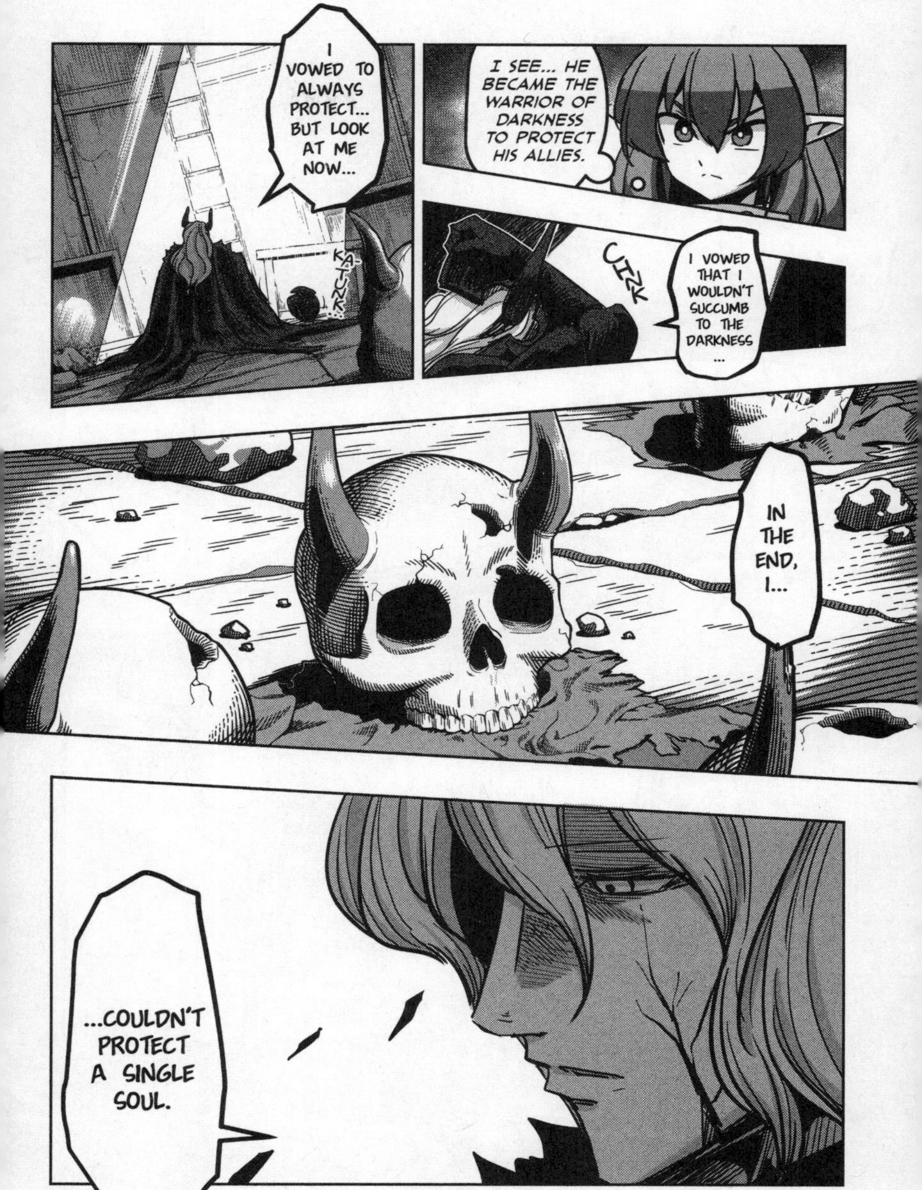
I SEE... HE BECAME THE WARRIOR OF DARKNESS TO PROTECT HIS ALLIES.
CLINK
I VOWED THAT I WOULDN'T SUCCUMB TO THE DARKNESS ...
I VOWED TO ALWAYS PROTECT... BUT LOOK AT ME NOW...
KA-TUNK...
IN THE END, I...
...COULDN'T PROTECT A SINGLE SOUL.

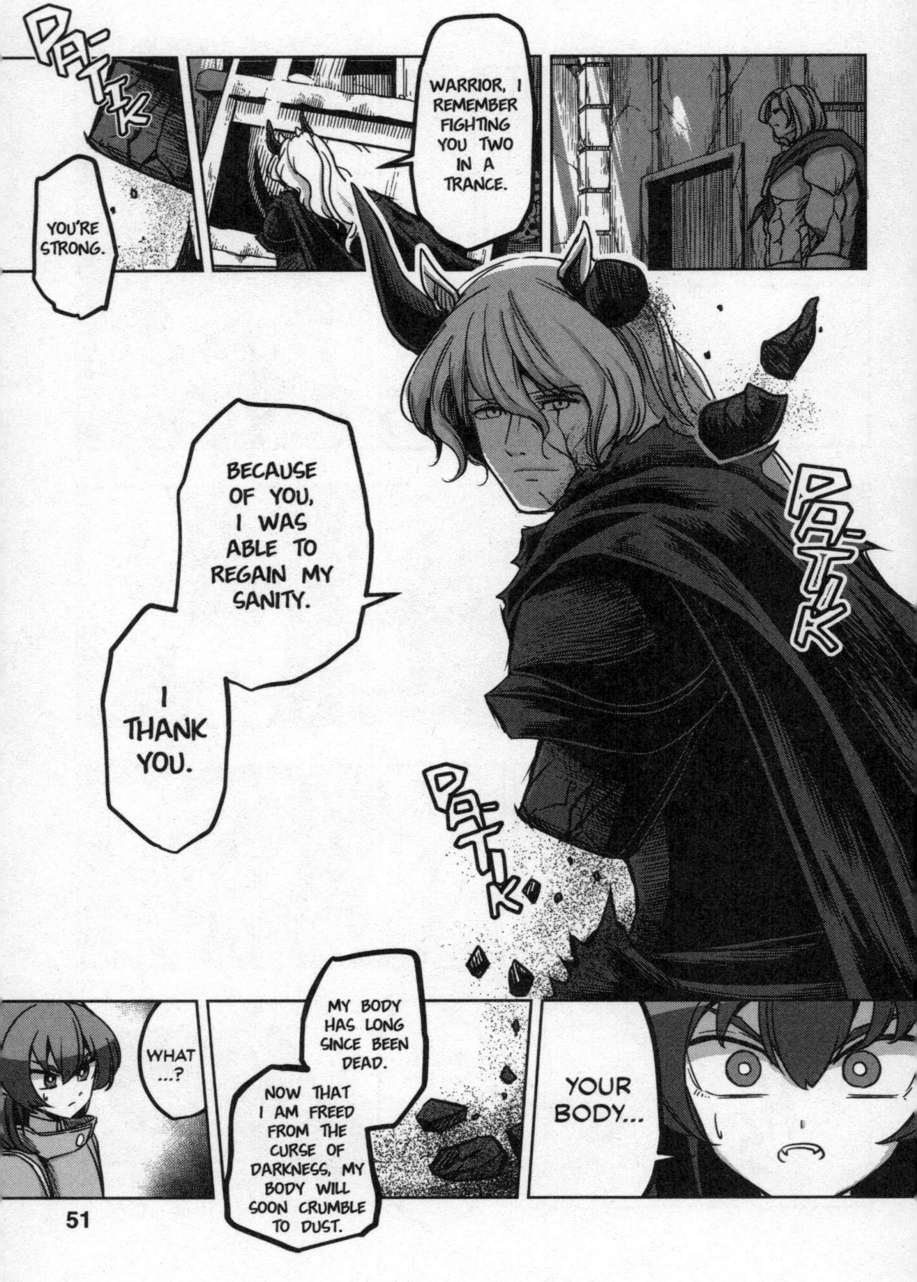
WARRIOR, I REMEMBER FIGHTING YOU TWO IN A TRANCE.
DA-TIK
YOU'RE STRONG.
DA-TIK
BECAUSE OF YOU, I WAS ABLE TO REGAIN MY SANITY.
I THANK YOU.
DA-TIK
YOUR BODY...
MY BODY HAS LONG SINCE BEEN DEAD.
NOW THAT I AM FREED FROM THE CURSE OF DARKNESS, MY BODY WILL SOON CRUMBLE TO DUST.
WHAT ...?

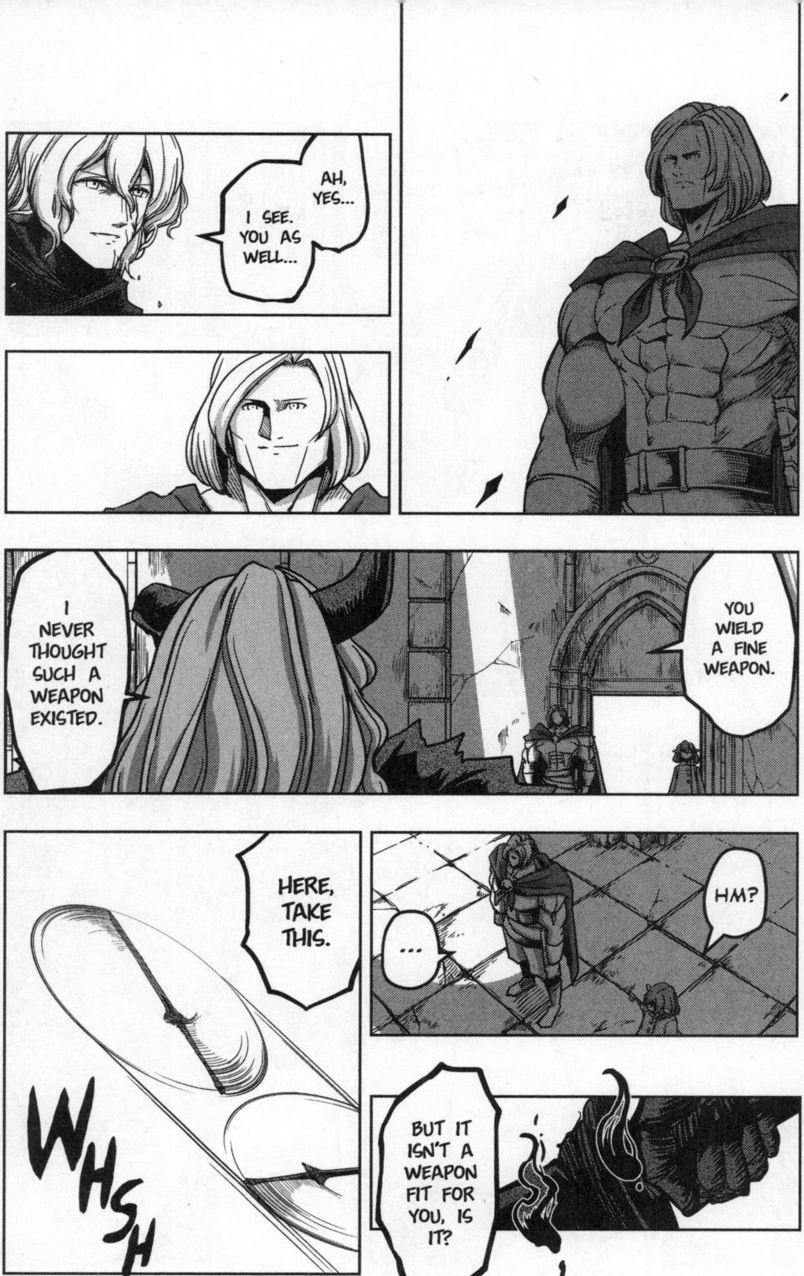
AH, YES... I SEE. YOU AS WELL...
YOU WIELD A FINE WEAPON.
I NEVER THOUGHT SUCH A WEAPON EXISTED.
HM?
...
BUT IT ISN'T A WEAPON FIT FOR YOU, IS IT?
HERE, TAKE THIS.
WHSH

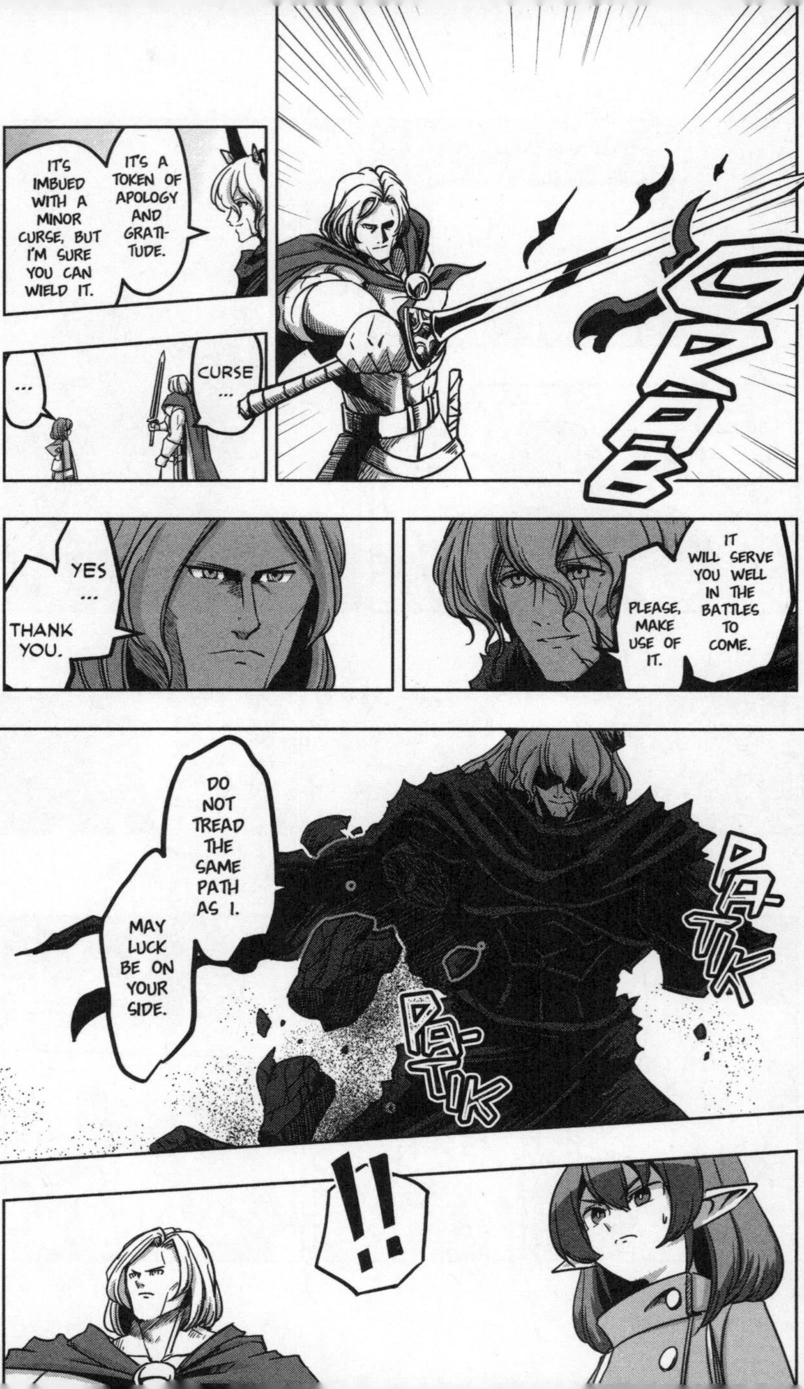
GRAB
IT'S A TOKEN OF APOLOGY AND GRATITUDE.
IT'S IMBUED WITH A MINOR CURSE, BUT I'M SURE YOU CAN WIELD IT.
CURSE ...
...
IT WILL SERVE YOU WELL IN THE BATTLES TO COME.
PLEASE, MAKE USE OF IT.
YES ...
THANK YOU.
DO NOT TREAD THE SAME PATH AS I.
MAY LUCK BE ON YOUR SIDE.
PA-TIK
PA-TIK
!!

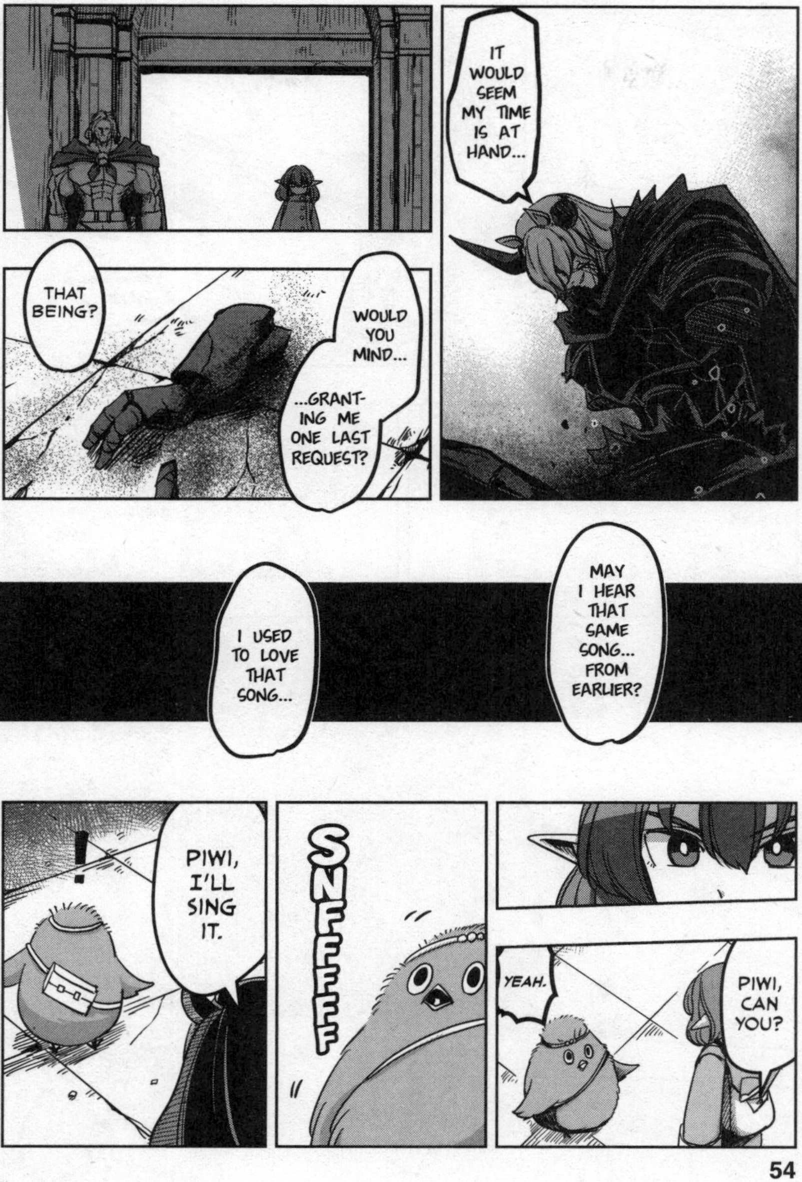
IT WOULD SEEM MY TIME IS AT HAND...
WOULD YOU MIND...
...GRANT-ING ME ONE LAST REQUEST?
THAT BEING?
MAY I HEAR THAT SAME SONG... FROM EARLIER?
I USED TO LOVE THAT SONG...
PIWI, CAN YOU?
YEAH.
SNFFFF
!
PIWI, I'LL SING IT.

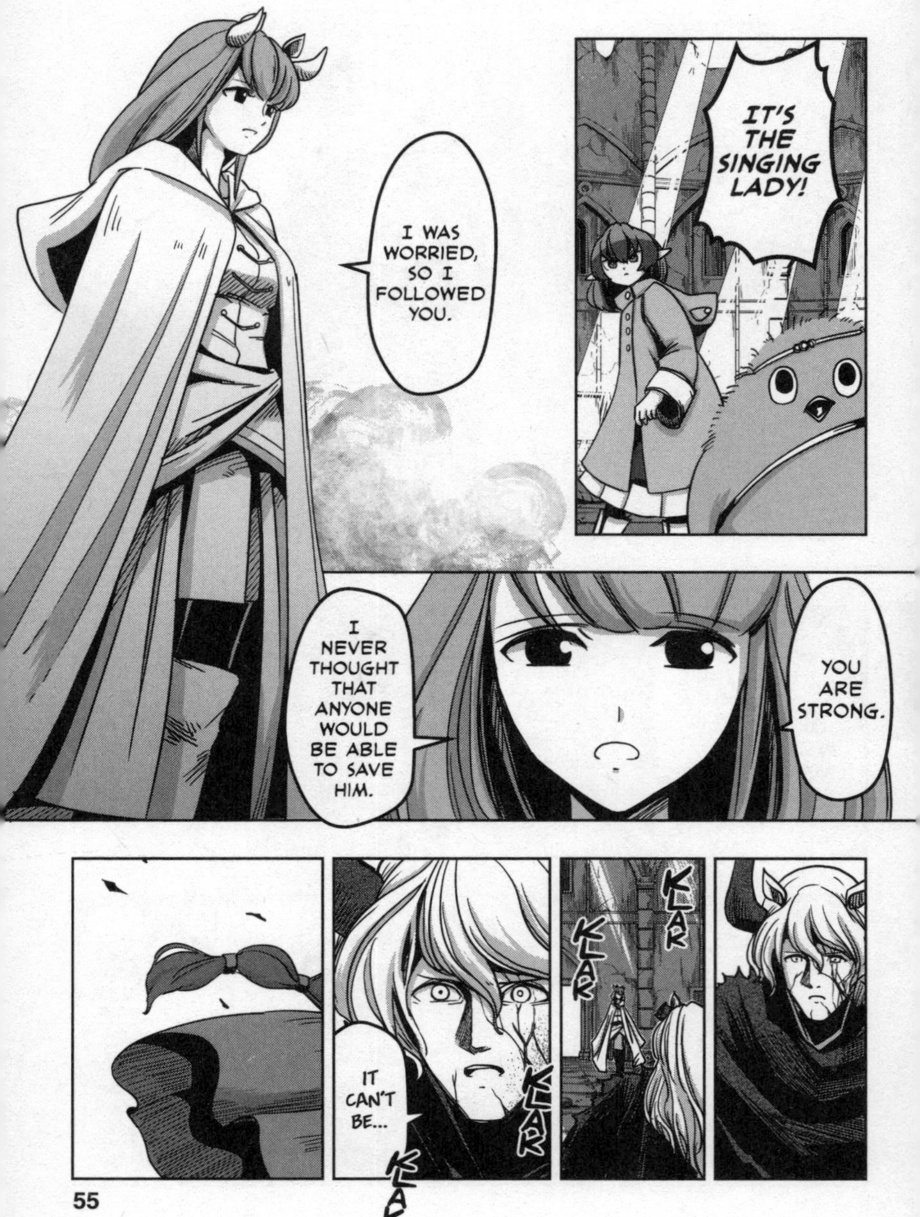
IT'S THE SINGING LADY!
I WAS WORRIED, SO I FOLLOWED YOU.
YOU ARE STRONG.
I NEVER THOUGHT THAT ANYONE WOULD BE ABLE TO SAVE HIM.
KLAK
KLAK
KLAK
IT CAN'T BE...
KLAK

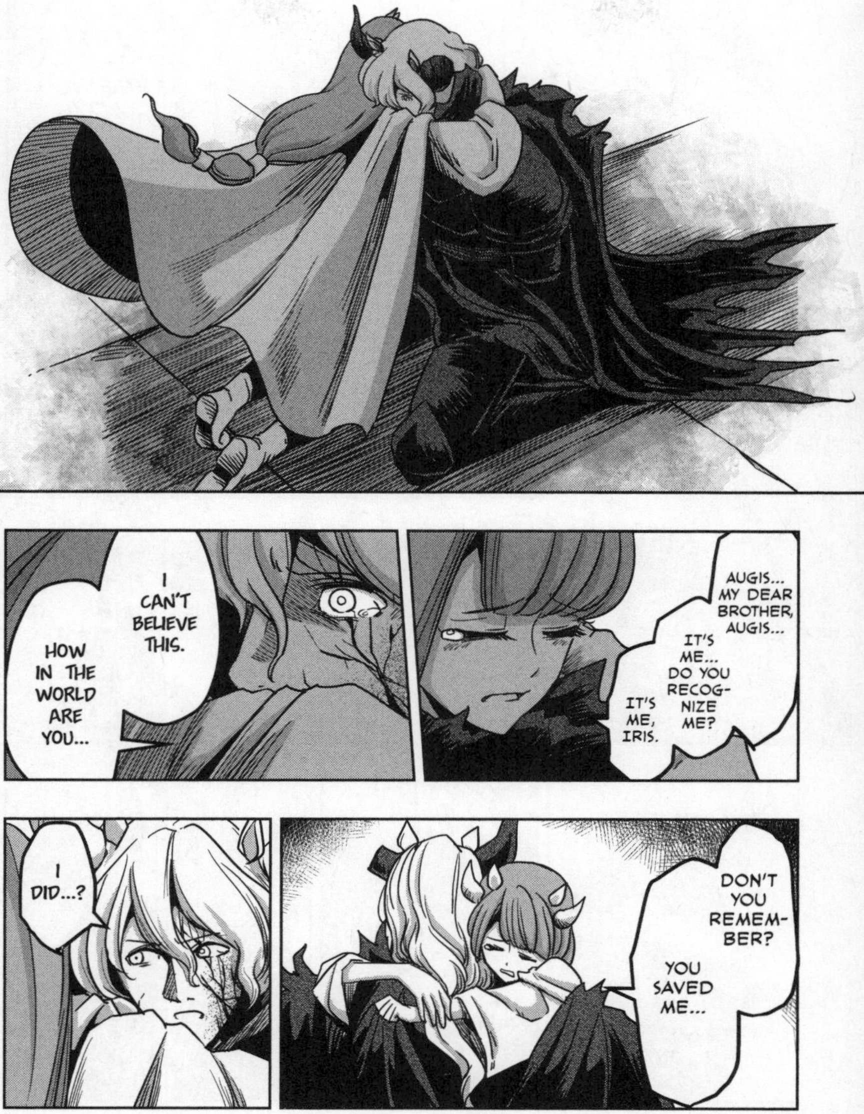
AUGIS... MY DEAR BROTHER, AUGIS...
IT'S ME... DO YOU RECOG-NIZE ME?
IT'S ME, IRIS.
I CAN'T BELIEVE THIS.
HOW IN THE WORLD ARE YOU...
DON'T YOU REMEM-BER?
YOU SAVED ME...
I DID...?

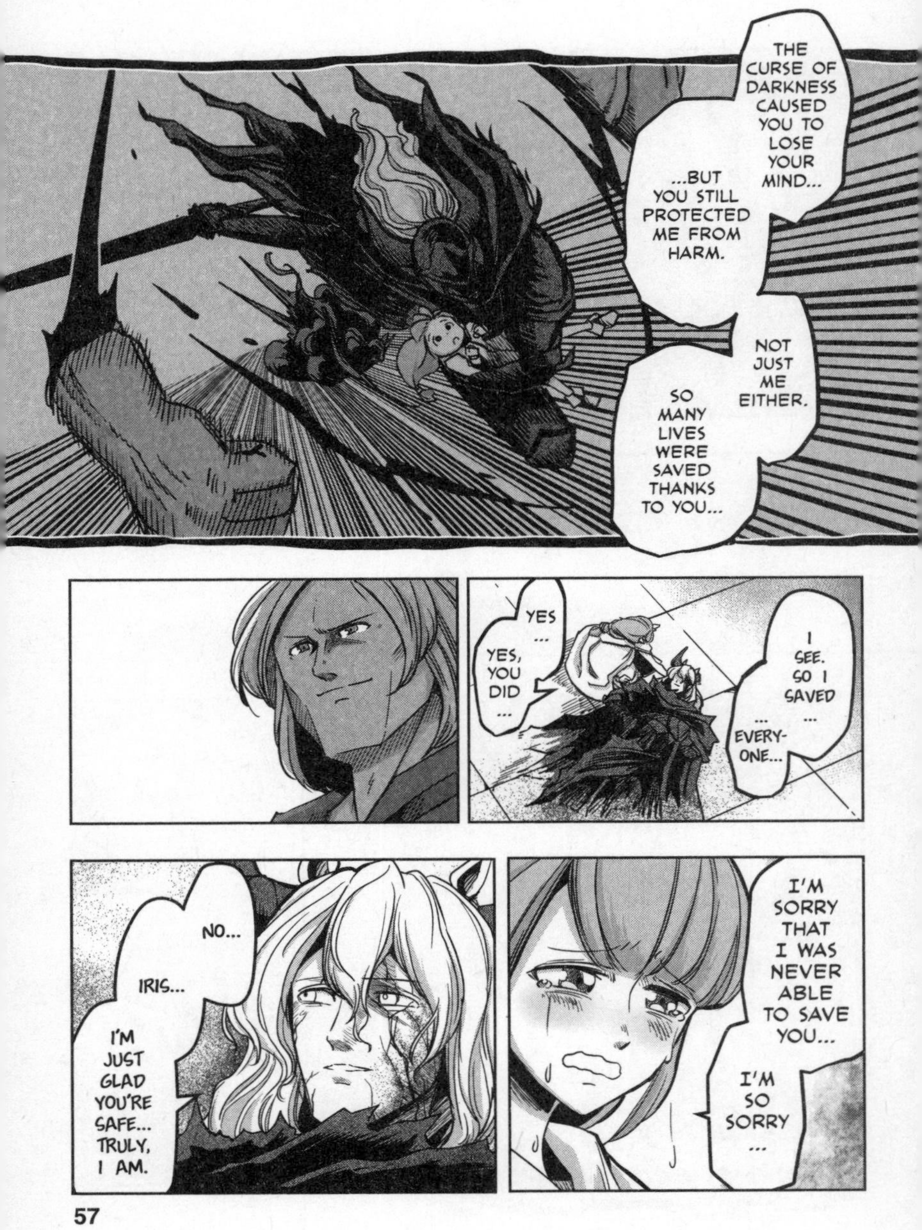
THE CURSE OF DARKNESS CAUSED YOU TO LOSE YOUR MIND...
...BUT YOU STILL PROTECTED ME FROM HARM.
NOT JUST ME EITHER.
SO MANY LIVES WERE SAVED THANKS TO YOU...
I SEE. SO I SAVED ...
... EVERY-ONE...
YES ...
YES, YOU DID ...
I'M SORRY THAT I WAS NEVER ABLE TO SAVE YOU...
I'M SO SORRY ...
NO...
IRIS...
I'M JUST GLAD YOU'RE SAFE... TRULY, I AM.

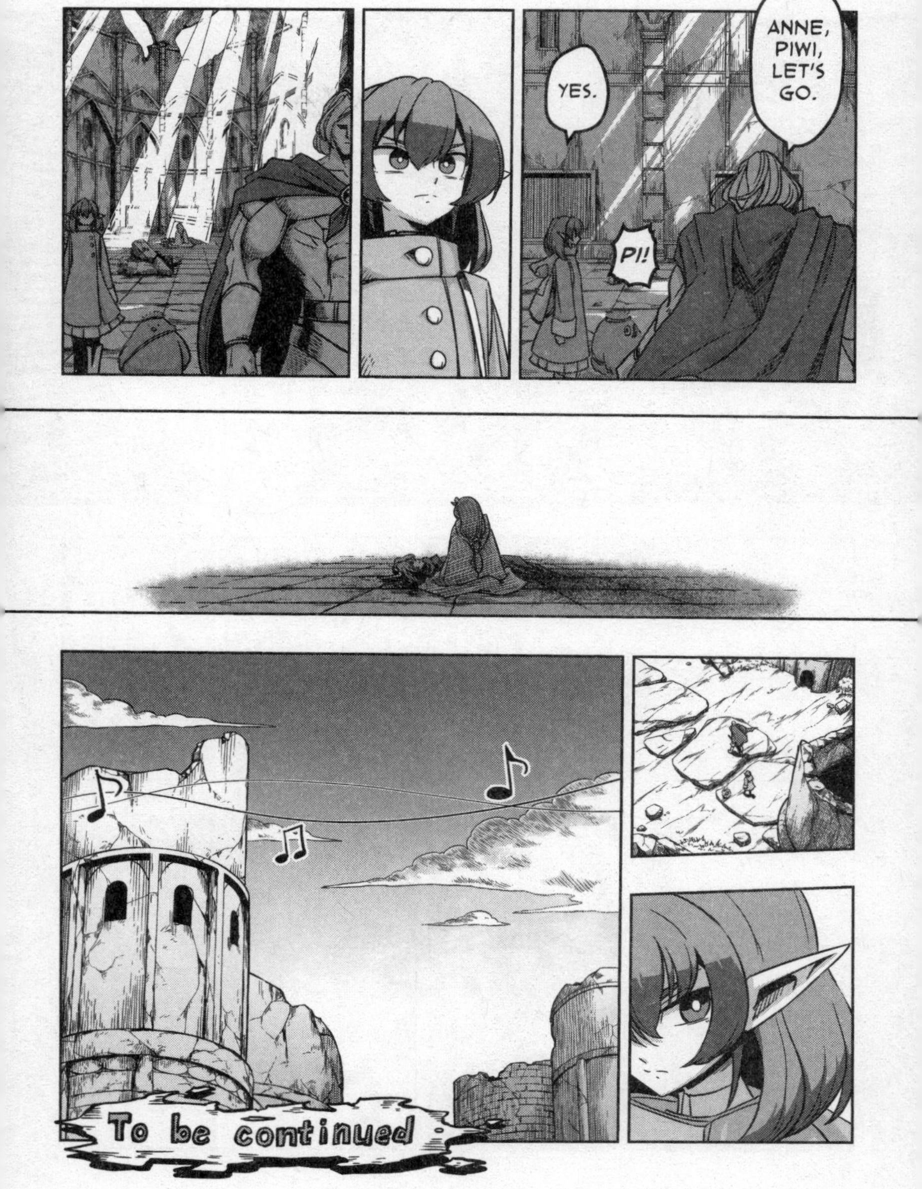
ANNE, PIWI, LET'S GO.
YES.
PI!
To be continued

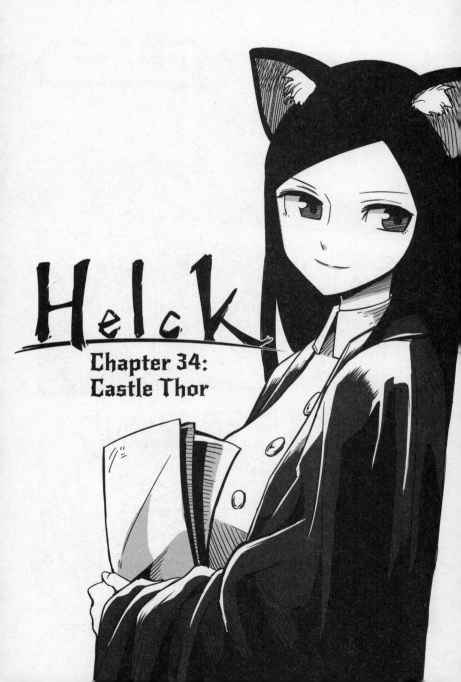

Helck

Chapter 34: Castle Thor

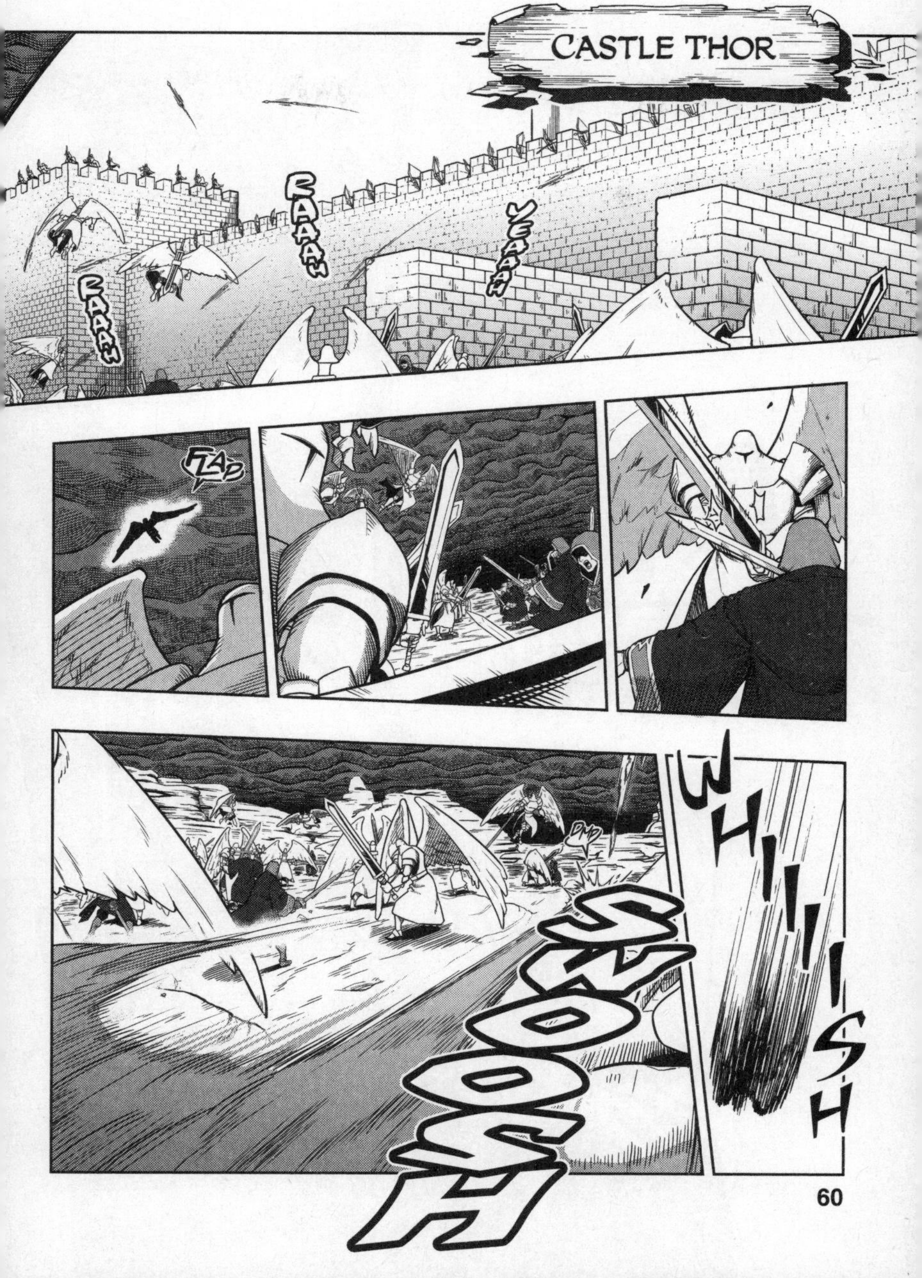
CASTLE THOR
YEAAAAH
RAAAAH
RAAAAH
FLAP
WHIIIIISH
SWOOSH
DMP

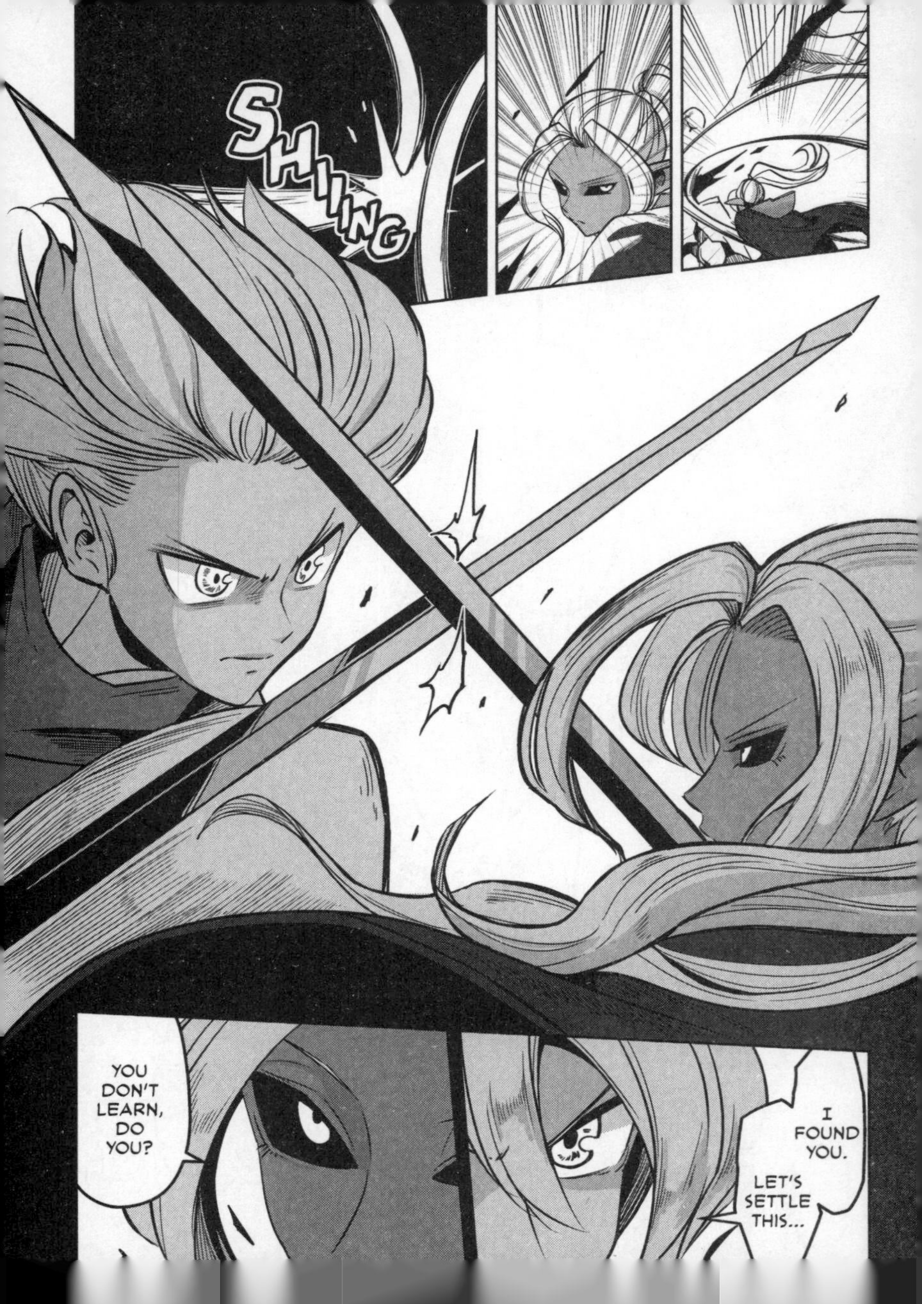
SHIIING
I FOUND YOU.
LET'S SETTLE THIS...
YOU DON'T LEARN, DO YOU?

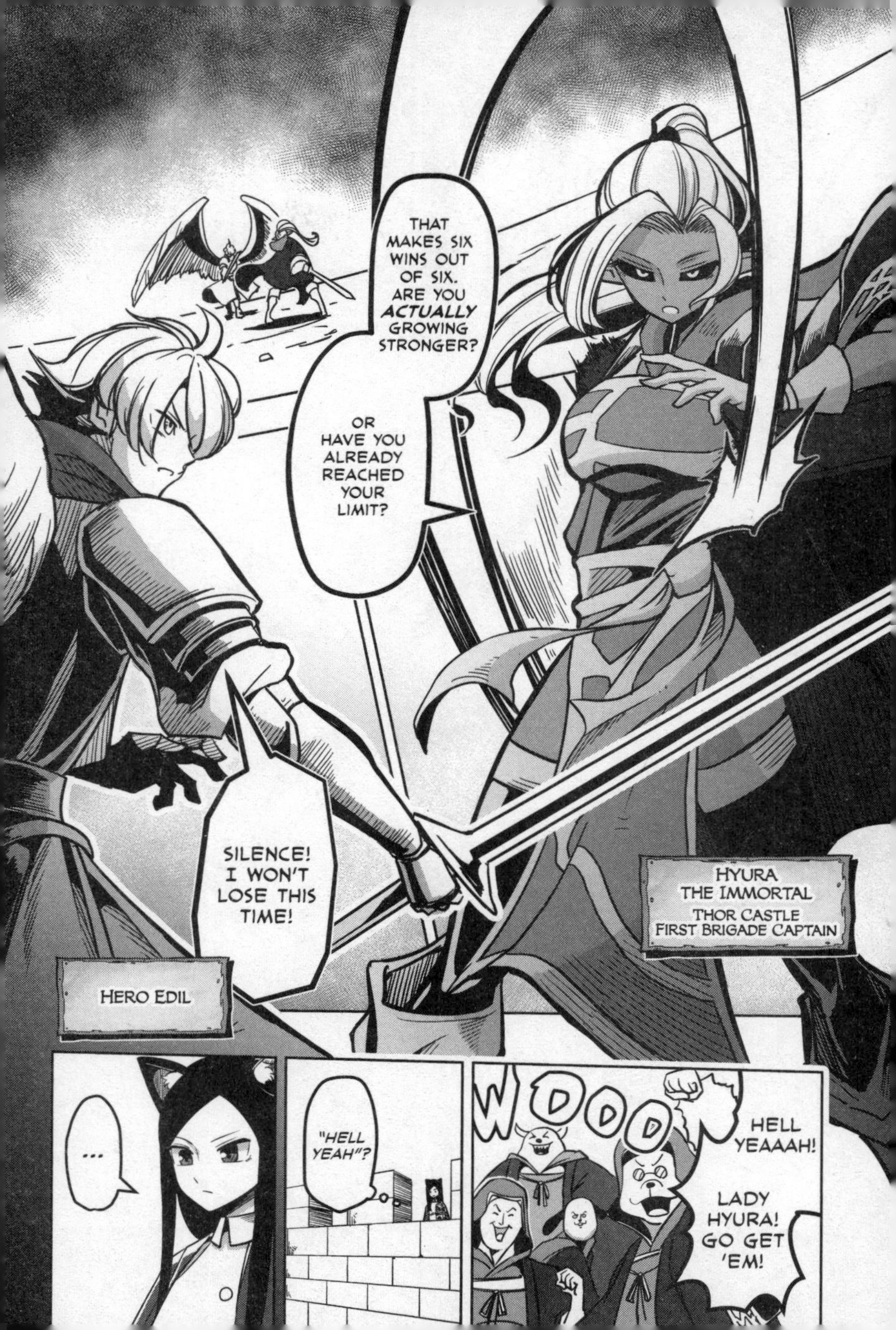
THAT MAKES SIX WINS OUT OF SIX. ARE YOU *ACTUALLY* GROWING STRONGER?
OR HAVE YOU ALREADY REACHED YOUR LIMIT?
HYURA THE IMMORTAL
THOR CASTLE FIRST BRIGADE CAPTAIN
SILENCE! I WON'T LOSE THIS TIME!
HERO EDIL
WOOO
HELL YEAAAH!
LADY HYURA! GO GET 'EM!
"HELL YEAH"?
...

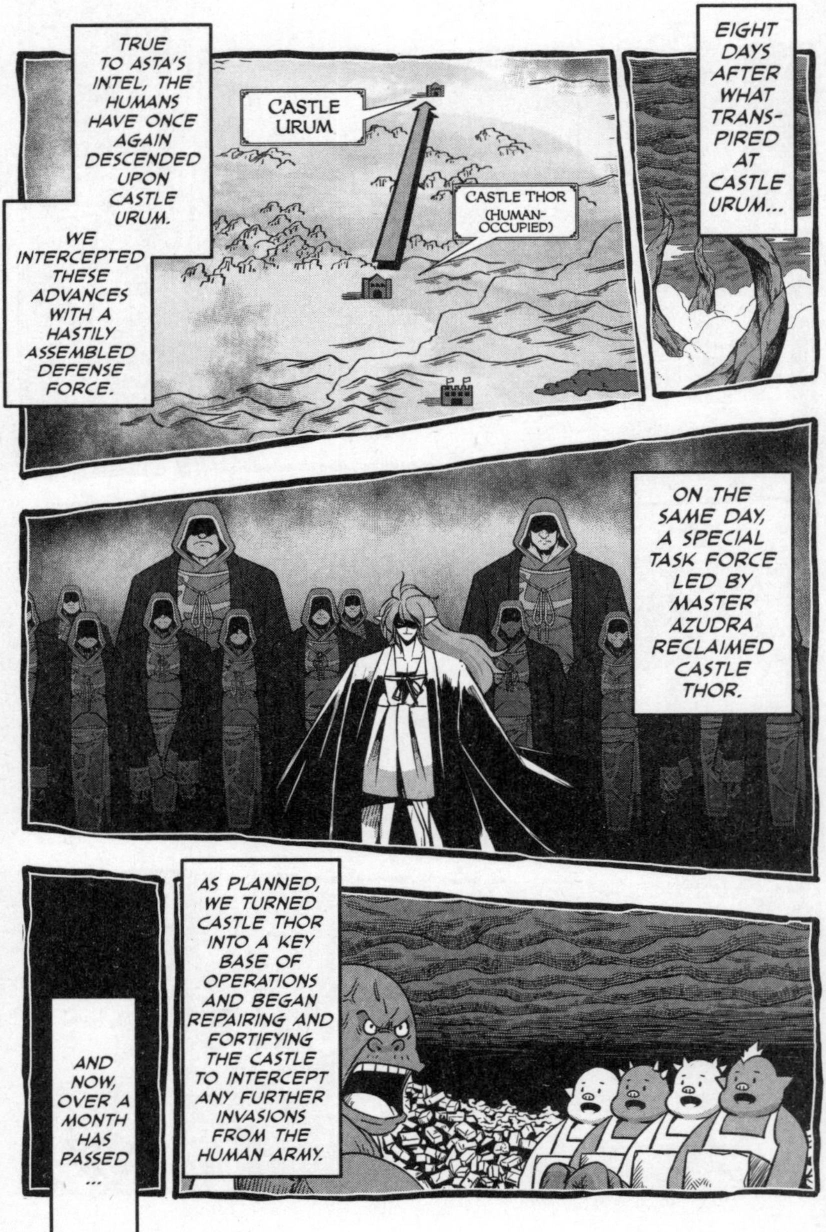
EIGHT DAYS AFTER WHAT TRANS-PIRED AT CASTLE URUM...
TRUE TO ASTA'S INTEL, THE HUMANS HAVE ONCE AGAIN DESCENDED UPON CASTLE URUM.
CASTLE URUM
CASTLE THOR (HUMAN-OCCUPIED)
WE INTERCEPTED THESE ADVANCES WITH A HASTILY ASSEMBLED DEFENSE FORCE.
ON THE SAME DAY, A SPECIAL TASK FORCE LED BY MASTER AZUDRA RECLAIMED CASTLE THOR.
AS PLANNED, WE TURNED CASTLE THOR INTO A KEY BASE OF OPERATIONS AND BEGAN REPAIRING AND FORTIFYING THE CASTLE TO INTERCEPT ANY FURTHER INVASIONS FROM THE HUMAN ARMY.
AND NOW, OVER A MONTH HAS PASSED ...

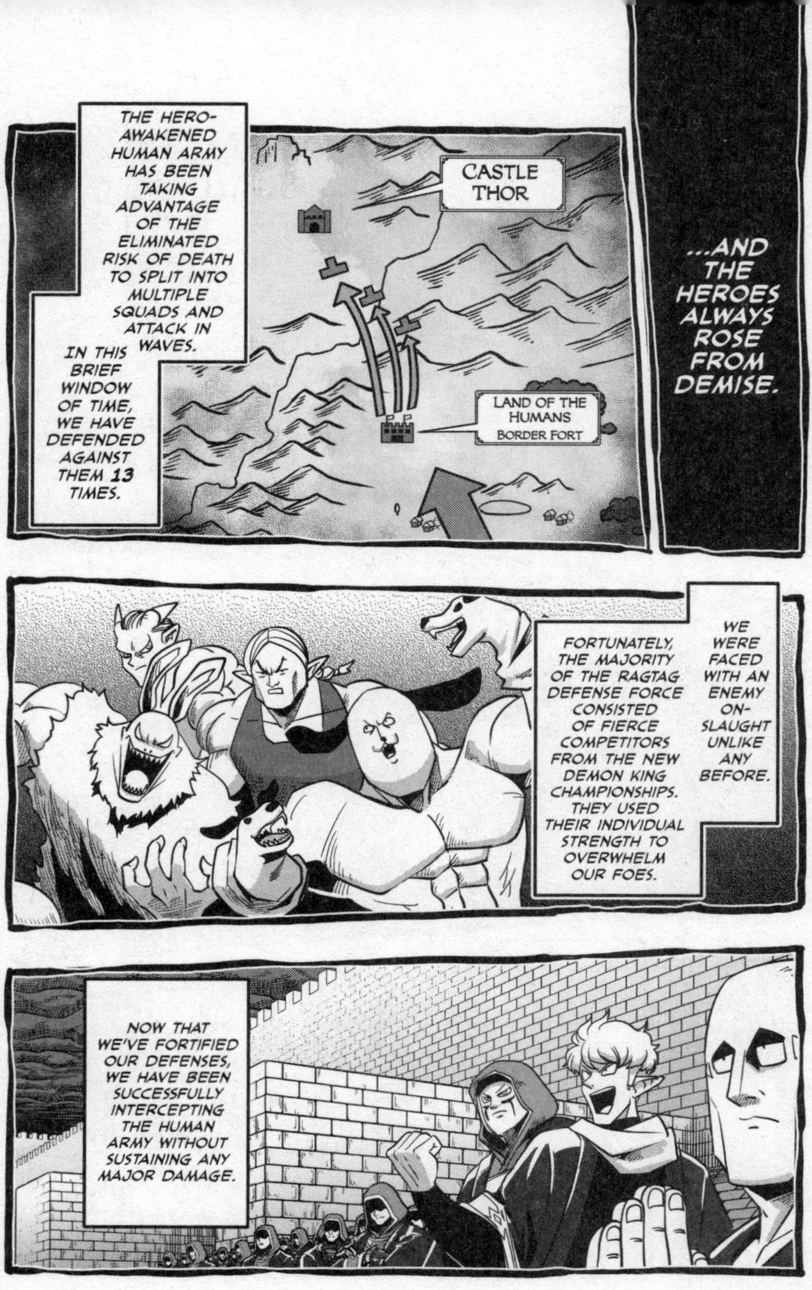
...AND THE HEROES ALWAYS ROSE FROM DEMISE.
THE HERO-AWAKENED HUMAN ARMY HAS BEEN TAKING ADVANTAGE OF THE ELIMINATED RISK OF DEATH TO SPLIT INTO MULTIPLE SQUADS AND ATTACK IN WAVES.
CASTLE THOR
LAND OF THE HUMANS BORDER FORT
IN THIS BRIEF WINDOW OF TIME, WE HAVE DEFENDED AGAINST THEM 13 TIMES.
WE WERE FACED WITH AN ENEMY ON-SLAUGHT UNLIKE ANY BEFORE.
FORTUNATELY, THE MAJORITY OF THE RAGTAG DEFENSE FORCE CONSISTED OF FIERCE COMPETITORS FROM THE NEW DEMON KING CHAMPIONSHIPS. THEY USED THEIR INDIVIDUAL STRENGTH TO OVERWHELM OUR FOES.
NOW THAT WE'VE FORTIFIED OUR DEFENSES, WE HAVE BEEN SUCCESSFULLY INTERCEPTING THE HUMAN ARMY WITHOUT SUSTAINING ANY MAJOR DAMAGE.

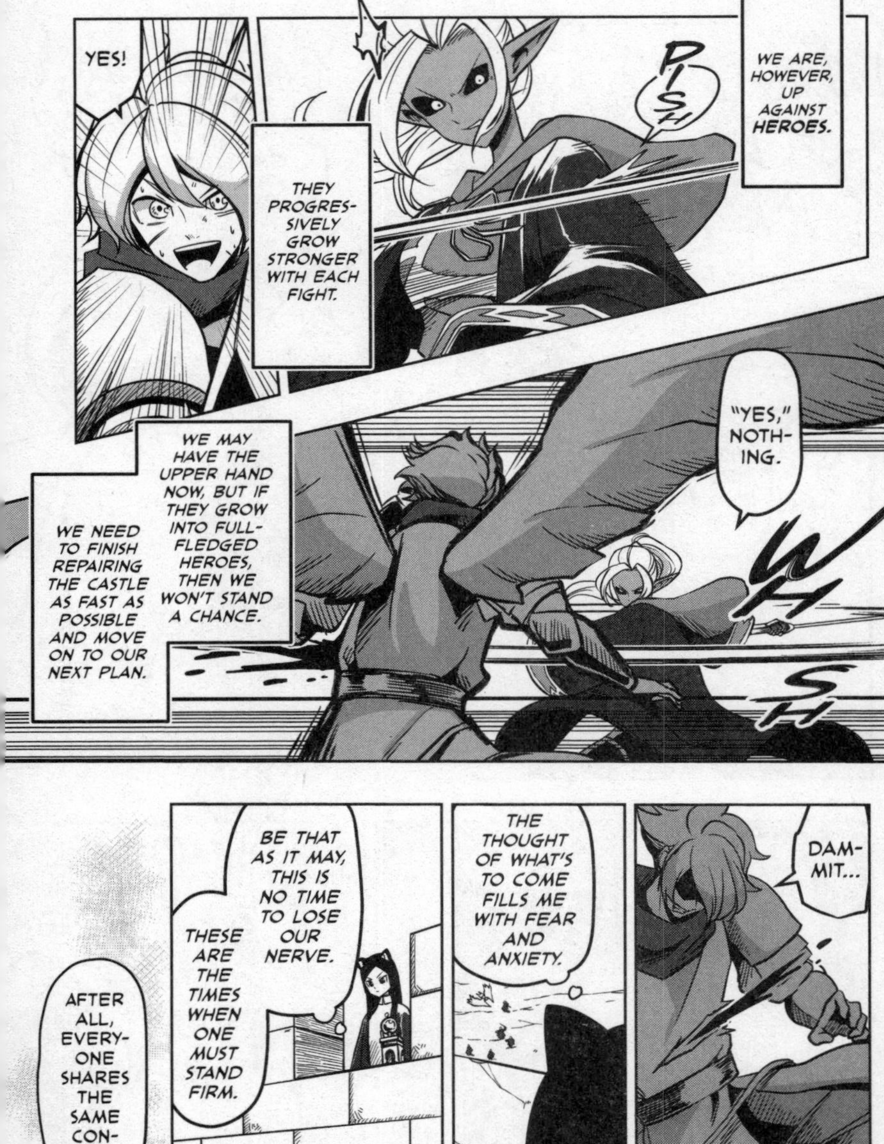
WE ARE, HOWEVER, UP AGAINST HEROES.
PISH
THEY PROGRES-SIVELY GROW STRONGER WITH EACH FIGHT.
YES!
"YES," NOTH-ING.
WHSH
WE MAY HAVE THE UPPER HAND NOW, BUT IF THEY GROW INTO FULL-FLEDGED HEROES, THEN WE WON'T STAND A CHANCE.
WE NEED TO FINISH REPAIRING THE CASTLE AS FAST AS POSSIBLE AND MOVE ON TO OUR NEXT PLAN.
DAM-MIT...
THE THOUGHT OF WHAT'S TO COME FILLS ME WITH FEAR AND ANXIETY.
BE THAT AS IT MAY, THIS IS NO TIME TO LOSE OUR NERVE.
THESE ARE THE TIMES WHEN ONE MUST STAND FIRM.
AFTER ALL, EVERY-ONE SHARES THE SAME CON-CERNS...

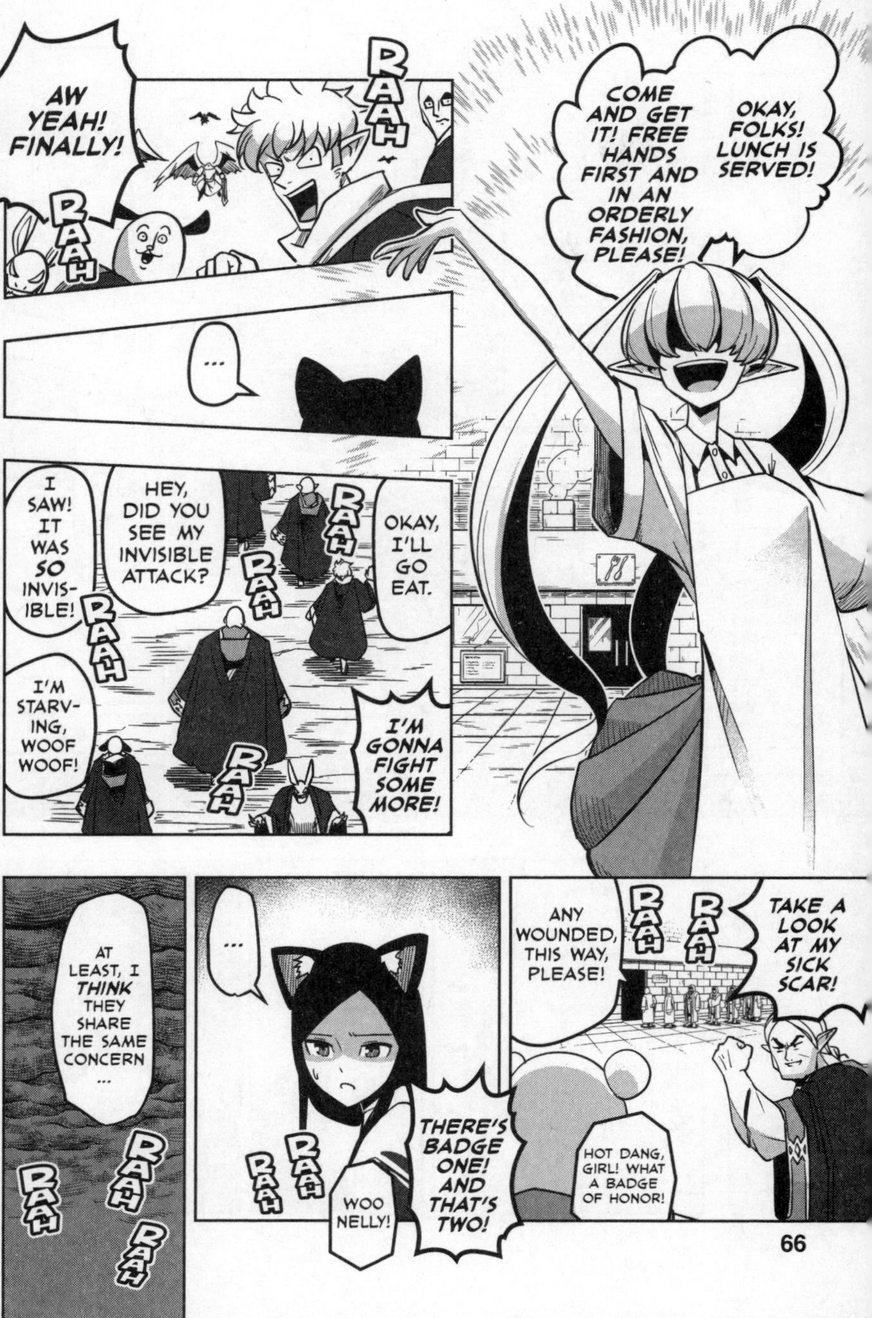
OKAY, FOLKS! LUNCH IS SERVED!
COME AND GET IT! FREE HANDS FIRST AND IN AN ORDERLY FASHION, PLEASE!
RAAAH
AW YEAH! FINALLY!
RAAH
...
OKAY, I'LL GO EAT.
RAAH
RAAH
HEY, DID YOU SEE MY INVISIBLE ATTACK?
I SAW! IT WAS *SO* INVISIBLE!
RAAH
I'M GONNA FIGHT SOME MORE!
RAAH
I'M STARVING, WOOF WOOF!
TAKE A LOOK AT MY SICK SCAR!
RAAH
RAAH
ANY WOUNDED, THIS WAY, PLEASE!
HOT DANG, GIRL! WHAT A BADGE OF HONOR!
...
RAAH
RAAH
THERE'S BADGE ONE! AND THAT'S TWO!
WOO NELLY!
AT LEAST, I *THINK* THEY SHARE THE SAME CONCERN ...
RAAH
RAAH
RAAH

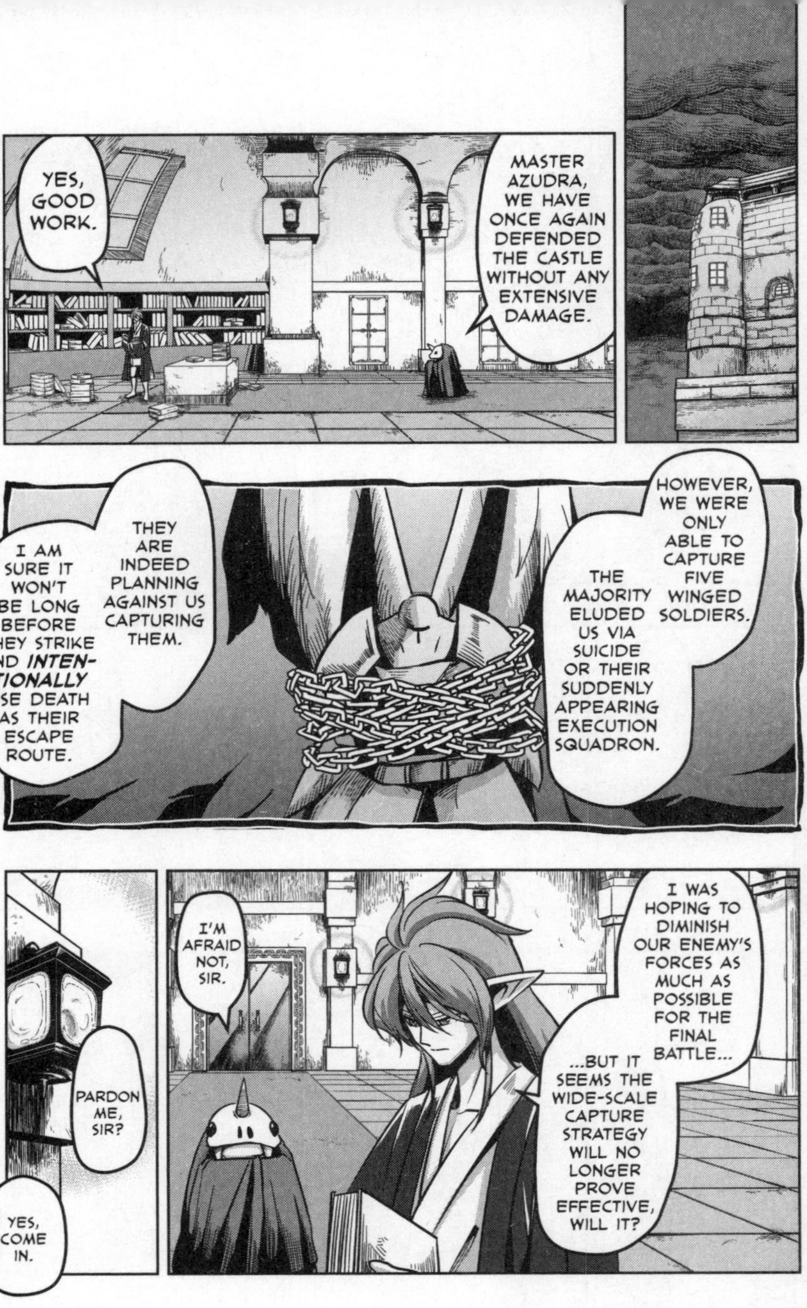
MASTER AZUDRA, WE HAVE ONCE AGAIN DEFENDED THE CASTLE WITHOUT ANY EXTENSIVE DAMAGE.
YES, GOOD WORK.
HOWEVER, WE WERE ONLY ABLE TO CAPTURE FIVE WINGED SOLDIERS.
THE MAJORITY ELUDED US VIA SUICIDE OR THEIR SUDDENLY APPEARING EXECUTION SQUADRON.
THEY ARE INDEED PLANNING AGAINST US CAPTURING THEM.
I AM SURE IT WON'T BE LONG BEFORE THEY STRIKE AND *INTENTIONALLY* USE DEATH AS THEIR ESCAPE ROUTE.
I WAS HOPING TO DIMINISH OUR ENEMY'S FORCES AS MUCH AS POSSIBLE FOR THE FINAL BATTLE...
...BUT IT SEEMS THE WIDE-SCALE CAPTURE STRATEGY WILL NO LONGER PROVE EFFECTIVE, WILL IT?
I'M AFRAID NOT, SIR.
PARDON ME, SIR?
YES, COME IN.

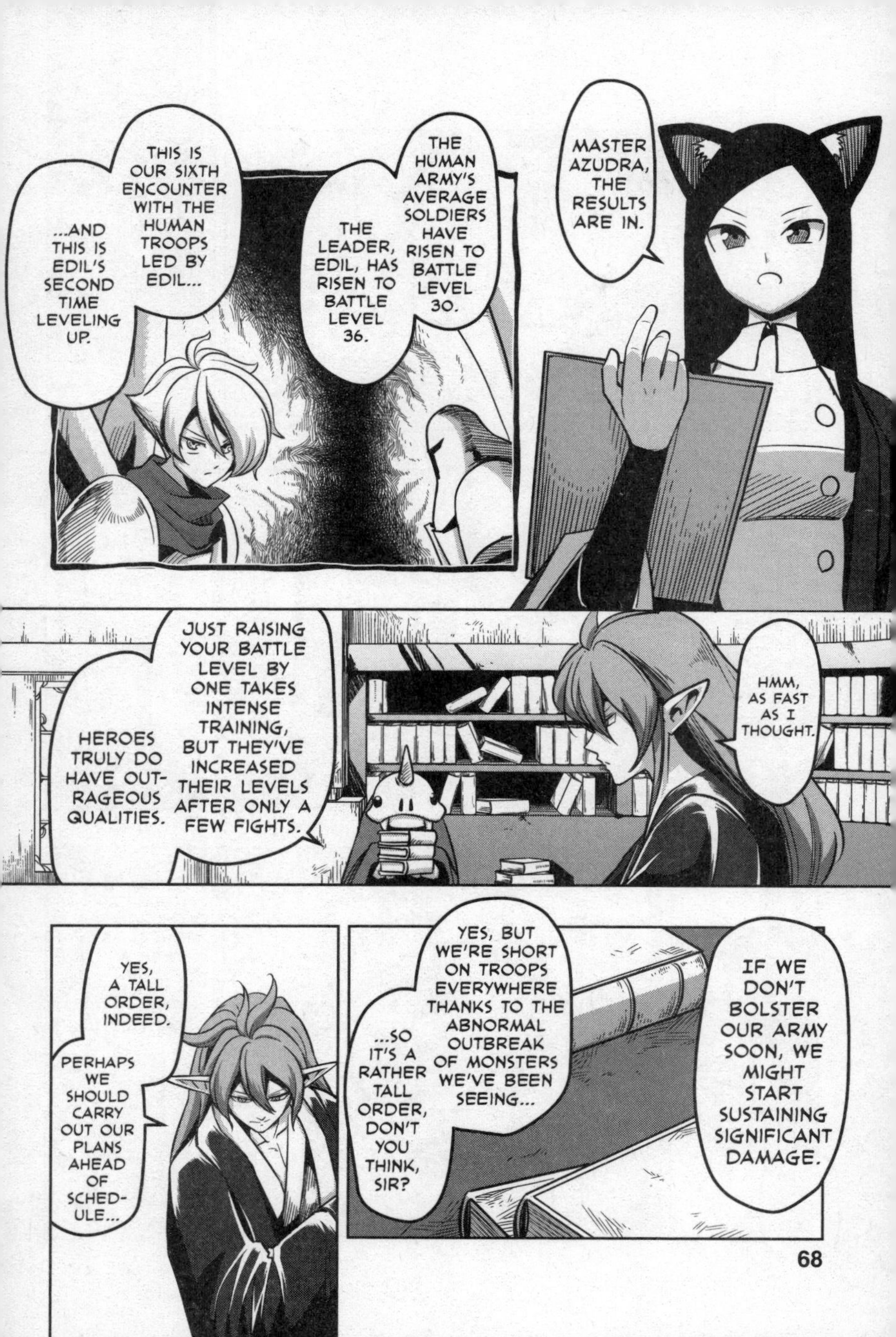
MASTER AZUDRA, THE RESULTS ARE IN.
THE HUMAN ARMY'S AVERAGE SOLDIERS HAVE RISEN TO BATTLE LEVEL 30.
THE LEADER, EDIL, HAS RISEN TO BATTLE LEVEL 36.
THIS IS OUR SIXTH ENCOUNTER WITH THE HUMAN TROOPS LED BY EDIL...
...AND THIS IS EDIL'S SECOND TIME LEVELING UP.
HMM, AS FAST AS I THOUGHT.
JUST RAISING YOUR BATTLE LEVEL BY ONE TAKES INTENSE TRAINING, BUT THEY'VE INCREASED THEIR LEVELS AFTER ONLY A FEW FIGHTS.
HEROES TRULY DO HAVE OUTRAGEOUS QUALITIES.
IF WE DON'T BOLSTER OUR ARMY SOON, WE MIGHT START SUSTAINING SIGNIFICANT DAMAGE.
YES, BUT WE'RE SHORT ON TROOPS EVERYWHERE THANKS TO THE ABNORMAL OUTBREAK OF MONSTERS WE'VE BEEN SEEING...
...SO IT'S A RATHER TALL ORDER, DON'T YOU THINK, SIR?
YES, A TALL ORDER, INDEED.
PERHAPS WE SHOULD CARRY OUT OUR PLANS AHEAD OF SCHEDULE...

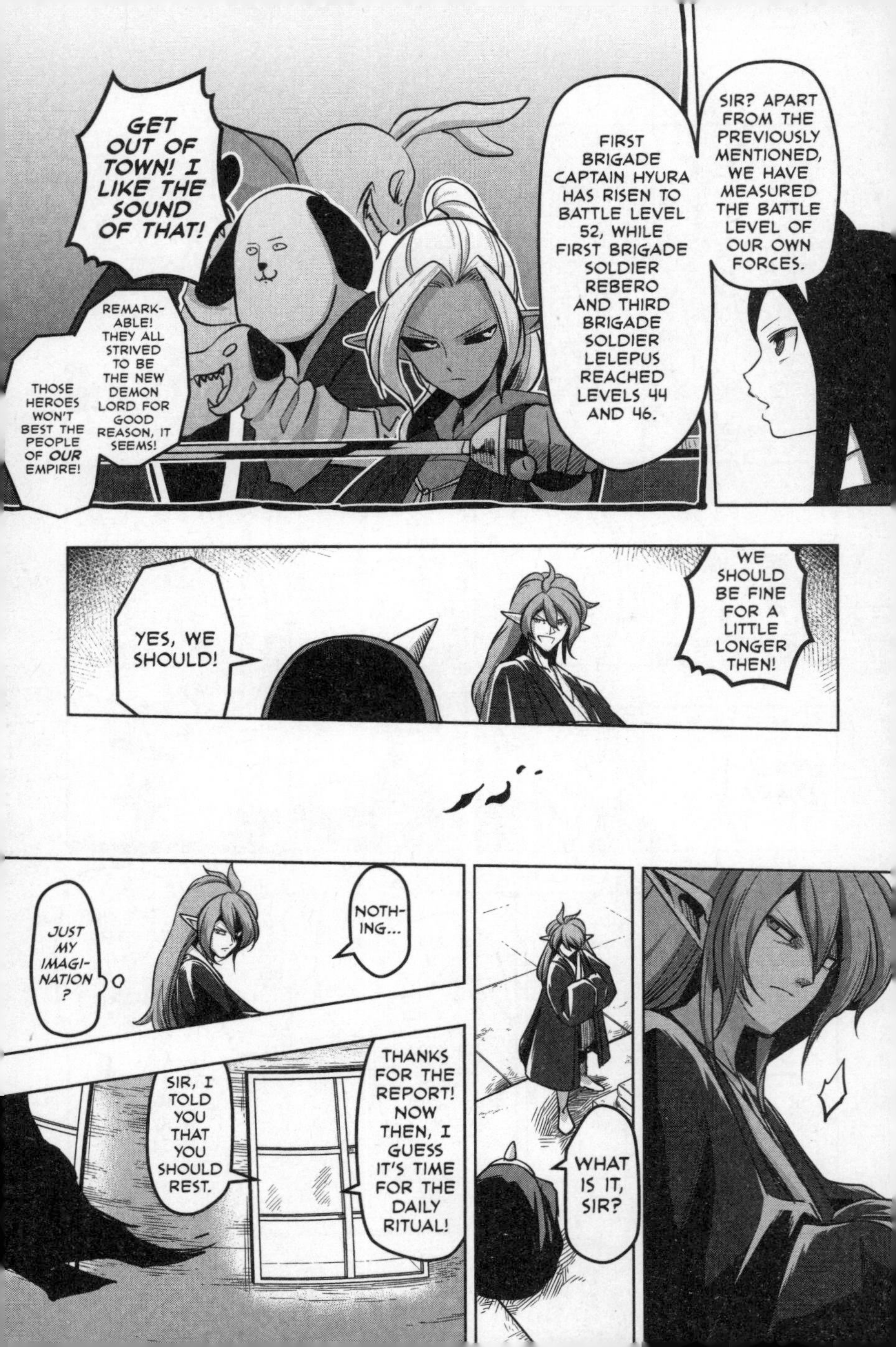
SIR? APART FROM THE PREVIOUSLY MENTIONED, WE HAVE MEASURED THE BATTLE LEVEL OF OUR OWN FORCES.
FIRST BRIGADE CAPTAIN HYURA HAS RISEN TO BATTLE LEVEL 52, WHILE FIRST BRIGADE SOLDIER REBERO AND THIRD BRIGADE SOLDIER LELEPUS REACHED LEVELS 44 AND 46.
GET OUT OF TOWN! I LIKE THE SOUND OF THAT!
REMARKABLE! THEY ALL STRIVED TO BE THE NEW DEMON LORD FOR GOOD REASON, IT SEEMS!
THOSE HEROES WON'T BEST THE PEOPLE OF OUR EMPIRE!
WE SHOULD BE FINE FOR A LITTLE LONGER THEN!
YES, WE SHOULD!
WHAT IS IT, SIR?
NOTHING...
JUST MY IMAGINATION?
THANKS FOR THE REPORT! NOW THEN, I GUESS IT'S TIME FOR THE DAILY RITUAL!
SIR, I TOLD YOU THAT YOU SHOULD REST.

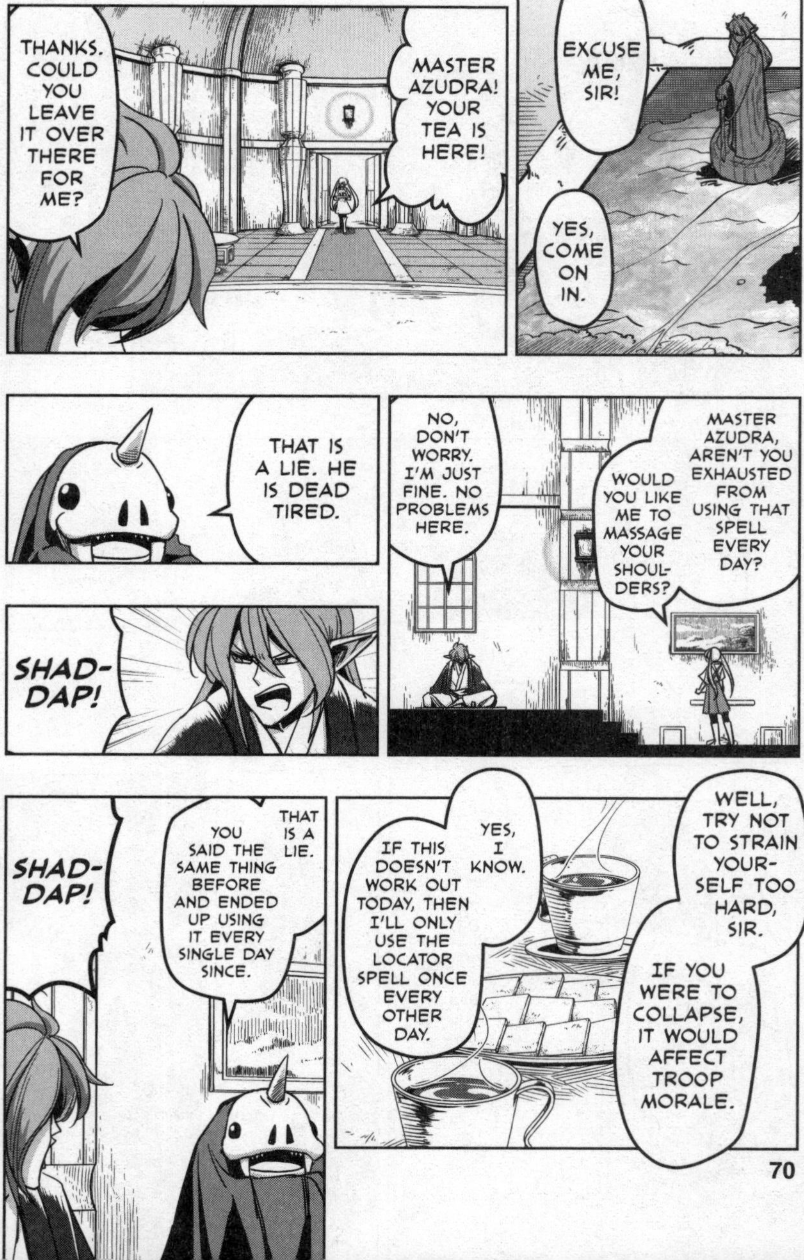
EXCUSE ME, SIR!
YES, COME ON IN.
MASTER AZUDRA! YOUR TEA IS HERE!
THANKS. COULD YOU LEAVE IT OVER THERE FOR ME?
MASTER AZUDRA, AREN'T YOU EXHAUSTED FROM USING THAT SPELL EVERY DAY?
WOULD YOU LIKE ME TO MASSAGE YOUR SHOULDERS?
NO, DON'T WORRY. I'M JUST FINE. NO PROBLEMS HERE.
THAT IS A LIE. HE IS DEAD TIRED.
SHAD-DAP!
WELL, TRY NOT TO STRAIN YOURSELF TOO HARD, SIR.
YES, I KNOW.
IF YOU WERE TO COLLAPSE, IT WOULD AFFECT TROOP MORALE.
IF THIS DOESN'T WORK OUT TODAY, THEN I'LL ONLY USE THE LOCATOR SPELL ONCE EVERY OTHER DAY.
THAT IS A LIE.
YOU SAID THE SAME THING BEFORE AND ENDED UP USING IT EVERY SINGLE DAY SINCE.
SHAD-DAP!

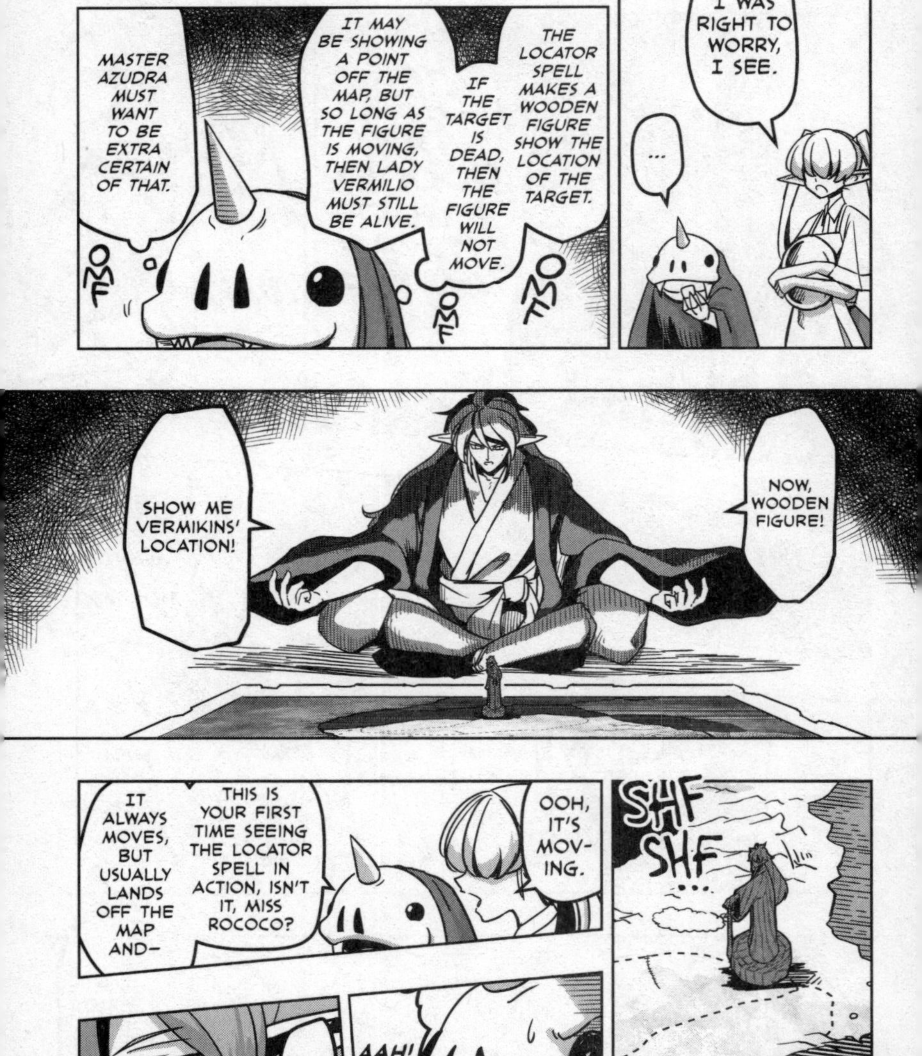
I WAS RIGHT TO WORRY, I SEE.
...
THE LOCATOR SPELL MAKES A WOODEN FIGURE SHOW THE LOCATION OF THE TARGET.
IF THE TARGET IS DEAD, THEN THE FIGURE WILL NOT MOVE.
OMF
OMF
IT MAY BE SHOWING A POINT OFF THE MAP, BUT SO LONG AS THE FIGURE IS MOVING, THEN LADY VERMILIO MUST STILL BE ALIVE.
MASTER AZUDRA MUST WANT TO BE EXTRA CERTAIN OF THAT.
OMF
NOW, WOODEN FIGURE!
SHOW ME VERMIKINS' LOCATION!
SHF
SHF
...
OOH, IT'S MOV-ING.
THIS IS YOUR FIRST TIME SEEING THE LOCATOR SPELL IN ACTION, ISN'T IT, MISS ROCOCO?
IT ALWAYS MOVES, BUT USUALLY LANDS OFF THE MAP AND–
AAH!
...

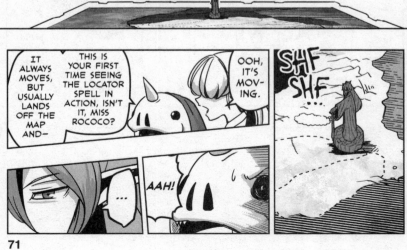

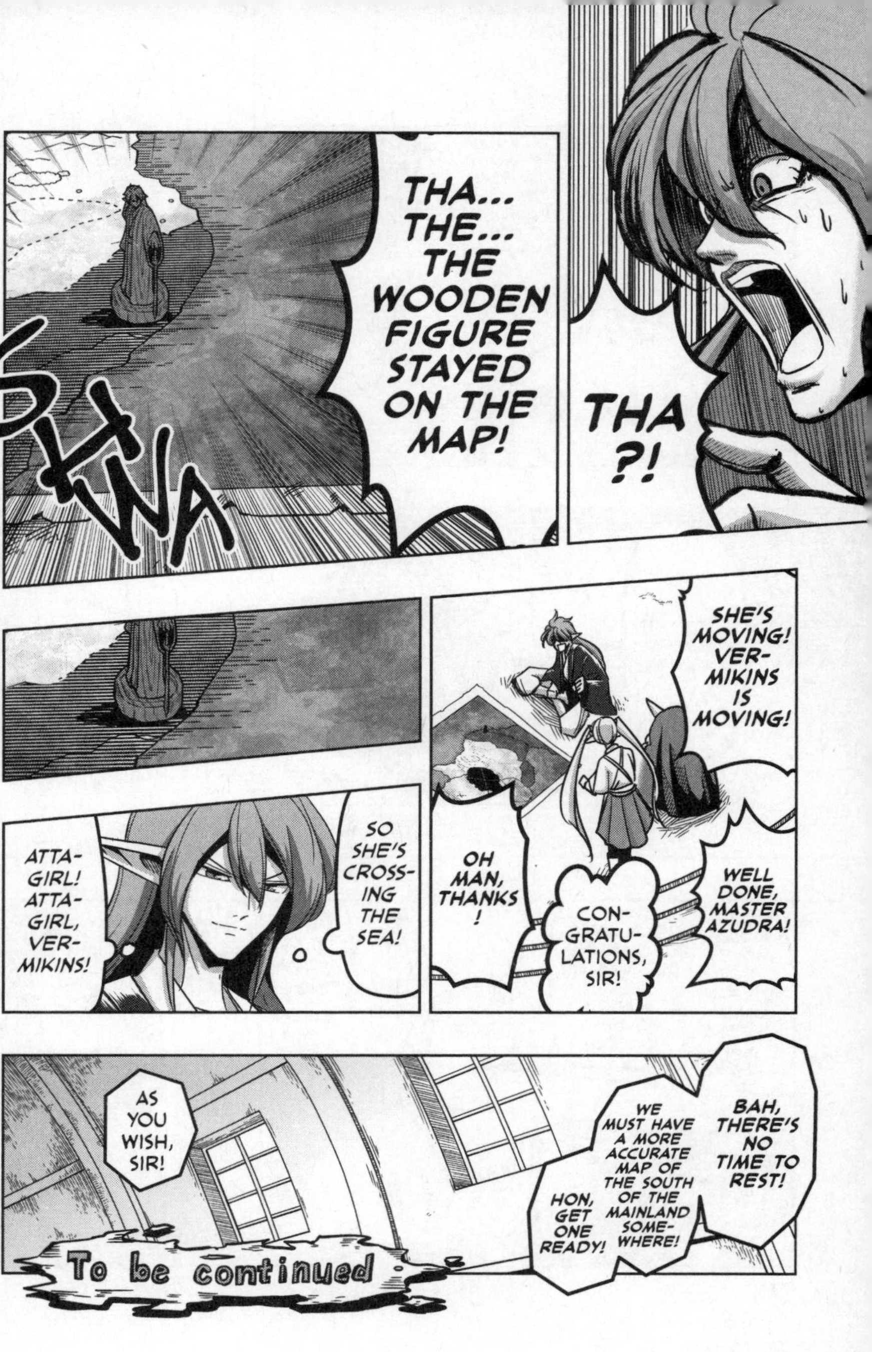
THA ?!
THA... THE... THE WOODEN FIGURE STAYED ON THE MAP!
SHWA
SHE'S MOVING! VER-MIKINS IS MOVING!
WELL DONE, MASTER AZUDRA!
CON-GRATU-LATIONS, SIR!
OH MAN, THANKS!
SO SHE'S CROSS-ING THE SEA!
ATTA-GIRL! ATTA-GIRL, VER-MIKINS!
BAH, THERE'S NO TIME TO REST!
WE MUST HAVE A MORE ACCURATE MAP OF THE SOUTH OF THE MAINLAND SOME-WHERE!
HON, GET ONE READY!
AS YOU WISH, SIR!
To be continued

Helck

Chapter 35: A Believing Heart

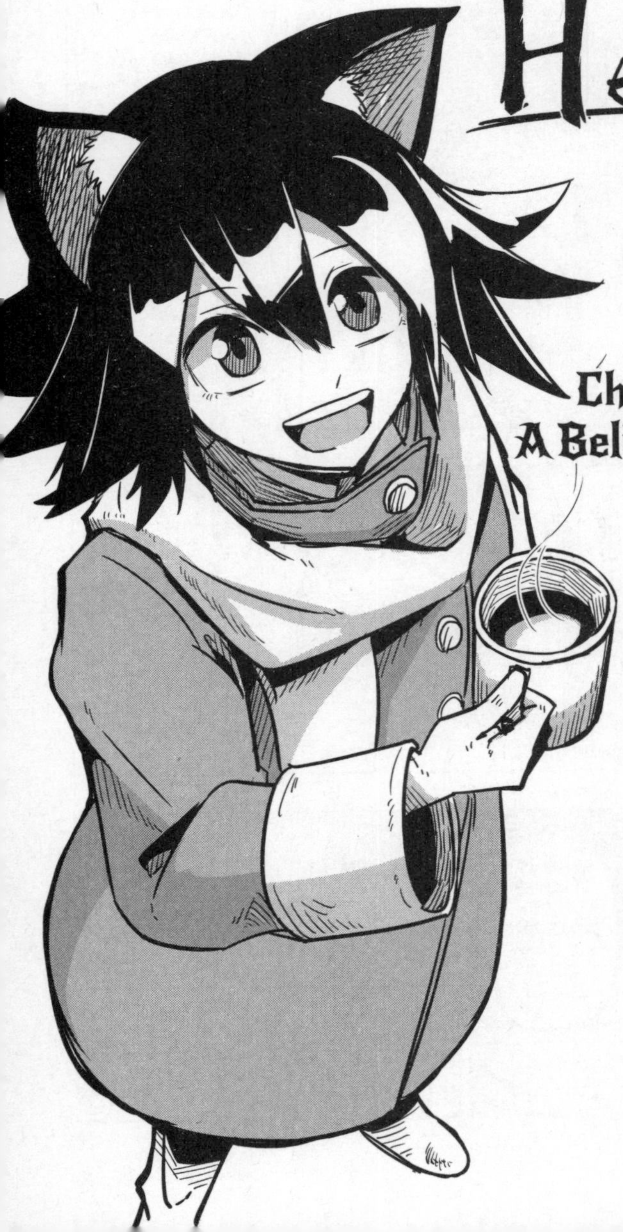

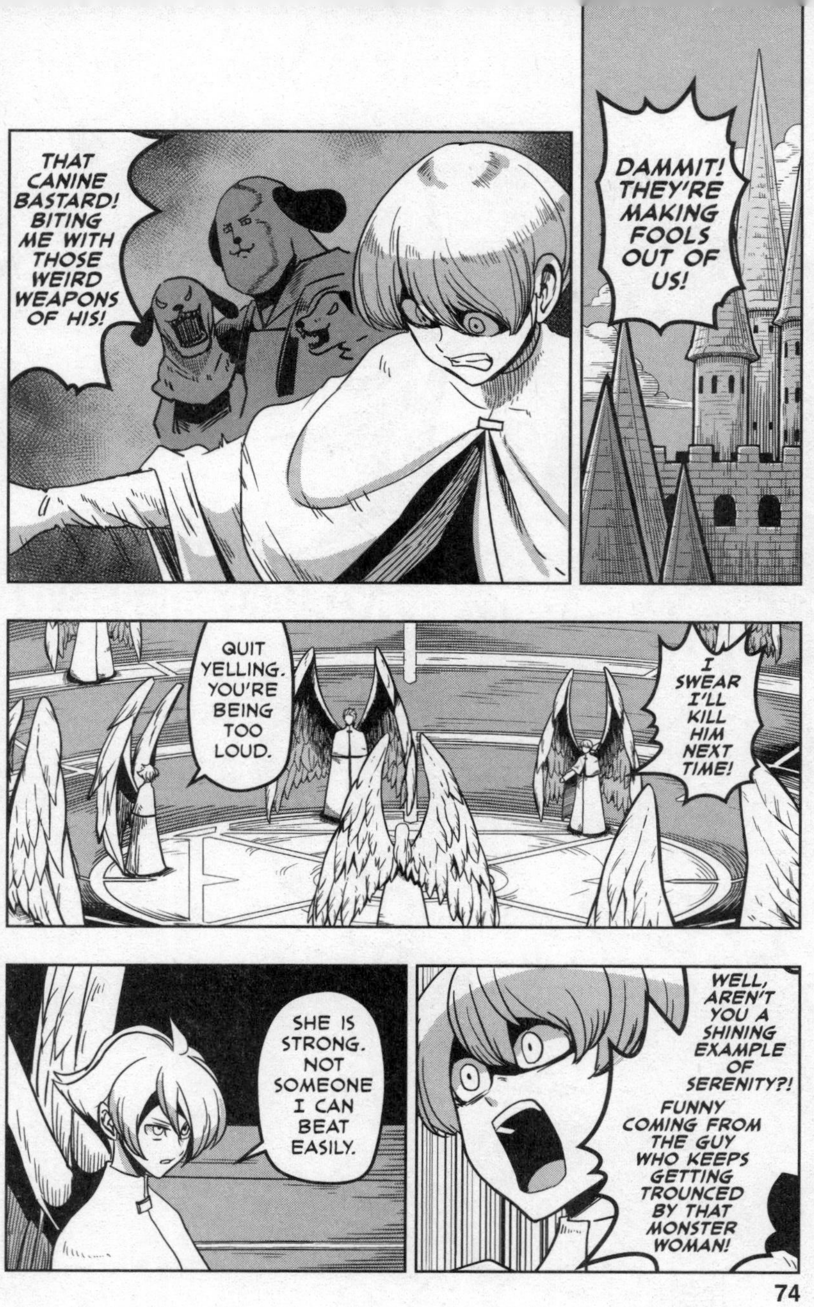
DAMMIT! THEY'RE MAKING FOOLS OUT OF US!
THAT CANINE BASTARD! BITING ME WITH THOSE WEIRD WEAPONS OF HIS!
I SWEAR I'LL KILL HIM NEXT TIME!
QUIT YELLING. YOU'RE BEING TOO LOUD.
WELL, AREN'T YOU A SHINING EXAMPLE OF SERENITY?!
FUNNY COMING FROM THE GUY WHO KEEPS GETTING TROUNCED BY THAT MONSTER WOMAN!
SHE IS STRONG. NOT SOMEONE I CAN BEAT EASILY.

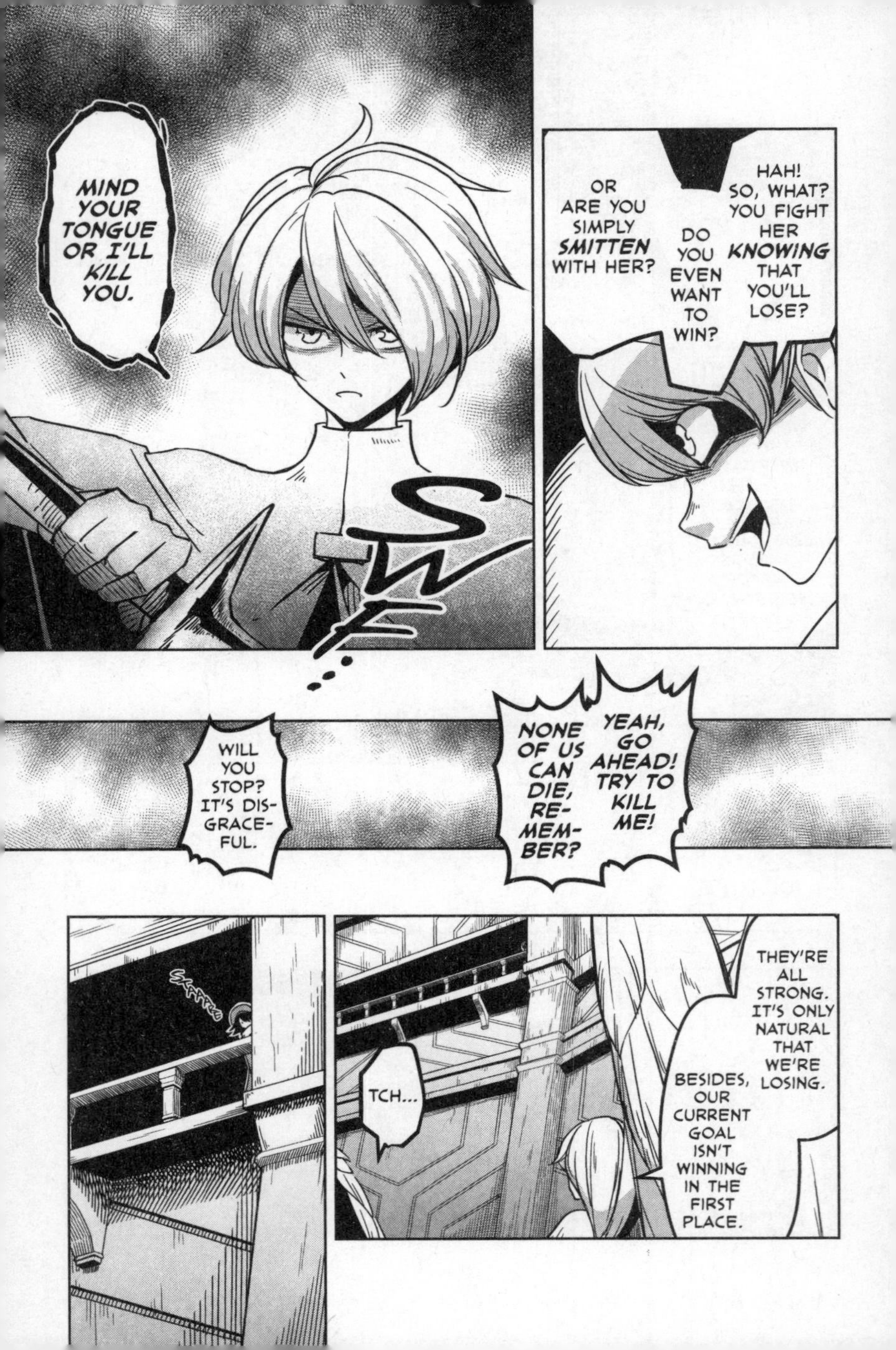
HAH! SO, WHAT? YOU FIGHT HER KNOWING THAT YOU'LL LOSE?
DO YOU EVEN WANT TO WIN?
OR ARE YOU SIMPLY SMITTEN WITH HER?
MIND YOUR TONGUE OR I'LL KILL YOU.
SWF
...
YEAH, GO AHEAD! TRY TO KILL ME!
NONE OF US CAN DIE, RE-MEM-BER?
WILL YOU STOP? IT'S DIS-GRACE-FUL.
THEY'RE ALL STRONG. IT'S ONLY NATURAL THAT WE'RE LOSING.
BESIDES, OUR CURRENT GOAL ISN'T WINNING IN THE FIRST PLACE.
TCH...

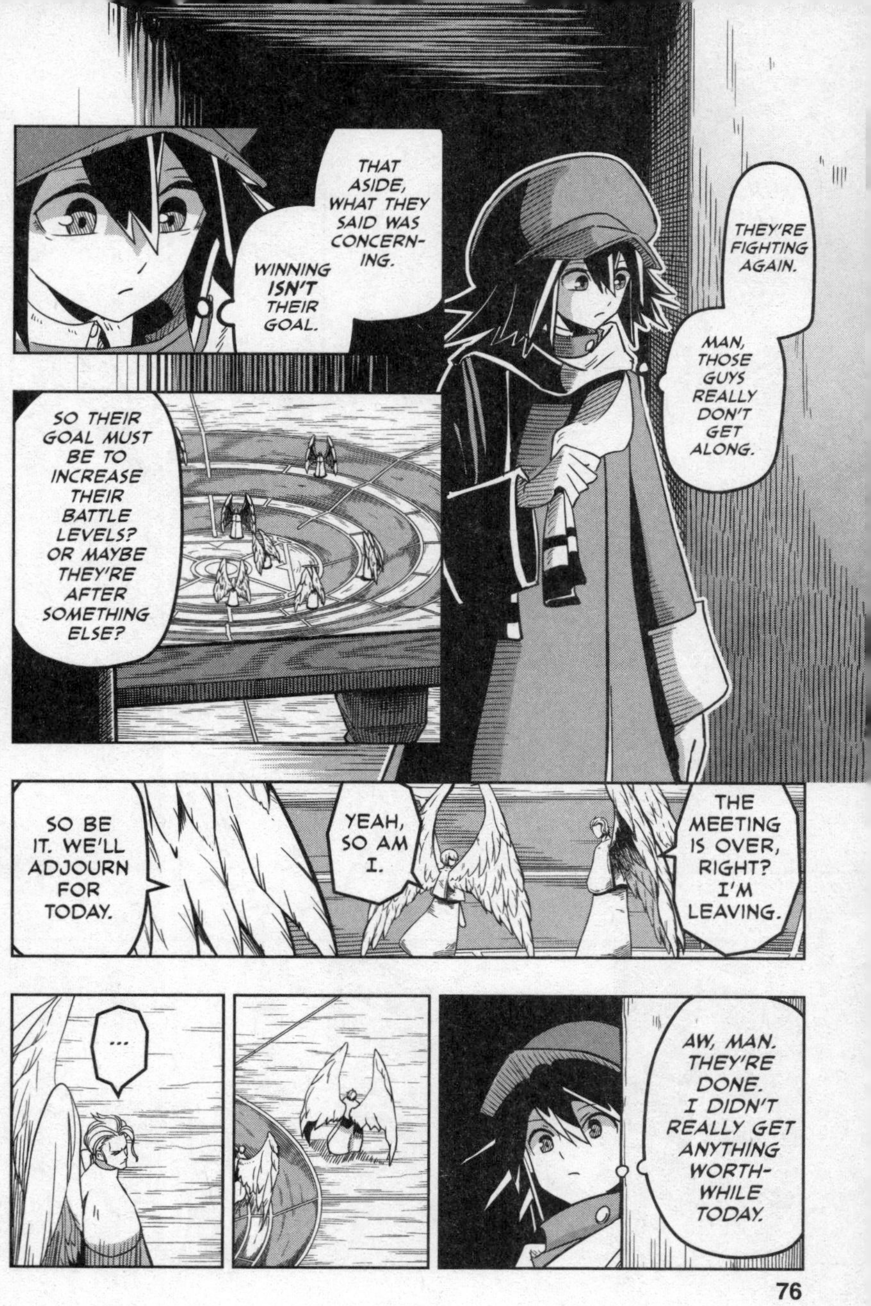
THEY'RE FIGHTING AGAIN.
MAN, THOSE GUYS REALLY DON'T GET ALONG.
THAT ASIDE, WHAT THEY SAID WAS CONCERN-ING.
WINNING ISN'T THEIR GOAL.
SO THEIR GOAL MUST BE TO INCREASE THEIR BATTLE LEVELS? OR MAYBE THEY'RE AFTER SOMETHING ELSE?
THE MEETING IS OVER, RIGHT? I'M LEAVING.
YEAH, SO AM I.
SO BE IT. WE'LL ADJOURN FOR TODAY.
AW, MAN. THEY'RE DONE. I DIDN'T REALLY GET ANYTHING WORTH-WHILE TODAY.
...

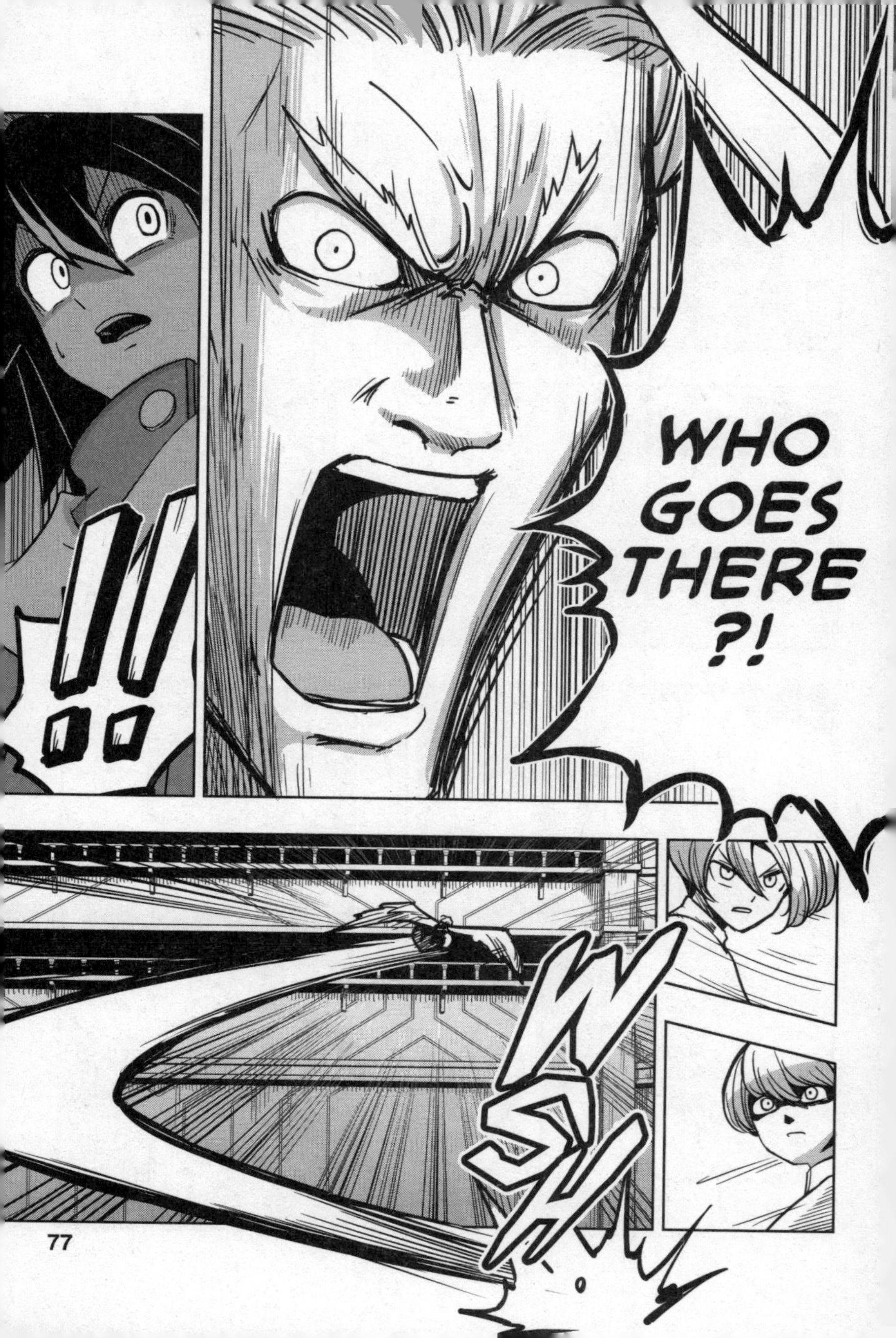
WHO GOES THERE ?!
!!
WHSH

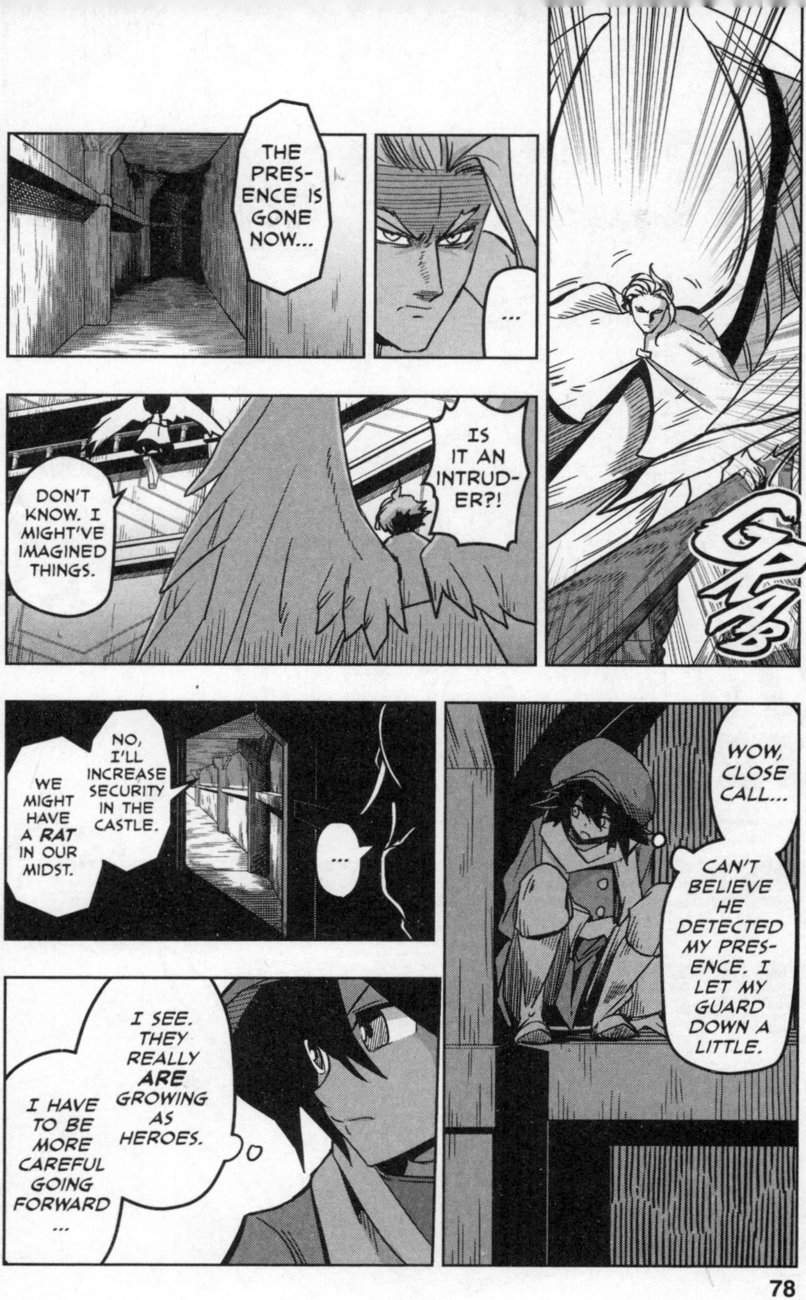
GRAB
THE PRESENCE IS GONE NOW...
...
IS IT AN INTRUDER?!
DON'T KNOW. I MIGHT'VE IMAGINED THINGS.
WOW, CLOSE CALL...
CAN'T BELIEVE HE DETECTED MY PRESENCE. I LET MY GUARD DOWN A LITTLE.
...
NO, I'LL INCREASE SECURITY IN THE CASTLE.
WE MIGHT HAVE A **RAT** IN OUR MIDST.
I SEE. THEY REALLY **ARE** GROWING AS HEROES.
I HAVE TO BE MORE CAREFUL GOING FORWARD...

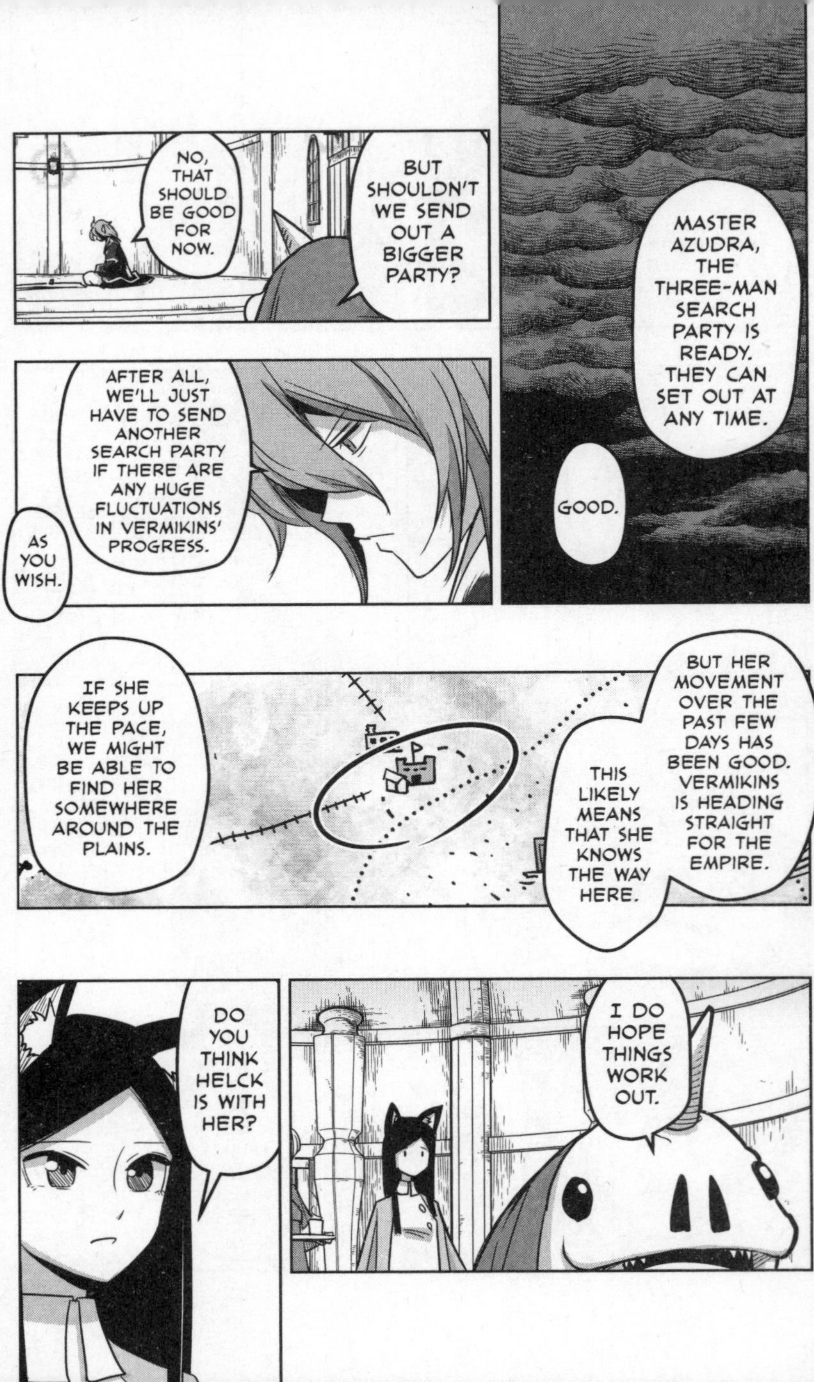
MASTER AZUDRA, THE THREE-MAN SEARCH PARTY IS READY. THEY CAN SET OUT AT ANY TIME.
GOOD.
BUT SHOULDN'T WE SEND OUT A BIGGER PARTY?
NO, THAT SHOULD BE GOOD FOR NOW.
AFTER ALL, WE'LL JUST HAVE TO SEND ANOTHER SEARCH PARTY IF THERE ARE ANY HUGE FLUCTUATIONS IN VERMIKINS' PROGRESS.
AS YOU WISH.
BUT HER MOVEMENT OVER THE PAST FEW DAYS HAS BEEN GOOD. VERMIKINS IS HEADING STRAIGHT FOR THE EMPIRE.
THIS LIKELY MEANS THAT SHE KNOWS THE WAY HERE.
IF SHE KEEPS UP THE PACE, WE MIGHT BE ABLE TO FIND HER SOMEWHERE AROUND THE PLAINS.
I DO HOPE THINGS WORK OUT.
DO YOU THINK HELCK IS WITH HER?

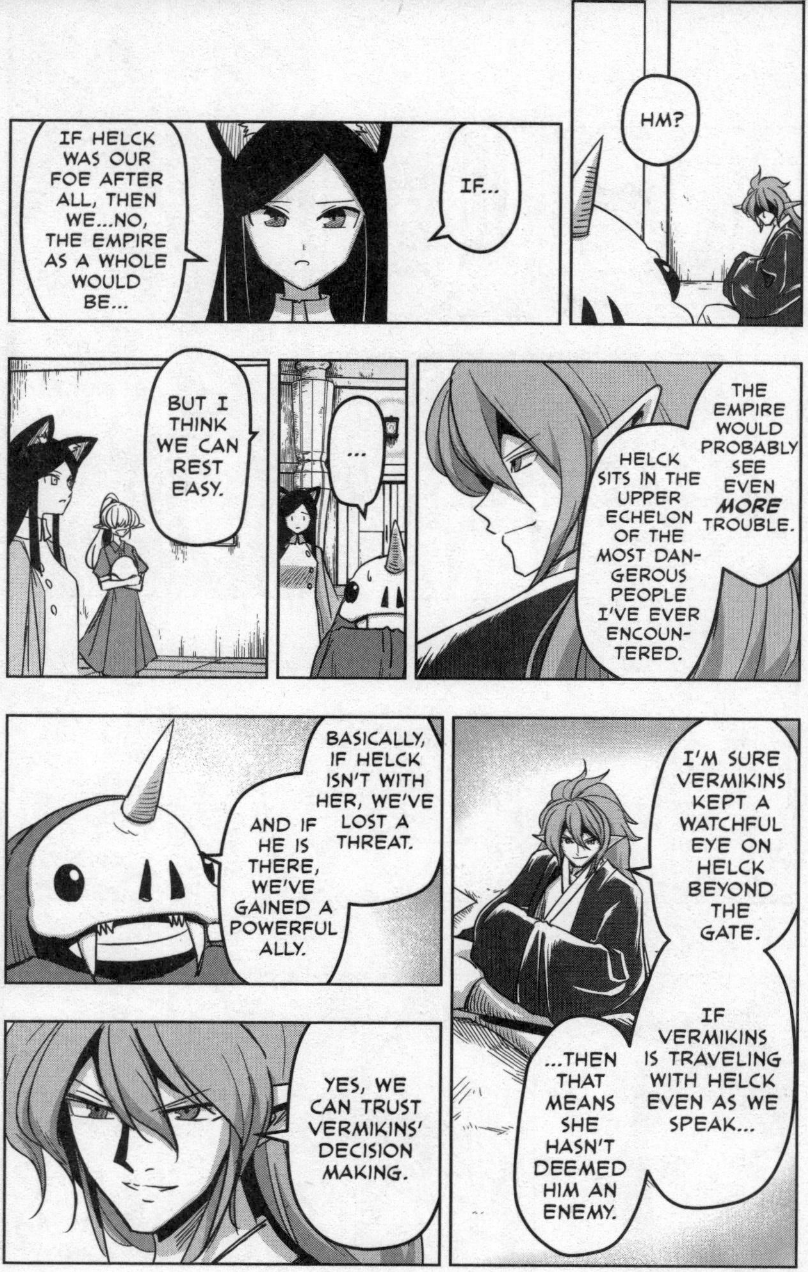

HM?
IF...
IF HELCK WAS OUR FOE AFTER ALL, THEN WE...NO, THE EMPIRE AS A WHOLE WOULD BE...
THE EMPIRE WOULD PROBABLY SEE EVEN *MORE* TROUBLE.
HELCK SITS IN THE UPPER ECHELON OF THE MOST DANGEROUS PEOPLE I'VE EVER ENCOUNTERED.
...
BUT I THINK WE CAN REST EASY.
I'M SURE VERMIKINS KEPT A WATCHFUL EYE ON HELCK BEYOND THE GATE.
IF VERMIKINS IS TRAVELING WITH HELCK EVEN AS WE SPEAK...
...THEN THAT MEANS SHE HASN'T DEEMED HIM AN ENEMY.
BASICALLY, IF HELCK ISN'T WITH HER, WE'VE LOST A THREAT.
AND IF HE IS THERE, WE'VE GAINED A POWERFUL ALLY.
YES, WE CAN TRUST VERMIKINS' DECISION MAKING.

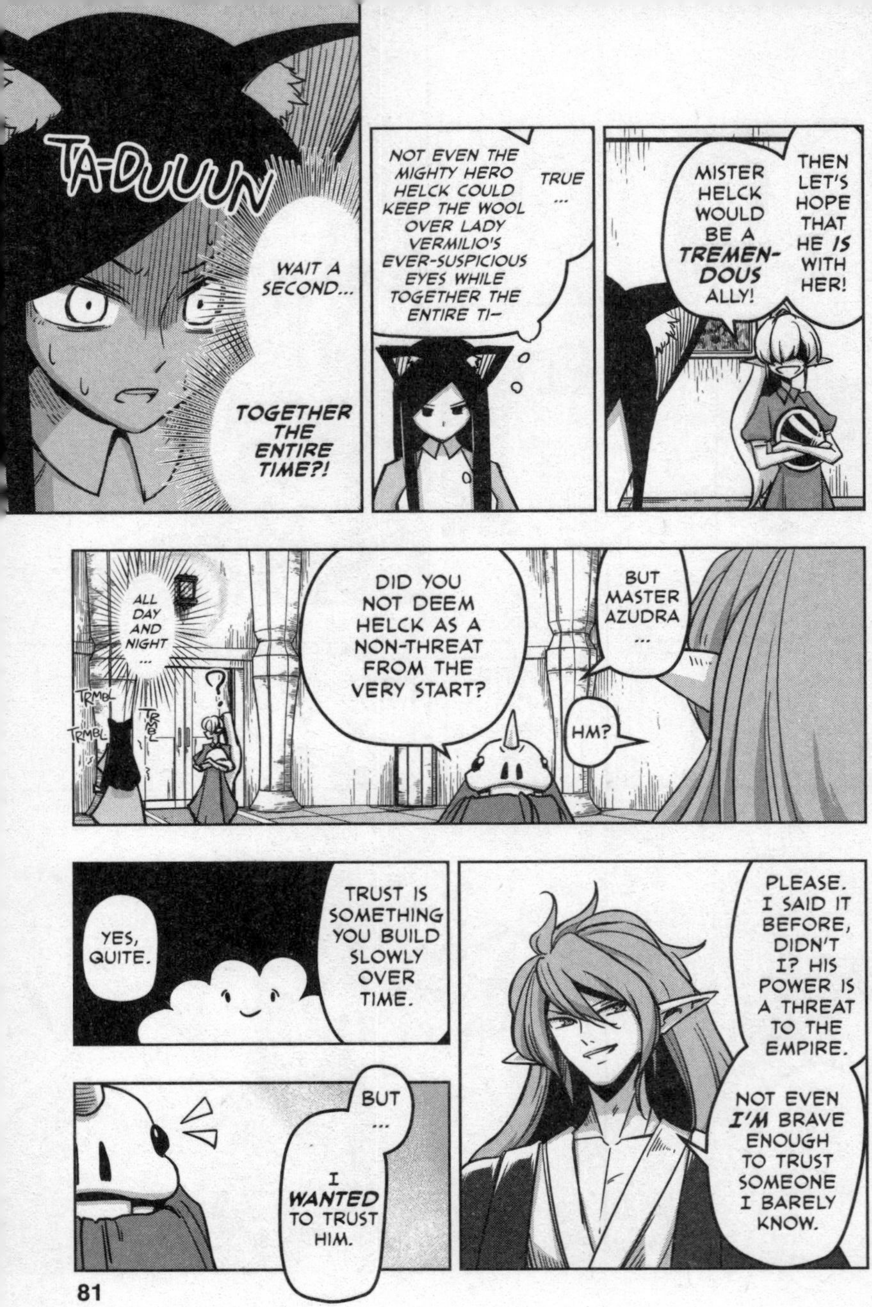
THEN LET'S HOPE THAT HE *IS* WITH HER!
MISTER HELCK WOULD BE A ***TREMENDOUS*** ALLY!
TRUE ...
NOT EVEN THE MIGHTY HERO HELCK COULD KEEP THE WOOL OVER LADY VERMILIO'S EVER-SUSPICIOUS EYES WHILE TOGETHER THE ENTIRE TI—
TA-DUUUN
WAIT A SECOND...
TOGETHER THE ENTIRE TIME?!
BUT MASTER AZUDRA ...
DID YOU NOT DEEM HELCK AS A NON-THREAT FROM THE VERY START?
HM?
?
ALL DAY AND NIGHT ...
TRMBL
TRMBL
TRMBL
PLEASE. I SAID IT BEFORE, DIDN'T I? HIS POWER IS A THREAT TO THE EMPIRE.
NOT EVEN ***I'M*** BRAVE ENOUGH TO TRUST SOMEONE I BARELY KNOW.
TRUST IS SOMETHING YOU BUILD SLOWLY OVER TIME.
YES, QUITE.
BUT ...
I ***WANTED*** TO TRUST HIM.

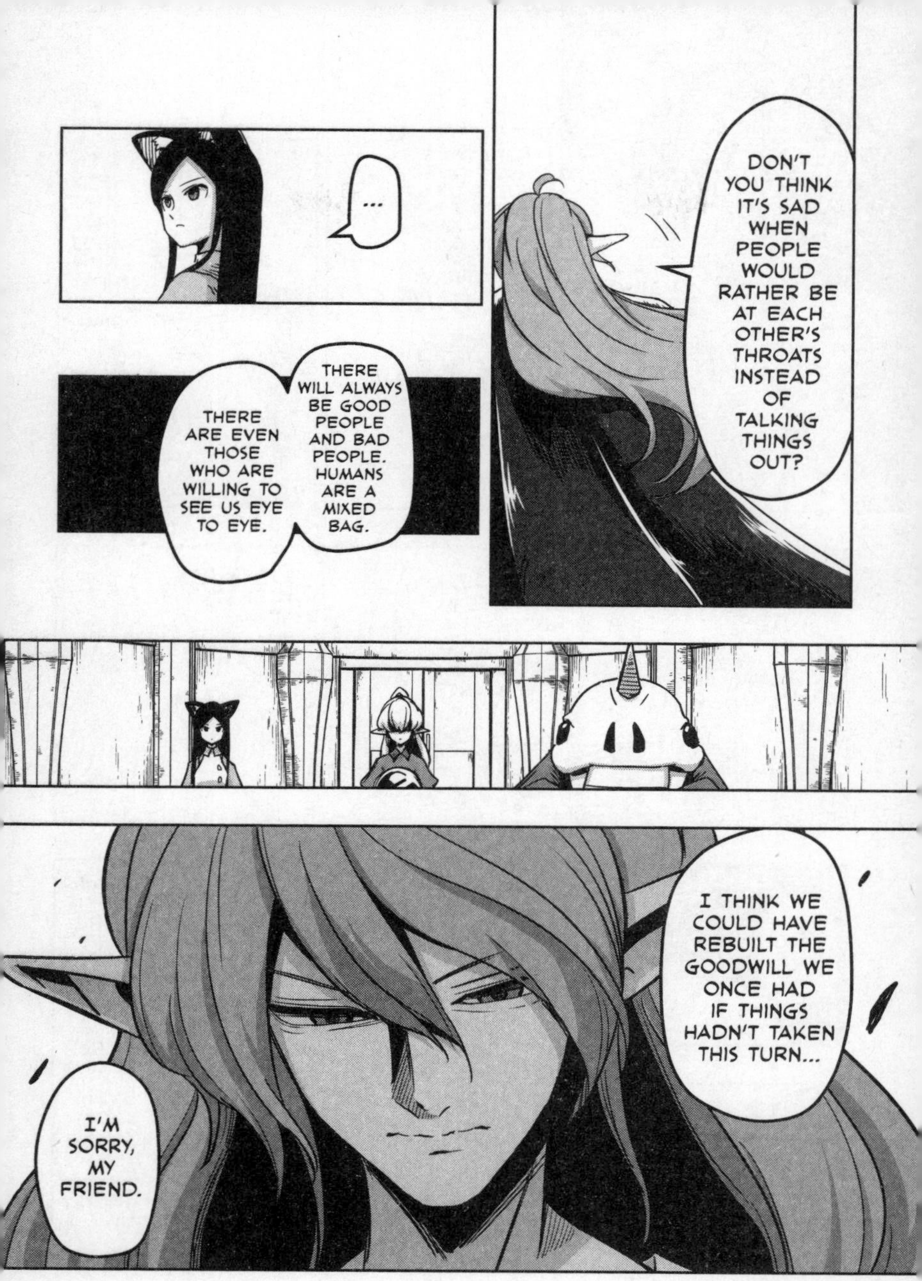
DON'T YOU THINK IT'S SAD WHEN PEOPLE WOULD RATHER BE AT EACH OTHER'S THROATS INSTEAD OF TALKING THINGS OUT?
...
THERE WILL ALWAYS BE GOOD PEOPLE AND BAD PEOPLE. HUMANS ARE A MIXED BAG.
THERE ARE EVEN THOSE WHO ARE WILLING TO SEE US EYE TO EYE.
I THINK WE COULD HAVE REBUILT THE GOODWILL WE ONCE HAD IF THINGS HADN'T TAKEN THIS TURN...
I'M SORRY, MY FRIEND.

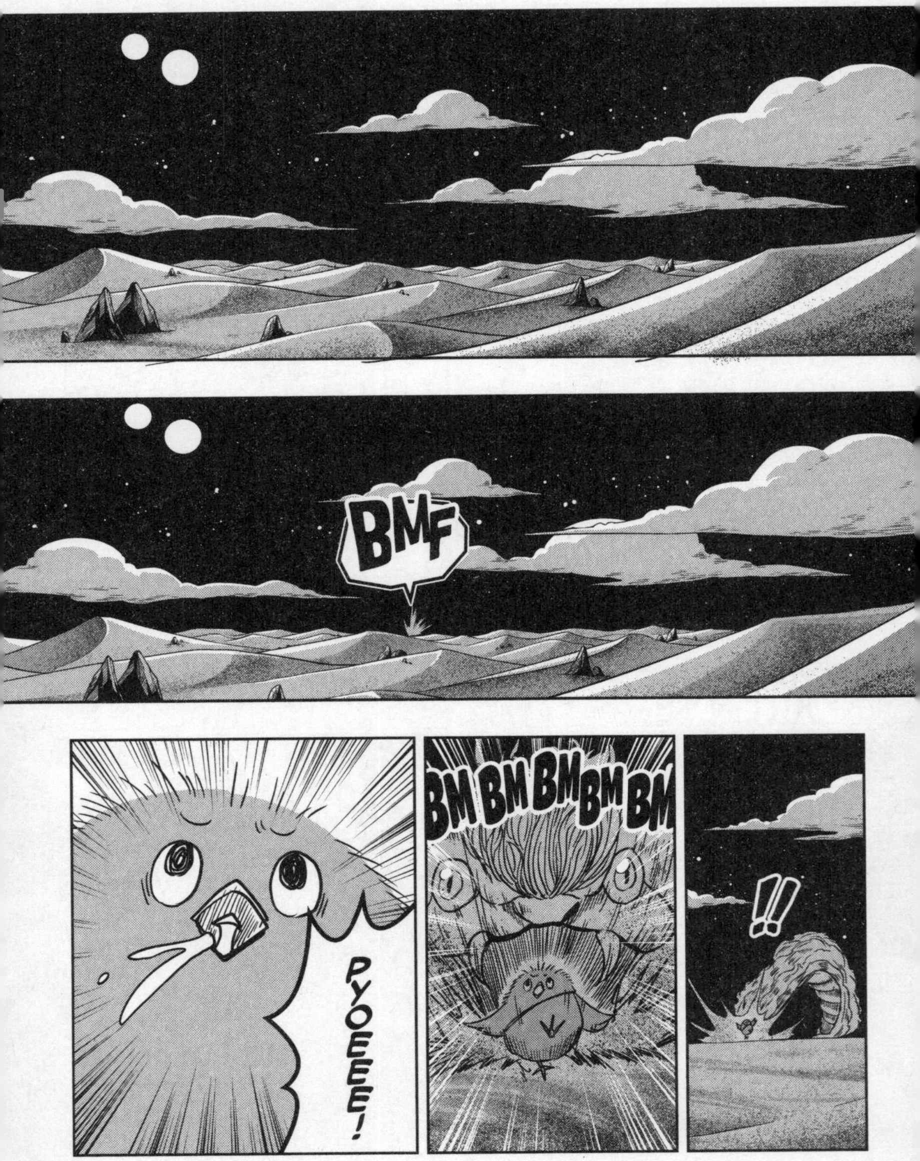
BMF
!!
BM BM BM BM BM
PYOEEE!

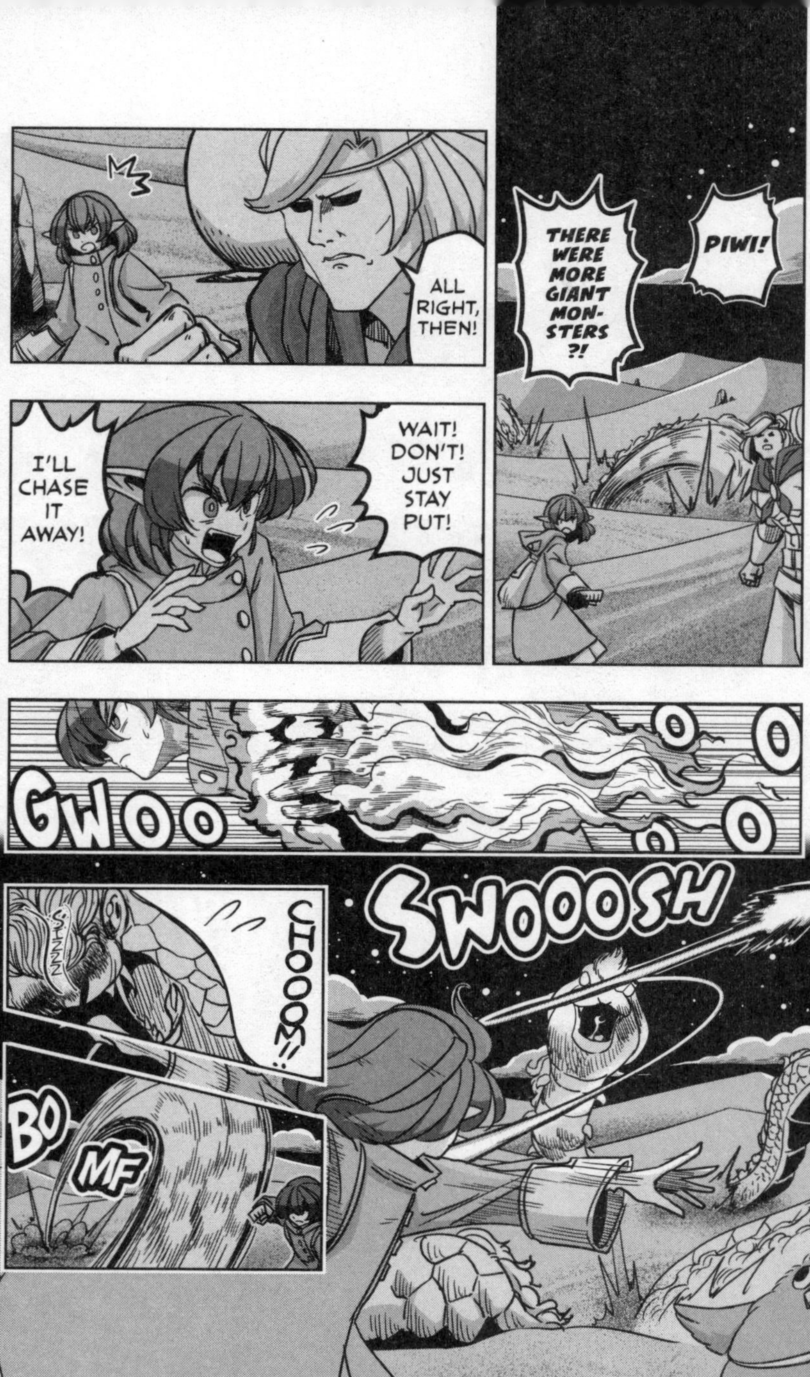
PIWI!
THERE WERE MORE GIANT MON-STERS ?!
ALL RIGHT, THEN!
WAIT! DON'T! JUST STAY PUT!
I'LL CHASE IT AWAY!
GWOOOOOO
SWOOOSH
CHOOOM!!
SIZZZ
BOMF

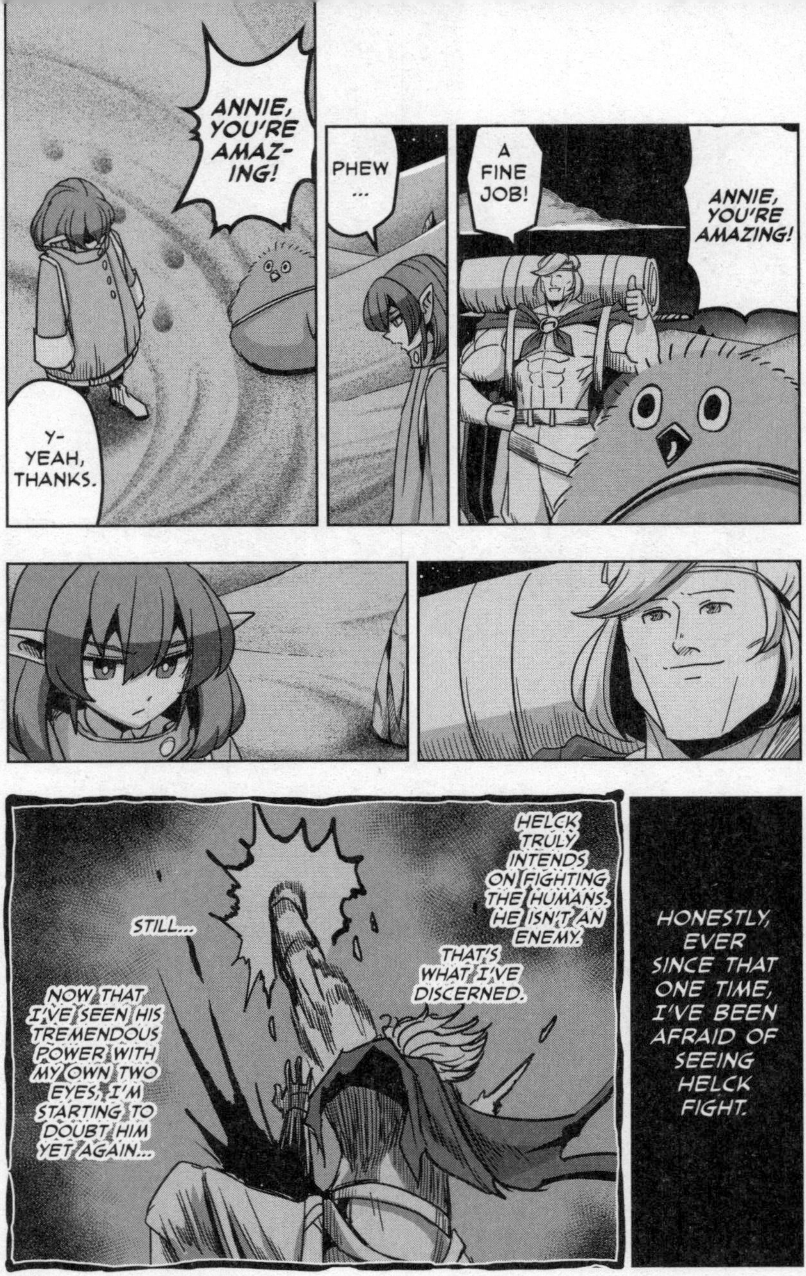
ANNIE, YOU'RE AMAZING!
A FINE JOB!
PHEW...
ANNIE, YOU'RE AMAZ-ING!
Y-YEAH, THANKS.
HONESTLY, EVER SINCE THAT ONE TIME, I'VE BEEN AFRAID OF SEEING HELCK FIGHT.
HELCK TRULY INTENDS ON FIGHTING THE HUMANS. HE ISN'T AN ENEMY.
THAT'S WHAT I'VE DISCERNED.
STILL...
NOW THAT I'VE SEEN HIS TREMENDOUS POWER WITH MY OWN TWO EYES, I'M STARTING TO DOUBT HIM YET AGAIN...

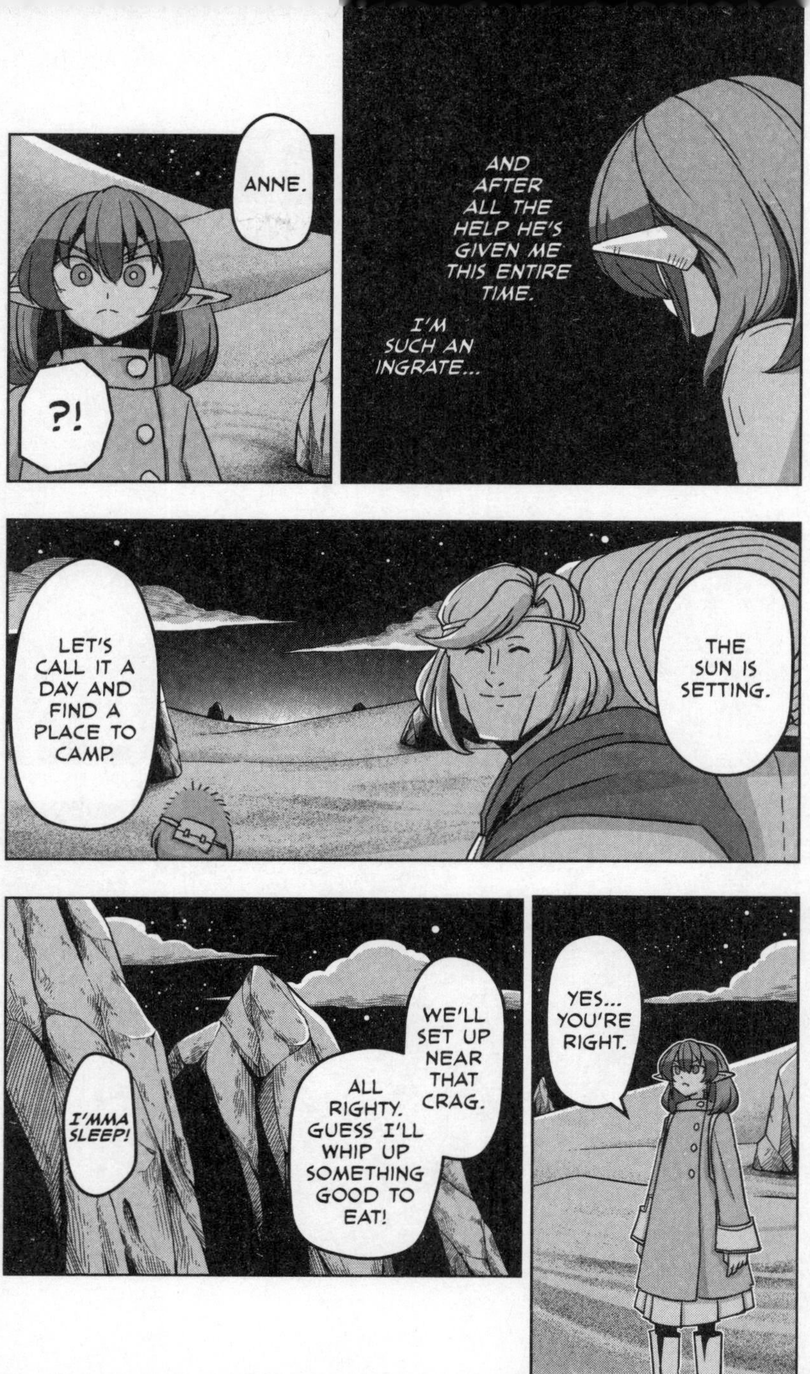
AND AFTER ALL THE HELP HE'S GIVEN ME THIS ENTIRE TIME.
I'M SUCH AN INGRATE...
ANNE.
?!
THE SUN IS SETTING.
LET'S CALL IT A DAY AND FIND A PLACE TO CAMP.
YES... YOU'RE RIGHT.
WE'LL SET UP NEAR THAT CRAG.
ALL RIGHTY. GUESS I'LL WHIP UP SOMETHING GOOD TO EAT!
I'MMA SLEEP!

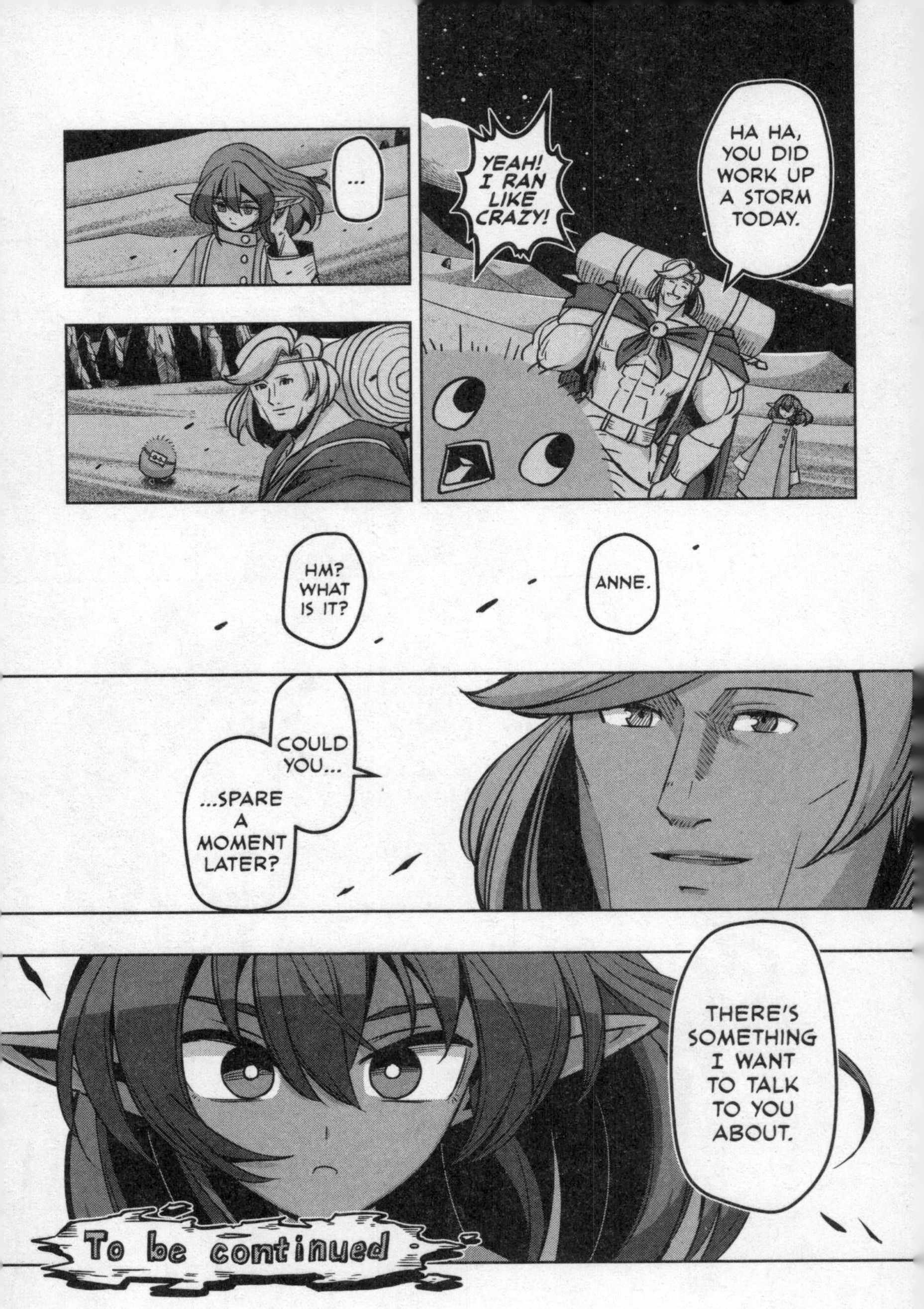
HA HA, YOU DID WORK UP A STORM TODAY.
YEAH! I RAN LIKE CRAZY!
...
ANNE.
HM? WHAT IS IT?
COULD YOU...
...SPARE A MOMENT LATER?
THERE'S SOMETHING I WANT TO TALK TO YOU ABOUT.
To be continued

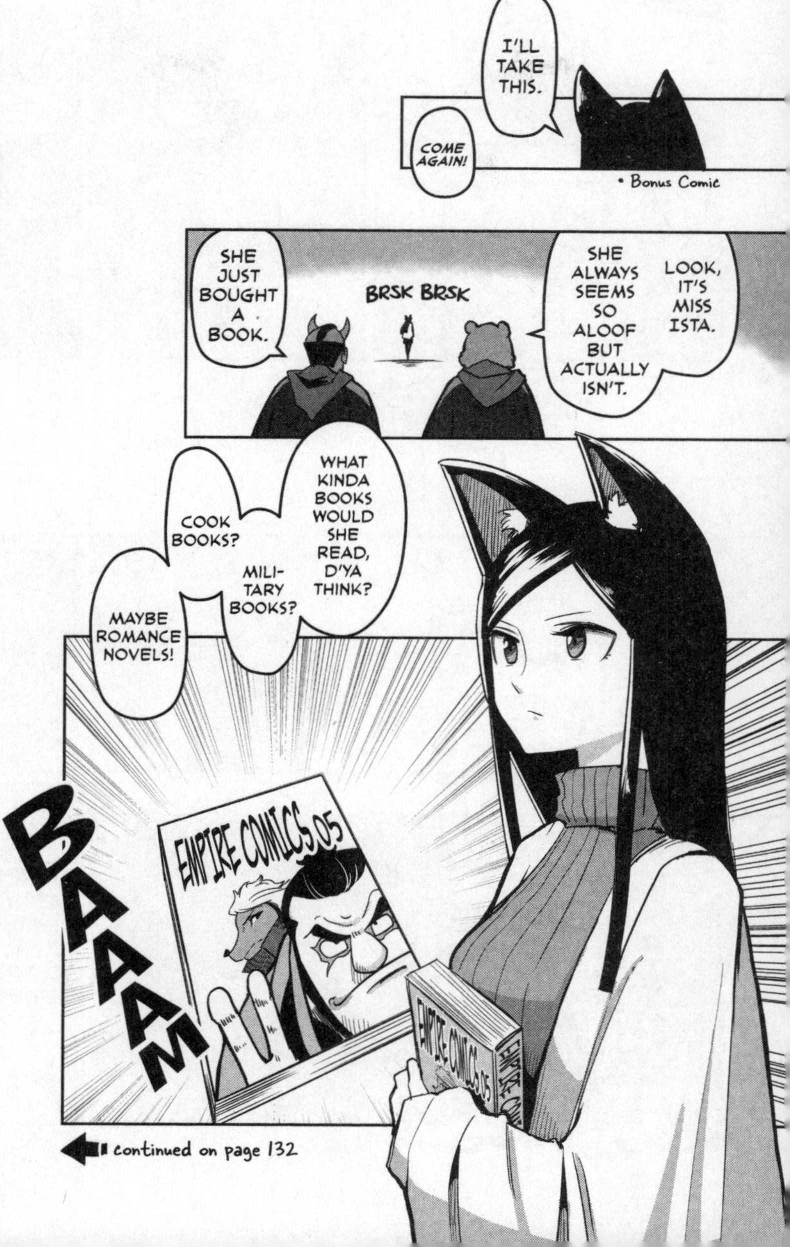
I'LL TAKE THIS.
COME AGAIN!
LOOK, IT'S MISS ISTA.
SHE ALWAYS SEEMS SO ALOOF BUT ACTUALLY ISN'T.
BRSK BRSK
SHE JUST BOUGHT A BOOK.
WHAT KINDA BOOKS WOULD SHE READ, D'YA THINK?
MILITARY BOOKS?
COOK BOOKS?
MAYBE ROMANCE NOVELS!
BAAAM
EMPIRE COMICS 05
EMPIRE COMICS 05

• Bonus Comic

continued on page 132

Chapter 36: Helck's Past 1

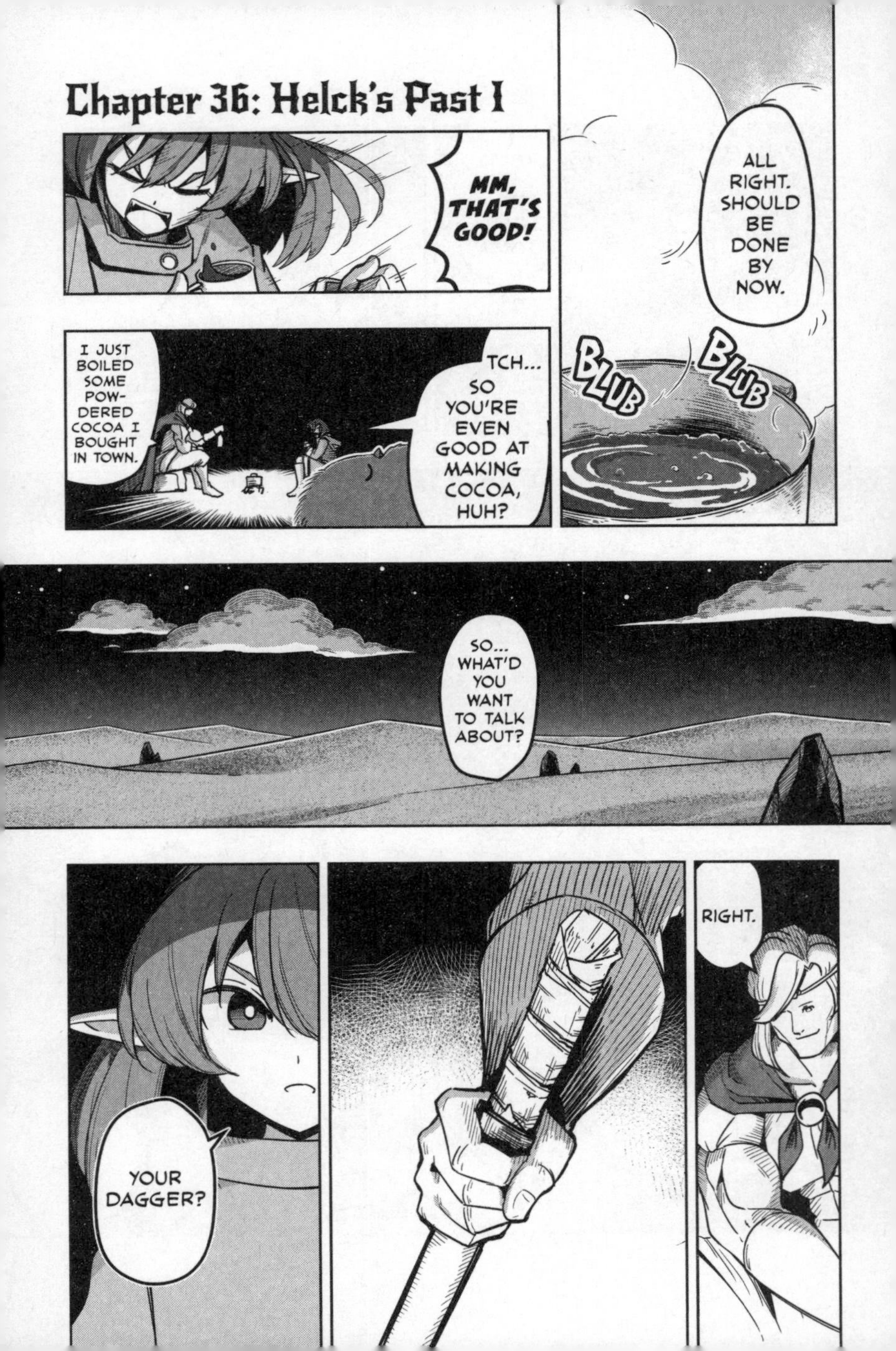
ALL RIGHT. SHOULD BE DONE BY NOW.
BLUB
BLUB
MM, THAT'S GOOD!
TCH... SO YOU'RE EVEN GOOD AT MAKING COCOA, HUH?
I JUST BOILED SOME POW-DERED COCOA I BOUGHT IN TOWN.
SO... WHAT'D YOU WANT TO TALK ABOUT?
RIGHT.
YOUR DAGGER?

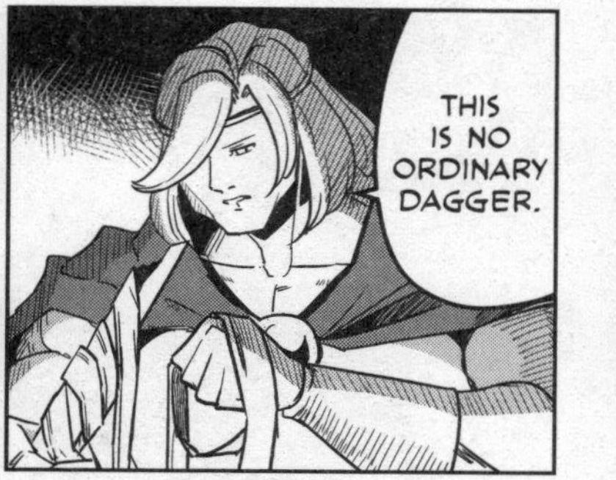
THIS IS NO ORDINARY DAGGER.
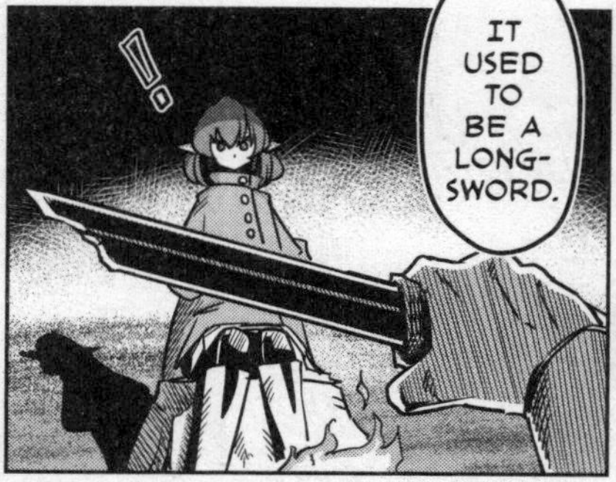
!
IT USED TO BE A LONG-SWORD.
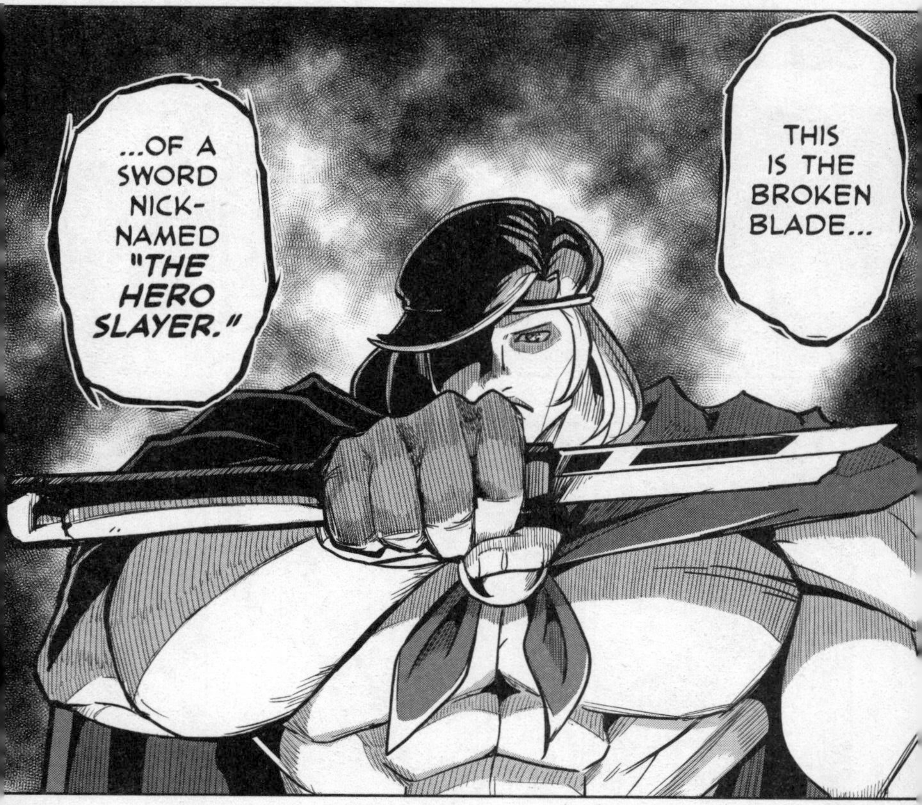
THIS IS THE BROKEN BLADE...
...OF A SWORD NICK-NAMED ***"THE HERO SLAYER."***

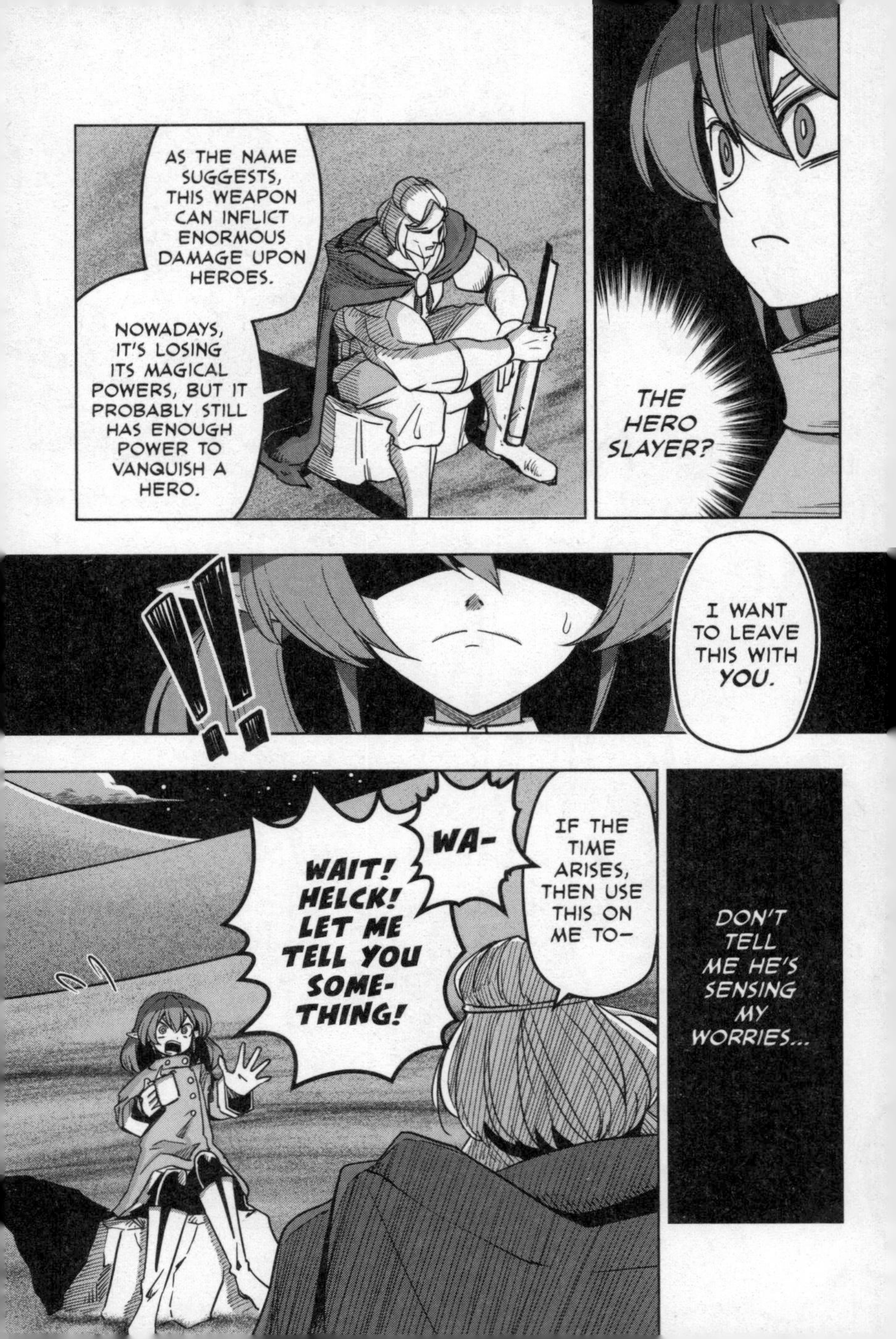
THE HERO SLAYER?
AS THE NAME SUGGESTS, THIS WEAPON CAN INFLICT ENORMOUS DAMAGE UPON HEROES.
NOWADAYS, IT'S LOSING ITS MAGICAL POWERS, BUT IT PROBABLY STILL HAS ENOUGH POWER TO VANQUISH A HERO.
I WANT TO LEAVE THIS WITH YOU.
!!
DON'T TELL ME HE'S SENSING MY WORRIES...
IF THE TIME ARISES, THEN USE THIS ON ME TO—
WA-
WAIT! HELCK! LET ME TELL YOU SOME-THING!

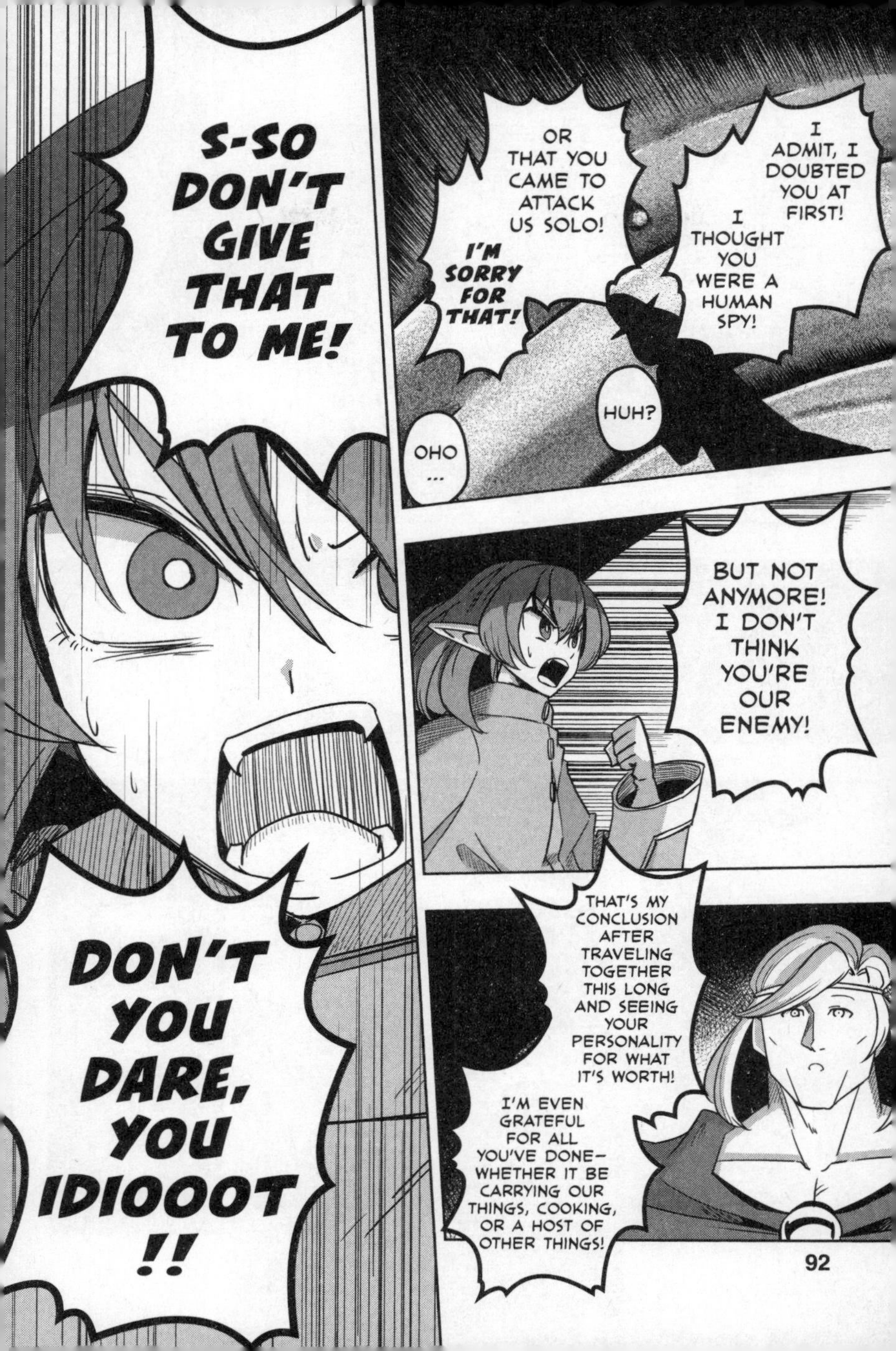
I ADMIT, I DOUBTED YOU AT FIRST!
I THOUGHT YOU WERE A HUMAN SPY!
OR THAT YOU CAME TO ATTACK US SOLO!
I'M SORRY FOR THAT!
HUH?
OHO ...
BUT NOT ANYMORE! I DON'T THINK YOU'RE OUR ENEMY!
THAT'S MY CONCLUSION AFTER TRAVELING TOGETHER THIS LONG AND SEEING YOUR PERSONALITY FOR WHAT IT'S WORTH!
I'M EVEN GRATEFUL FOR ALL YOU'VE DONE—WHETHER IT BE CARRYING OUR THINGS, COOKING, OR A HOST OF OTHER THINGS!
S-SO DON'T GIVE THAT TO ME!
DON'T YOU DARE, YOU IDIOOOT !!

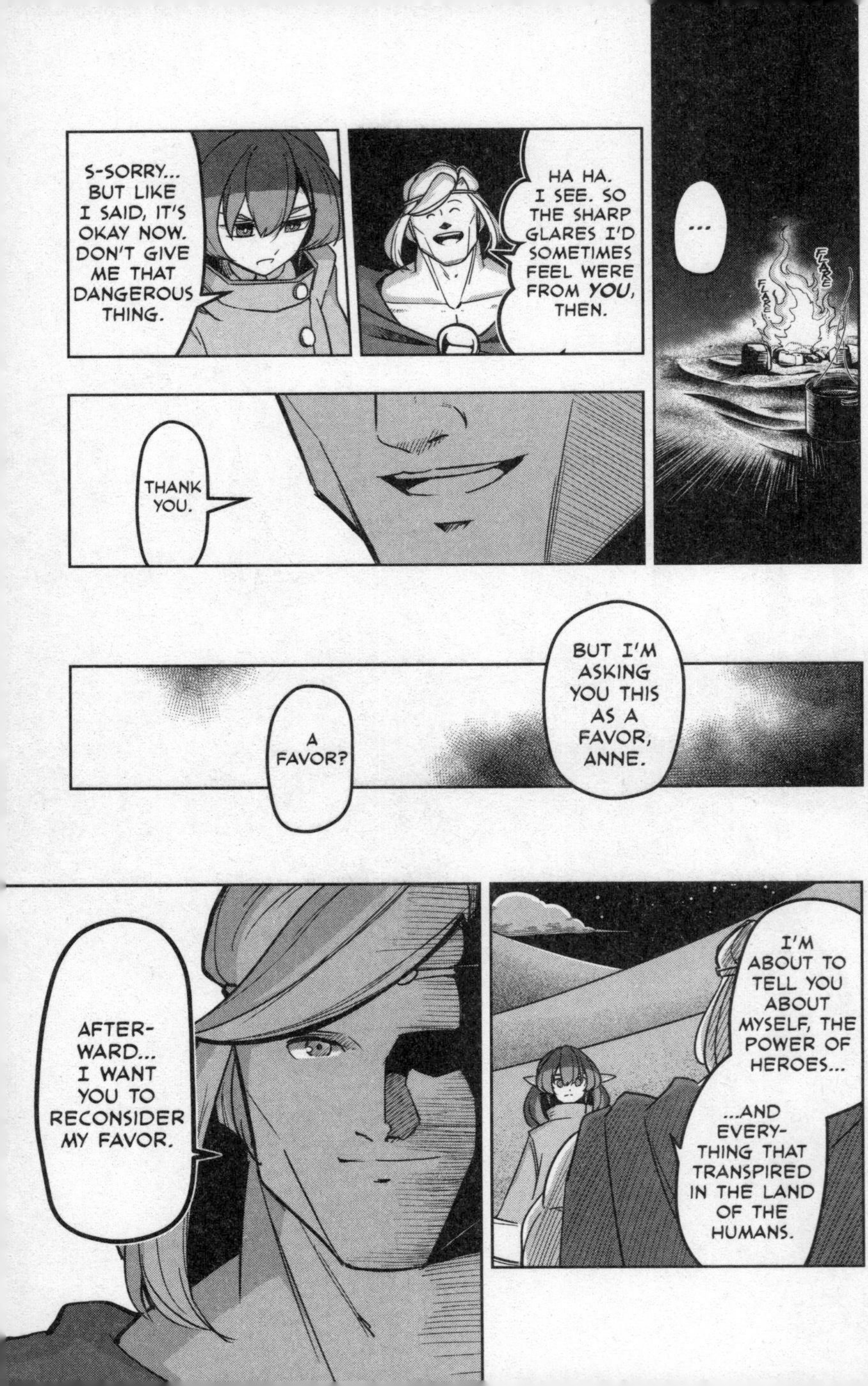
...
FLARE
FLARE
HA HA. I SEE. SO THE SHARP GLARES I'D SOMETIMES FEEL WERE FROM *YOU*, THEN.
S-SORRY... BUT LIKE I SAID, IT'S OKAY NOW. DON'T GIVE ME THAT DANGEROUS THING.
THANK YOU.
BUT I'M ASKING YOU THIS AS A FAVOR, ANNE.
A FAVOR?
I'M ABOUT TO TELL YOU ABOUT MYSELF, THE POWER OF HEROES...
...AND EVERYTHING THAT TRANSPIRED IN THE LAND OF THE HUMANS.
AFTERWARD... I WANT YOU TO RECONSIDER MY FAVOR.

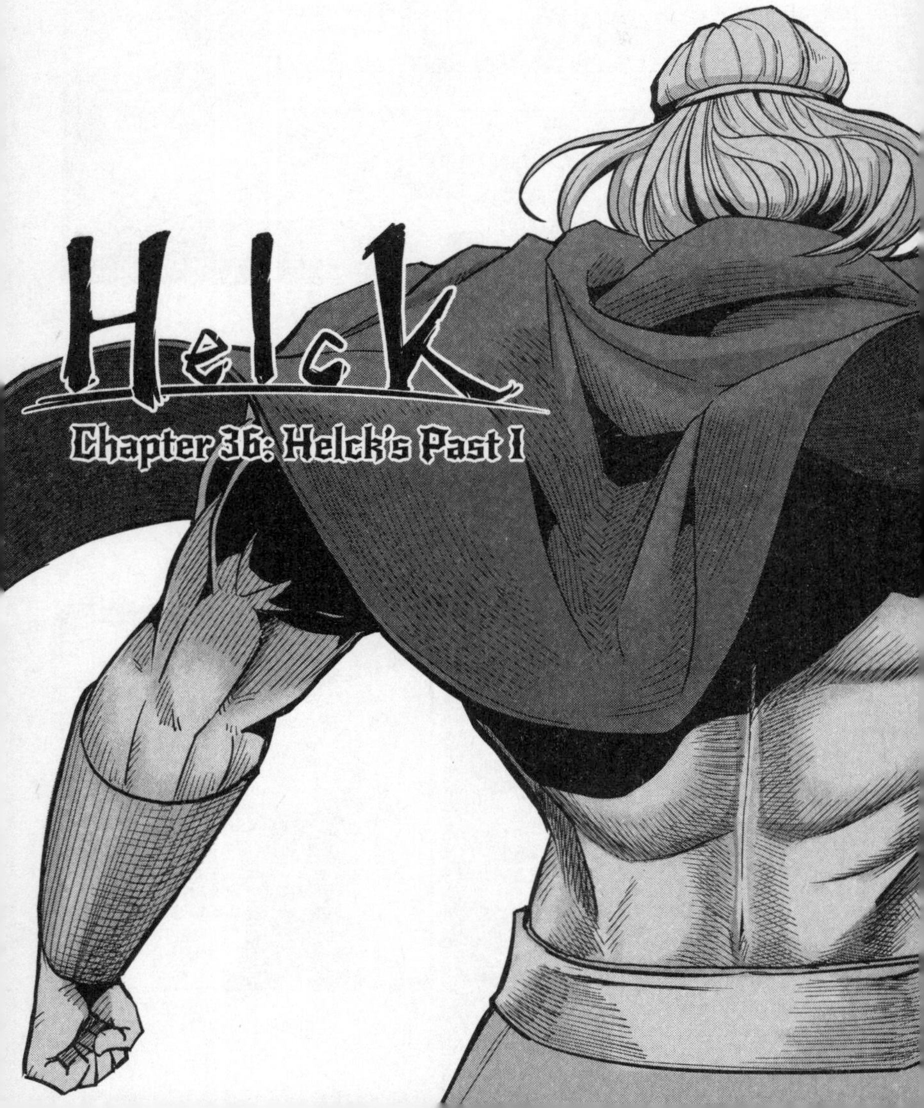
Helck
Chapter 36: Helck's Past 1

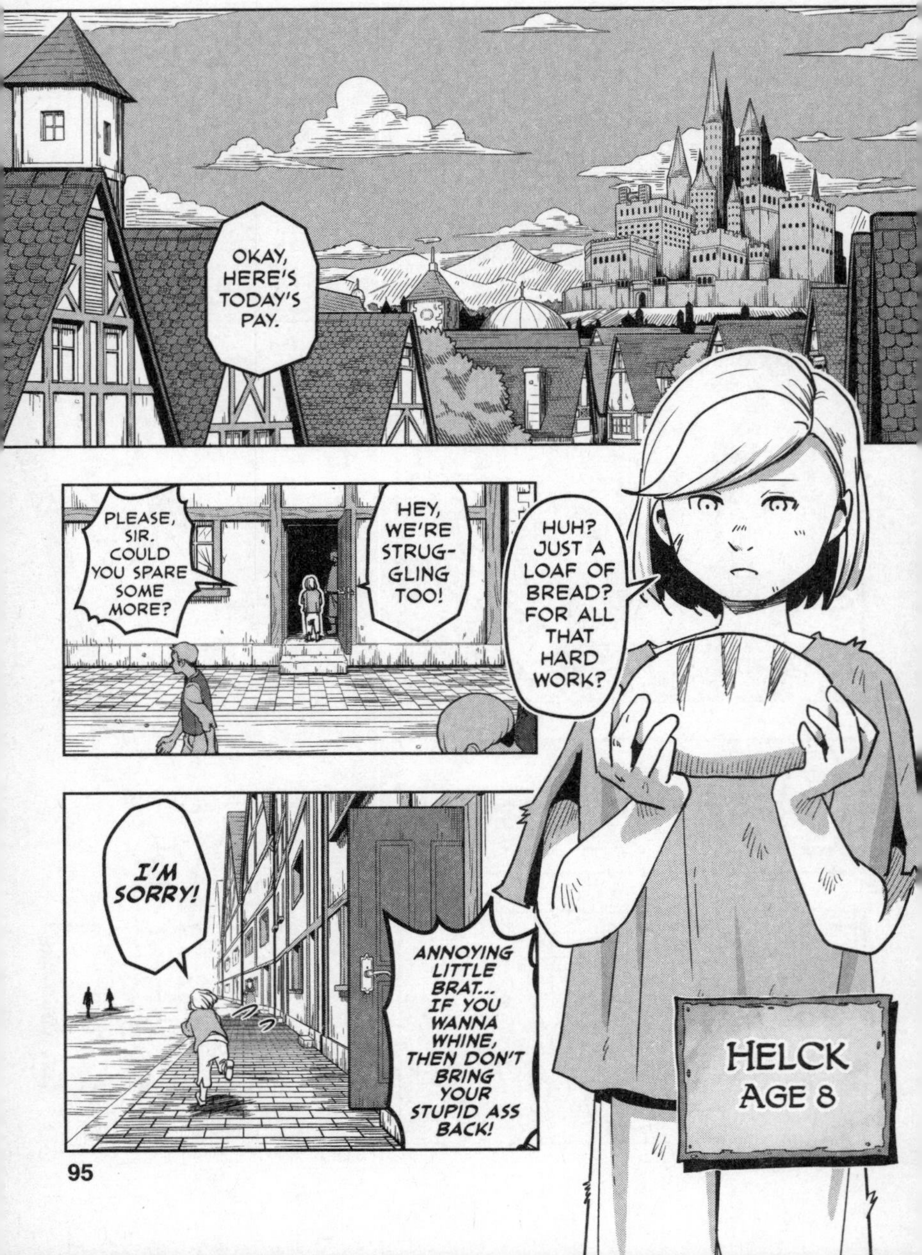

OKAY, HERE'S TODAY'S PAY.
HUH? JUST A LOAF OF BREAD? FOR ALL THAT HARD WORK?
HELCK
AGE 8
HEY, WE'RE STRUG-GLING TOO!
PLEASE, SIR. COULD YOU SPARE SOME MORE?
ANNOYING LITTLE BRAT... IF YOU WANNA WHINE, THEN DON'T BRING YOUR STUPID ASS BACK!
I'M SORRY!

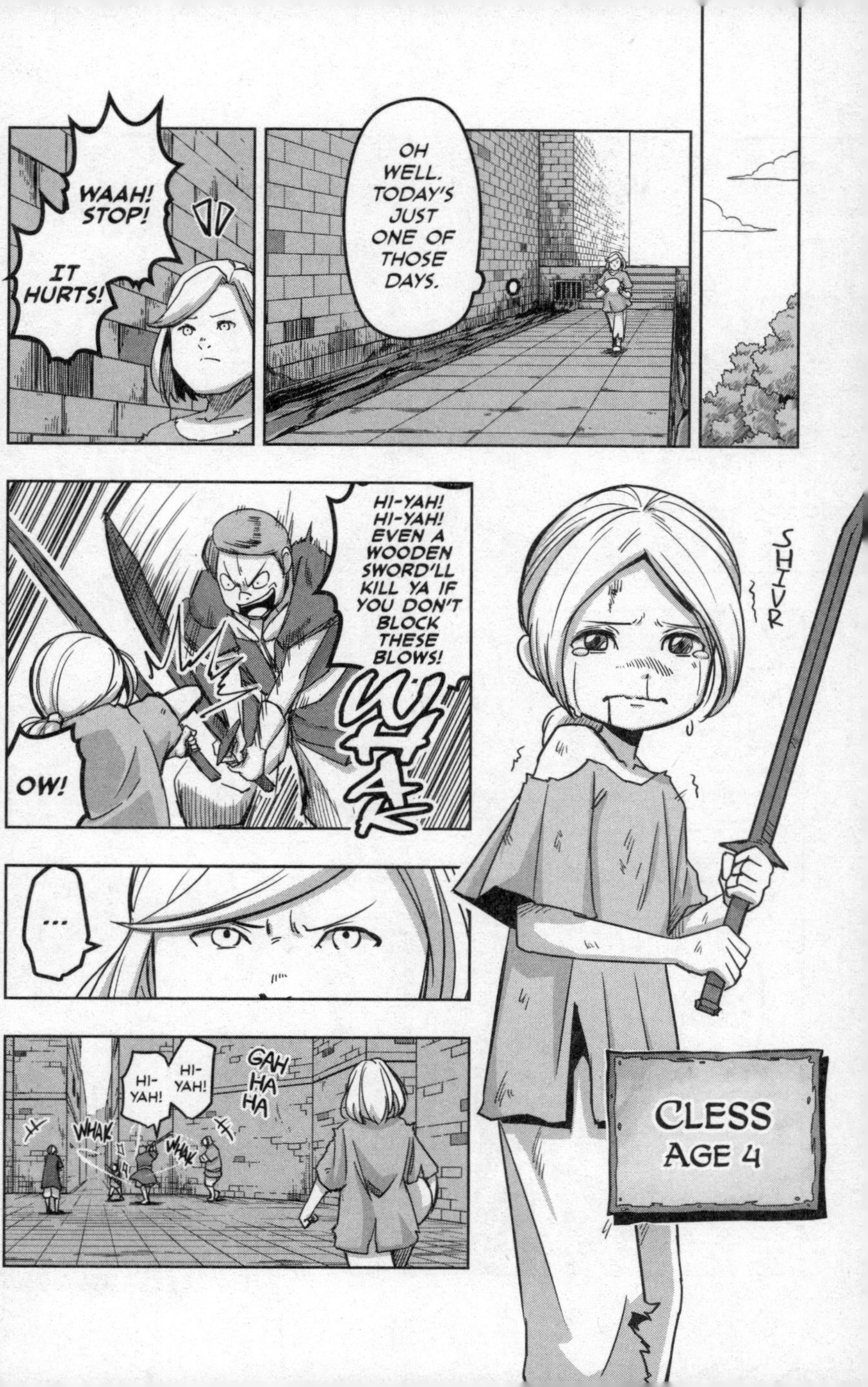
OH WELL. TODAY'S JUST ONE OF THOSE DAYS.
WAAH! STOP!
IT HURTS!
SHIVR
CLESS
AGE 4
HI-YAH! HI-YAH! EVEN A WOODEN SWORD'LL KILL YA IF YOU DON'T BLOCK THESE BLOWS!
WHAK
OW!
...
GAH HA HA
HI-YAH!
HI-YAH!
WHAK
WHAK

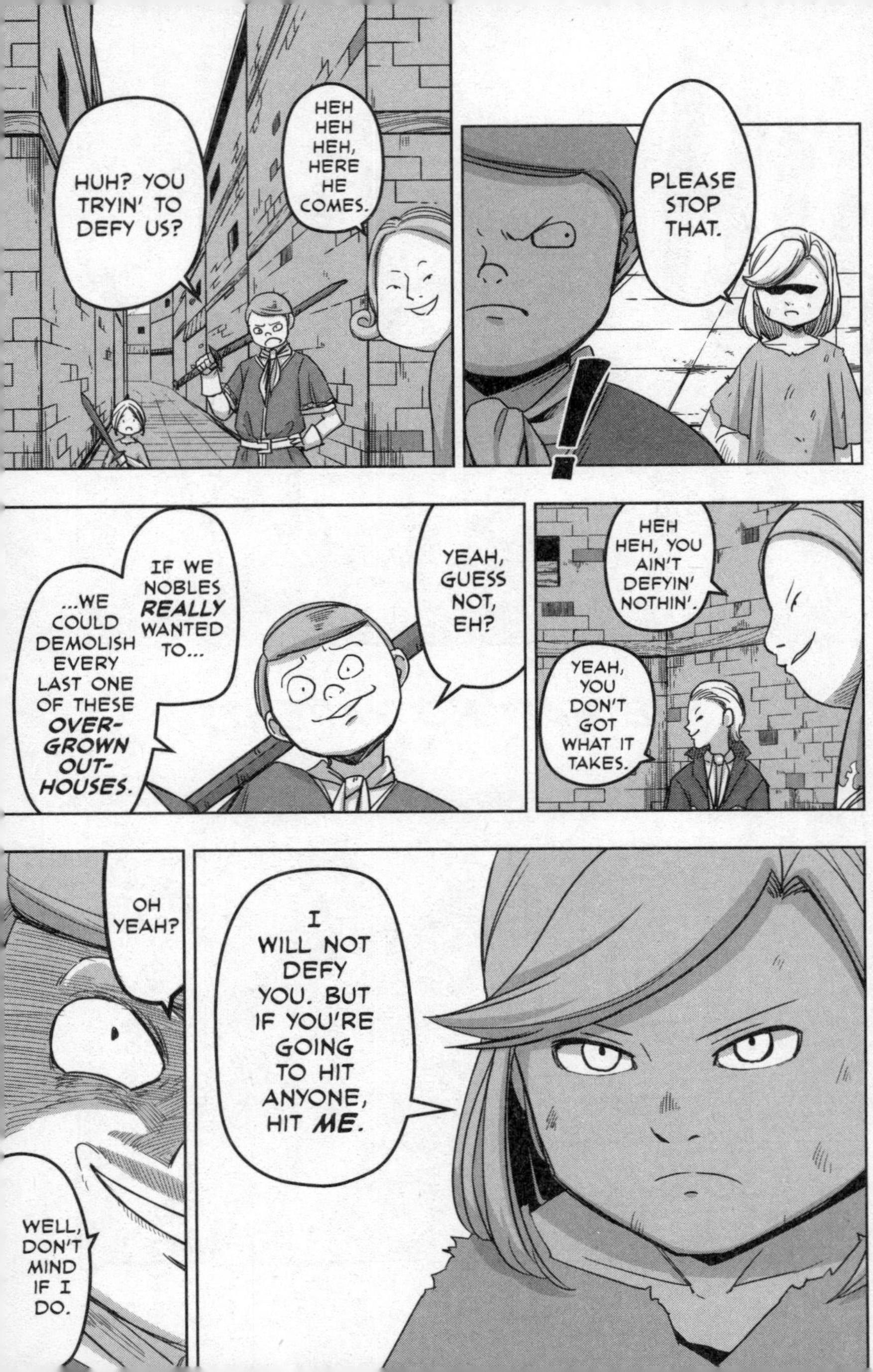
PLEASE STOP THAT.
HEH HEH HEH, HERE HE COMES.
HUH? YOU TRYIN' TO DEFY US?
HEH HEH, YOU AIN'T DEFYIN' NOTHIN'.
YEAH, YOU DON'T GOT WHAT IT TAKES.
YEAH, GUESS NOT, EH?
IF WE NOBLES REALLY WANTED TO...
...WE COULD DEMOLISH EVERY LAST ONE OF THESE OVER-GROWN OUT-HOUSES.
I WILL NOT DEFY YOU. BUT IF YOU'RE GOING TO HIT ANYONE, HIT ME.
OH YEAH?
WELL, DON'T MIND IF I DO.

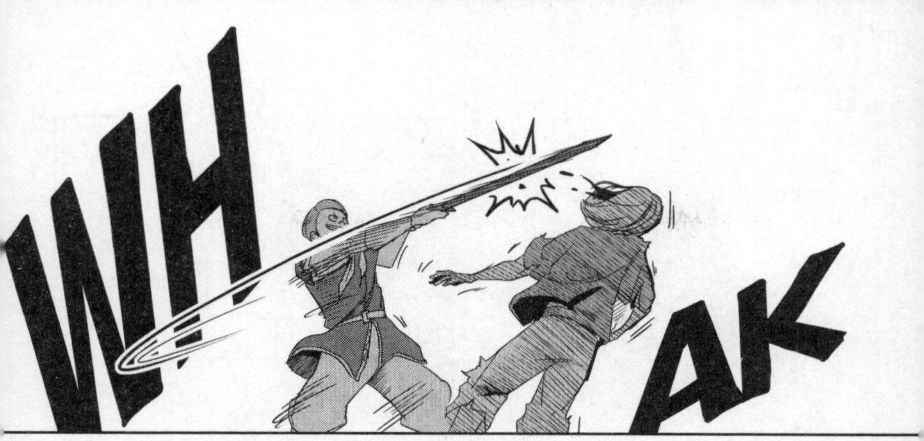
WH
AK

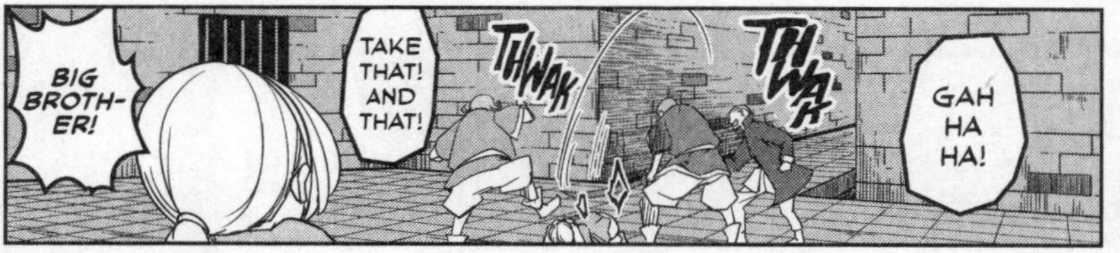
GAH HA HA!
THWAK
TAKE THAT! AND THAT!
THWAK
BIG BROTHER!

WE HAD NO PARENTS.

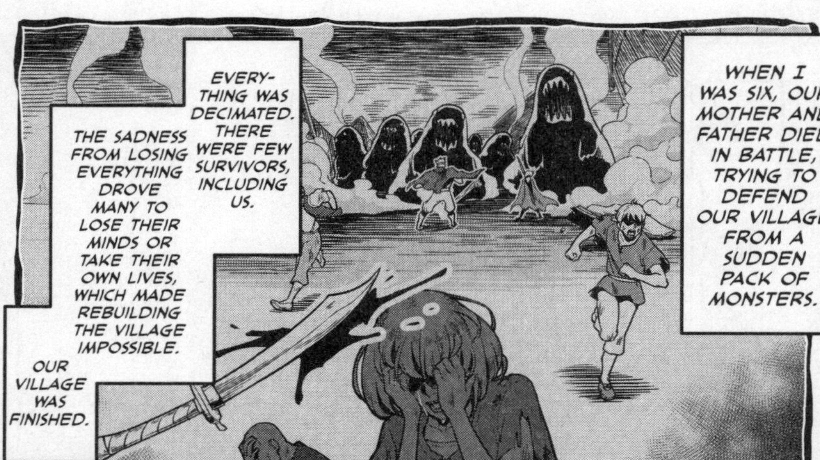
WHEN I WAS SIX, OUR MOTHER AND FATHER DIED IN BATTLE, TRYING TO DEFEND OUR VILLAGE FROM A SUDDEN PACK OF MONSTERS.
EVERYTHING WAS DECIMATED. THERE WERE FEW SURVIVORS, INCLUDING US.
THE SADNESS FROM LOSING EVERYTHING DROVE MANY TO LOSE THEIR MINDS OR TAKE THEIR OWN LIVES, WHICH MADE REBUILDING THE VILLAGE IMPOSSIBLE.
OUR VILLAGE WAS FINISHED.

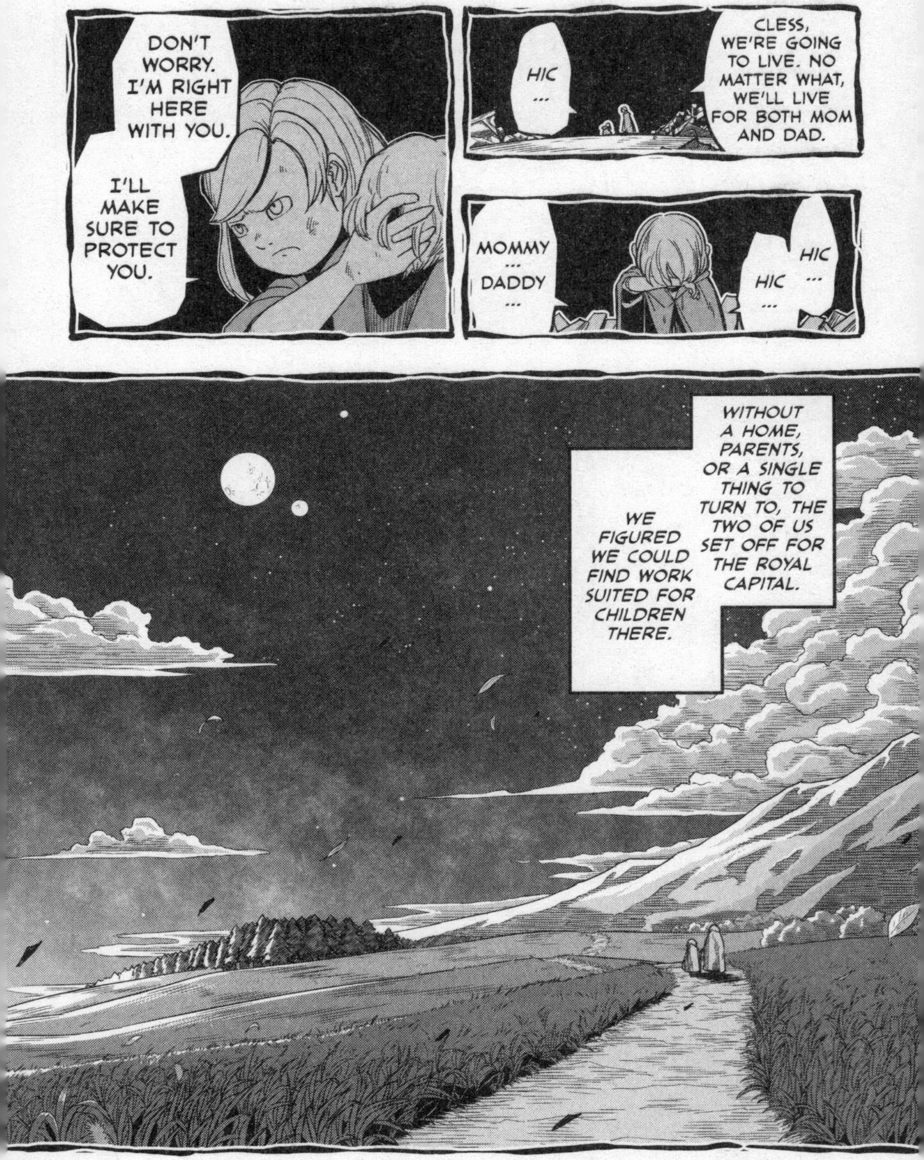
CLESS, WE'RE GOING TO LIVE. NO MATTER WHAT, WE'LL LIVE FOR BOTH MOM AND DAD.
HIC ...
HIC ...
HIC ...
MOMMY ... DADDY ...
DON'T WORRY. I'M RIGHT HERE WITH YOU.
I'LL MAKE SURE TO PROTECT YOU.
WITHOUT A HOME, PARENTS, OR A SINGLE THING TO TURN TO, THE TWO OF US SET OFF FOR THE ROYAL CAPITAL.
WE FIGURED WE COULD FIND WORK SUITED FOR CHILDREN THERE.

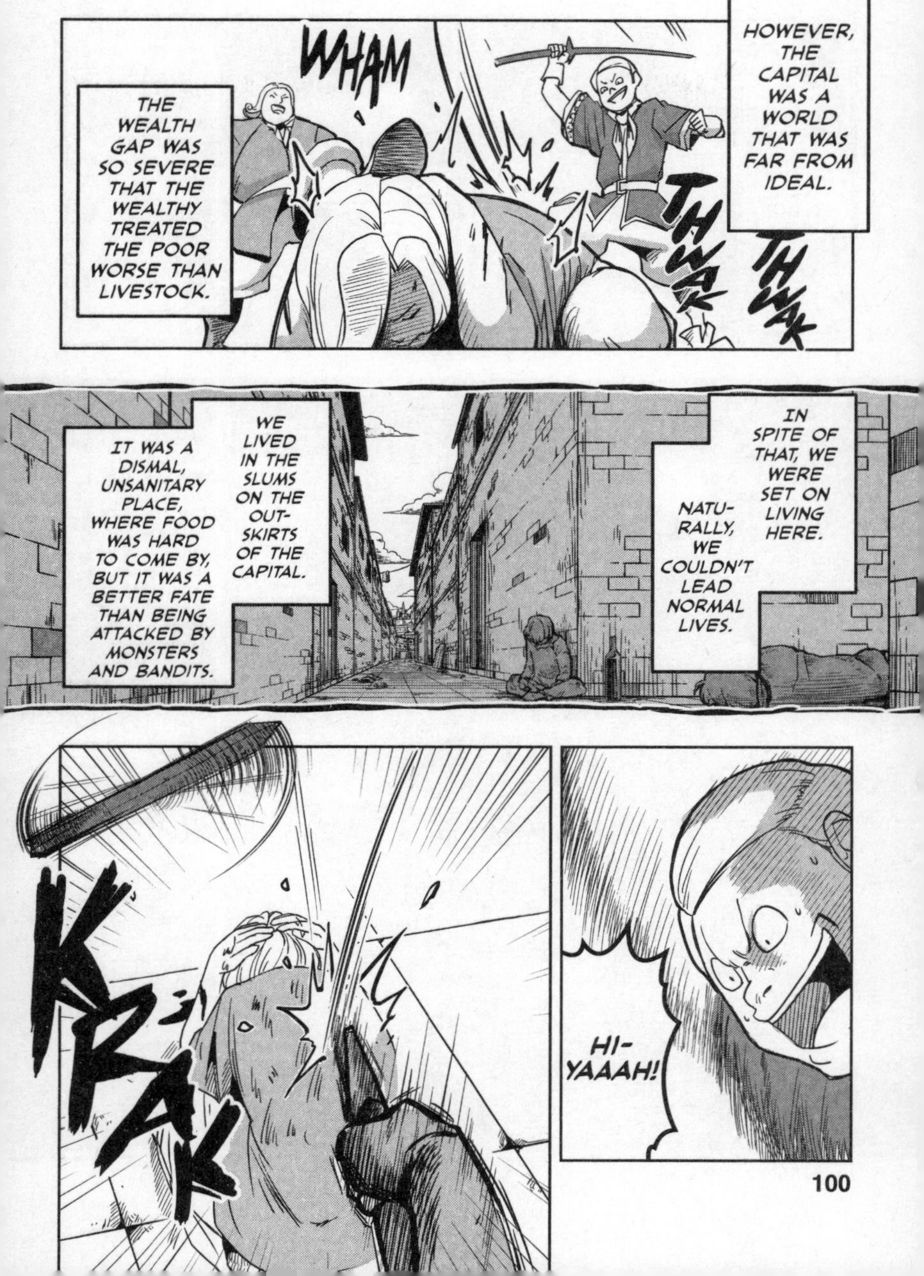
HOWEVER, THE CAPITAL WAS A WORLD THAT WAS FAR FROM IDEAL.
THE WEALTH GAP WAS SO SEVERE THAT THE WEALTHY TREATED THE POOR WORSE THAN LIVESTOCK.
WHAM
THWAK
THWAK
IN SPITE OF THAT, WE WERE SET ON LIVING HERE.
NATU-RALLY, WE COULDN'T LEAD NORMAL LIVES.
WE LIVED IN THE SLUMS ON THE OUT-SKIRTS OF THE CAPITAL.
IT WAS A DISMAL, UNSANITARY PLACE, WHERE FOOD WAS HARD TO COME BY, BUT IT WAS A BETTER FATE THAN BEING ATTACKED BY MONSTERS AND BANDITS.
HI-YAAAH!
KRAK

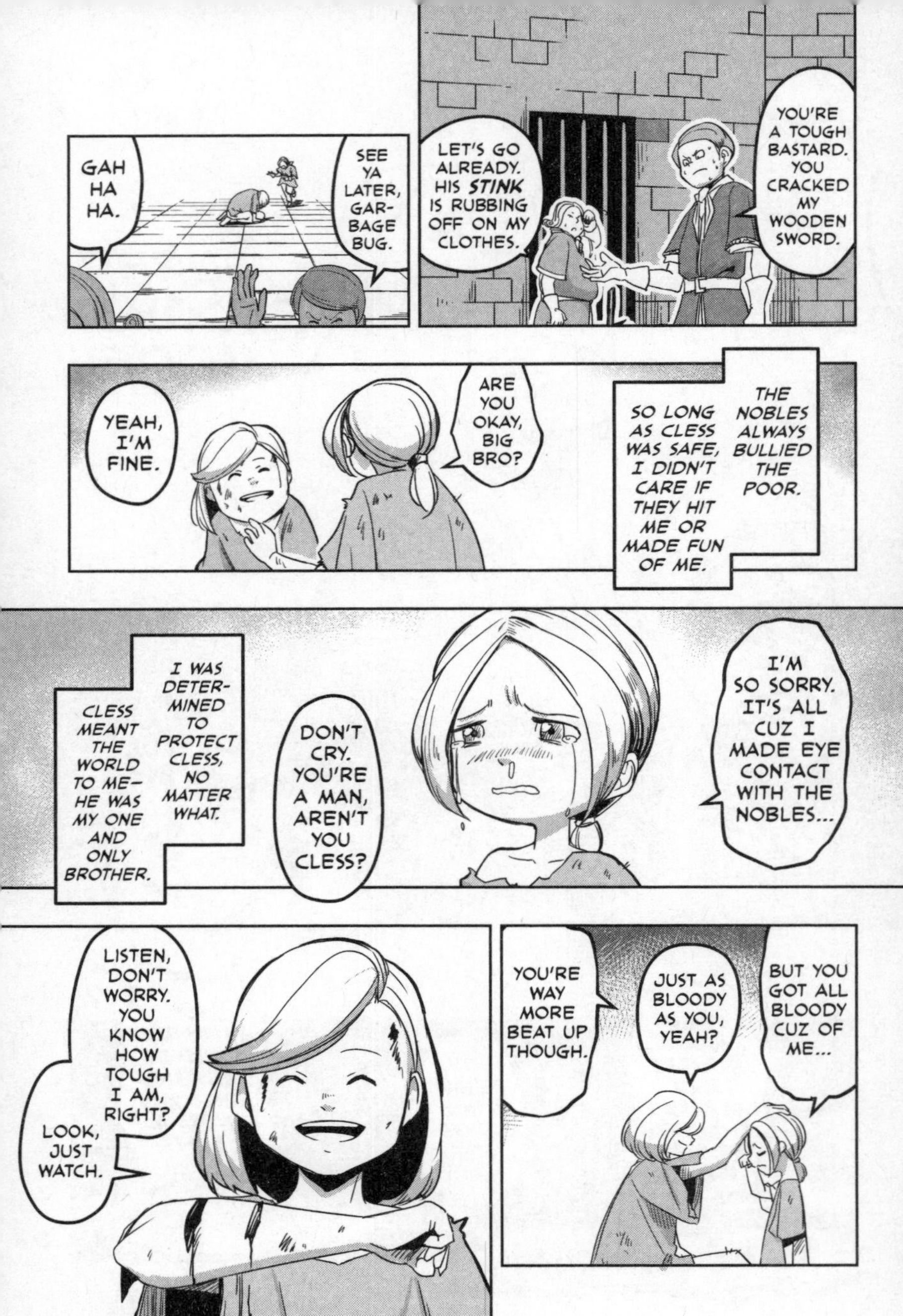
YOU'RE A TOUGH BASTARD. YOU CRACKED MY WOODEN SWORD.
LET'S GO ALREADY. HIS **STINK** IS RUBBING OFF ON MY CLOTHES.
SEE YA LATER, GARBAGE BUG.
GAH HA HA.
THE NOBLES ALWAYS BULLIED THE POOR.
SO LONG AS CLESS WAS SAFE, I DIDN'T CARE IF THEY HIT ME OR MADE FUN OF ME.
ARE YOU OKAY, BIG BRO?
YEAH, I'M FINE.
I'M SO SORRY. IT'S ALL CUZ I MADE EYE CONTACT WITH THE NOBLES...
DON'T CRY. YOU'RE A MAN, AREN'T YOU CLESS?
I WAS DETERMINED TO PROTECT CLESS, NO MATTER WHAT.
CLESS MEANT THE WORLD TO ME—HE WAS MY ONE AND ONLY BROTHER.
BUT YOU GOT ALL BLOODY CUZ OF ME...
JUST AS BLOODY AS YOU, YEAH?
YOU'RE WAY MORE BEAT UP THOUGH.
LISTEN, DON'T WORRY. YOU KNOW HOW TOUGH I AM, RIGHT?
LOOK, JUST WATCH.

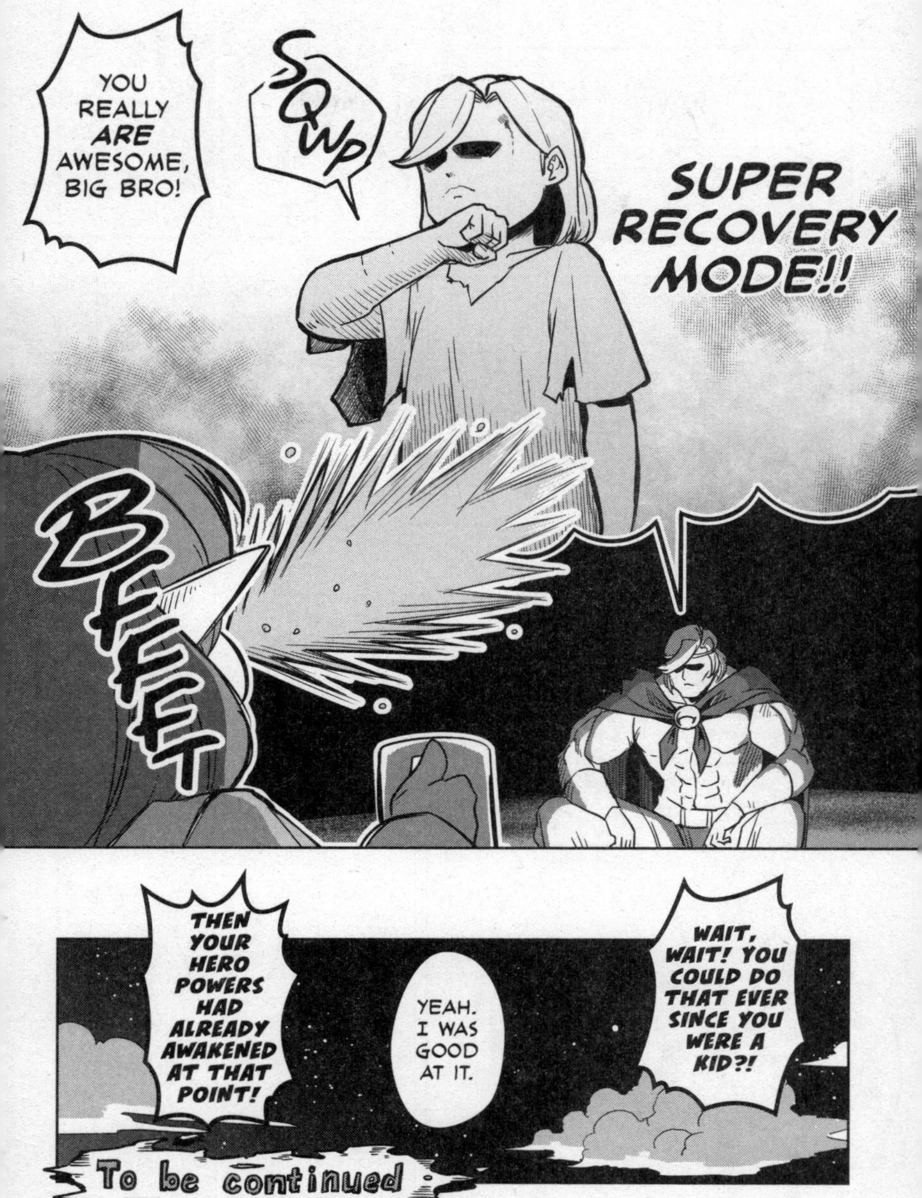
SUPER RECOVERY MODE!!
SQWP
YOU REALLY ARE AWESOME, BIG BRO!
WAIT, WAIT! YOU COULD DO THAT EVER SINCE YOU WERE A KID?!
YEAH. I WAS GOOD AT IT.
THEN YOUR HERO POWERS HAD ALREADY AWAKENED AT THAT POINT!
To be continued

Chapter 37: Helck's Past II

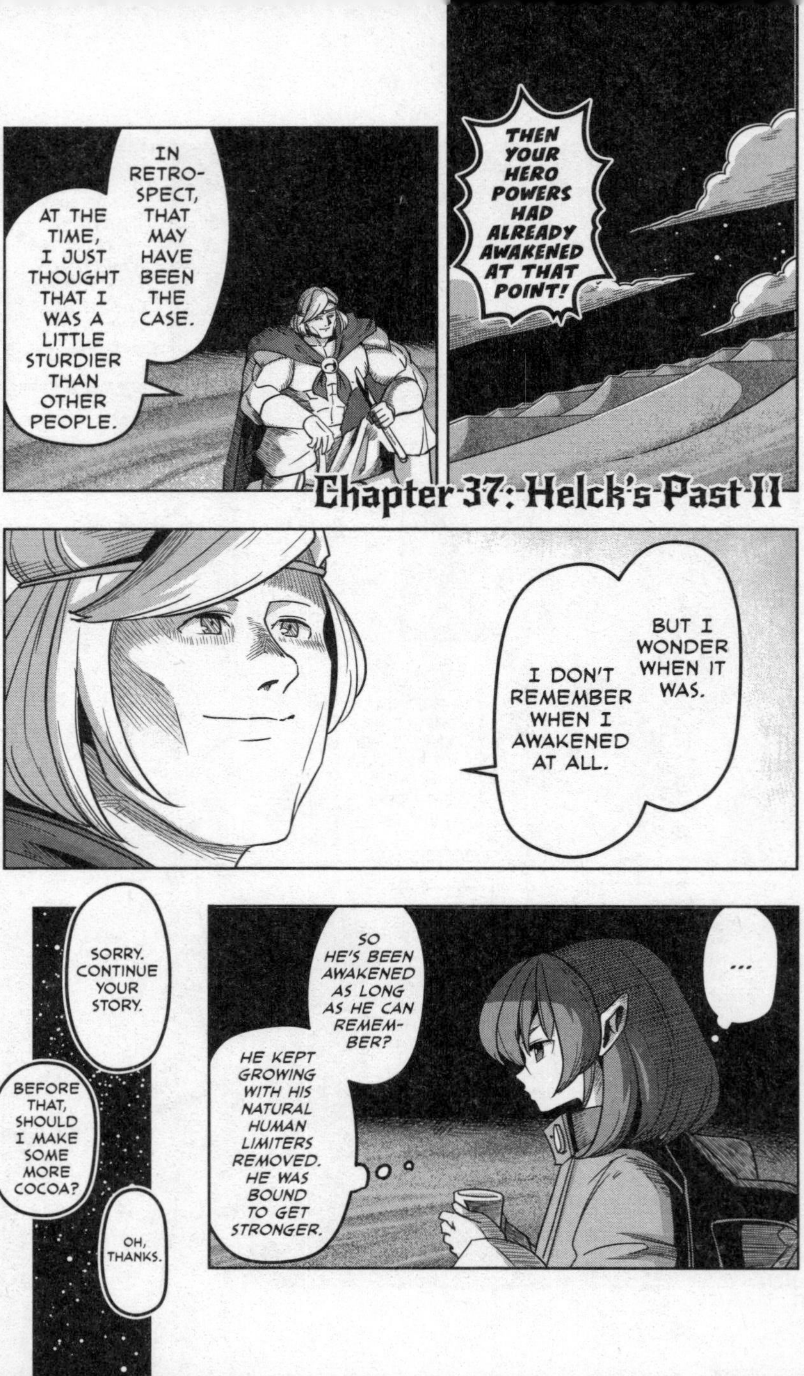
THEN YOUR HERO POWERS HAD ALREADY AWAKENED AT THAT POINT!
IN RETROSPECT, THAT MAY HAVE BEEN THE CASE.
AT THE TIME, I JUST THOUGHT THAT I WAS A LITTLE STURDIER THAN OTHER PEOPLE.
BUT I WONDER WHEN IT WAS.
I DON'T REMEMBER WHEN I AWAKENED AT ALL.
...
SO HE'S BEEN AWAKENED AS LONG AS HE CAN REMEMBER?
HE KEPT GROWING WITH HIS NATURAL HUMAN LIMITERS REMOVED. HE WAS BOUND TO GET STRONGER.
SORRY. CONTINUE YOUR STORY.
BEFORE THAT, SHOULD I MAKE SOME MORE COCOA?
OH, THANKS.

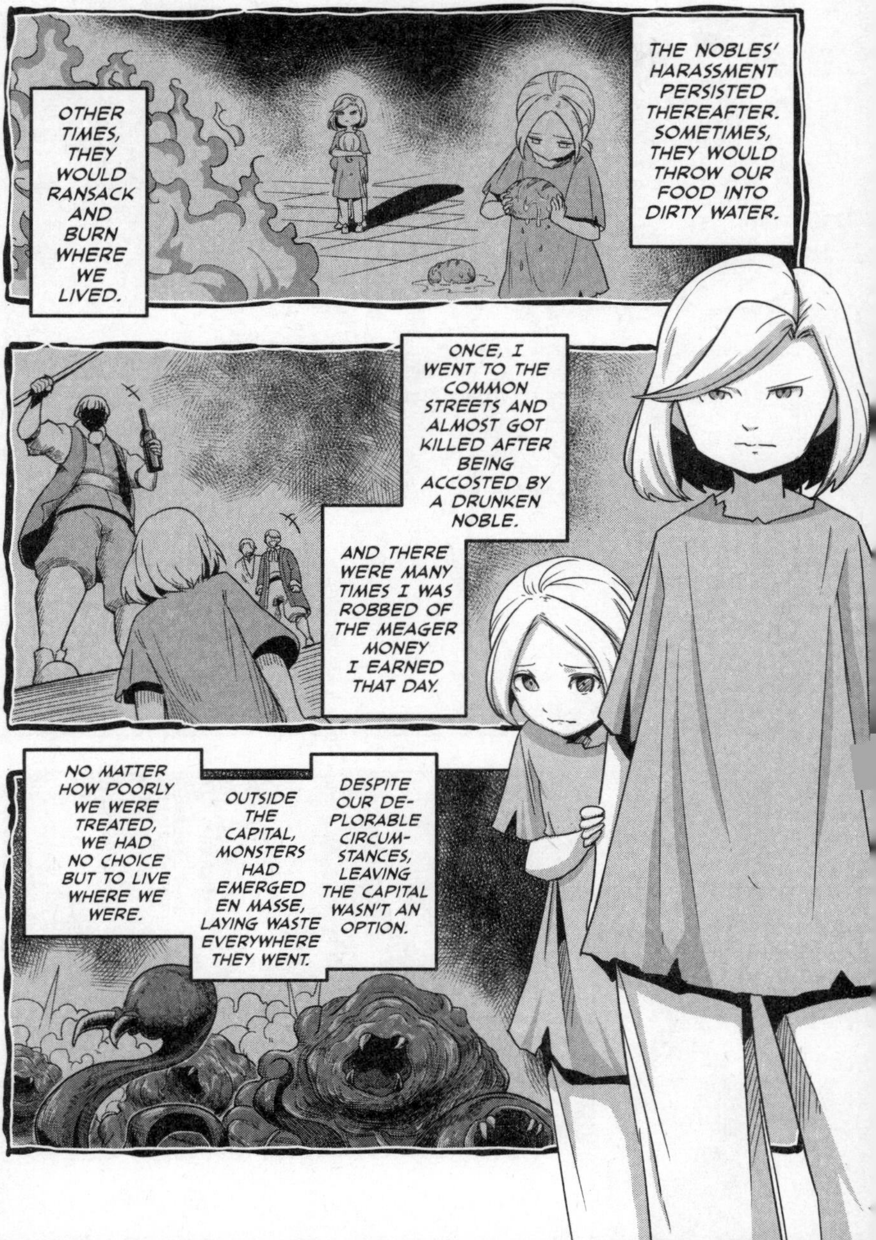
THE NOBLES' HARASSMENT PERSISTED THEREAFTER. SOMETIMES, THEY WOULD THROW OUR FOOD INTO DIRTY WATER.
OTHER TIMES, THEY WOULD RANSACK AND BURN WHERE WE LIVED.
ONCE, I WENT TO THE COMMON STREETS AND ALMOST GOT KILLED AFTER BEING ACCOSTED BY A DRUNKEN NOBLE.
AND THERE WERE MANY TIMES I WAS ROBBED OF THE MEAGER MONEY I EARNED THAT DAY.
DESPITE OUR DE-PLORABLE CIRCUM-STANCES, LEAVING THE CAPITAL WASN'T AN OPTION.
OUTSIDE THE CAPITAL, MONSTERS HAD EMERGED EN MASSE, LAYING WASTE EVERYWHERE THEY WENT.
NO MATTER HOW POORLY WE WERE TREATED, WE HAD NO CHOICE BUT TO LIVE WHERE WE WERE.

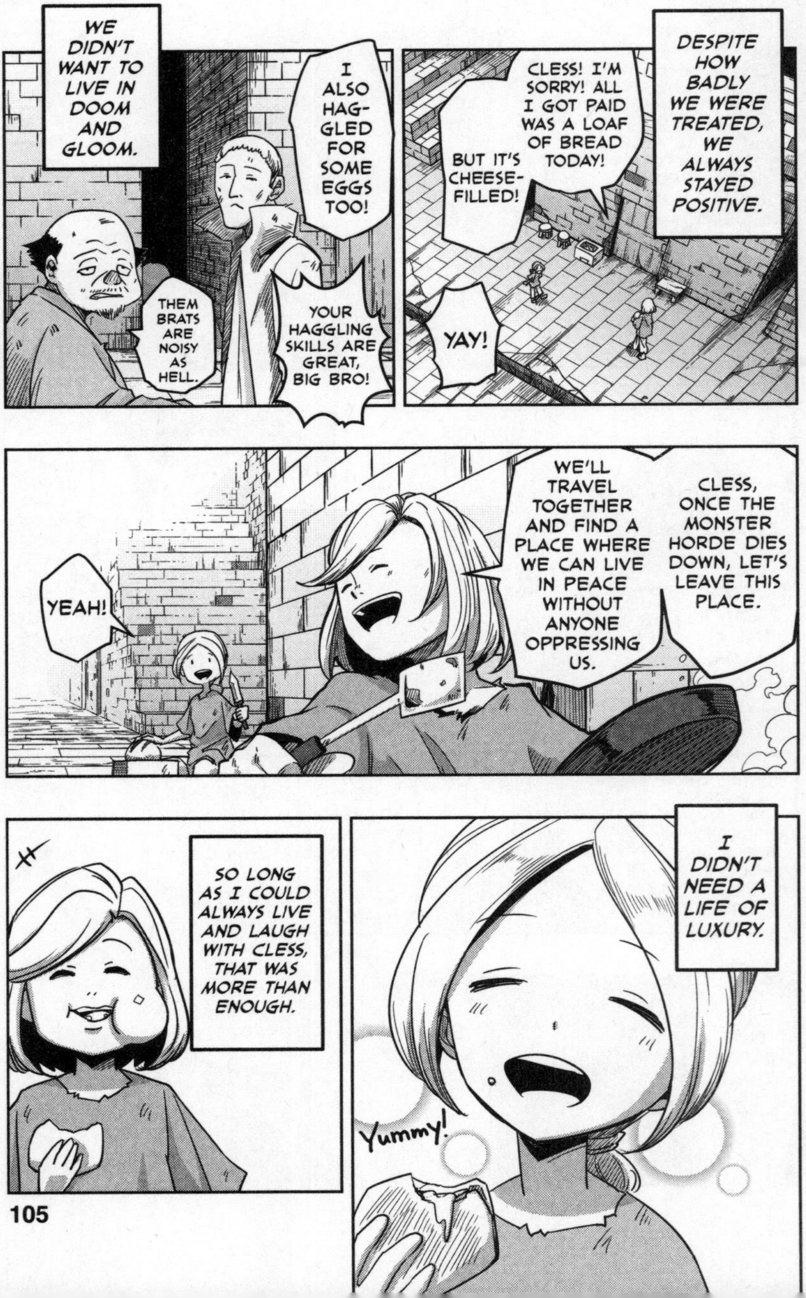
DESPITE HOW BADLY WE WERE TREATED, WE ALWAYS STAYED POSITIVE.
CLESS! I'M SORRY! ALL I GOT PAID WAS A LOAF OF BREAD TODAY!
BUT IT'S CHEESE-FILLED!
YAY!
WE DIDN'T WANT TO LIVE IN DOOM AND GLOOM.
I ALSO HAGGLED FOR SOME EGGS TOO!
YOUR HAGGLING SKILLS ARE GREAT, BIG BRO!
THEM BRATS ARE NOISY AS HELL.
CLESS, ONCE THE MONSTER HORDE DIES DOWN, LET'S LEAVE THIS PLACE.
WE'LL TRAVEL TOGETHER AND FIND A PLACE WHERE WE CAN LIVE IN PEACE WITHOUT ANYONE OPPRESSING US.
YEAH!
I DIDN'T NEED A LIFE OF LUXURY.
Yummy!
SO LONG AS I COULD ALWAYS LIVE AND LAUGH WITH CLESS, THAT WAS MORE THAN ENOUGH.

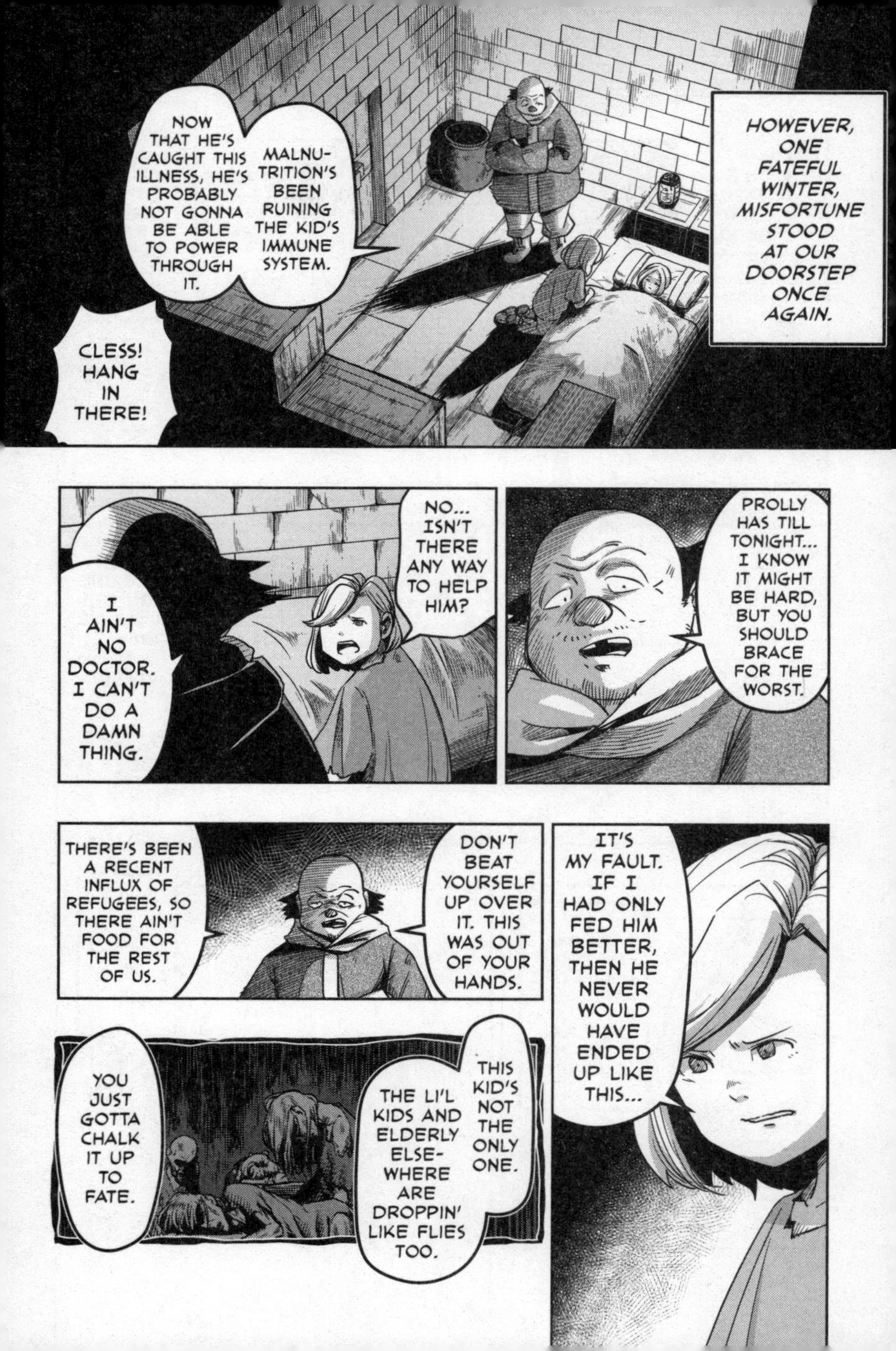
HOWEVER, ONE FATEFUL WINTER, MISFORTUNE STOOD AT OUR DOORSTEP ONCE AGAIN.
MALNUTRITION'S BEEN RUINING THE KID'S IMMUNE SYSTEM.
NOW THAT HE'S CAUGHT THIS ILLNESS, HE'S PROBABLY NOT GONNA BE ABLE TO POWER THROUGH IT.
CLESS! HANG IN THERE!
PROLLY HAS TILL TONIGHT... I KNOW IT MIGHT BE HARD, BUT YOU SHOULD BRACE FOR THE WORST.
NO... ISN'T THERE ANY WAY TO HELP HIM?
I AIN'T NO DOCTOR. I CAN'T DO A DAMN THING.
IT'S MY FAULT. IF I HAD ONLY FED HIM BETTER, THEN HE NEVER WOULD HAVE ENDED UP LIKE THIS...
DON'T BEAT YOURSELF UP OVER IT. THIS WAS OUT OF YOUR HANDS.
THERE'S BEEN A RECENT INFLUX OF REFUGEES, SO THERE AIN'T FOOD FOR THE REST OF US.
THIS KID'S NOT THE ONLY ONE.
THE LI'L KIDS AND ELDERLY ELSEWHERE ARE DROPPIN' LIKE FLIES TOO.
YOU JUST GOTTA CHALK IT UP TO FATE.

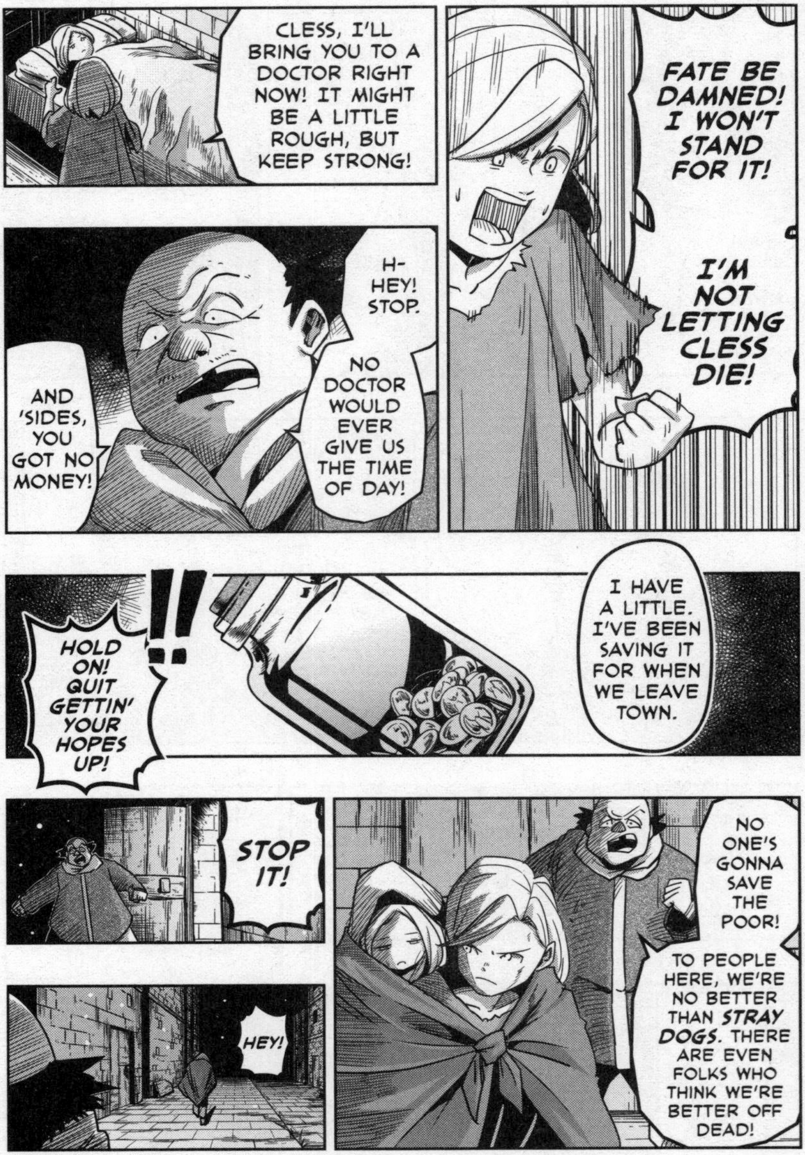
FATE BE DAMNED! I WON'T STAND FOR IT!
I'M NOT LETTING CLESS DIE!
CLESS, I'LL BRING YOU TO A DOCTOR RIGHT NOW! IT MIGHT BE A LITTLE ROUGH, BUT KEEP STRONG!
H-HEY! STOP.
NO DOCTOR WOULD EVER GIVE US THE TIME OF DAY!
AND 'SIDES, YOU GOT NO MONEY!
I HAVE A LITTLE. I'VE BEEN SAVING IT FOR WHEN WE LEAVE TOWN.
!!
HOLD ON! QUIT GETTIN' YOUR HOPES UP!
NO ONE'S GONNA SAVE THE POOR!
TO PEOPLE HERE, WE'RE NO BETTER THAN STRAY DOGS. THERE ARE EVEN FOLKS WHO THINK WE'RE BETTER OFF DEAD!
STOP IT!
HEY!

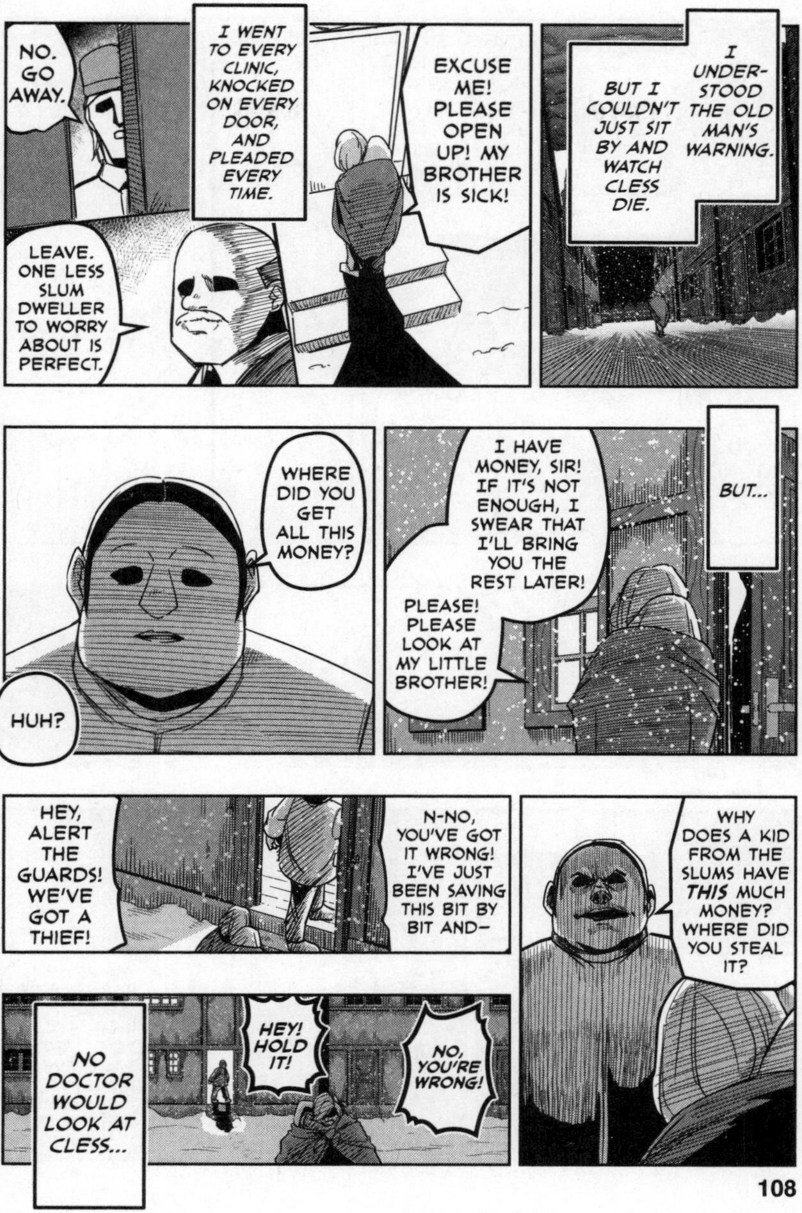
I UNDERSTOOD THE OLD MAN'S WARNING.
BUT I COULDN'T JUST SIT BY AND WATCH CLESS DIE.
EXCUSE ME! PLEASE OPEN UP! MY BROTHER IS SICK!
I WENT TO EVERY CLINIC, KNOCKED ON EVERY DOOR, AND PLEADED EVERY TIME.
NO. GO AWAY.
LEAVE. ONE LESS SLUM DWELLER TO WORRY ABOUT IS PERFECT.
BUT...
I HAVE MONEY, SIR! IF IT'S NOT ENOUGH, I SWEAR THAT I'LL BRING YOU THE REST LATER!
PLEASE! PLEASE LOOK AT MY LITTLE BROTHER!
WHERE DID YOU GET ALL THIS MONEY?
HUH?
WHY DOES A KID FROM THE SLUMS HAVE *THIS* MUCH MONEY? WHERE DID YOU STEAL IT?
N-NO, YOU'VE GOT IT WRONG! I'VE JUST BEEN SAVING THIS BIT BY BIT AND—
HEY, ALERT THE GUARDS! WE'VE GOT A THIEF!
NO, YOU'RE WRONG!
HEY! HOLD IT!
NO DOCTOR WOULD LOOK AT CLESS...

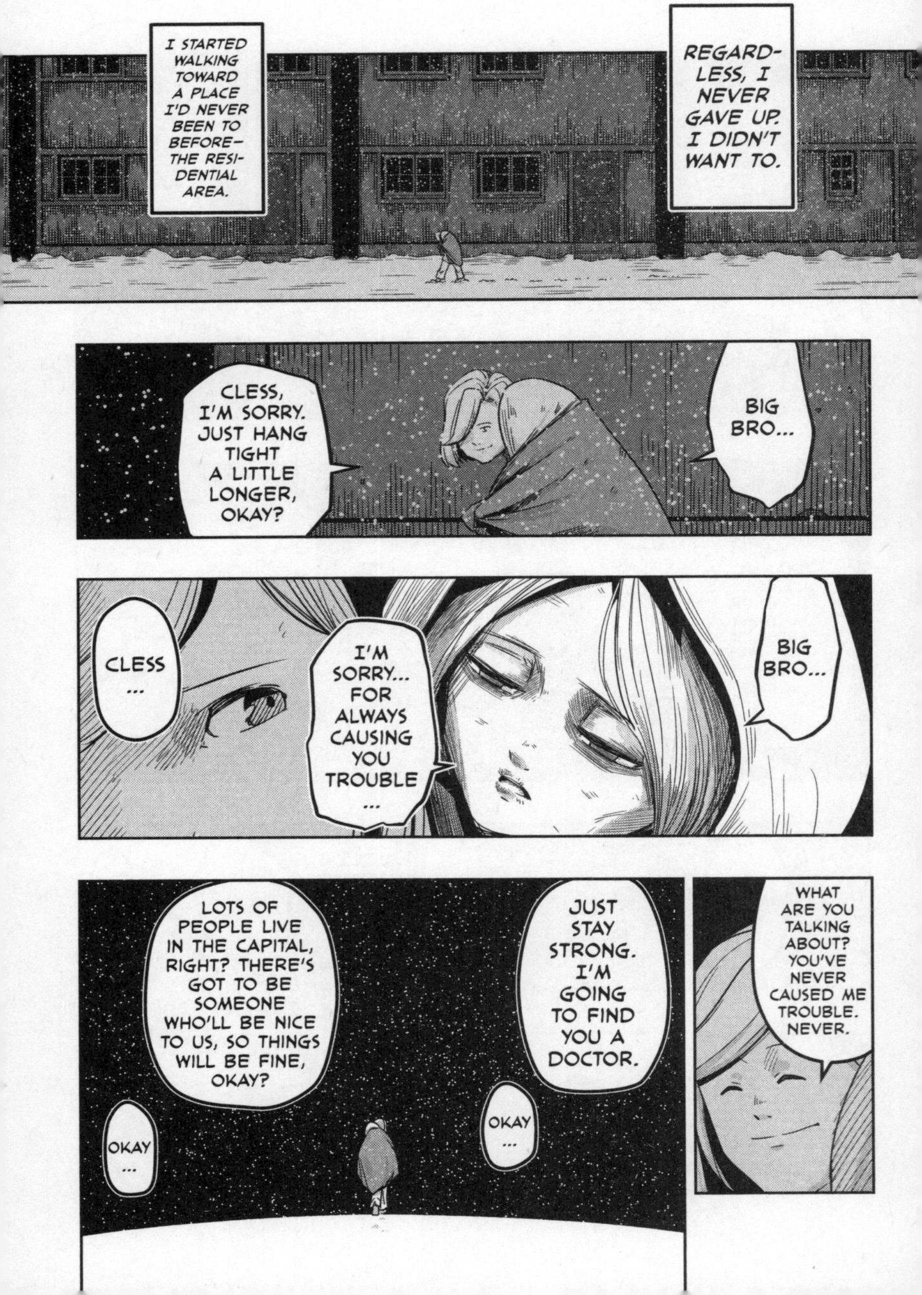
REGARD-LESS, I NEVER GAVE UP. I DIDN'T WANT TO.
I STARTED WALKING TOWARD A PLACE I'D NEVER BEEN TO BEFORE—THE RESI-DENTIAL AREA.
BIG BRO...
CLESS, I'M SORRY. JUST HANG TIGHT A LITTLE LONGER, OKAY?
BIG BRO...
I'M SORRY... FOR ALWAYS CAUSING YOU TROUBLE...
CLESS...
WHAT ARE YOU TALKING ABOUT? YOU'VE NEVER CAUSED ME TROUBLE. NEVER.
JUST STAY STRONG. I'M GOING TO FIND YOU A DOCTOR.
LOTS OF PEOPLE LIVE IN THE CAPITAL, RIGHT? THERE'S GOT TO BE SOMEONE WHO'LL BE NICE TO US, SO THINGS WILL BE FINE, OKAY?
OKAY...
OKAY...

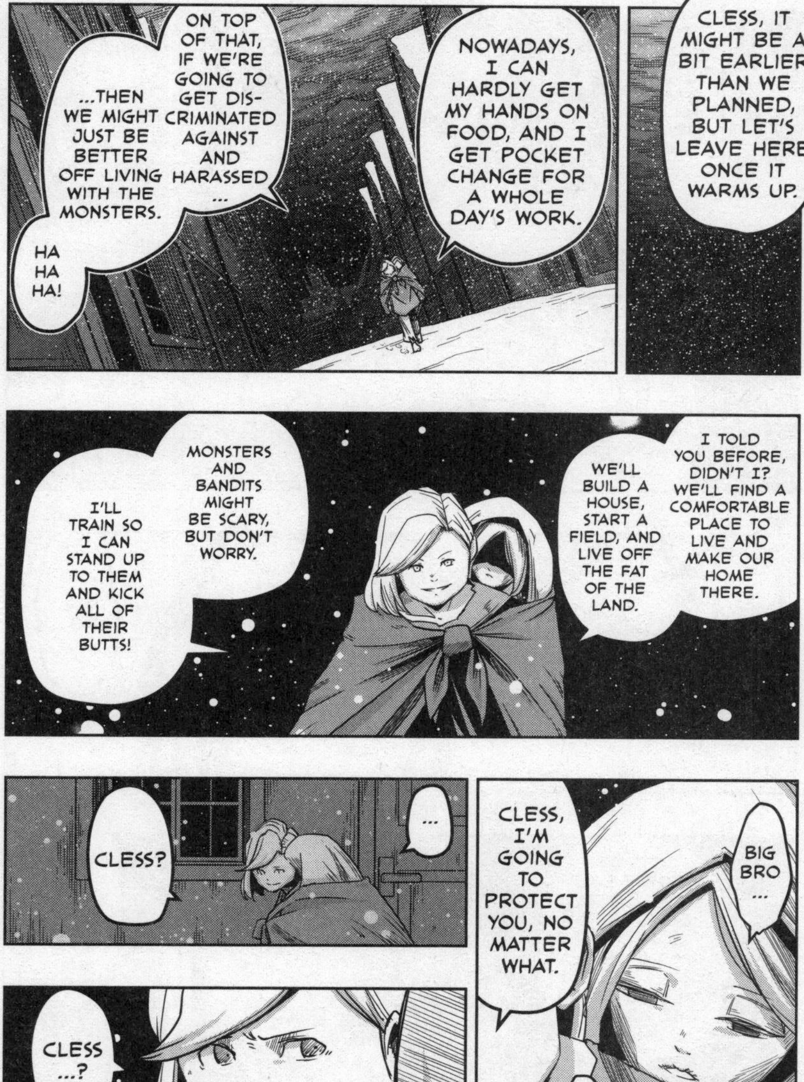
CLESS, IT MIGHT BE A BIT EARLIER THAN WE PLANNED, BUT LET'S LEAVE HERE ONCE IT WARMS UP.
NOWADAYS, I CAN HARDLY GET MY HANDS ON FOOD, AND I GET POCKET CHANGE FOR A WHOLE DAY'S WORK.
ON TOP OF THAT, IF WE'RE GOING TO GET DIS-CRIMINATED AGAINST AND HARASSED...
...THEN WE MIGHT JUST BE BETTER OFF LIVING WITH THE MONSTERS.
HA HA HA!
I TOLD YOU BEFORE, DIDN'T I? WE'LL FIND A COMFORTABLE PLACE TO LIVE AND MAKE OUR HOME THERE.
WE'LL BUILD A HOUSE, START A FIELD, AND LIVE OFF THE FAT OF THE LAND.
MONSTERS AND BANDITS MIGHT BE SCARY, BUT DON'T WORRY.
I'LL TRAIN SO I CAN STAND UP TO THEM AND KICK ALL OF THEIR BUTTS!
BIG BRO...
CLESS, I'M GOING TO PROTECT YOU, NO MATTER WHAT.
...
...
CLESS?
CLESS...?

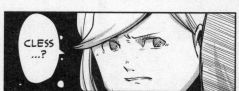

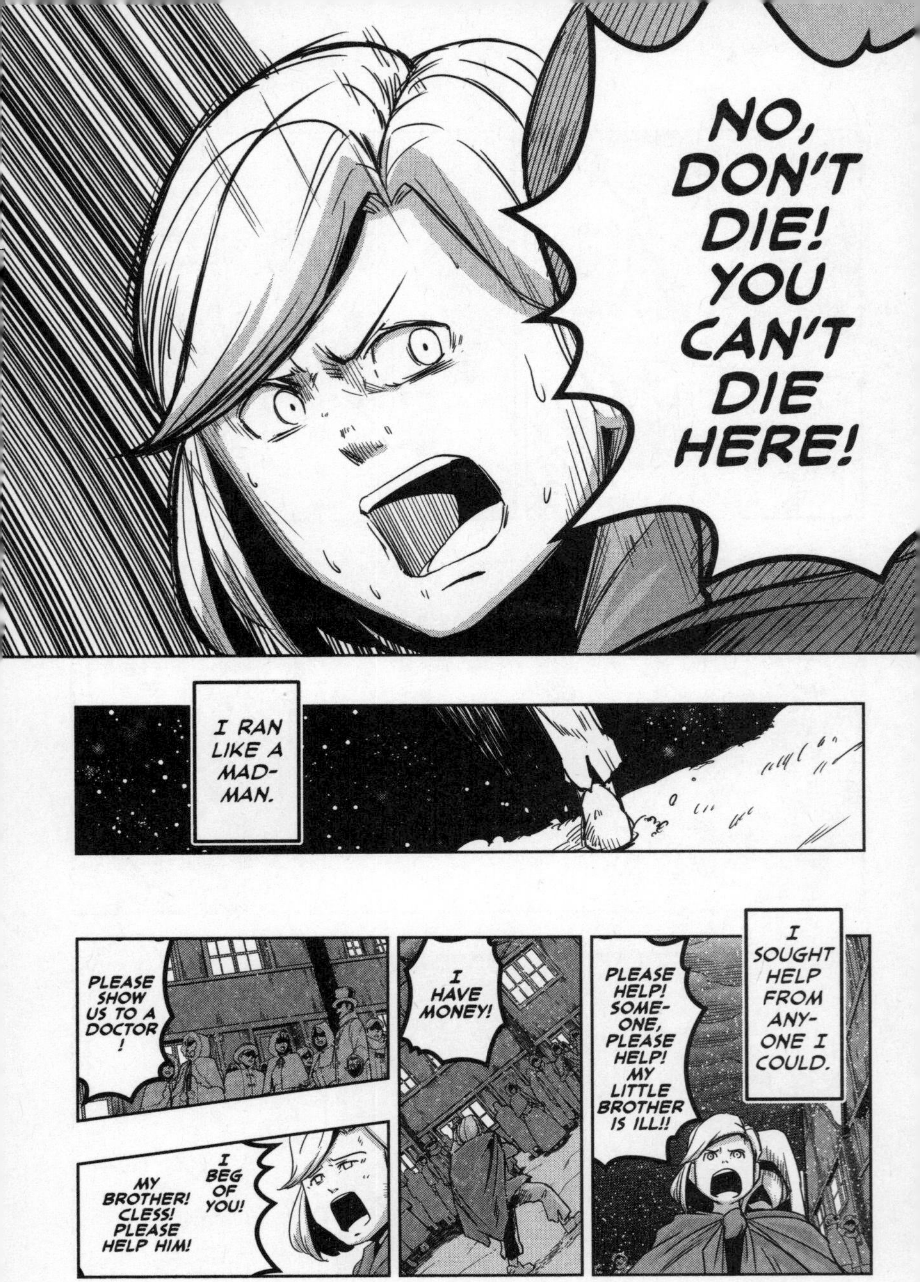
NO, DON'T DIE! YOU CAN'T DIE HERE!
I RAN LIKE A MADMAN.
I SOUGHT HELP FROM ANYONE I COULD.
PLEASE HELP! SOMEONE, PLEASE HELP! MY LITTLE BROTHER IS ILL!!
I HAVE MONEY!
PLEASE SHOW US TO A DOCTOR!
I BEG OF YOU!
MY BROTHER! CLESS! PLEASE HELP HIM!

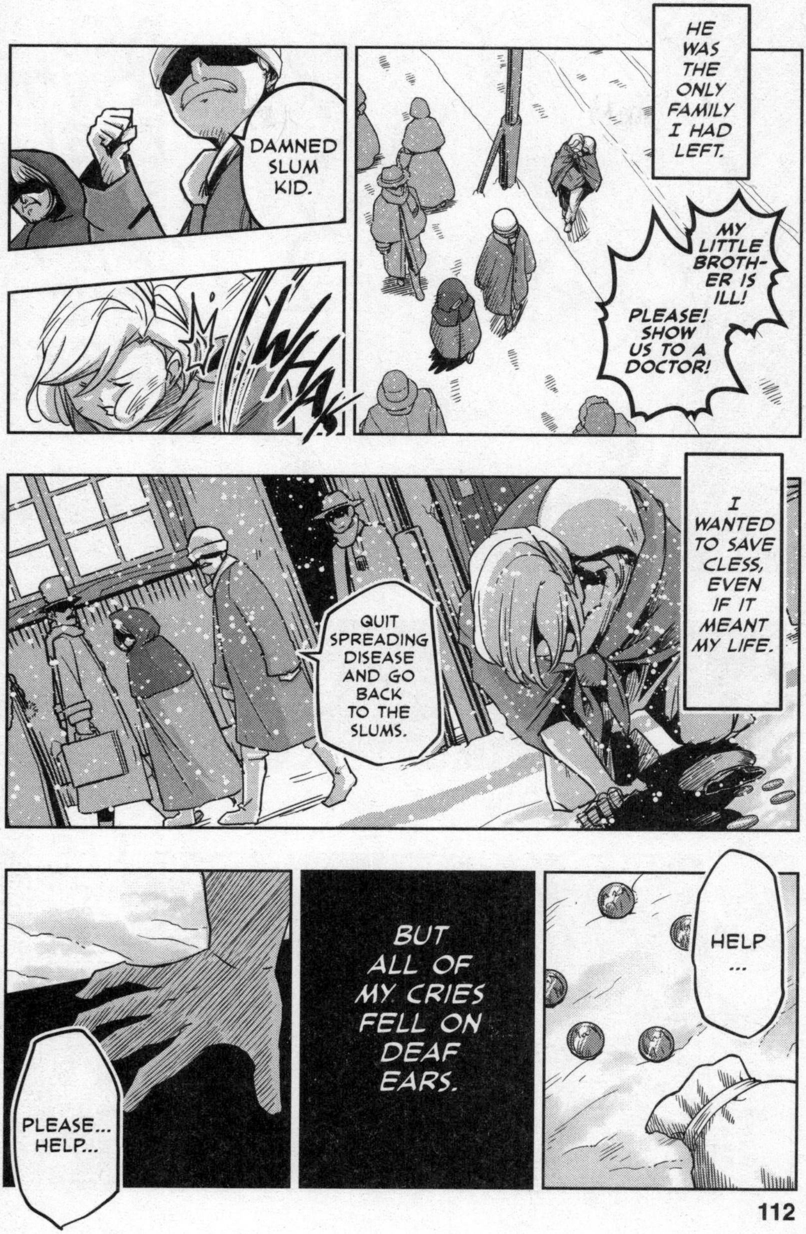
HE WAS THE ONLY FAMILY I HAD LEFT.
MY LITTLE BROTHER IS ILL!
PLEASE! SHOW US TO A DOCTOR!
DAMNED SLUM KID.
WHAK
I WANTED TO SAVE CLESS, EVEN IF IT MEANT MY LIFE.
QUIT SPREADING DISEASE AND GO BACK TO THE SLUMS.
HELP...
BUT ALL OF MY CRIES FELL ON DEAF EARS.
PLEASE... HELP...

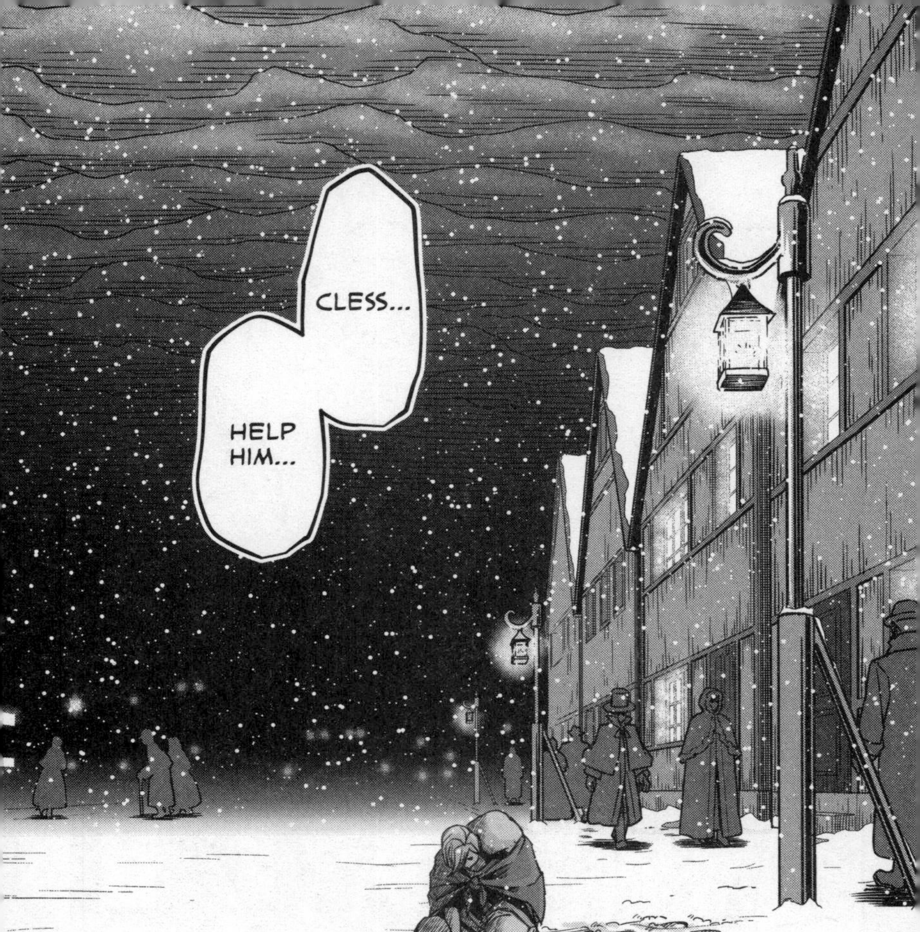
CLESS...
HELP HIM...

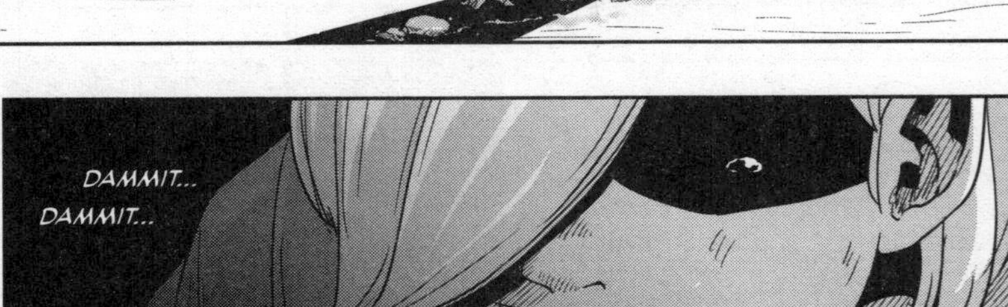
DAMMIT...
DAMMIT...

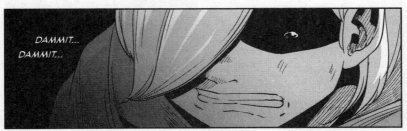

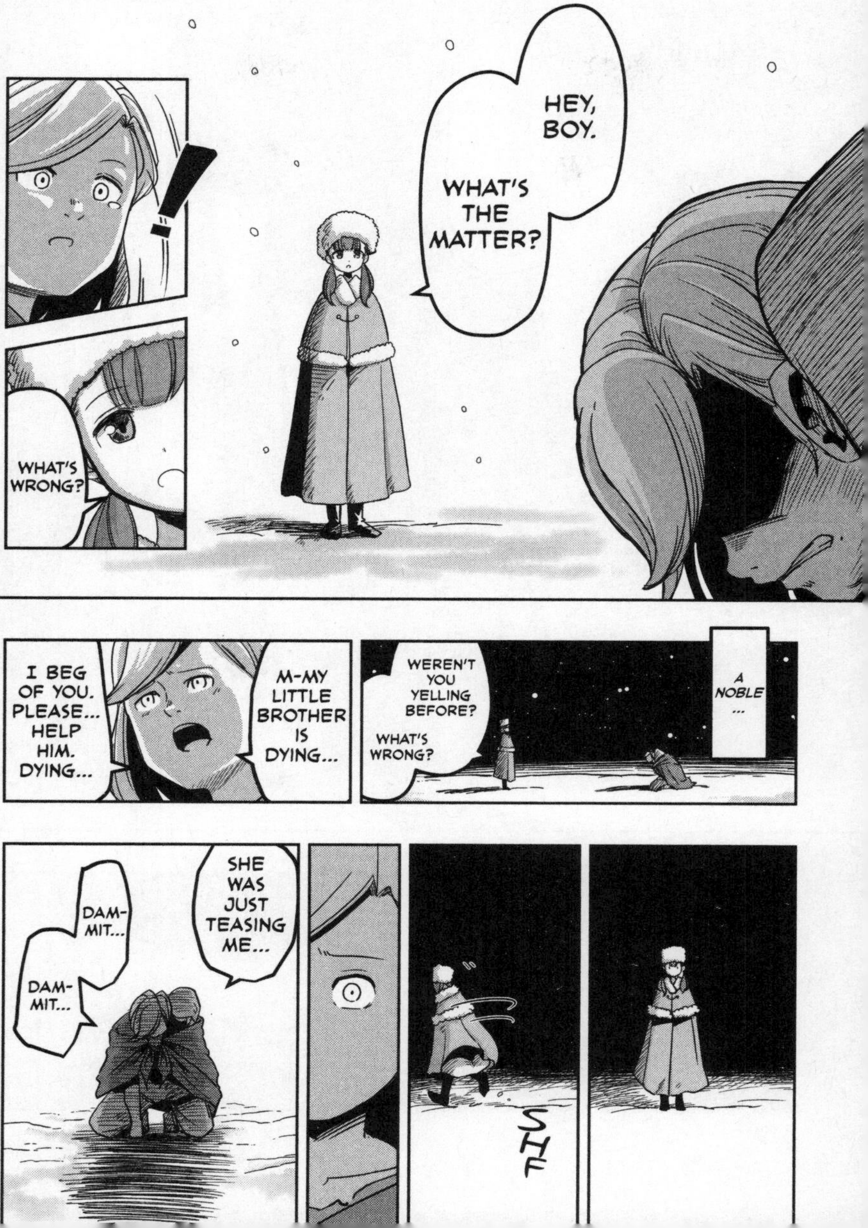
HEY, BOY.
WHAT'S THE MATTER?
!
WHAT'S WRONG?
A NOBLE...
WEREN'T YOU YELLING BEFORE?
WHAT'S WRONG?
M-MY LITTLE BROTHER IS DYING...
I BEG OF YOU. PLEASE... HELP HIM. DYING...
SHF
SHE WAS JUST TEASING ME...
DAM-MIT...
DAM-MIT...

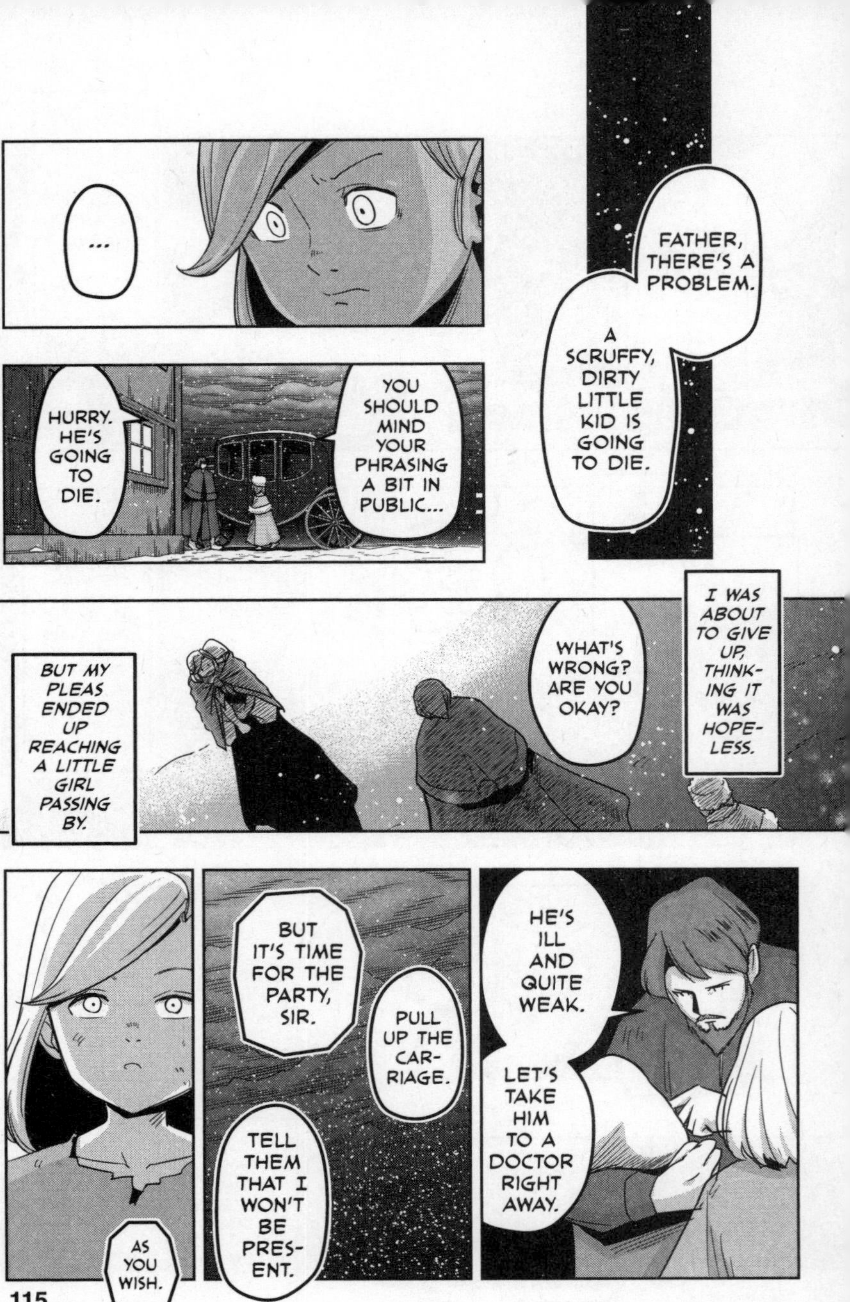
FATHER, THERE'S A PROBLEM.
A SCRUFFY, DIRTY LITTLE KID IS GOING TO DIE.
...
YOU SHOULD MIND YOUR PHRASING A BIT IN PUBLIC...
HURRY. HE'S GOING TO DIE.
I WAS ABOUT TO GIVE UP, THINKING IT WAS HOPELESS.
WHAT'S WRONG? ARE YOU OKAY?
BUT MY PLEAS ENDED UP REACHING A LITTLE GIRL PASSING BY.
HE'S ILL AND QUITE WEAK.
LET'S TAKE HIM TO A DOCTOR RIGHT AWAY.
BUT IT'S TIME FOR THE PARTY, SIR.
PULL UP THE CARRIAGE.
TELL THEM THAT I WON'T BE PRESENT.
AS YOU WISH.

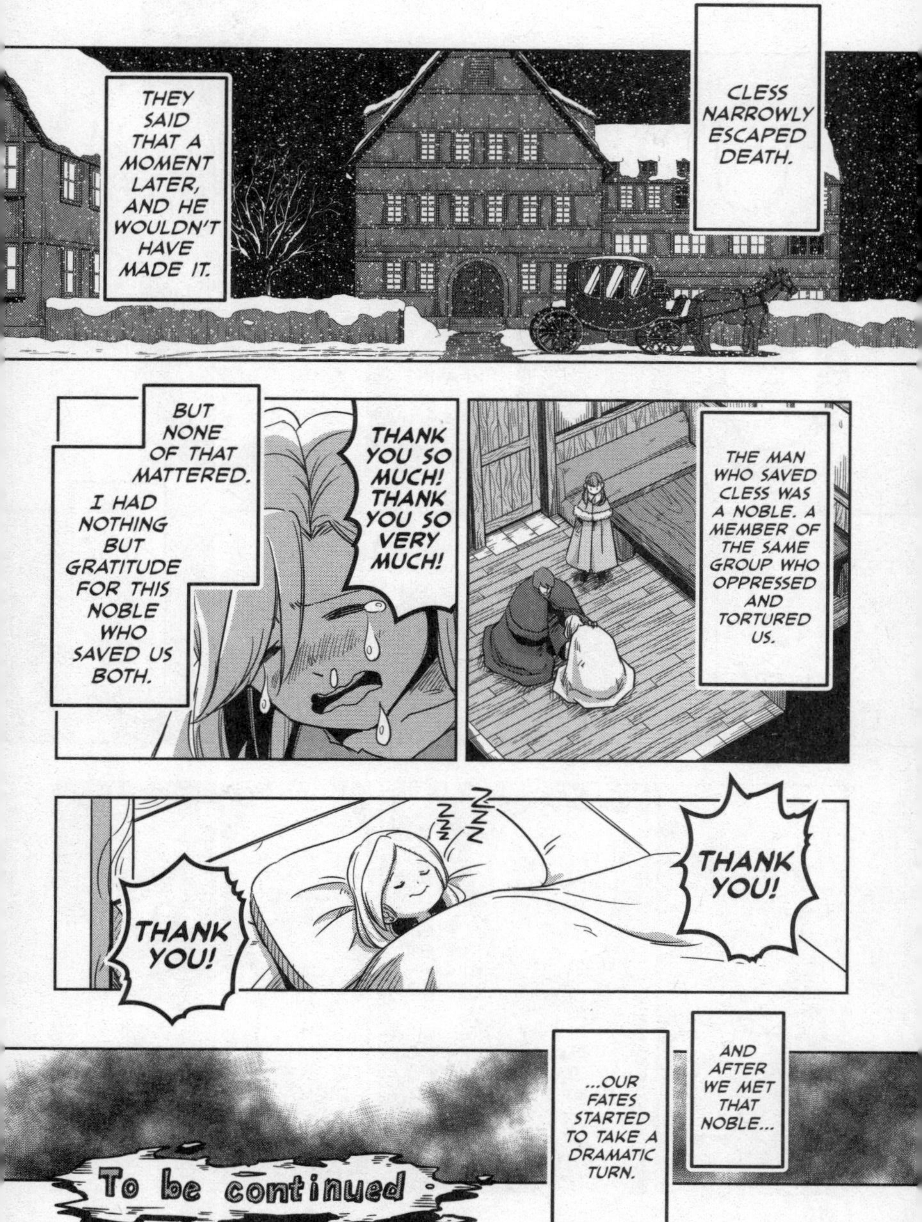
CLESS NARROWLY ESCAPED DEATH.
THEY SAID THAT A MOMENT LATER, AND HE WOULDN'T HAVE MADE IT.
THE MAN WHO SAVED CLESS WAS A NOBLE. A MEMBER OF THE SAME GROUP WHO OPPRESSED AND TORTURED US.
THANK YOU SO MUCH! THANK YOU SO VERY MUCH!
BUT NONE OF THAT MATTERED.
I HAD NOTHING BUT GRATITUDE FOR THIS NOBLE WHO SAVED US BOTH.
THANK YOU!
THANK YOU!
AND AFTER WE MET THAT NOBLE...
...OUR FATES STARTED TO TAKE A DRAMATIC TURN.
To be continued

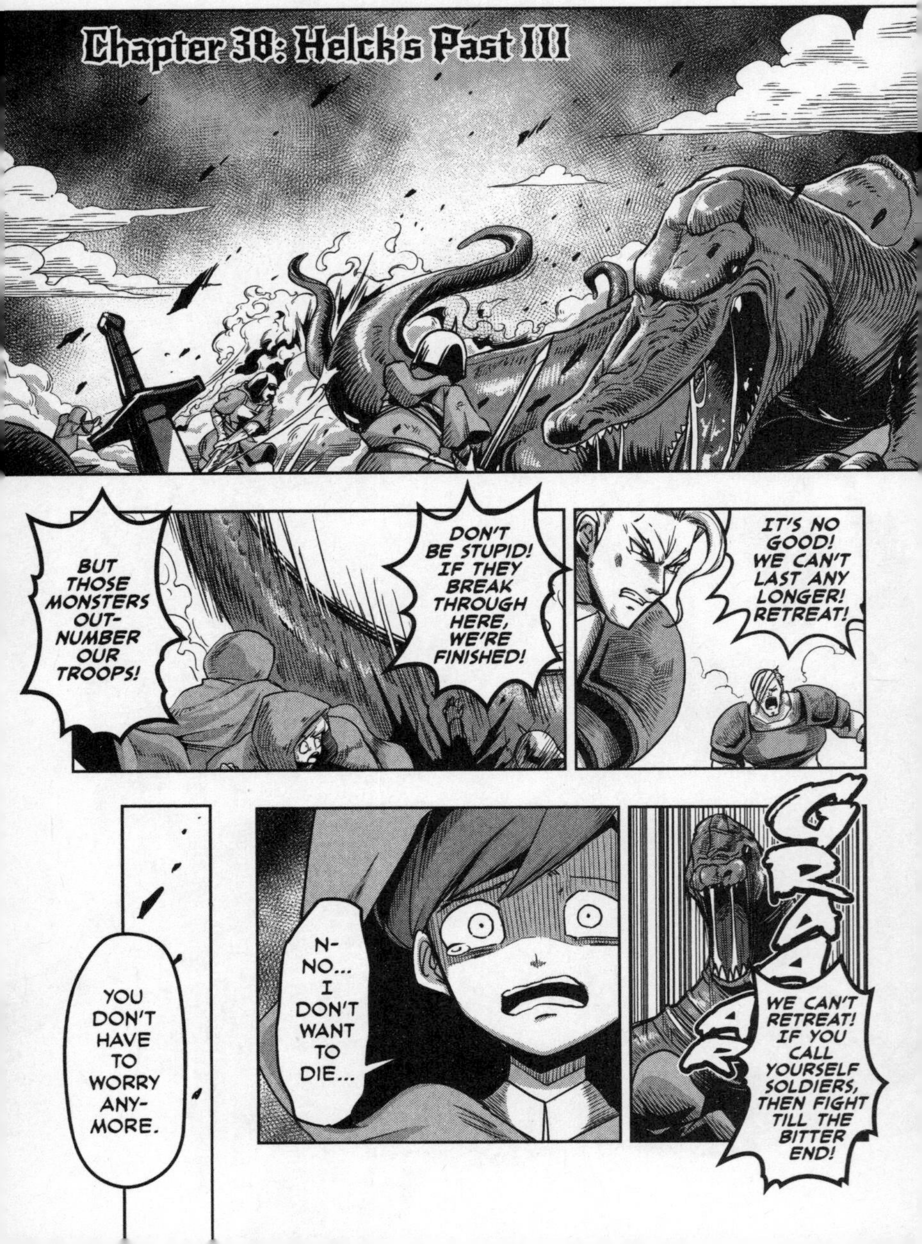
Chapter 38: Helck's Past III
IT'S NO GOOD! WE CAN'T LAST ANY LONGER! RETREAT!
DON'T BE STUPID! IF THEY BREAK THROUGH HERE, WE'RE FINISHED!
BUT THOSE MONSTERS OUT-NUMBER OUR TROOPS!
GRAAR
WE CAN'T RETREAT! IF YOU CALL YOURSELF SOLDIERS, THEN FIGHT TILL THE BITTER END!
N-NO... I DON'T WANT TO DIE...
YOU DON'T HAVE TO WORRY ANY-MORE.

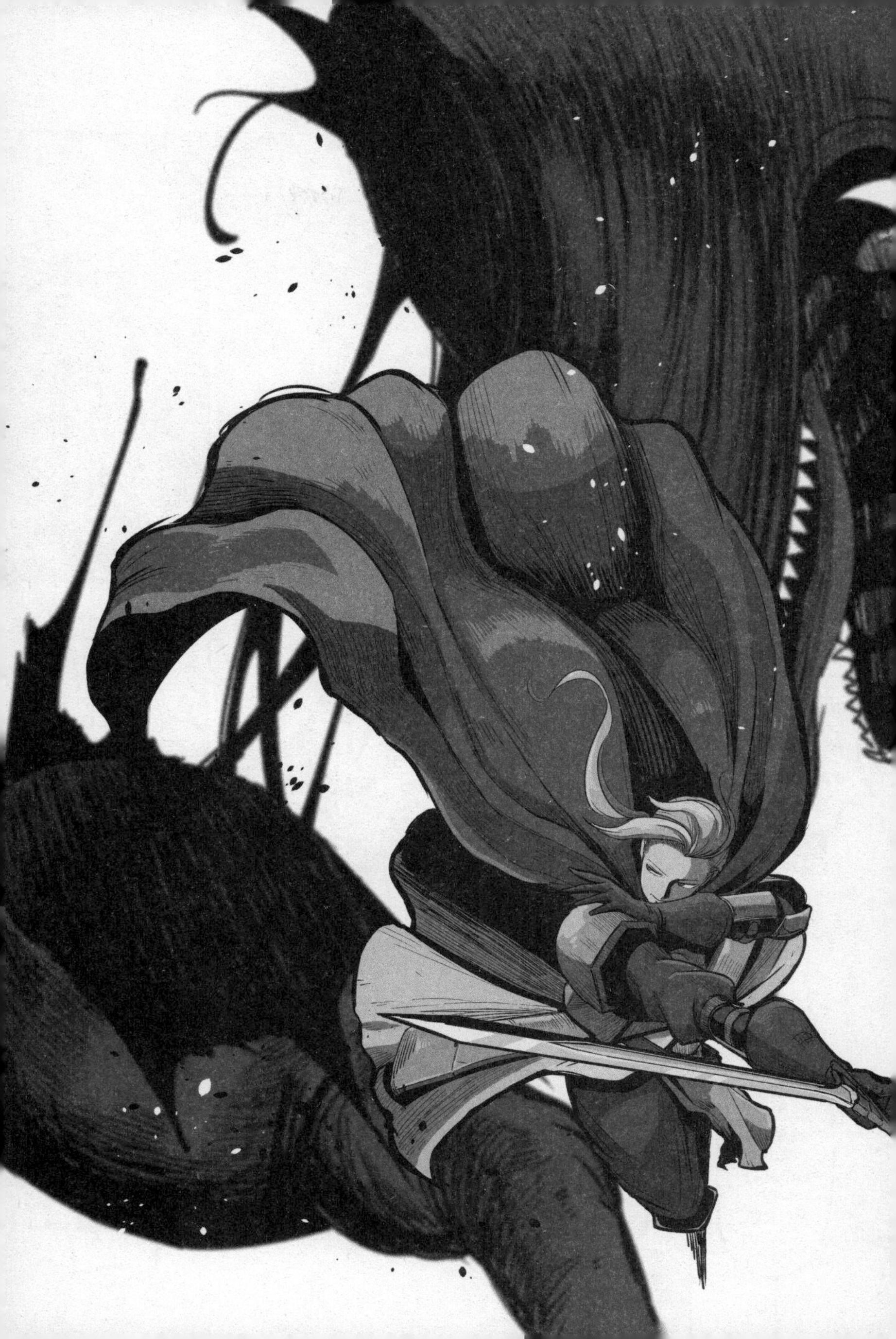

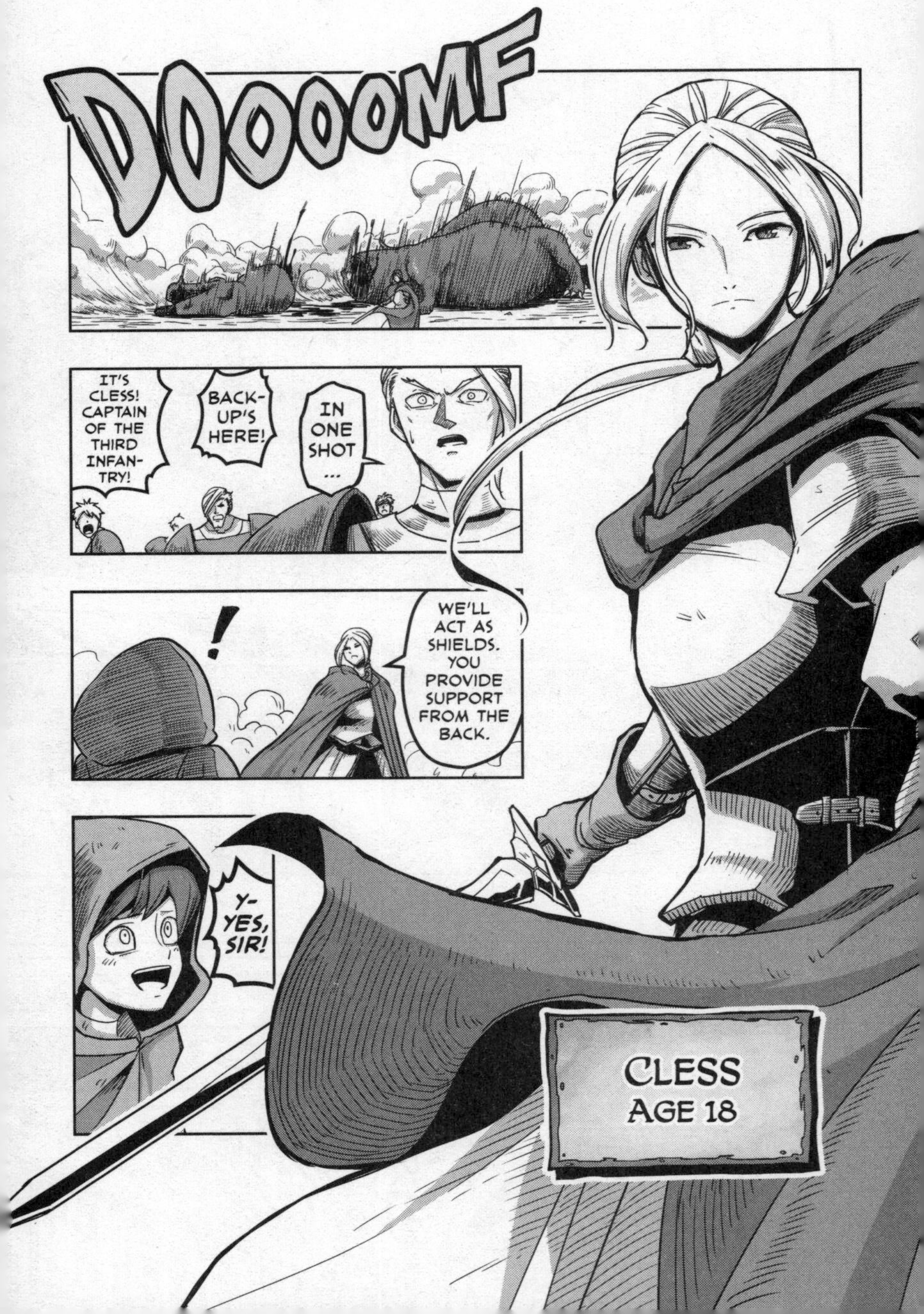
CLESS
AGE 18
DOOOOMF
IN ONE SHOT ...
BACK-UP'S HERE!
IT'S CLESS! CAPTAIN OF THE THIRD INFANTRY!
WE'LL ACT AS SHIELDS. YOU PROVIDE SUPPORT FROM THE BACK.
!
Y-YES, SIR!

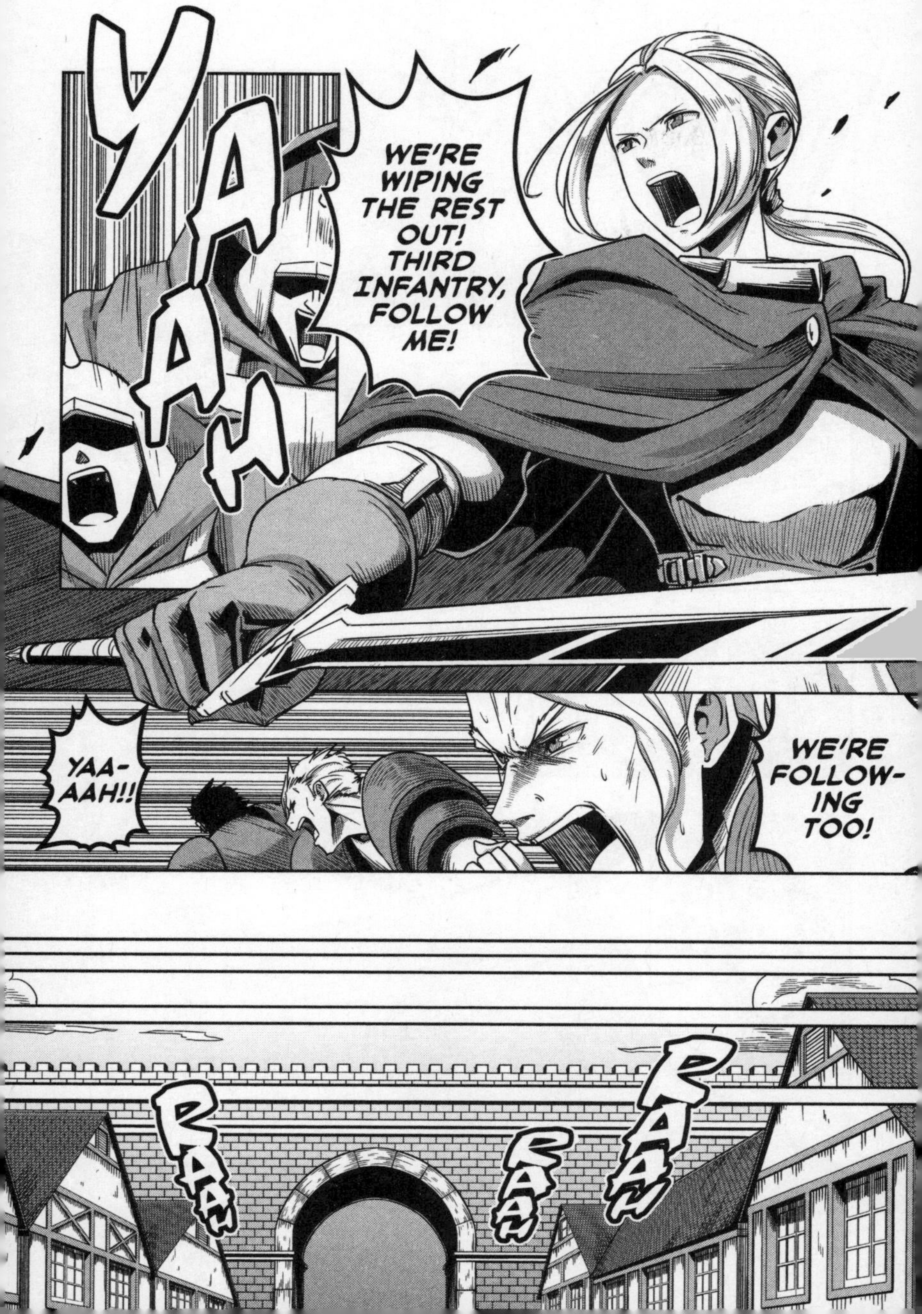
WE'RE WIPING THE REST OUT! THIRD INFANTRY, FOLLOW ME!
YAAAH
WE'RE FOLLOW-ING TOO!
YAA-AAH!!
RAAH
RAAH
RAAH

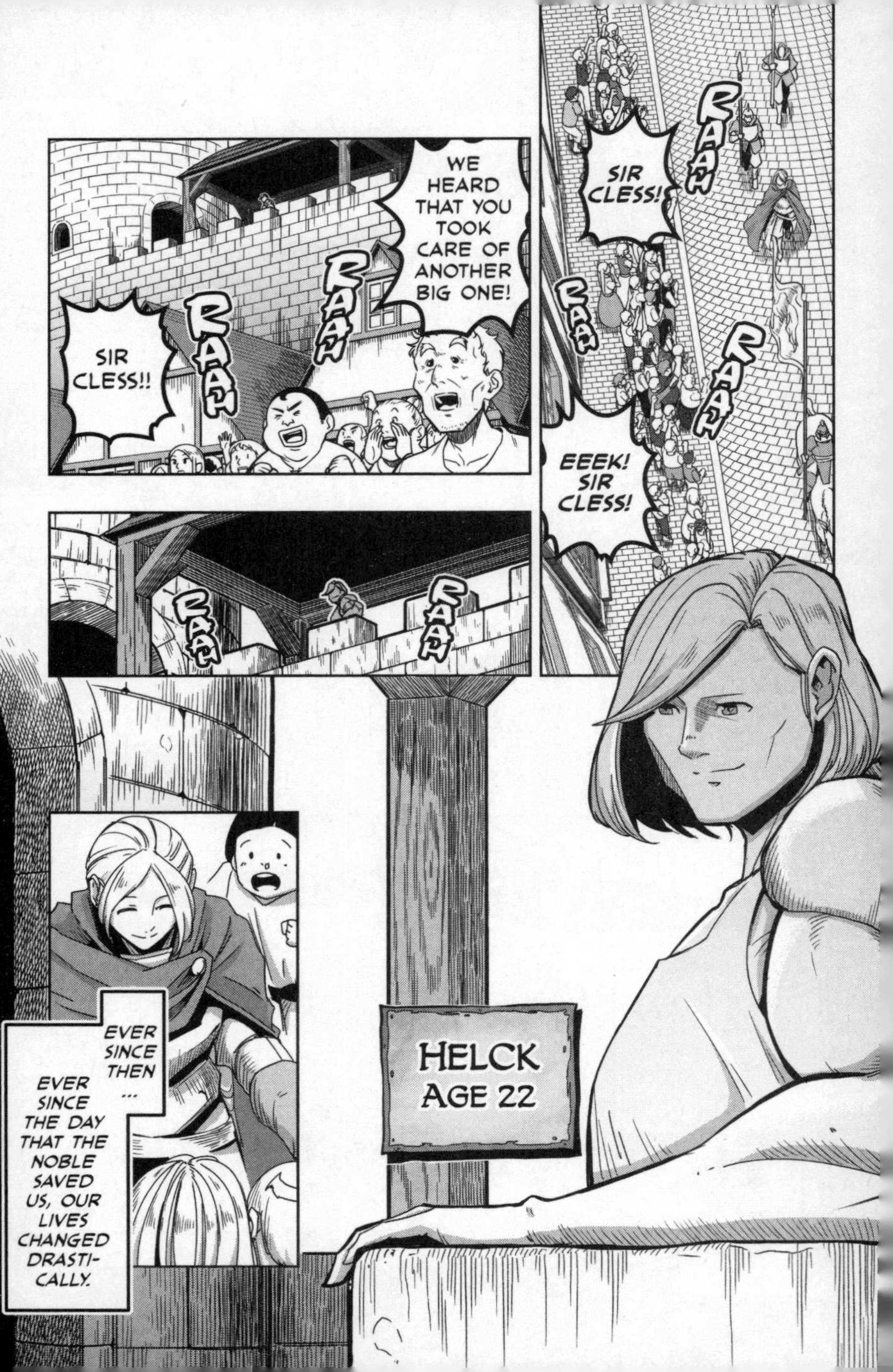
SIR CLESS!
RAAAH
RAAH
RAAAH
EEEK! SIR CLESS!
WE HEARD THAT YOU TOOK CARE OF ANOTHER BIG ONE!
RAAAH
RAAAH
SIR CLESS!!
RAAAH
RAAAH
HELCK AGE 22
EVER SINCE THEN...
EVER SINCE THE DAY THAT THE NOBLE SAVED US, OUR LIVES CHANGED DRASTICALLY.

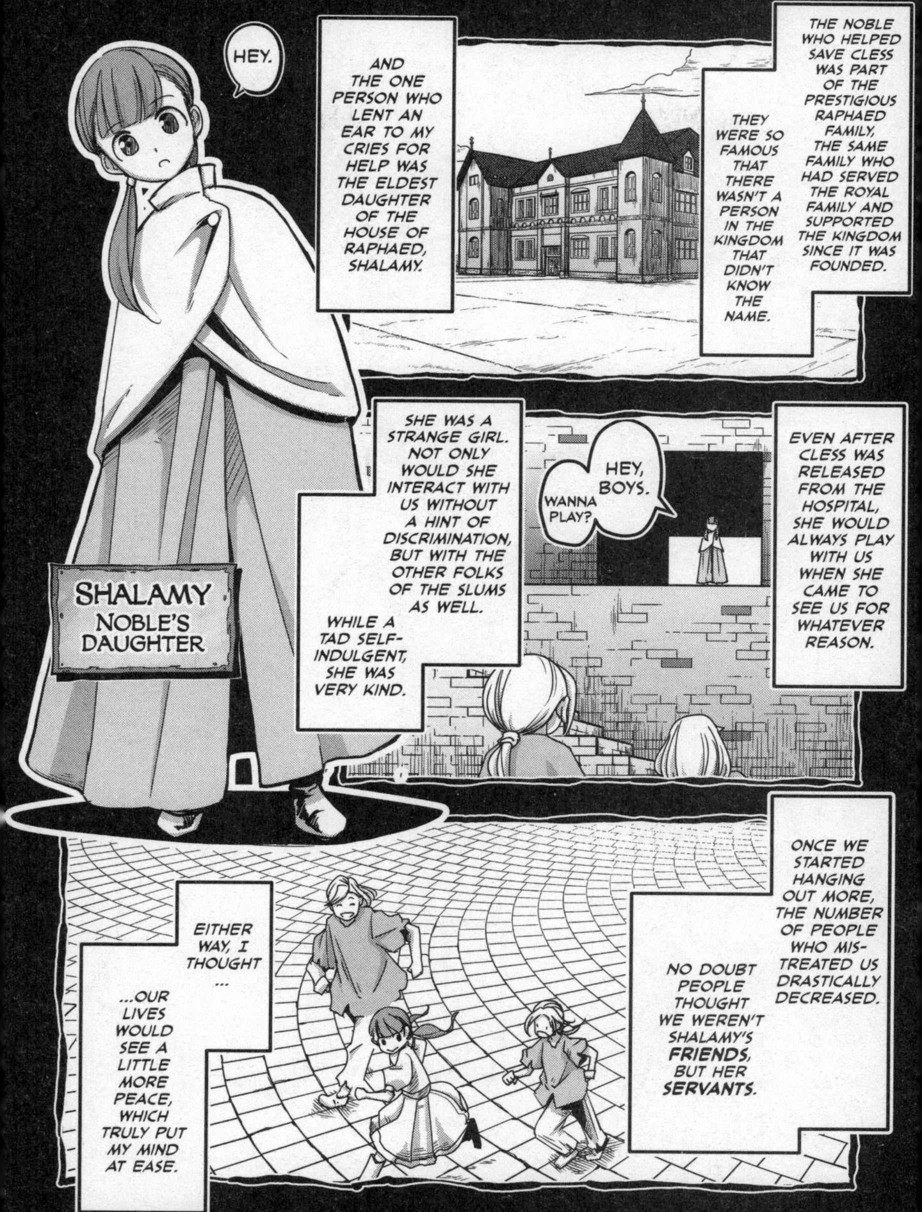
THE NOBLE WHO HELPED SAVE CLESS WAS PART OF THE PRESTIGIOUS RAPHAED FAMILY, THE SAME FAMILY WHO HAD SERVED THE ROYAL FAMILY AND SUPPORTED THE KINGDOM SINCE IT WAS FOUNDED.
THEY WERE SO FAMOUS THAT THERE WASN'T A PERSON IN THE KINGDOM THAT DIDN'T KNOW THE NAME.
AND THE ONE PERSON WHO LENT AN EAR TO MY CRIES FOR HELP WAS THE ELDEST DAUGHTER OF THE HOUSE OF RAPHAED, SHALAMY.
EVEN AFTER CLESS WAS RELEASED FROM THE HOSPITAL, SHE WOULD ALWAYS PLAY WITH US WHEN SHE CAME TO SEE US FOR WHATEVER REASON.
HEY, BOYS.
WANNA PLAY?
SHE WAS A STRANGE GIRL. NOT ONLY WOULD SHE INTERACT WITH US WITHOUT A HINT OF DISCRIMINATION, BUT WITH THE OTHER FOLKS OF THE SLUMS AS WELL.
WHILE A TAD SELF-INDULGENT, SHE WAS VERY KIND.
HEY.
SHALAMY
NOBLE'S DAUGHTER
ONCE WE STARTED HANGING OUT MORE, THE NUMBER OF PEOPLE WHO MIS-TREATED US DRASTICALLY DECREASED.
NO DOUBT PEOPLE THOUGHT WE WEREN'T SHALAMY'S FRIENDS, BUT HER SERVANTS.
EITHER WAY, I THOUGHT ...
...OUR LIVES WOULD SEE A LITTLE MORE PEACE, WHICH TRULY PUT MY MIND AT EASE.

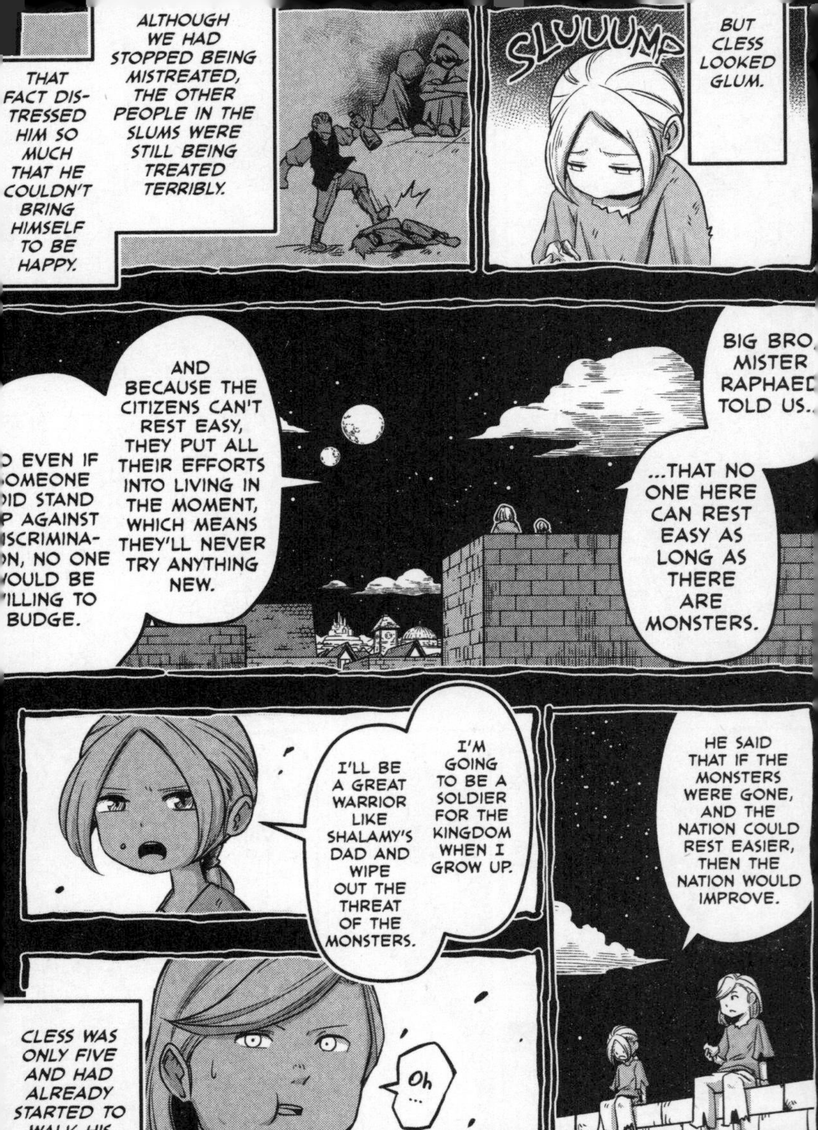
SLUUUMP
BUT CLESS LOOKED GLUM.
ALTHOUGH WE HAD STOPPED BEING MISTREATED, THE OTHER PEOPLE IN THE SLUMS WERE STILL BEING TREATED TERRIBLY.
THAT FACT DISTRESSED HIM SO MUCH THAT HE COULDN'T BRING HIMSELF TO BE HAPPY.
BIG BRO, MISTER RAPHAEL TOLD US...
...THAT NO ONE HERE CAN REST EASY AS LONG AS THERE ARE MONSTERS.
AND BECAUSE THE CITIZENS CAN'T REST EASY, THEY PUT ALL THEIR EFFORTS INTO LIVING IN THE MOMENT, WHICH MEANS THEY'LL NEVER TRY ANYTHING NEW.
O EVEN IF OMEONE DID STAND P AGAINST ISCRIMINA-ON, NO ONE VOULD BE ILLING TO BUDGE.
HE SAID THAT IF THE MONSTERS WERE GONE, AND THE NATION COULD REST EASIER, THEN THE NATION WOULD IMPROVE.
I'M GOING TO BE A SOLDIER FOR THE KINGDOM WHEN I GROW UP.
I'LL BE A GREAT WARRIOR LIKE SHALAMY'S DAD AND WIPE OUT THE THREAT OF THE MONSTERS.
Oh...
CLESS WAS ONLY FIVE AND HAD ALREADY STARTED TO WALK HIS OWN PATH

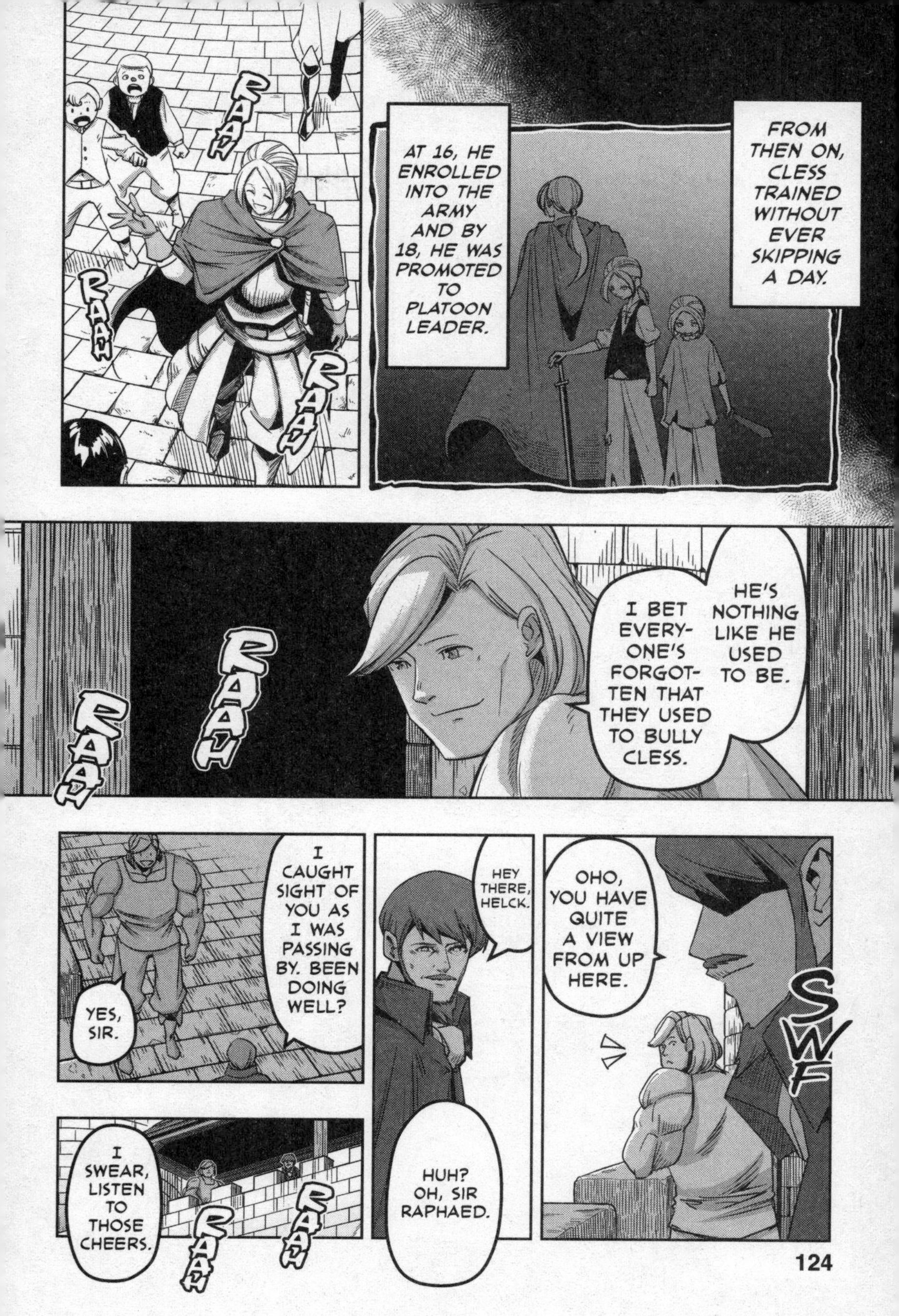
FROM THEN ON, CLESS TRAINED WITHOUT EVER SKIPPING A DAY.
AT 16, HE ENROLLED INTO THE ARMY AND BY 18, HE WAS PROMOTED TO PLATOON LEADER.
RAAAH
RAAAH
RAAAH
HE'S NOTHING LIKE HE USED TO BE.
I BET EVERYONE'S FORGOTTEN THAT THEY USED TO BULLY CLESS.
RAAAH
RAAAH
OHO, YOU HAVE QUITE A VIEW FROM UP HERE.
SWF
HEY THERE, HELCK.
HUH? OH, SIR RAPHAED.
I CAUGHT SIGHT OF YOU AS I WAS PASSING BY. BEEN DOING WELL?
YES, SIR.
I SWEAR, LISTEN TO THOSE CHEERS.
RAAAH
RAAAH

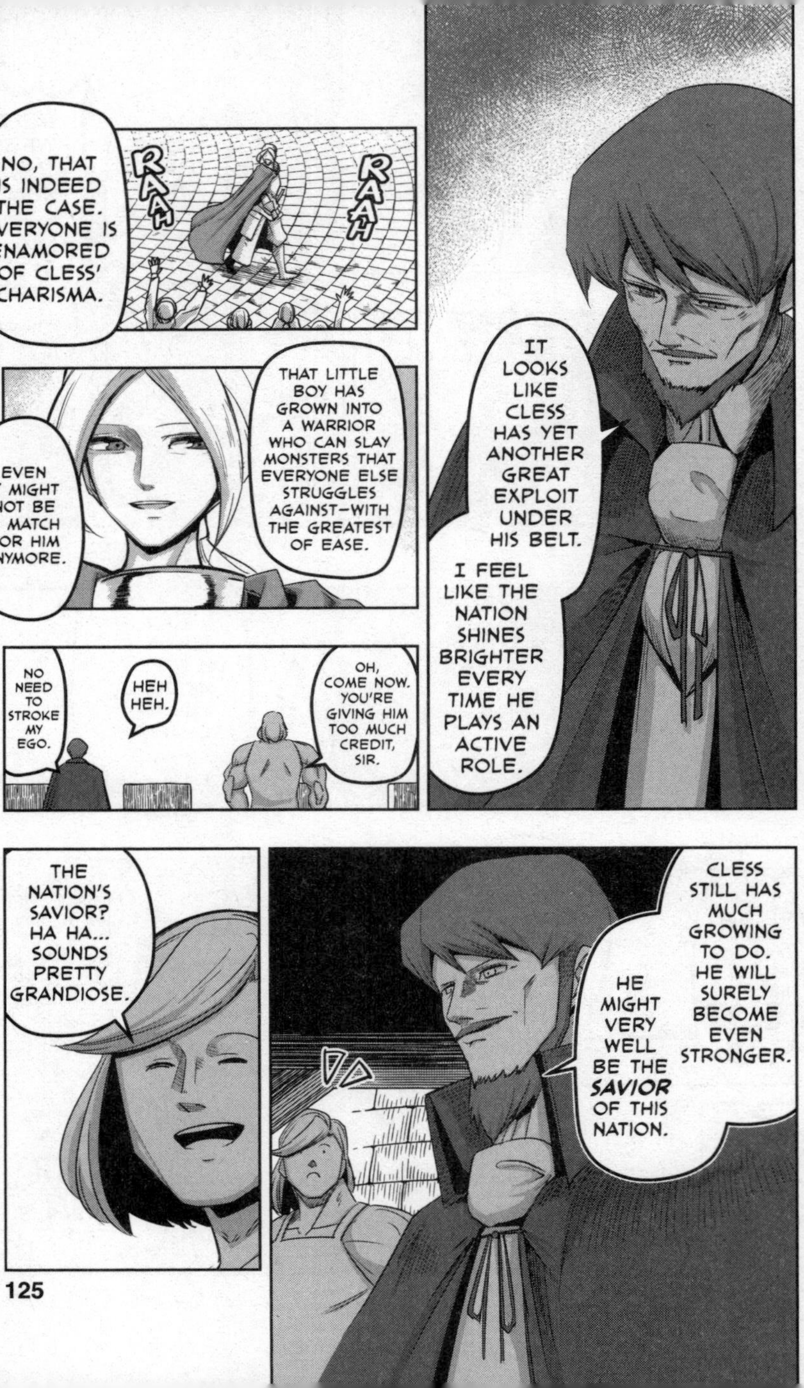

IT LOOKS LIKE CLESS HAS YET ANOTHER GREAT EXPLOIT UNDER HIS BELT.
I FEEL LIKE THE NATION SHINES BRIGHTER EVERY TIME HE PLAYS AN ACTIVE ROLE.
RAAH
RAAH
NO, THAT IS INDEED THE CASE. EVERYONE IS ENAMORED OF CLESS' CHARISMA.
THAT LITTLE BOY HAS GROWN INTO A WARRIOR WHO CAN SLAY MONSTERS THAT EVERYONE ELSE STRUGGLES AGAINST—WITH THE GREATEST OF EASE.
EVEN *I* MIGHT NOT BE A MATCH FOR HIM ANYMORE.
OH, COME NOW. YOU'RE GIVING HIM TOO MUCH CREDIT, SIR.
HEH HEH.
NO NEED TO STROKE MY EGO.
CLESS STILL HAS MUCH GROWING TO DO. HE WILL SURELY BECOME EVEN STRONGER.
HE MIGHT VERY WELL BE THE *SAVIOR* OF THIS NATION.
THE NATION'S SAVIOR? HA HA... SOUNDS PRETTY GRANDIOSE.

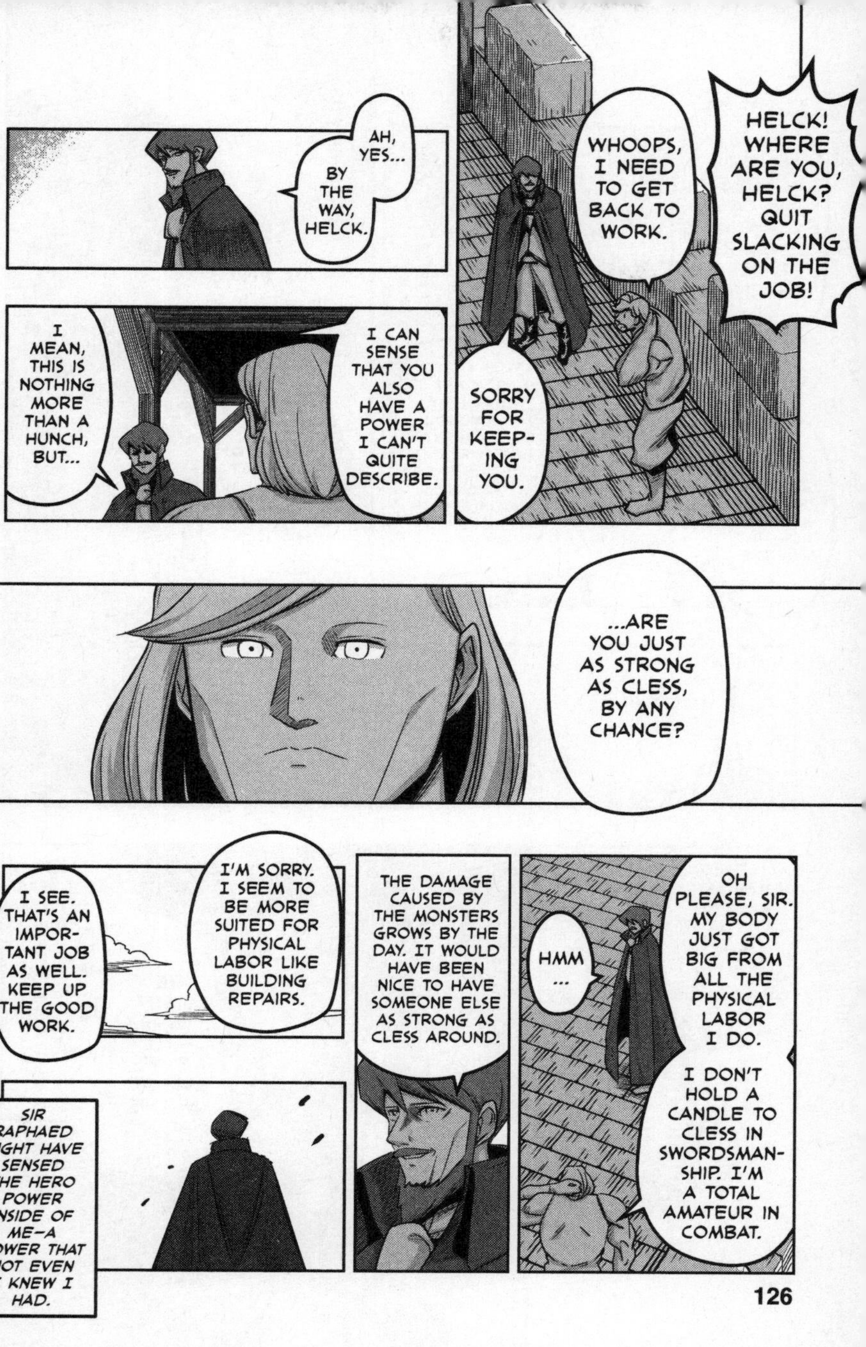
HELCK! WHERE ARE YOU, HELCK? QUIT SLACKING ON THE JOB!
WHOOPS, I NEED TO GET BACK TO WORK.
SORRY FOR KEEP-ING YOU.
AH, YES... BY THE WAY, HELCK.
I MEAN, THIS IS NOTHING MORE THAN A HUNCH, BUT...
I CAN SENSE THAT YOU ALSO HAVE A POWER I CAN'T QUITE DESCRIBE.
...ARE YOU JUST AS STRONG AS CLESS, BY ANY CHANCE?
OH PLEASE, SIR. MY BODY JUST GOT BIG FROM ALL THE PHYSICAL LABOR I DO.
HMM ...
I DON'T HOLD A CANDLE TO CLESS IN SWORDSMAN-SHIP. I'M A TOTAL AMATEUR IN COMBAT.
THE DAMAGE CAUSED BY THE MONSTERS GROWS BY THE DAY. IT WOULD HAVE BEEN NICE TO HAVE SOMEONE ELSE AS STRONG AS CLESS AROUND.
I'M SORRY. I SEEM TO BE MORE SUITED FOR PHYSICAL LABOR LIKE BUILDING REPAIRS.
I SEE. THAT'S AN IMPOR-TANT JOB AS WELL. KEEP UP THE GOOD WORK.
SIR RAPHAED MIGHT HAVE SENSED THE HERO POWER INSIDE OF ME—A POWER THAT NOT EVEN I KNEW I HAD.

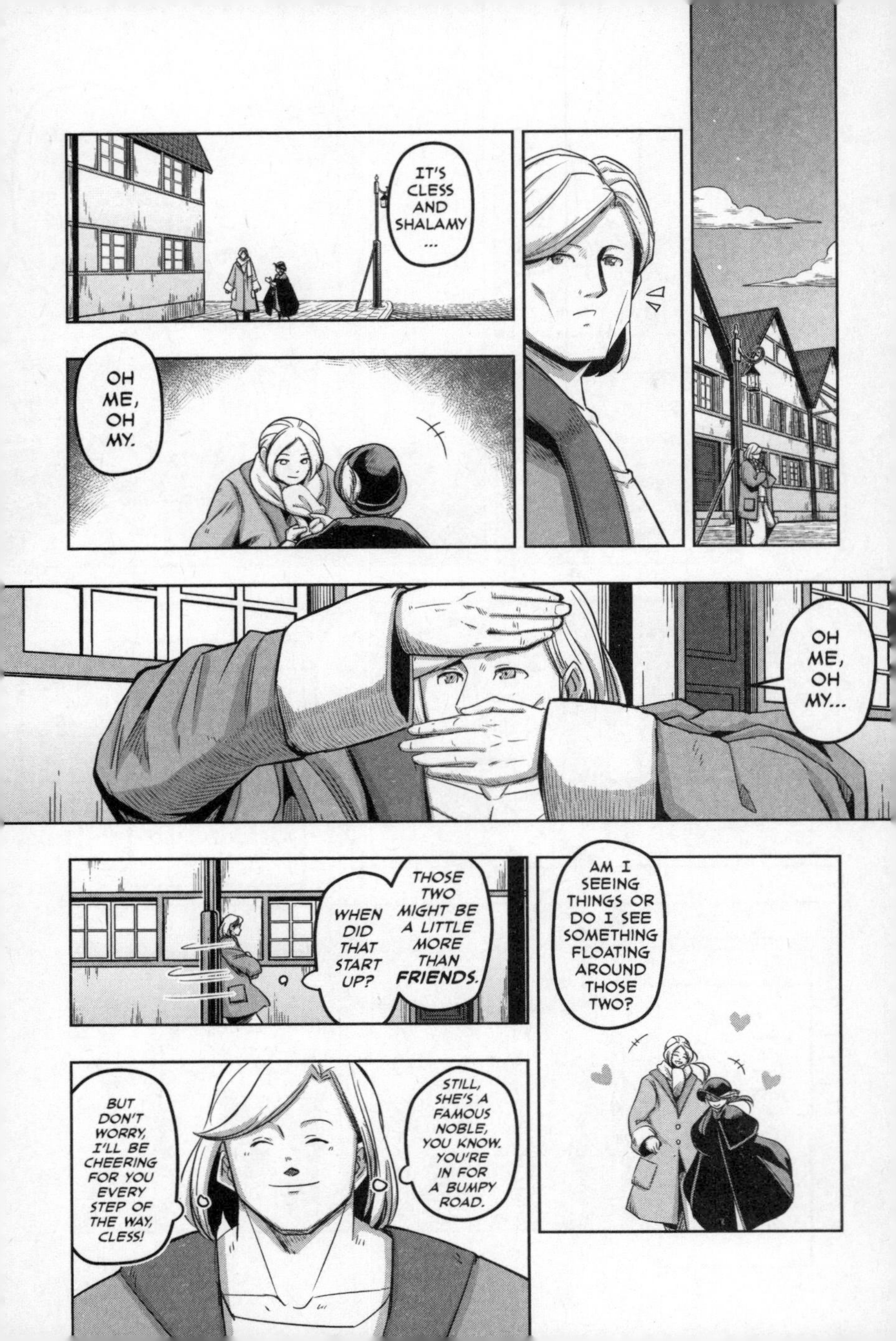
IT'S CLESS AND SHALAMY...
OH ME, OH MY.
OH ME, OH MY...
AM I SEEING THINGS OR DO I SEE SOMETHING FLOATING AROUND THOSE TWO?
THOSE TWO MIGHT BE A LITTLE MORE THAN FRIENDS.
WHEN DID THAT START UP?
STILL, SHE'S A FAMOUS NOBLE, YOU KNOW. YOU'RE IN FOR A BUMPY ROAD.
BUT DON'T WORRY, I'LL BE CHEERING FOR YOU EVERY STEP OF THE WAY, CLESS!

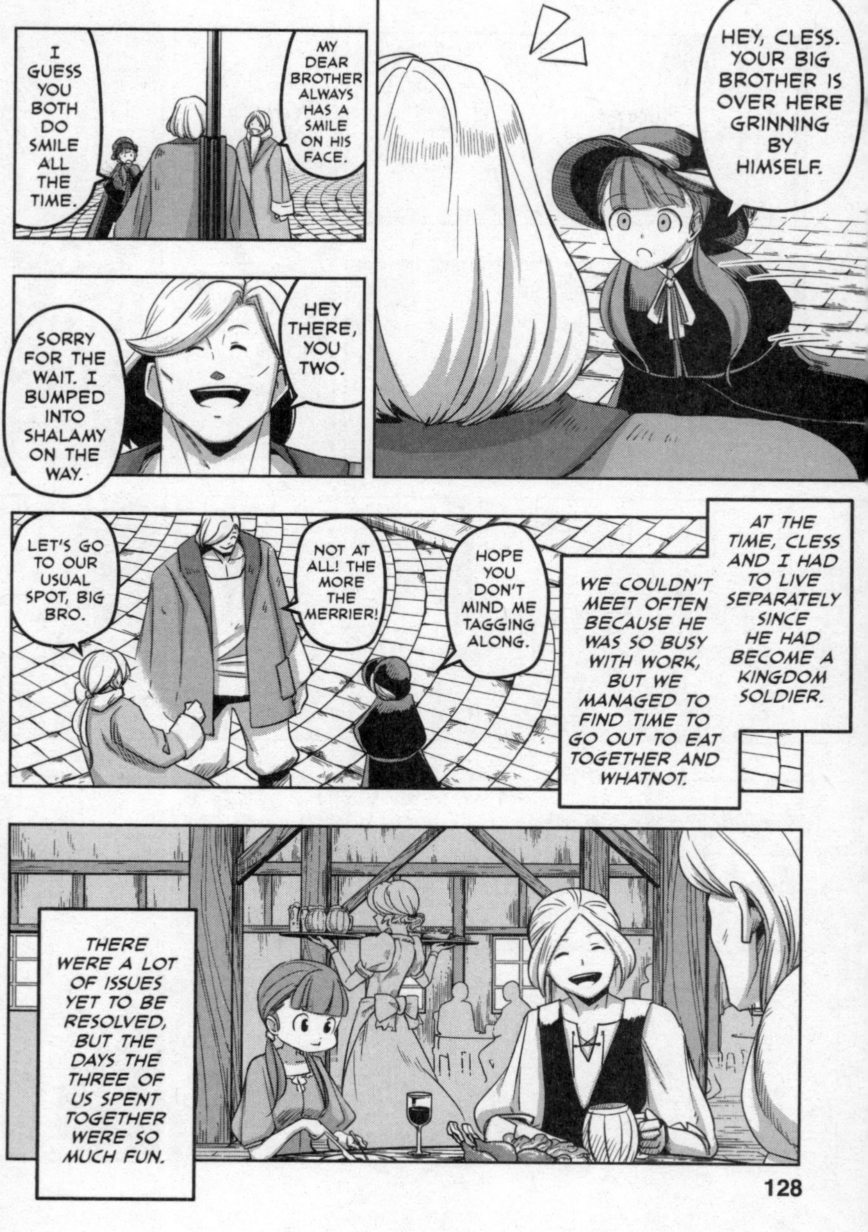

HEY, CLESS. YOUR BIG BROTHER IS OVER HERE GRINNING BY HIMSELF.
MY DEAR BROTHER ALWAYS HAS A SMILE ON HIS FACE.
I GUESS YOU BOTH DO SMILE ALL THE TIME.
HEY THERE, YOU TWO.
SORRY FOR THE WAIT. I BUMPED INTO SHALAMY ON THE WAY.
AT THE TIME, CLESS AND I HAD TO LIVE SEPARATELY SINCE HE HAD BECOME A KINGDOM SOLDIER.
WE COULDN'T MEET OFTEN BECAUSE HE WAS SO BUSY WITH WORK, BUT WE MANAGED TO FIND TIME TO GO OUT TO EAT TOGETHER AND WHATNOT.
HOPE YOU DON'T MIND ME TAGGING ALONG.
NOT AT ALL! THE MORE THE MERRIER!
LET'S GO TO OUR USUAL SPOT, BIG BRO.
THERE WERE A LOT OF ISSUES YET TO BE RESOLVED, BUT THE DAYS THE THREE OF US SPENT TOGETHER WERE SO MUCH FUN.

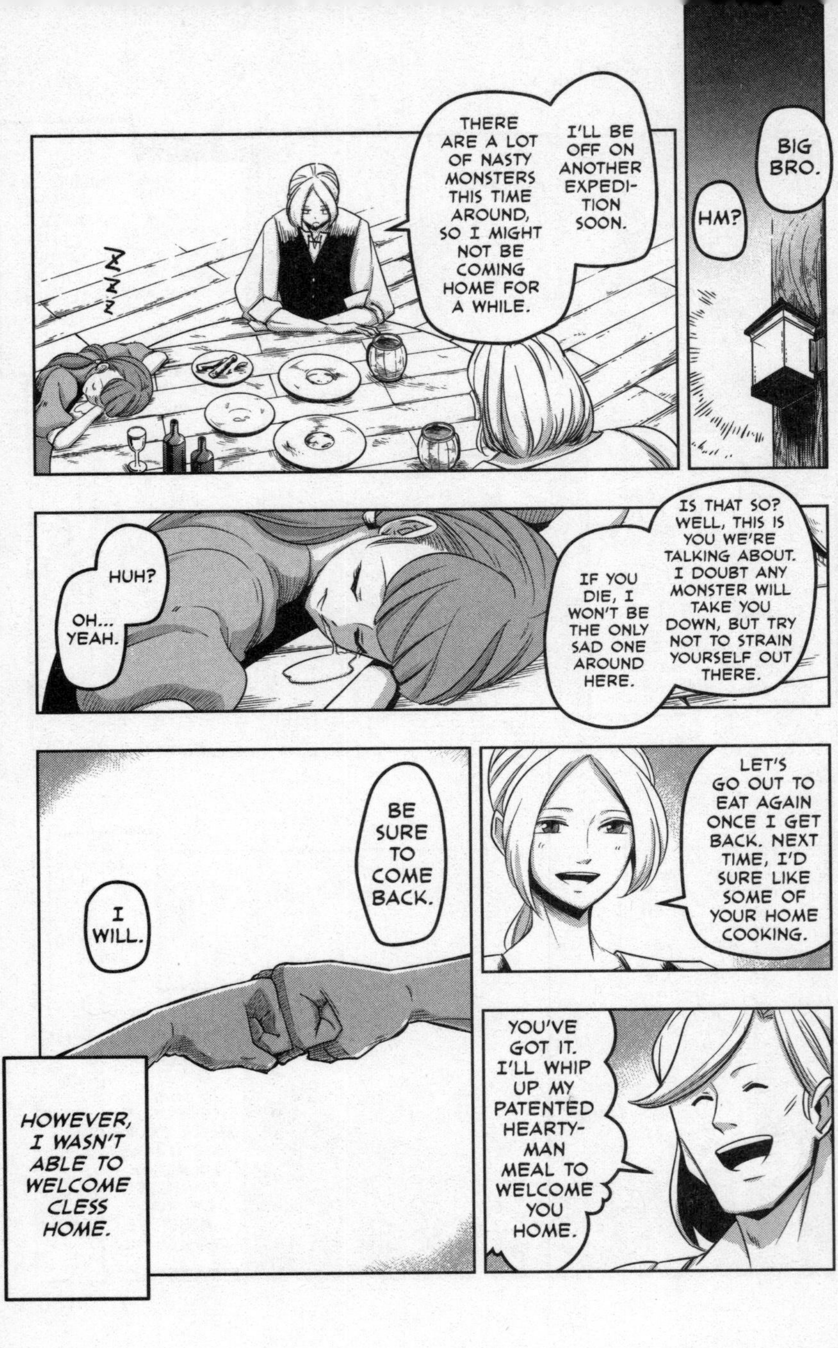
BIG BRO.
HM?
I'LL BE OFF ON ANOTHER EXPEDITION SOON.
THERE ARE A LOT OF NASTY MONSTERS THIS TIME AROUND, SO I MIGHT NOT BE COMING HOME FOR A WHILE.
ZZZ
IS THAT SO? WELL, THIS IS YOU WE'RE TALKING ABOUT. I DOUBT ANY MONSTER WILL TAKE YOU DOWN, BUT TRY NOT TO STRAIN YOURSELF OUT THERE.
IF YOU DIE, I WON'T BE THE ONLY SAD ONE AROUND HERE.
HUH?
OH... YEAH.
LET'S GO OUT TO EAT AGAIN ONCE I GET BACK. NEXT TIME, I'D SURE LIKE SOME OF YOUR HOME COOKING.
YOU'VE GOT IT. I'LL WHIP UP MY PATENTED HEARTY-MAN MEAL TO WELCOME YOU HOME.
BE SURE TO COME BACK.
I WILL.
HOWEVER, I WASN'T ABLE TO WELCOME CLESS HOME.

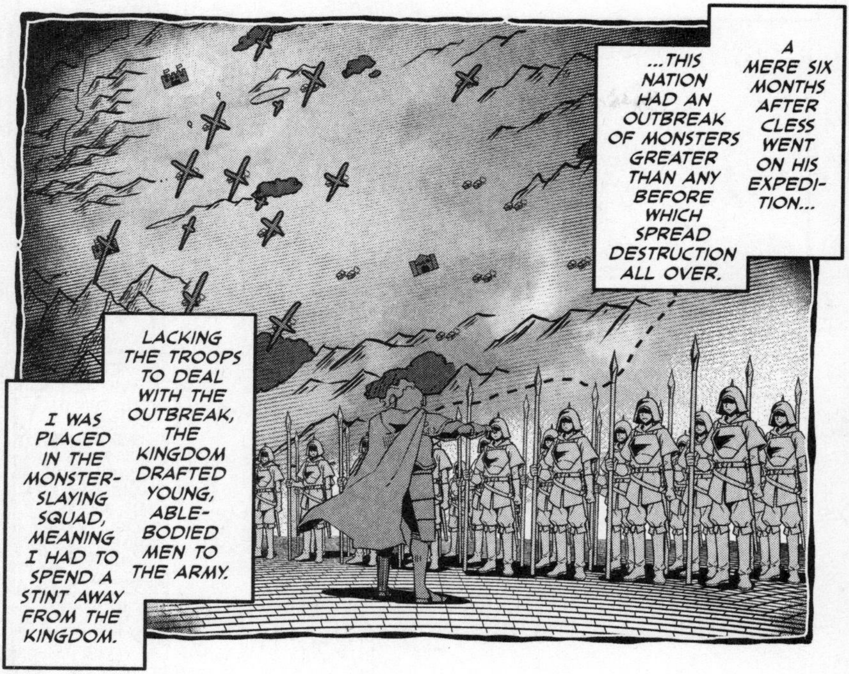
A MERE SIX MONTHS AFTER CLESS WENT ON HIS EXPEDITION...
...THIS NATION HAD AN OUTBREAK OF MONSTERS GREATER THAN ANY BEFORE WHICH SPREAD DESTRUCTION ALL OVER.
LACKING THE TROOPS TO DEAL WITH THE OUTBREAK, THE KINGDOM DRAFTED YOUNG, ABLE-BODIED MEN TO THE ARMY.
I WAS PLACED IN THE MONSTER-SLAYING SQUAD, MEANING I HAD TO SPEND A STINT AWAY FROM THE KINGDOM.

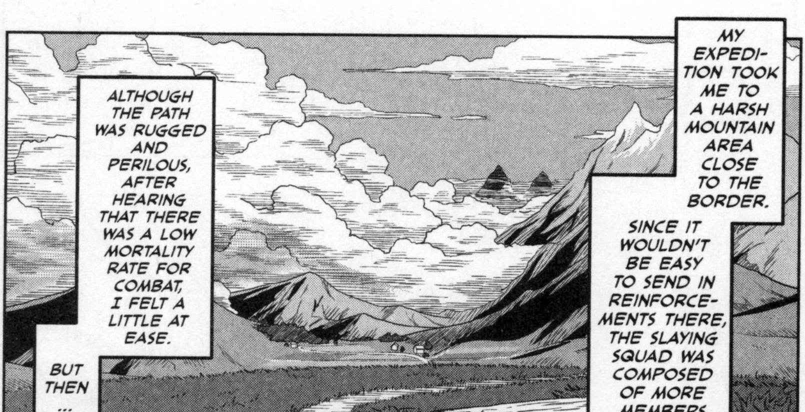
MY EXPEDITION TOOK ME TO A HARSH MOUNTAIN AREA CLOSE TO THE BORDER.
SINCE IT WOULDN'T BE EASY TO SEND IN REINFORCEMENTS THERE, THE SLAYING SQUAD WAS COMPOSED OF MORE MEMBERS THAN USUAL.
ALTHOUGH THE PATH WAS RUGGED AND PERILOUS, AFTER HEARING THAT THERE WAS A LOW MORTALITY RATE FOR COMBAT, I FELT A LITTLE AT EASE.
BUT THEN ...

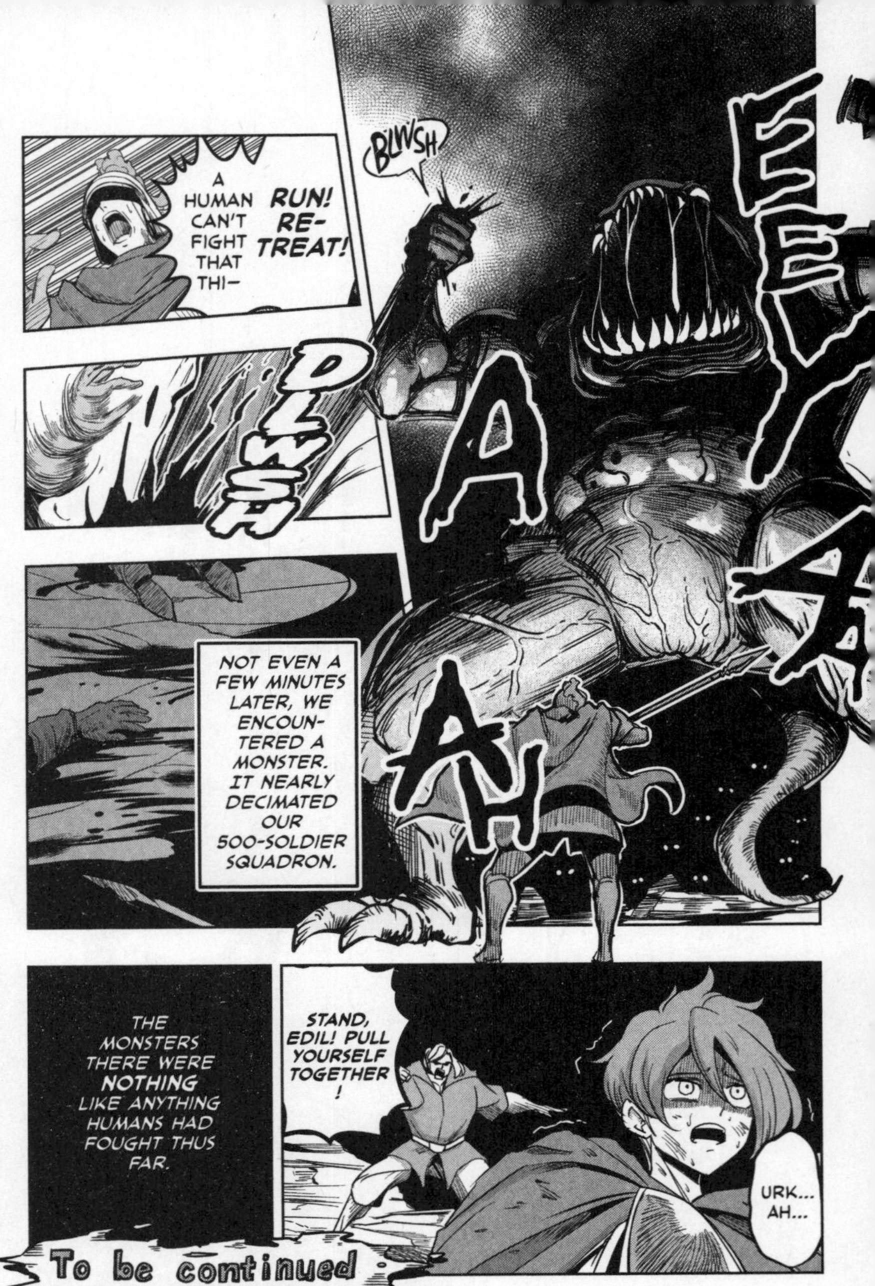

BLWSH
EEYAAAAH
RUN! RE-TREAT!
A HUMAN CAN'T FIGHT THAT THI—
DLWSH
NOT EVEN A FEW MINUTES LATER, WE ENCOUNTERED A MONSTER. IT NEARLY DECIMATED OUR 500-SOLDIER SQUADRON.
URK... AH...
STAND, EDIL! PULL YOURSELF TOGETHER!
THE MONSTERS THERE WERE NOTHING LIKE ANYTHING HUMANS HAD FOUGHT THUS FAR.
To be continued

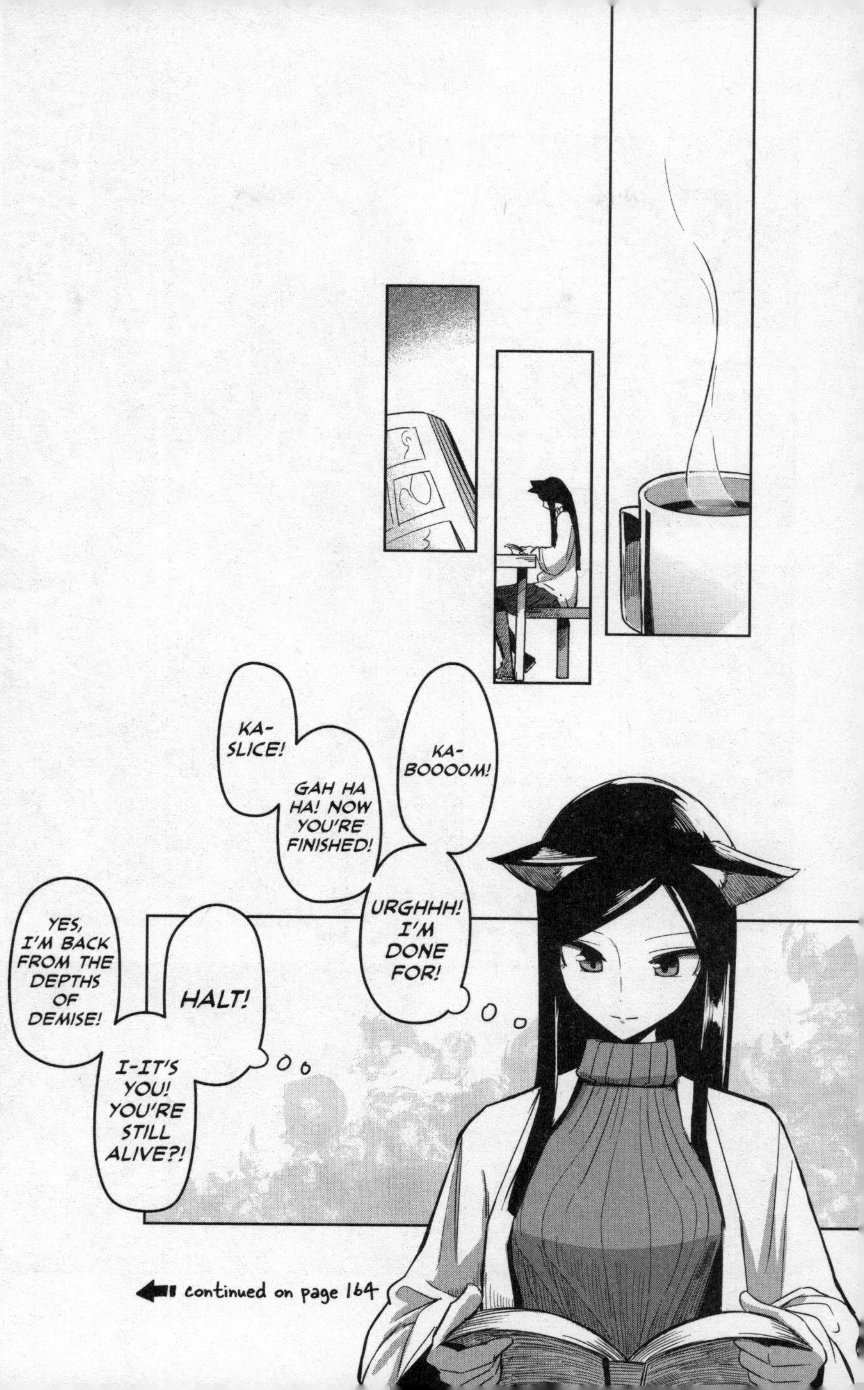
KA-BOOOOM!
KA-SLICE!
GAH HA HA! NOW YOU'RE FINISHED!
URGHHH! I'M DONE FOR!
HALT!
I-IT'S YOU! YOU'RE STILL ALIVE?!
YES, I'M BACK FROM THE DEPTHS OF DEMISE!

continued on page 164

Chapter 39: Helck's Past IV

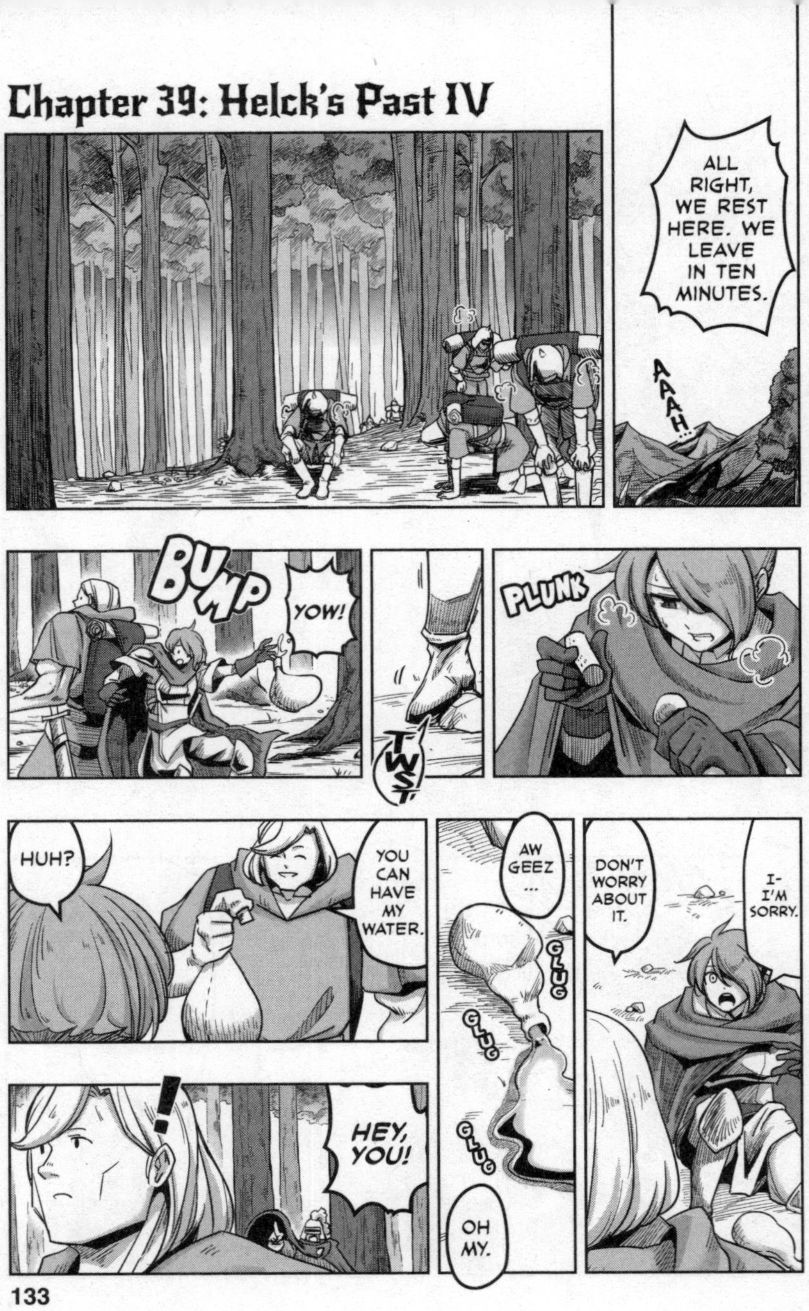
ALL RIGHT, WE REST HERE. WE LEAVE IN TEN MINUTES.
AAAH...
PLUNK
TWST
BUMP
YOW!
I- I'M SORRY.
DON'T WORRY ABOUT IT.
AW GEEZ ...
GLUG
GLUG
GLUG
OH MY.
YOU CAN HAVE MY WATER.
HUH?
!
HEY, YOU!

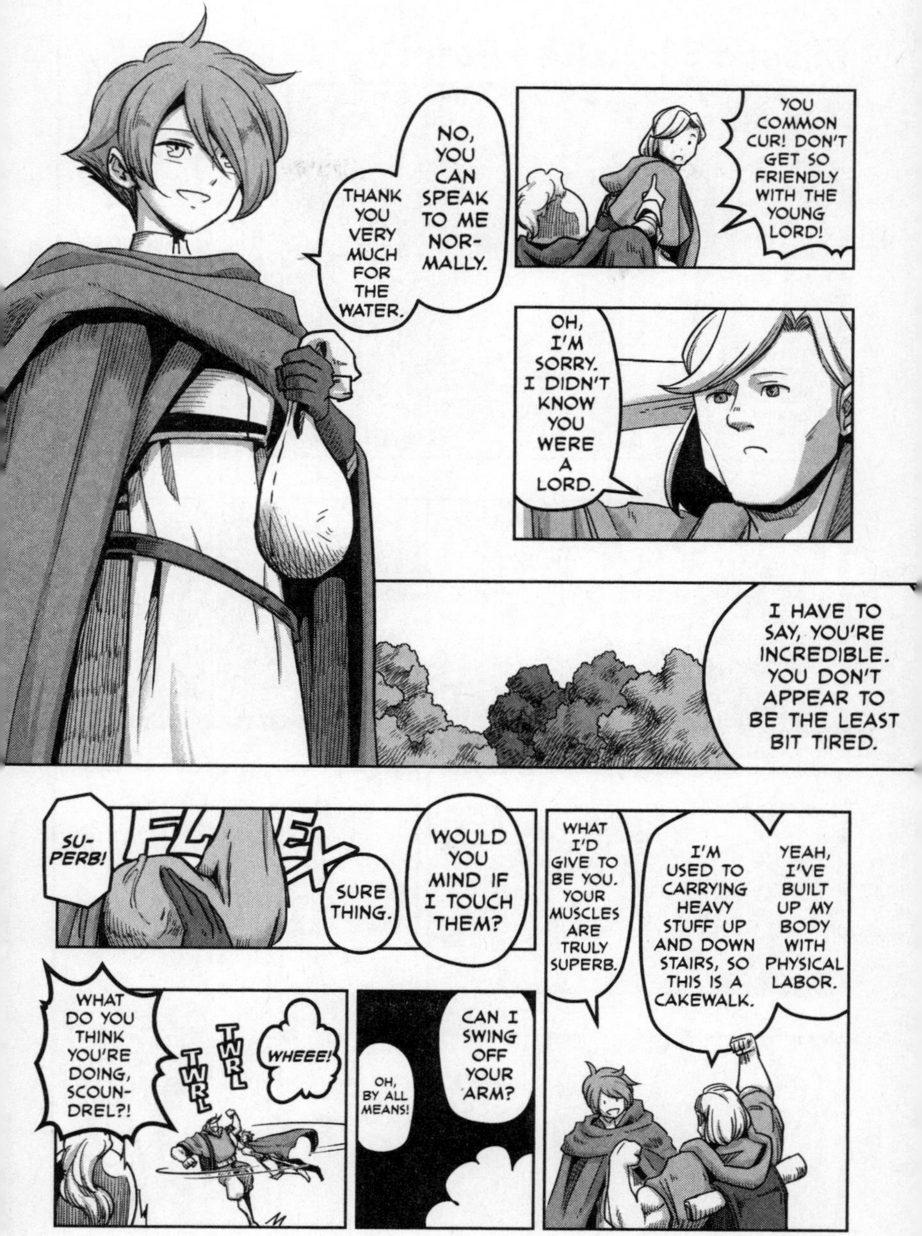
YOU COMMON CUR! DON'T GET SO FRIENDLY WITH THE YOUNG LORD!
OH, I'M SORRY. I DIDN'T KNOW YOU WERE A LORD.
NO, YOU CAN SPEAK TO ME NOR-MALLY.
THANK YOU VERY MUCH FOR THE WATER.
I HAVE TO SAY, YOU'RE INCREDIBLE. YOU DON'T APPEAR TO BE THE LEAST BIT TIRED.
YEAH, I'VE BUILT UP MY BODY WITH PHYSICAL LABOR.
I'M USED TO CARRYING HEAVY STUFF UP AND DOWN STAIRS, SO THIS IS A CAKEWALK.
WHAT I'D GIVE TO BE YOU. YOUR MUSCLES ARE TRULY SUPERB.
WOULD YOU MIND IF I TOUCH THEM?
SURE THING.
FLEX
SU-PERB!
CAN I SWING OFF YOUR ARM?
OH, BY ALL MEANS!
WHEEE!
TWRL
TWRL
WHAT DO YOU THINK YOU'RE DOING, SCOUN-DREL?!

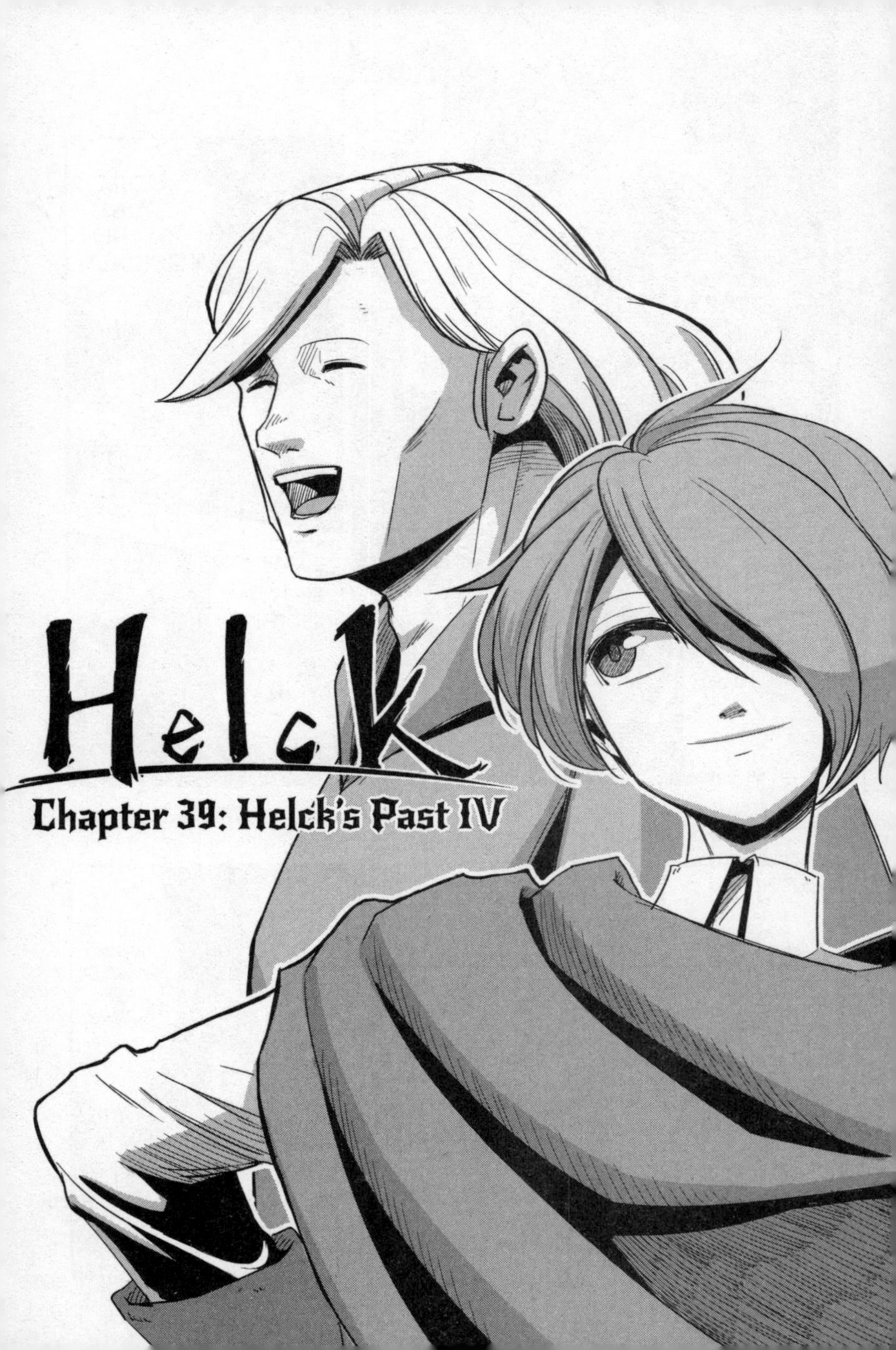
Helck
Chapter 39: Helck's Past IV

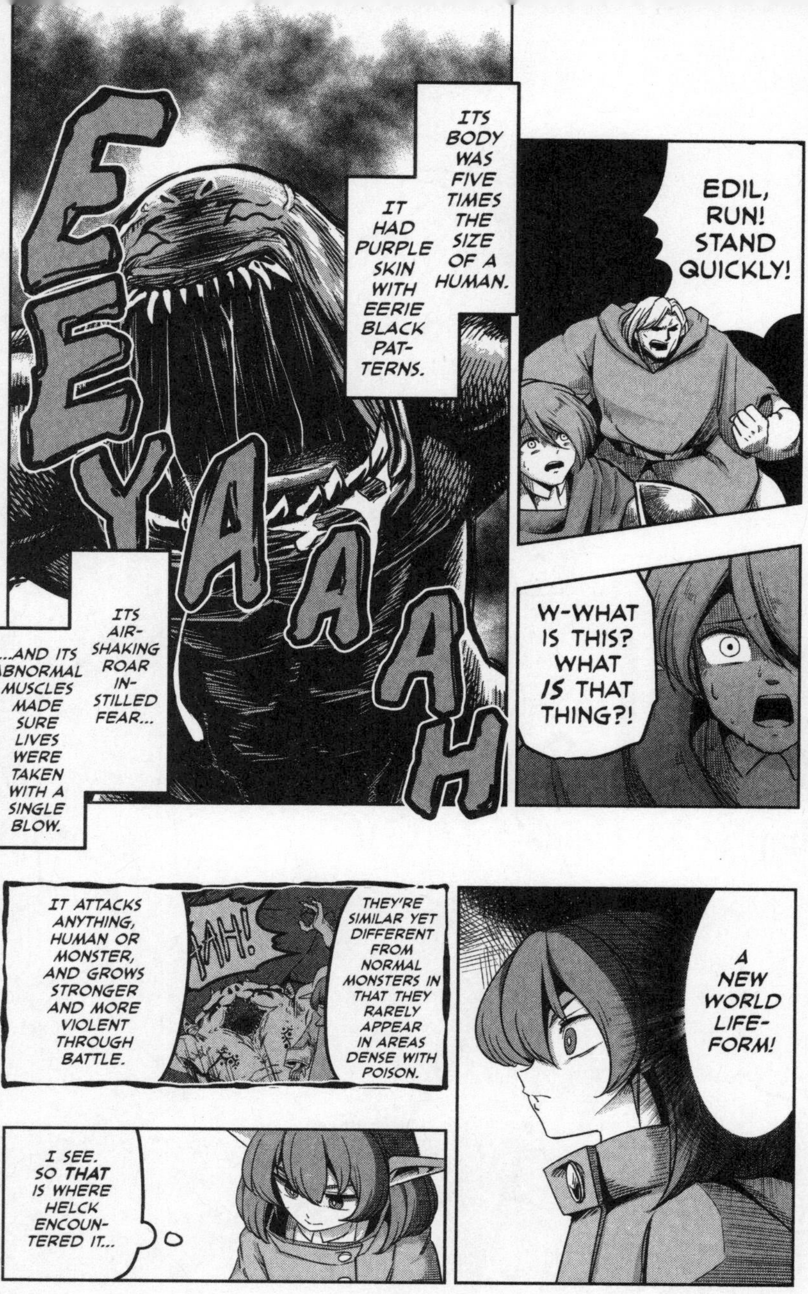
EDIL, RUN! STAND QUICKLY!
W-WHAT IS THIS? WHAT *IS* THAT THING?!
ITS BODY WAS FIVE TIMES THE SIZE OF A HUMAN.
IT HAD PURPLE SKIN WITH EERIE BLACK PAT-TERNS.
EEEYAAAAH
ITS AIR-SHAKING ROAR IN-STILLED FEAR...
...AND ITS ABNORMAL MUSCLES MADE SURE LIVES WERE TAKEN WITH A SINGLE BLOW.
A NEW WORLD LIFE-FORM!
THEY'RE SIMILAR YET DIFFERENT FROM NORMAL MONSTERS IN THAT THEY RARELY APPEAR IN AREAS DENSE WITH POISON.
IT ATTACKS ANYTHING, HUMAN OR MONSTER, AND GROWS STRONGER AND MORE VIOLENT THROUGH BATTLE.
I SEE. SO **THAT** IS WHERE HELCK ENCOUN-TERED IT...

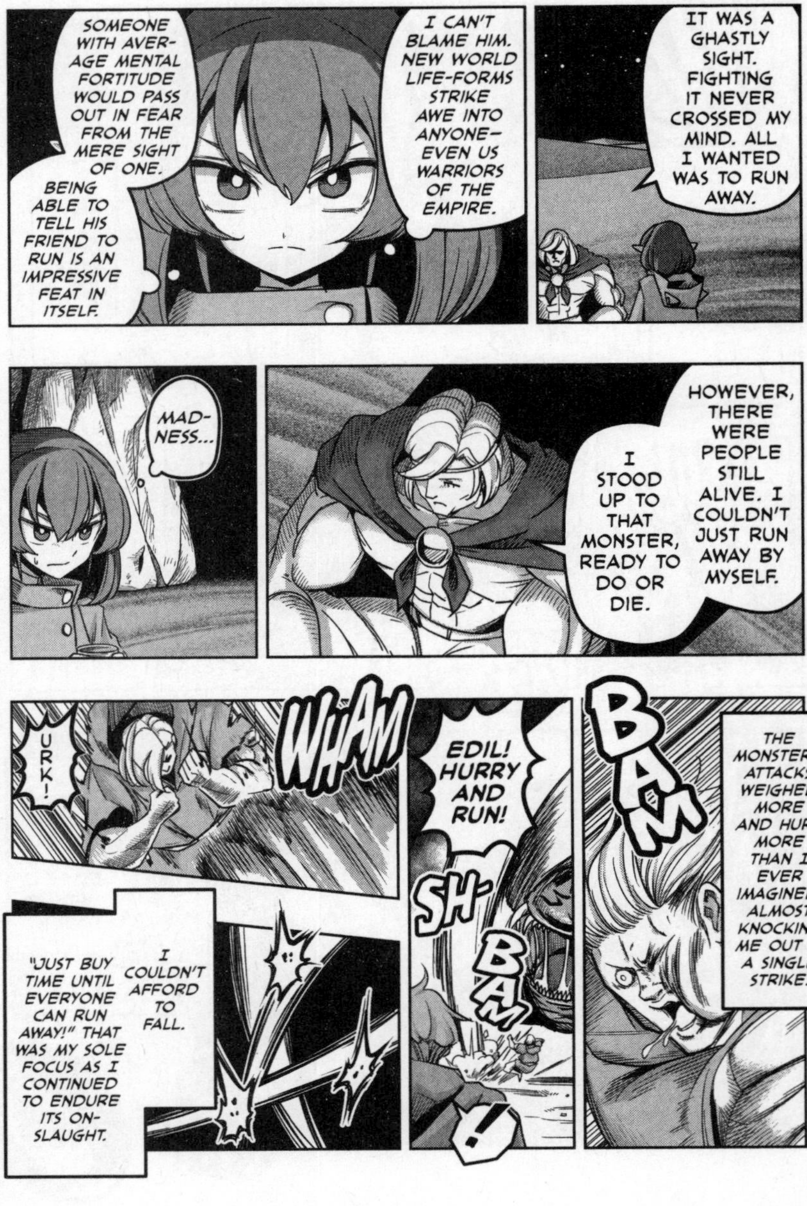
IT WAS A GHASTLY SIGHT. FIGHTING IT NEVER CROSSED MY MIND. ALL I WANTED WAS TO RUN AWAY.
I CAN'T BLAME HIM. NEW WORLD LIFE-FORMS STRIKE AWE INTO ANYONE—EVEN US WARRIORS OF THE EMPIRE.
SOMEONE WITH AVER-AGE MENTAL FORTITUDE WOULD PASS OUT IN FEAR FROM THE MERE SIGHT OF ONE.
BEING ABLE TO TELL HIS FRIEND TO RUN IS AN IMPRESSIVE FEAT IN ITSELF.
HOWEVER, THERE WERE PEOPLE STILL ALIVE. I COULDN'T JUST RUN AWAY BY MYSELF.
I STOOD UP TO THAT MONSTER, READY TO DO OR DIE.
MAD-NESS...
BAM
THE MONSTER'S ATTACKS WEIGHED MORE AND HURT MORE THAN I EVER IMAGINED, ALMOST KNOCKING ME OUT IN A SINGLE STRIKE.
EDIL! HURRY AND RUN!
SH-BAM
!
WHAM
URK!
I COULDN'T AFFORD TO FALL.
"JUST BUY TIME UNTIL EVERYONE CAN RUN AWAY!" THAT WAS MY SOLE FOCUS AS I CONTINUED TO ENDURE ITS ON-SLAUGHT.

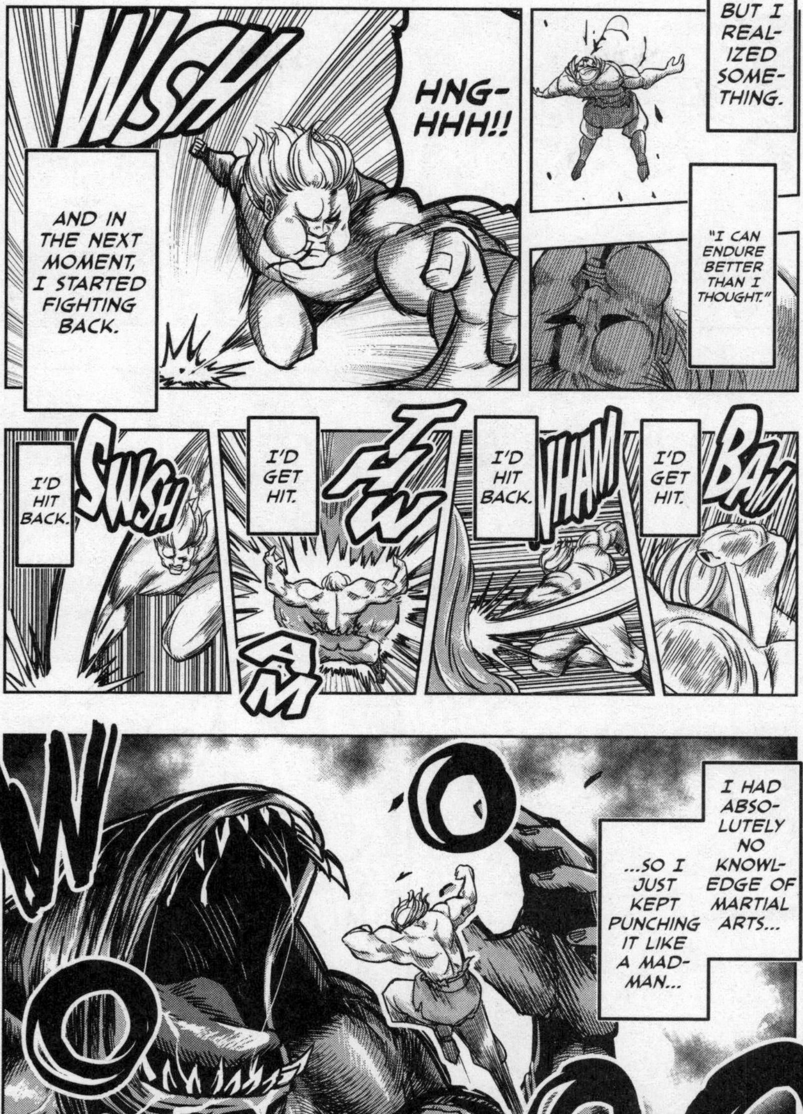
BUT I REAL-IZED SOME-THING.
"I CAN ENDURE BETTER THAN I THOUGHT."
HNG-HHH!!
WSH
AND IN THE NEXT MOMENT, I STARTED FIGHTING BACK.
I'D GET HIT.
BAM
I'D HIT BACK.
WHAM
I'D GET HIT.
THWAM
I'D HIT BACK.
SWSH
I HAD ABSOLUTELY NO KNOWLEDGE OF MARTIAL ARTS...
...SO I JUST KEPT PUNCHING IT LIKE A MADMAN...

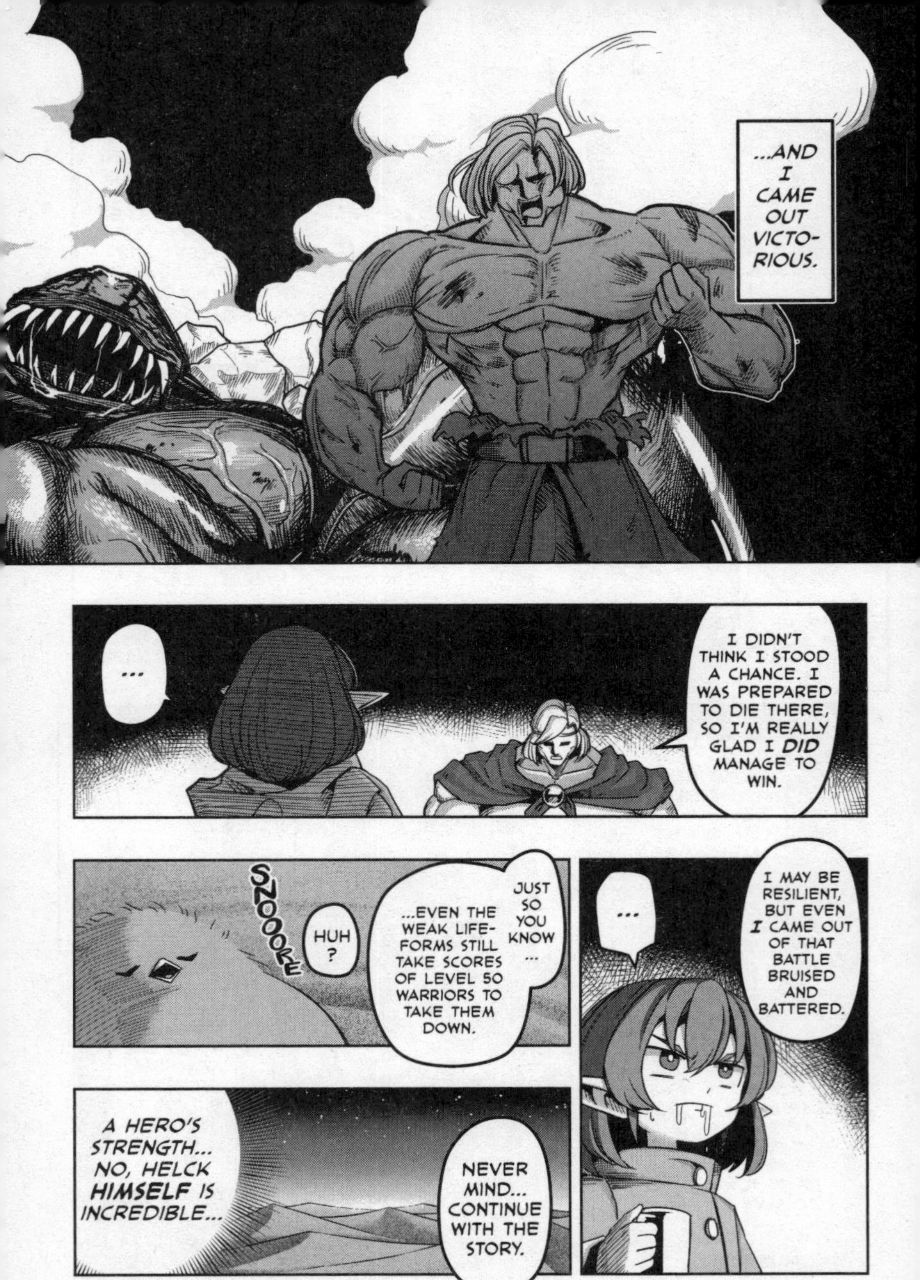
...AND I CAME OUT VICTO-RIOUS.
I DIDN'T THINK I STOOD A CHANCE. I WAS PREPARED TO DIE THERE, SO I'M REALLY GLAD I DID MANAGE TO WIN.
...
I MAY BE RESILIENT, BUT EVEN I CAME OUT OF THAT BATTLE BRUISED AND BATTERED.
...
JUST SO YOU KNOW ...
...EVEN THE WEAK LIFE-FORMS STILL TAKE SCORES OF LEVEL 50 WARRIORS TO TAKE THEM DOWN.
HUH?
SNOOORE
NEVER MIND... CONTINUE WITH THE STORY.
A HERO'S STRENGTH... NO, HELCK HIMSELF IS INCREDIBLE...

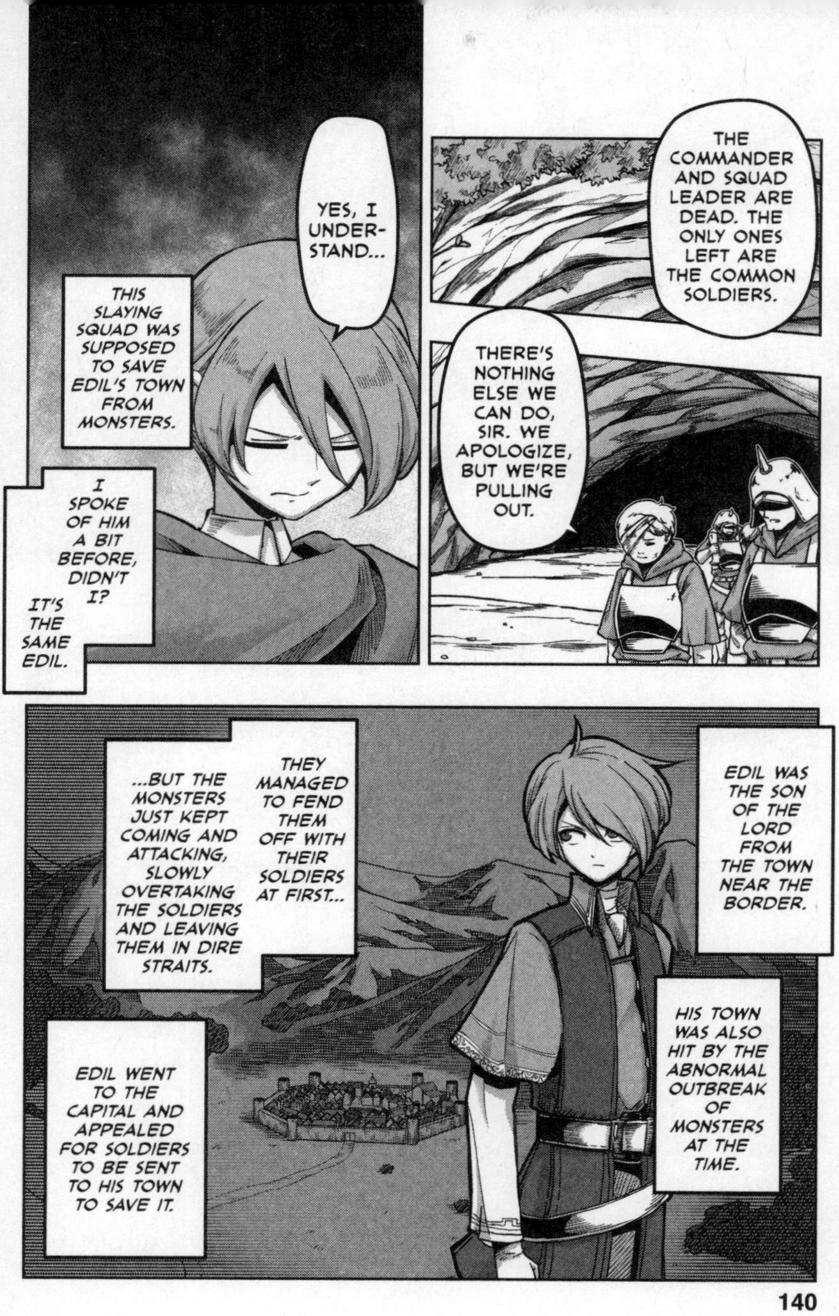
THE COMMANDER AND SQUAD LEADER ARE DEAD. THE ONLY ONES LEFT ARE THE COMMON SOLDIERS.
THERE'S NOTHING ELSE WE CAN DO, SIR. WE APOLOGIZE, BUT WE'RE PULLING OUT.
YES, I UNDERSTAND...
THIS SLAYING SQUAD WAS SUPPOSED TO SAVE EDIL'S TOWN FROM MONSTERS.
I SPOKE OF HIM A BIT BEFORE, DIDN'T I?
IT'S THE SAME EDIL.
EDIL WAS THE SON OF THE LORD FROM THE TOWN NEAR THE BORDER.
HIS TOWN WAS ALSO HIT BY THE ABNORMAL OUTBREAK OF MONSTERS AT THE TIME.
THEY MANAGED TO FEND THEM OFF WITH THEIR SOLDIERS AT FIRST...
...BUT THE MONSTERS JUST KEPT COMING AND ATTACKING, SLOWLY OVERTAKING THE SOLDIERS AND LEAVING THEM IN DIRE STRAITS.
EDIL WENT TO THE CAPITAL AND APPEALED FOR SOLDIERS TO BE SENT TO HIS TOWN TO SAVE IT.

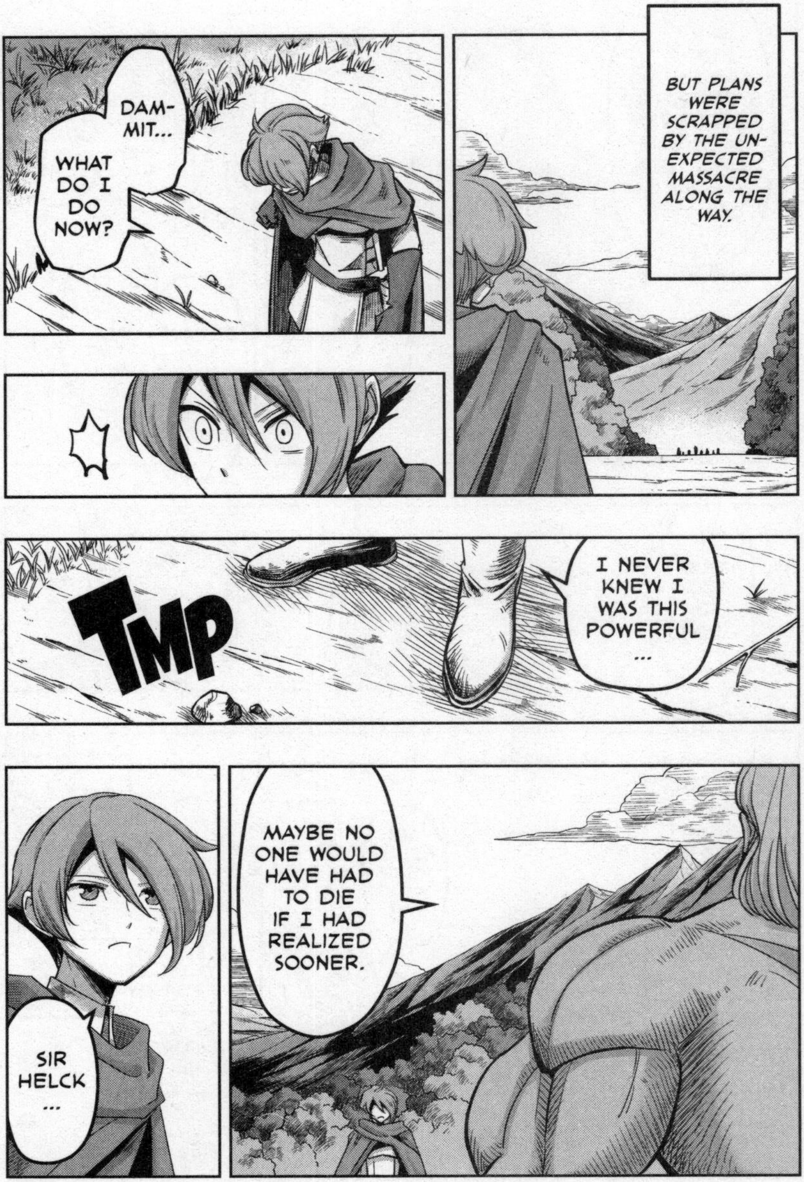
BUT PLANS WERE SCRAPPED BY THE UN-EXPECTED MASSACRE ALONG THE WAY.
DAM-MIT...
WHAT DO I DO NOW?
I NEVER KNEW I WAS THIS POWERFUL...
TMP
MAYBE NO ONE WOULD HAVE HAD TO DIE IF I HAD REALIZED SOONER.
SIR HELCK...

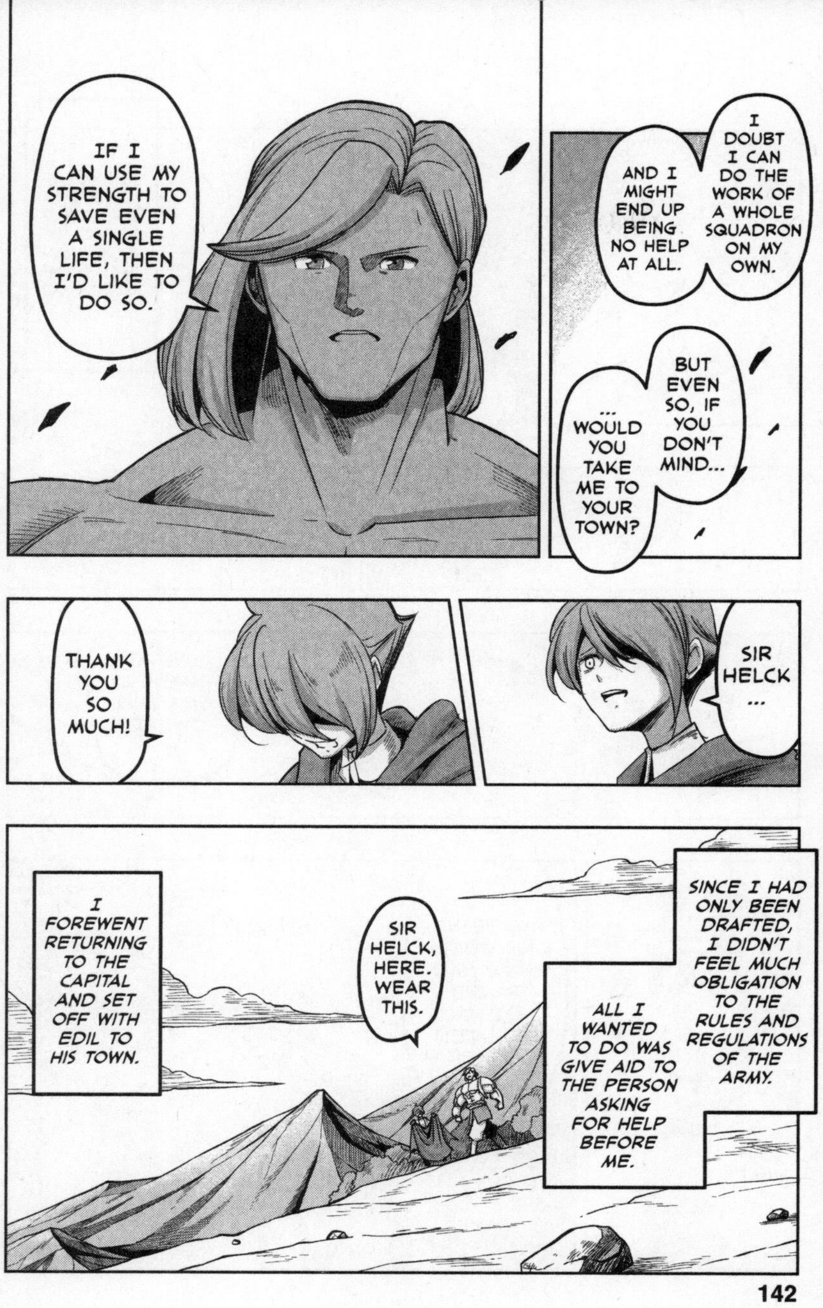
I DOUBT I CAN DO THE WORK OF A WHOLE SQUADRON ON MY OWN.
AND I MIGHT END UP BEING NO HELP AT ALL.
BUT EVEN SO, IF YOU DON'T MIND...
...WOULD YOU TAKE ME TO YOUR TOWN?
IF I CAN USE MY STRENGTH TO SAVE EVEN A SINGLE LIFE, THEN I'D LIKE TO DO SO.
SIR HELCK...
THANK YOU SO MUCH!
SINCE I HAD ONLY BEEN DRAFTED, I DIDN'T FEEL MUCH OBLIGATION TO THE RULES AND REGULATIONS OF THE ARMY.
ALL I WANTED TO DO WAS GIVE AID TO THE PERSON ASKING FOR HELP BEFORE ME.
SIR HELCK, HERE. WEAR THIS.
I FOREWENT RETURNING TO THE CAPITAL AND SET OFF WITH EDIL TO HIS TOWN.

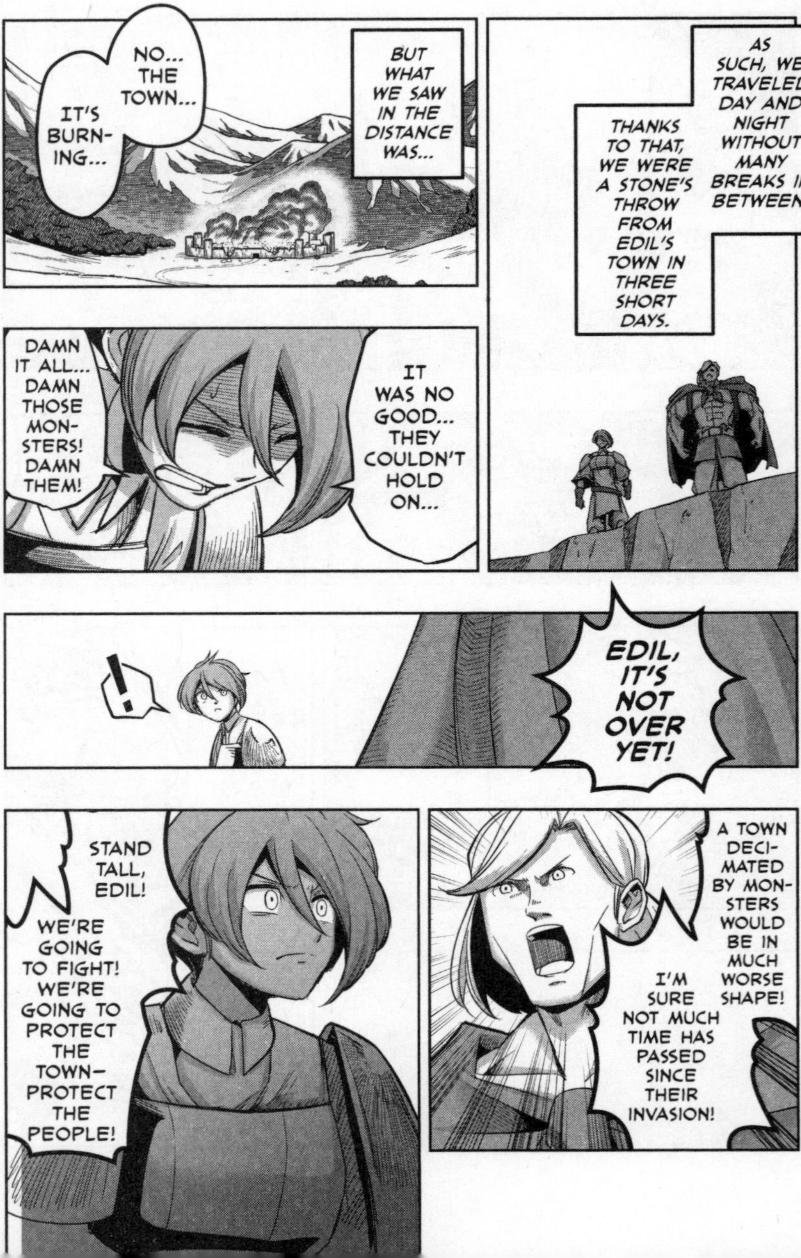

AS SUCH, WE TRAVELED DAY AND NIGHT WITHOUT MANY BREAKS IN BETWEEN.
THANKS TO THAT, WE WERE A STONE'S THROW FROM EDIL'S TOWN IN THREE SHORT DAYS.
BUT WHAT WE SAW IN THE DISTANCE WAS...
NO... THE TOWN...
IT'S BURNING...
IT WAS NO GOOD... THEY COULDN'T HOLD ON...
DAMN IT ALL... DAMN THOSE MONSTERS! DAMN THEM!
EDIL, IT'S NOT OVER YET!
!
A TOWN DECIMATED BY MONSTERS WOULD BE IN MUCH WORSE SHAPE!
I'M SURE NOT MUCH TIME HAS PASSED SINCE THEIR INVASION!
STAND TALL, EDIL!
WE'RE GOING TO FIGHT! WE'RE GOING TO PROTECT THE TOWN—PROTECT THE PEOPLE!

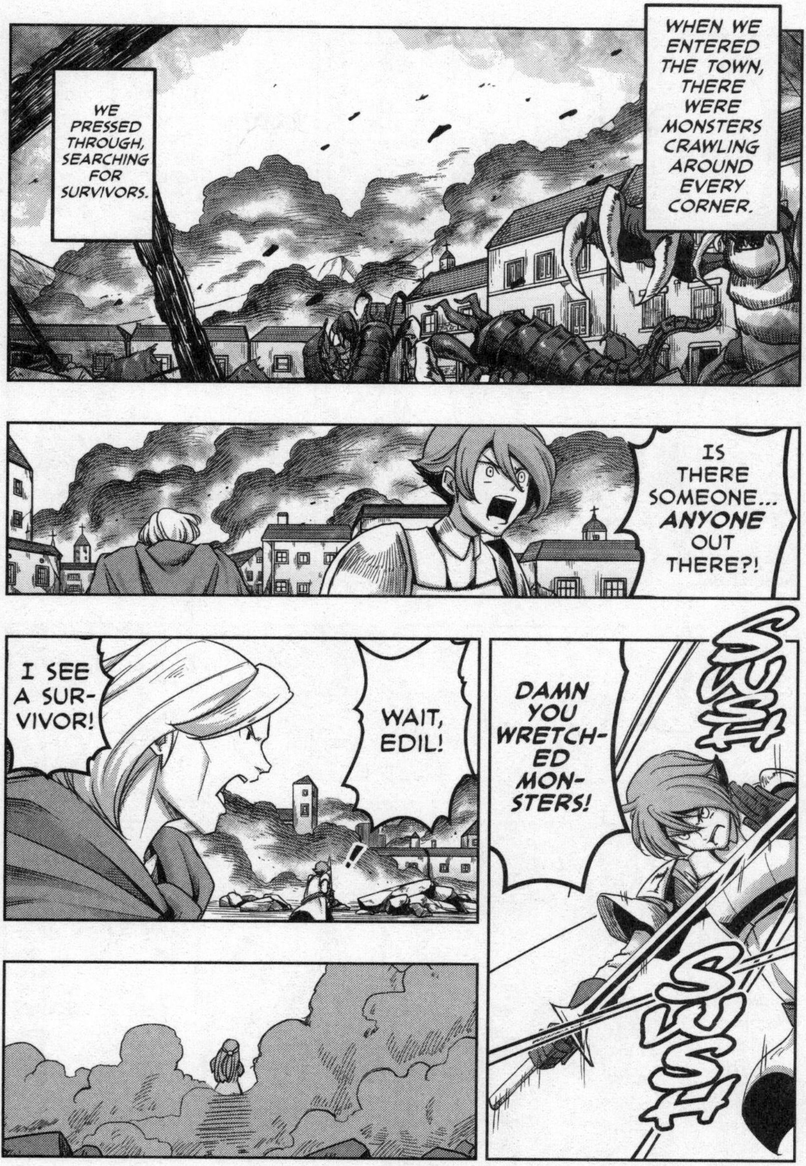
WHEN WE ENTERED THE TOWN, THERE WERE MONSTERS CRAWLING AROUND EVERY CORNER.
WE PRESSED THROUGH, SEARCHING FOR SURVIVORS.
IS THERE SOMEONE... ANYONE OUT THERE?!
SWISH
DAMN YOU WRETCH-ED MON-STERS!
SWISH
I SEE A SUR-VIVOR!
WAIT, EDIL!
!

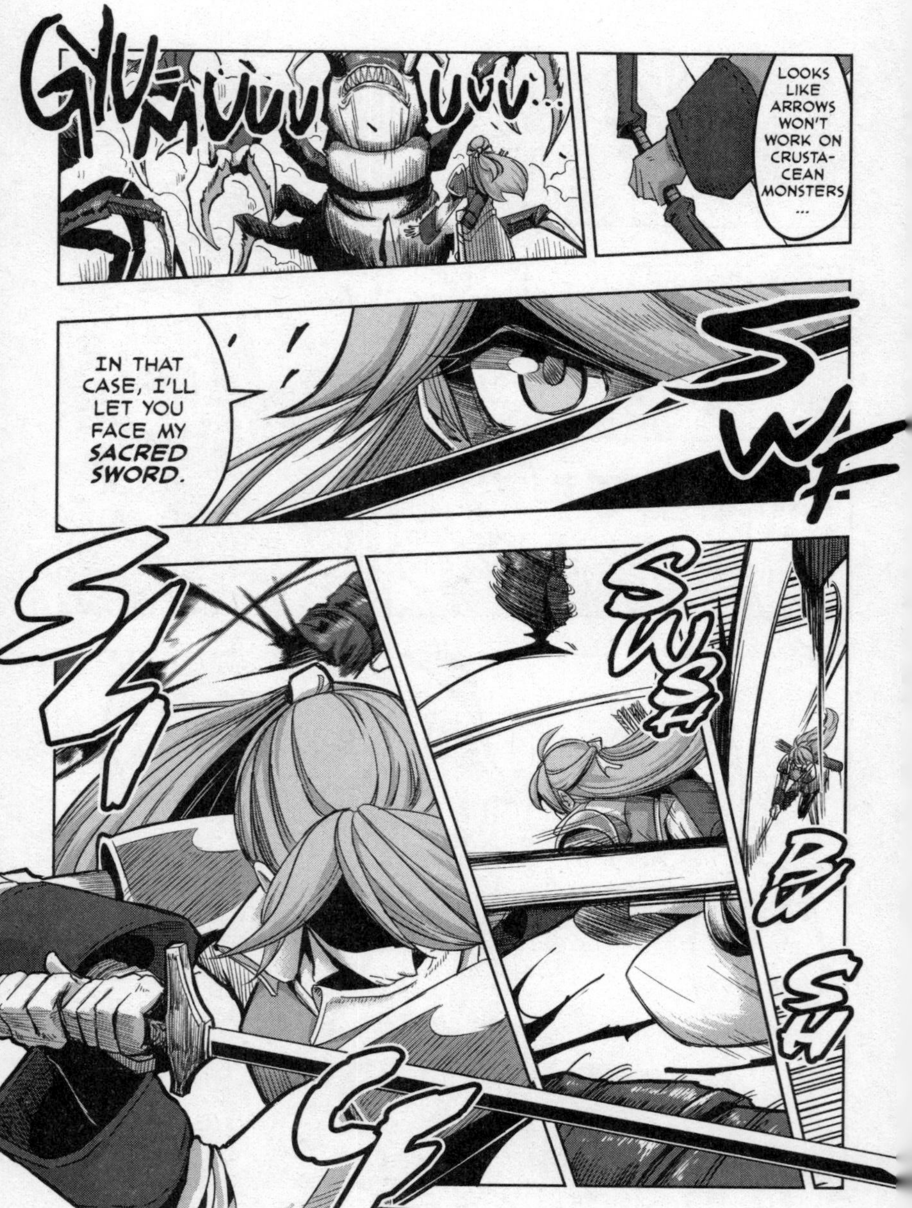
LOOKS LIKE ARROWS WON'T WORK ON CRUSTA-CEAN MONSTERS ...
GYU-MUUUUUUU...
IN THAT CASE, I'LL LET YOU FACE MY *SACRED SWORD.*
SWF
BWSHSH
SWISH

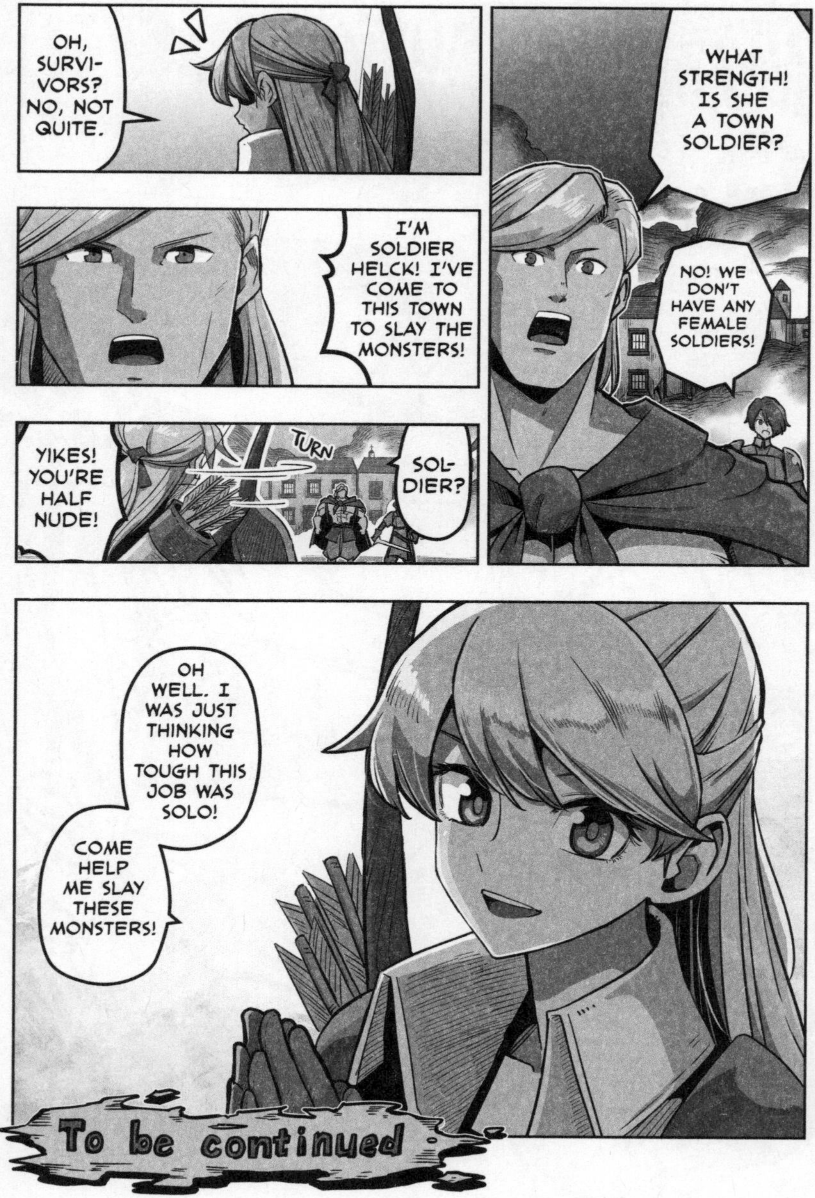
WHAT STRENGTH! IS SHE A TOWN SOLDIER?
NO! WE DON'T HAVE ANY FEMALE SOLDIERS!
OH, SURVIVORS? NO, NOT QUITE.
I'M SOLDIER HELCK! I'VE COME TO THIS TOWN TO SLAY THE MONSTERS!
SOL-DIER?
TURN
YIKES! YOU'RE HALF NUDE!
OH WELL. I WAS JUST THINKING HOW TOUGH THIS JOB WAS SOLO!
COME HELP ME SLAY THESE MONSTERS!
To be continued

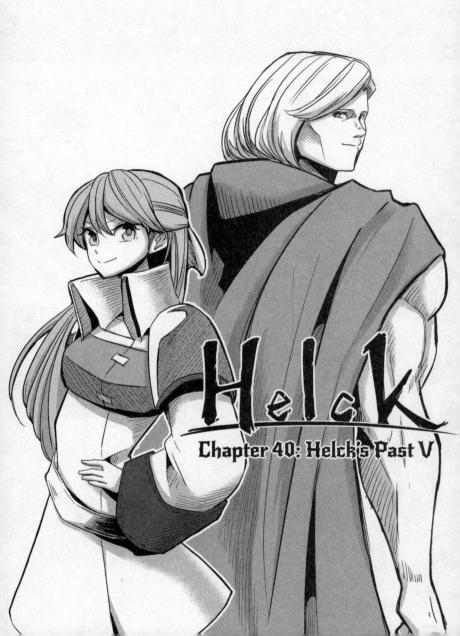

Helck

Chapter 40: Helck's Past V

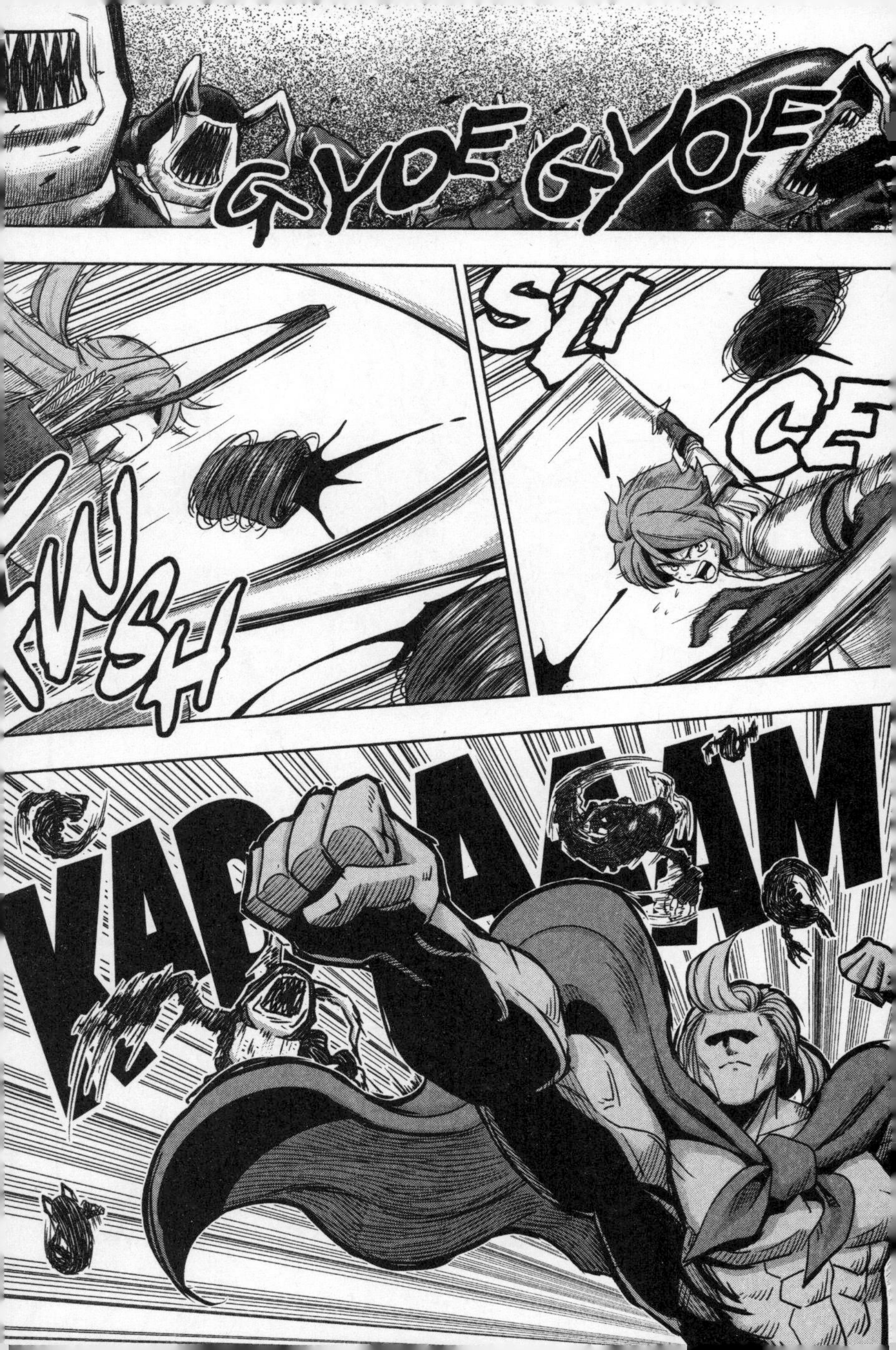
GYOE GYOE
SLICE
SWISH

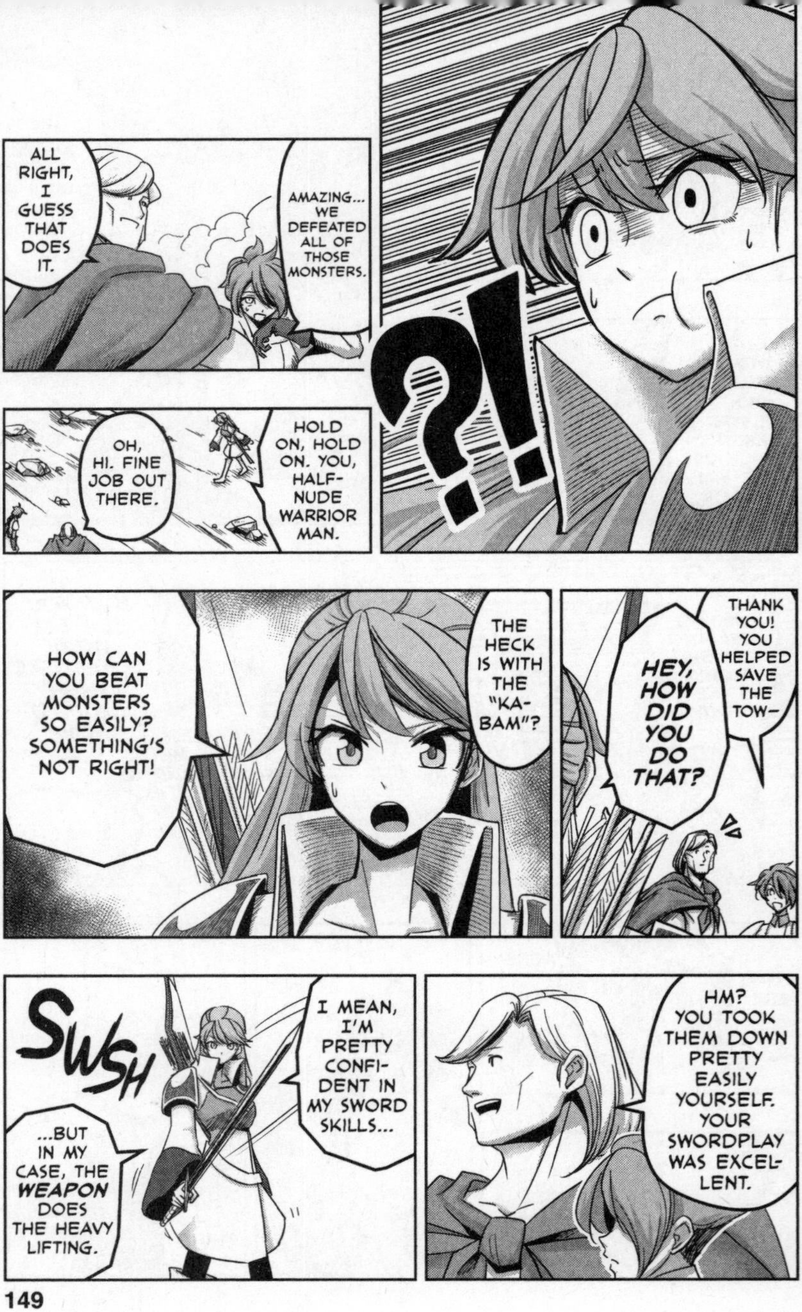
?!!
AMAZING... WE DEFEATED ALL OF THOSE MONSTERS.
ALL RIGHT, I GUESS THAT DOES IT.
HOLD ON, HOLD ON. YOU, HALF-NUDE WARRIOR MAN.
OH, HI. FINE JOB OUT THERE.
THANK YOU! YOU HELPED SAVE THE TOW—
HEY, HOW DID YOU DO THAT?
THE HECK IS WITH THE "KA-BAM"?
HOW CAN YOU BEAT MONSTERS SO EASILY? SOMETHING'S NOT RIGHT!
HM? YOU TOOK THEM DOWN PRETTY EASILY YOURSELF. YOUR SWORDPLAY WAS EXCELLENT.
I MEAN, I'M PRETTY CONFIDENT IN MY SWORD SKILLS...
SWISH
...BUT IN MY CASE, THE ***WEAPON*** DOES THE HEAVY LIFTING.

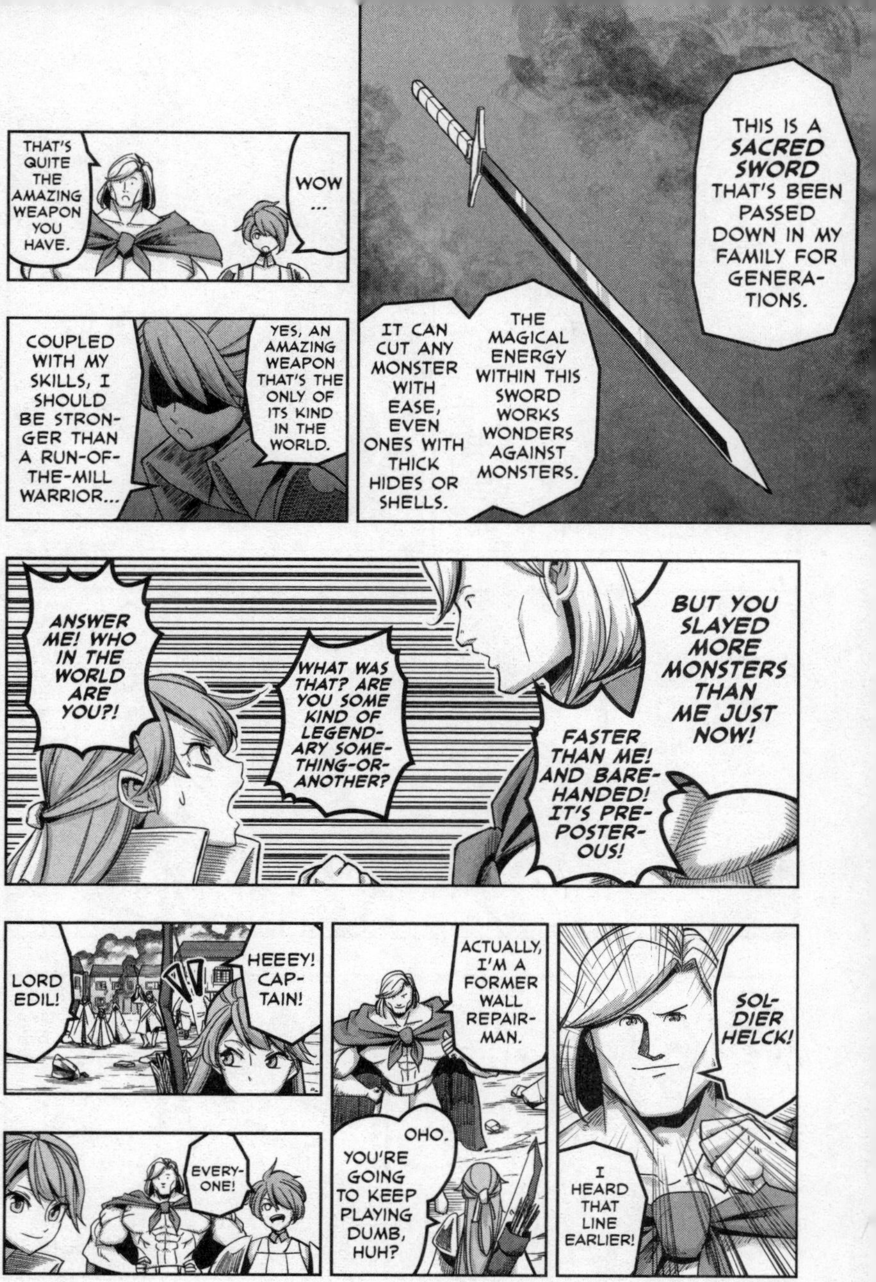
THIS IS A SACRED SWORD THAT'S BEEN PASSED DOWN IN MY FAMILY FOR GENERATIONS.
THE MAGICAL ENERGY WITHIN THIS SWORD WORKS WONDERS AGAINST MONSTERS.
IT CAN CUT ANY MONSTER WITH EASE, EVEN ONES WITH THICK HIDES OR SHELLS.
WOW...
THAT'S QUITE THE AMAZING WEAPON YOU HAVE.
YES, AN AMAZING WEAPON THAT'S THE ONLY OF ITS KIND IN THE WORLD.
COUPLED WITH MY SKILLS, I SHOULD BE STRONGER THAN A RUN-OF-THE-MILL WARRIOR...
BUT YOU SLAYED MORE MONSTERS THAN ME JUST NOW!
FASTER THAN ME! AND BAREHANDED! IT'S PREPOSTEROUS!
WHAT WAS THAT? ARE YOU SOME KIND OF LEGENDARY SOMETHING-OR-ANOTHER?
ANSWER ME! WHO IN THE WORLD ARE YOU?!
SOLDIER HELCK!
I HEARD THAT LINE EARLIER!
ACTUALLY, I'M A FORMER WALL REPAIRMAN.
OHO. YOU'RE GOING TO KEEP PLAYING DUMB, HUH?
HEEEY! CAPTAIN!
LORD EDIL!
EVERYONE!

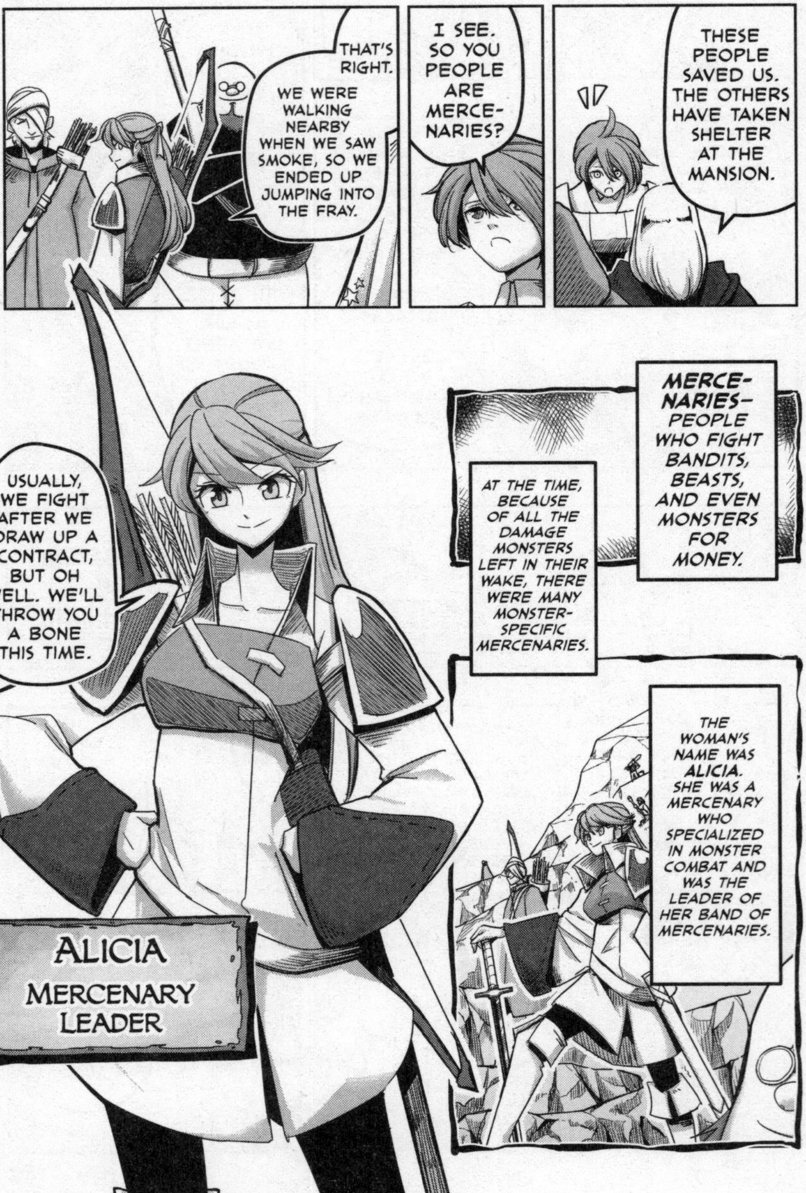
THESE PEOPLE SAVED US. THE OTHERS HAVE TAKEN SHELTER AT THE MANSION.
I SEE. SO YOU PEOPLE ARE MERCE-NARIES?
THAT'S RIGHT.
WE WERE WALKING NEARBY WHEN WE SAW SMOKE, SO WE ENDED UP JUMPING INTO THE FRAY.
MERCE-NARIES— PEOPLE WHO FIGHT BANDITS, BEASTS, AND EVEN MONSTERS FOR MONEY.
AT THE TIME, BECAUSE OF ALL THE DAMAGE MONSTERS LEFT IN THEIR WAKE, THERE WERE MANY MONSTER-SPECIFIC MERCENARIES.
THE WOMAN'S NAME WAS ALICIA. SHE WAS A MERCENARY WHO SPECIALIZED IN MONSTER COMBAT AND WAS THE LEADER OF HER BAND OF MERCENARIES.
USUALLY, WE FIGHT AFTER WE DRAW UP A CONTRACT, BUT OH WELL. WE'LL THROW YOU A BONE THIS TIME.
ALICIA
MERCENARY LEADER

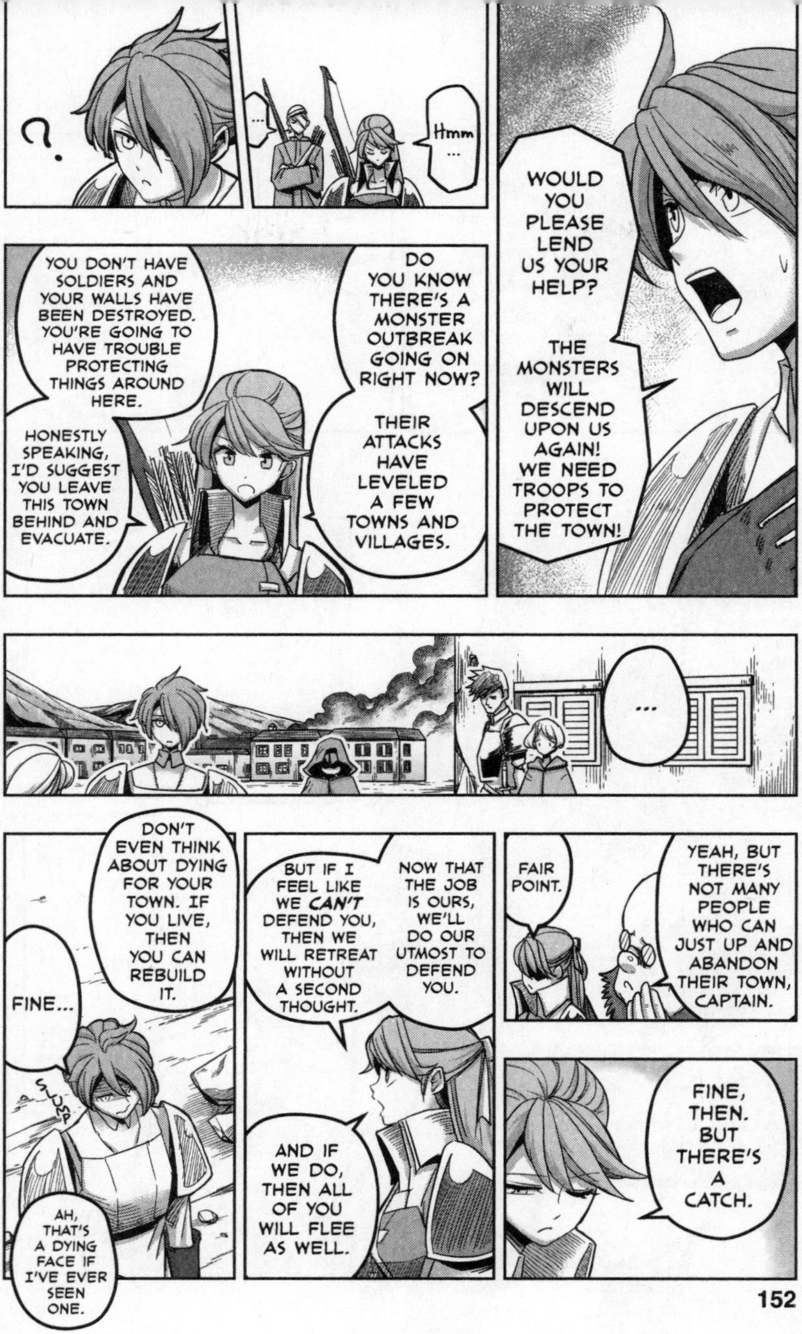
WOULD YOU PLEASE LEND US YOUR HELP?
THE MONSTERS WILL DESCEND UPON US AGAIN! WE NEED TROOPS TO PROTECT THE TOWN!
Hmmm ...
...
?
DO YOU KNOW THERE'S A MONSTER OUTBREAK GOING ON RIGHT NOW?
THEIR ATTACKS HAVE LEVELED A FEW TOWNS AND VILLAGES.
YOU DON'T HAVE SOLDIERS AND YOUR WALLS HAVE BEEN DESTROYED. YOU'RE GOING TO HAVE TROUBLE PROTECTING THINGS AROUND HERE.
HONESTLY SPEAKING, I'D SUGGEST YOU LEAVE THIS TOWN BEHIND AND EVACUATE.
...
YEAH, BUT THERE'S NOT MANY PEOPLE WHO CAN JUST UP AND ABANDON THEIR TOWN, CAPTAIN.
FAIR POINT.
FINE, THEN. BUT THERE'S A CATCH.
NOW THAT THE JOB IS OURS, WE'LL DO OUR UTMOST TO DEFEND YOU.
BUT IF I FEEL LIKE WE *CAN'T* DEFEND YOU, THEN WE WILL RETREAT WITHOUT A SECOND THOUGHT.
AND IF WE DO, THEN ALL OF YOU WILL FLEE AS WELL.
DON'T EVEN THINK ABOUT DYING FOR YOUR TOWN. IF YOU LIVE, THEN YOU CAN REBUILD IT.
FINE...
SLUMP
AH, THAT'S A DYING FACE IF I'VE EVER SEEN ONE.

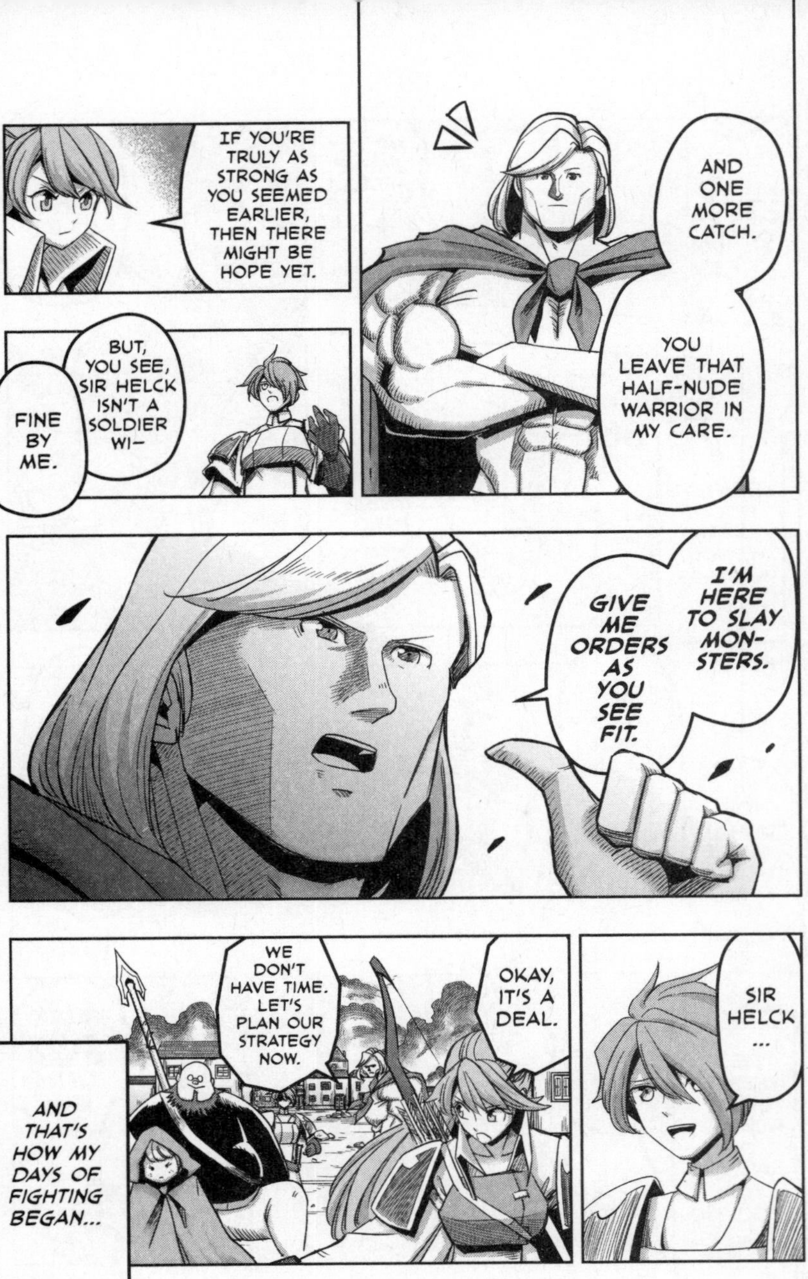
AND ONE MORE CATCH.
YOU LEAVE THAT HALF-NUDE WARRIOR IN MY CARE.
IF YOU'RE TRULY AS STRONG AS YOU SEEMED EARLIER, THEN THERE MIGHT BE HOPE YET.
BUT, YOU SEE, SIR HELCK ISN'T A SOLDIER WI—
FINE BY ME.
I'M HERE TO SLAY MONSTERS.
GIVE ME ORDERS AS YOU SEE FIT.
SIR HELCK ...
OKAY, IT'S A DEAL.
WE DON'T HAVE TIME. LET'S PLAN OUR STRATEGY NOW.
AND THAT'S HOW MY DAYS OF FIGHTING BEGAN...

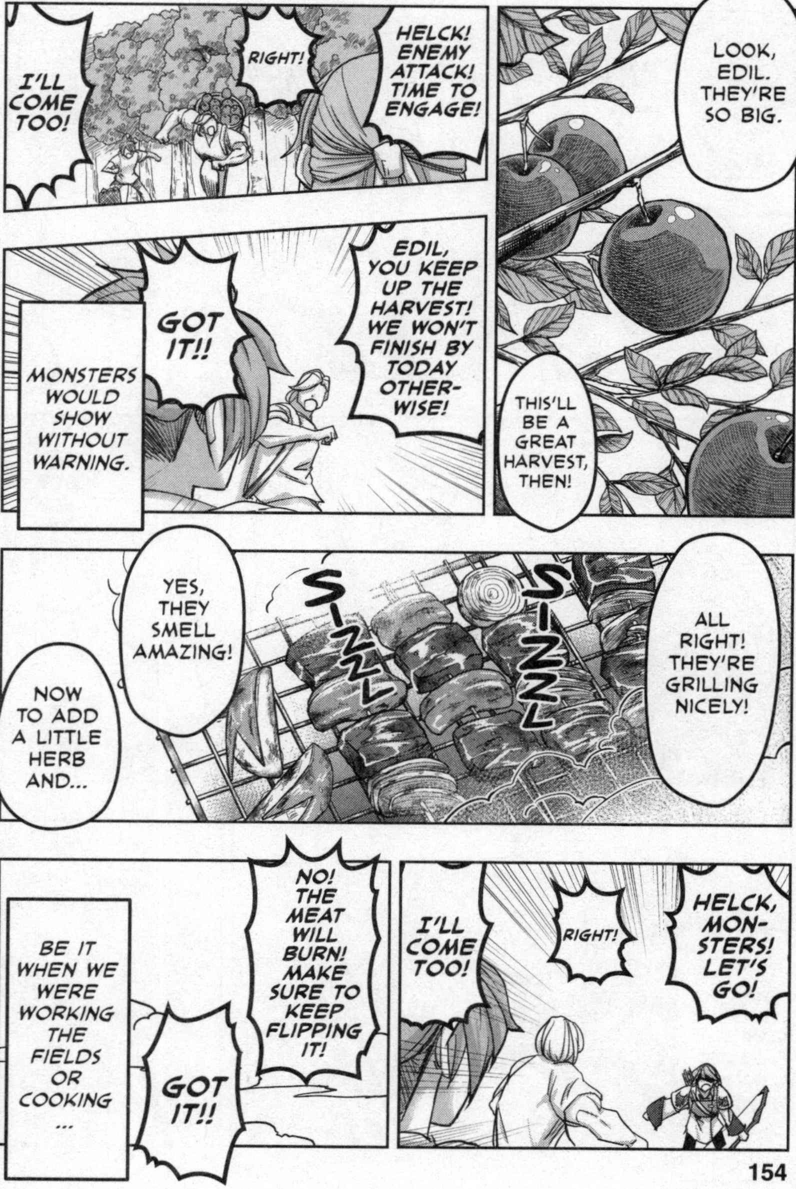
LOOK, EDIL. THEY'RE SO BIG.
THIS'LL BE A GREAT HARVEST, THEN!
HELCK! ENEMY ATTACK! TIME TO ENGAGE!
RIGHT!
I'LL COME TOO!
EDIL, YOU KEEP UP THE HARVEST! WE WON'T FINISH BY TODAY OTHERWISE!
GOT IT!!
MONSTERS WOULD SHOW WITHOUT WARNING.
ALL RIGHT! THEY'RE GRILLING NICELY!
SIZZL
SIZZL
YES, THEY SMELL AMAZING!
NOW TO ADD A LITTLE HERB AND...
HELCK, MONSTERS! LET'S GO!
RIGHT!
I'LL COME TOO!
NO! THE MEAT WILL BURN! MAKE SURE TO KEEP FLIPPING IT!
GOT IT!!
BE IT WHEN WE WERE WORKING THE FIELDS OR COOKING...

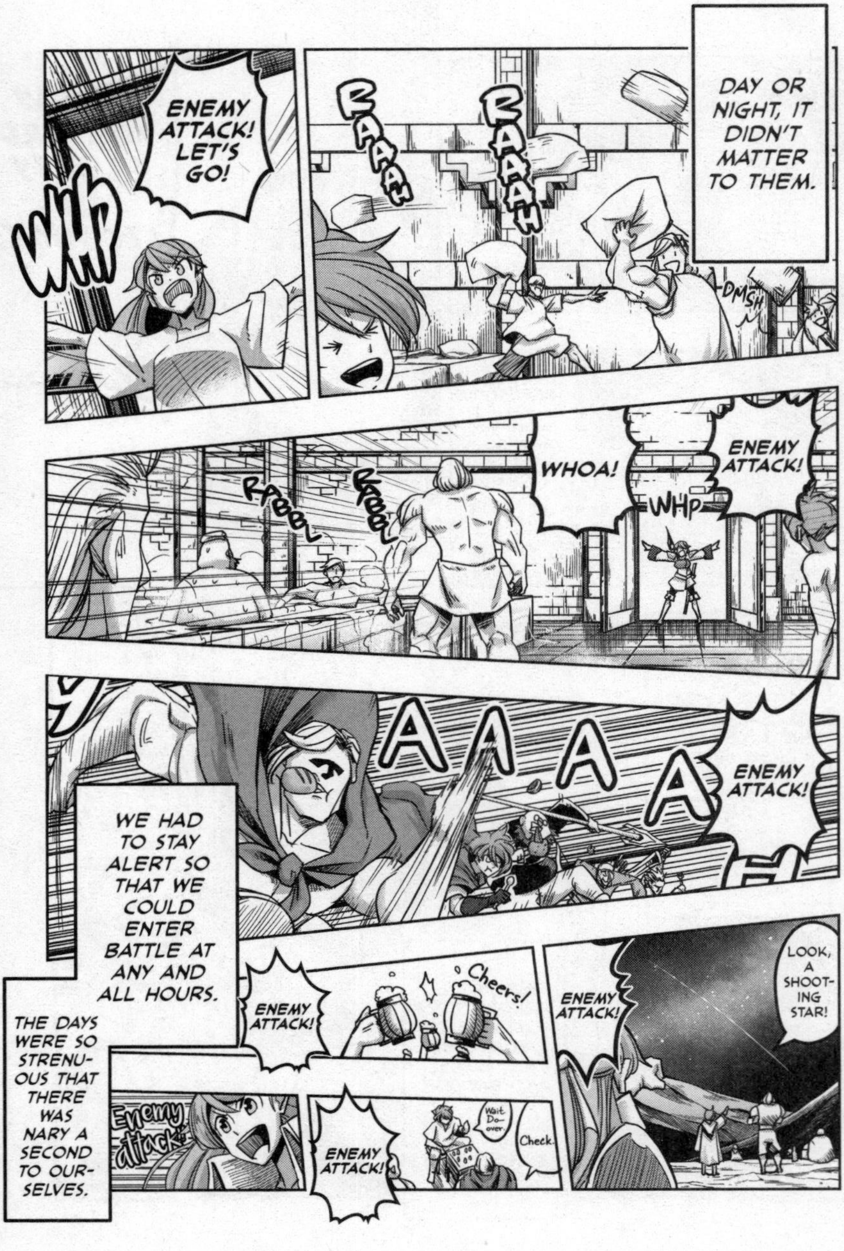
DAY OR NIGHT, IT DIDN'T MATTER TO THEM.
RAAAAH
RAAAAH
DMSH
ENEMY ATTACK! LET'S GO!
WHP
ENEMY ATTACK!
WHOA!
WHP
RABBL
RABBL
ENEMY ATTACK!
AAAAH
WE HAD TO STAY ALERT SO THAT WE COULD ENTER BATTLE AT ANY AND ALL HOURS.
LOOK, A SHOOTING STAR!
ENEMY ATTACK!
Cheers!
ENEMY ATTACK!
Check.
Wait Do-over.
ENEMY ATTACK!
Enemy attack!
THE DAYS WERE SO STRENUOUS THAT THERE WAS NARY A SECOND TO OURSELVES.

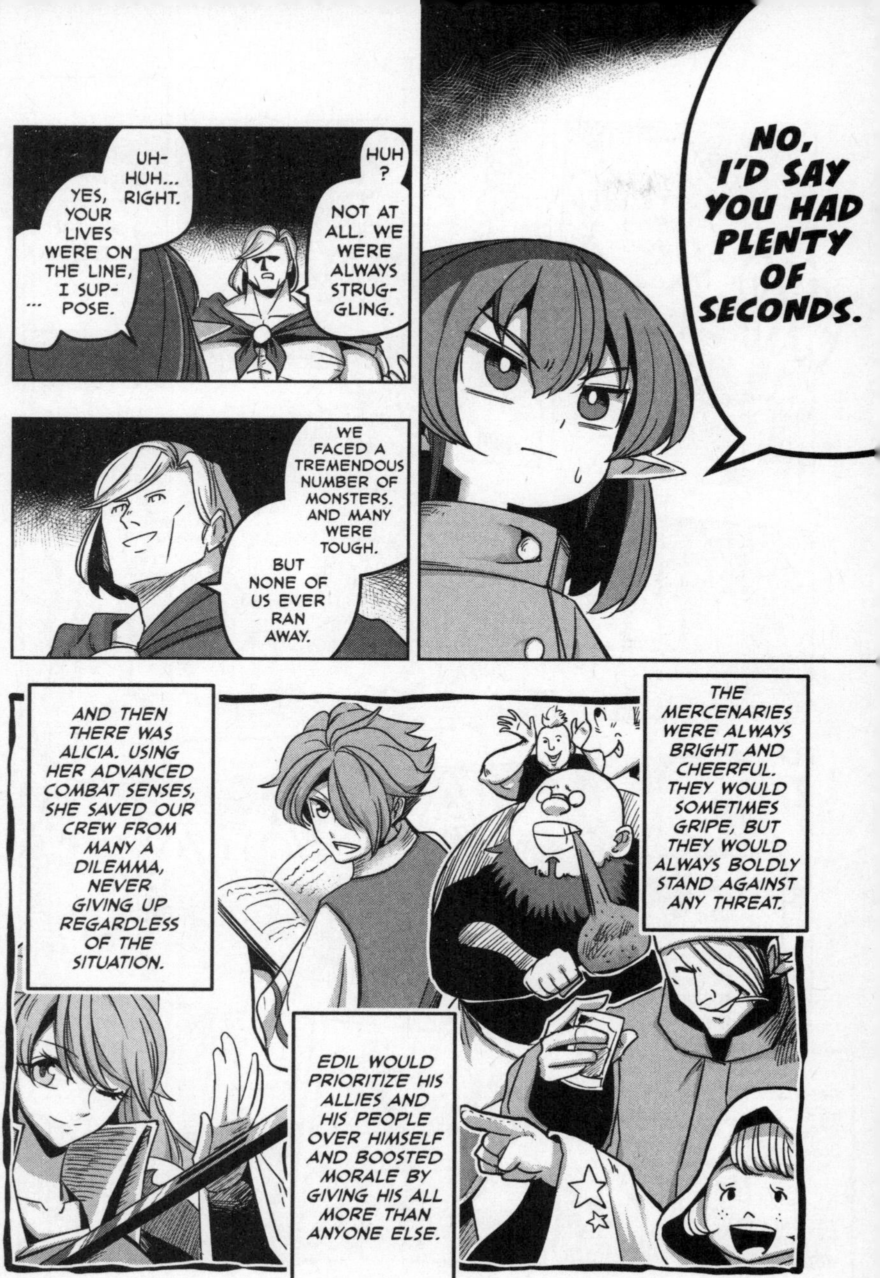

NO, I'D SAY YOU HAD PLENTY OF SECONDS.
HUH? NOT AT ALL. WE WERE ALWAYS STRUGGLING.
UH-HUH... RIGHT.
YES, YOUR LIVES WERE ON THE LINE, I SUPPOSE...
WE FACED A TREMENDOUS NUMBER OF MONSTERS. AND MANY WERE TOUGH.
BUT NONE OF US EVER RAN AWAY.
THE MERCENARIES WERE ALWAYS BRIGHT AND CHEERFUL. THEY WOULD SOMETIMES GRIPE, BUT THEY WOULD ALWAYS BOLDLY STAND AGAINST ANY THREAT.
AND THEN THERE WAS ALICIA. USING HER ADVANCED COMBAT SENSES, SHE SAVED OUR CREW FROM MANY A DILEMMA, NEVER GIVING UP REGARDLESS OF THE SITUATION.
EDIL WOULD PRIORITIZE HIS ALLIES AND HIS PEOPLE OVER HIMSELF AND BOOSTED MORALE BY GIVING HIS ALL MORE THAN ANYONE ELSE.

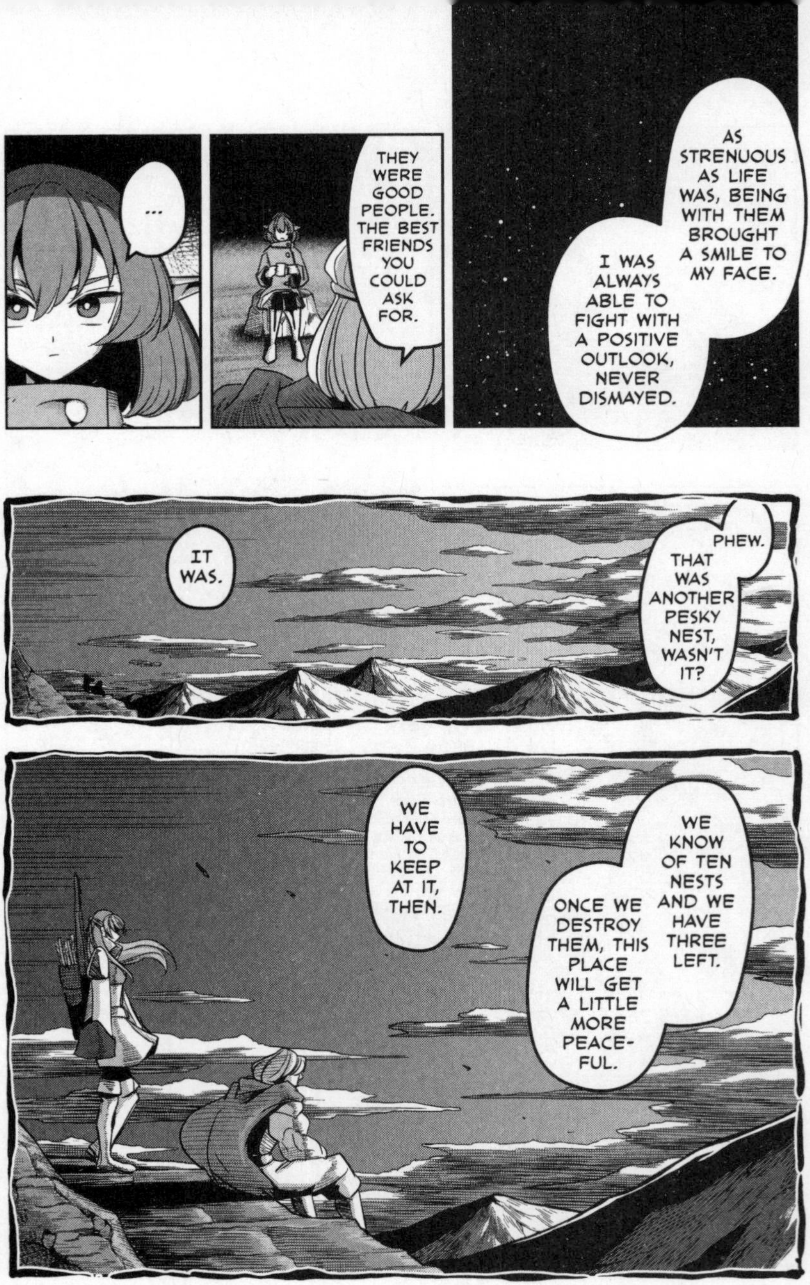
AS STRENUOUS AS LIFE WAS, BEING WITH THEM BROUGHT A SMILE TO MY FACE.
I WAS ALWAYS ABLE TO FIGHT WITH A POSITIVE OUTLOOK, NEVER DISMAYED.
THEY WERE GOOD PEOPLE. THE BEST FRIENDS YOU COULD ASK FOR.
...
PHEW. THAT WAS ANOTHER PESKY NEST, WASN'T IT?
IT WAS.
WE KNOW OF TEN NESTS AND WE HAVE THREE LEFT.
ONCE WE DESTROY THEM, THIS PLACE WILL GET A LITTLE MORE PEACE-FUL.
WE HAVE TO KEEP AT IT, THEN.

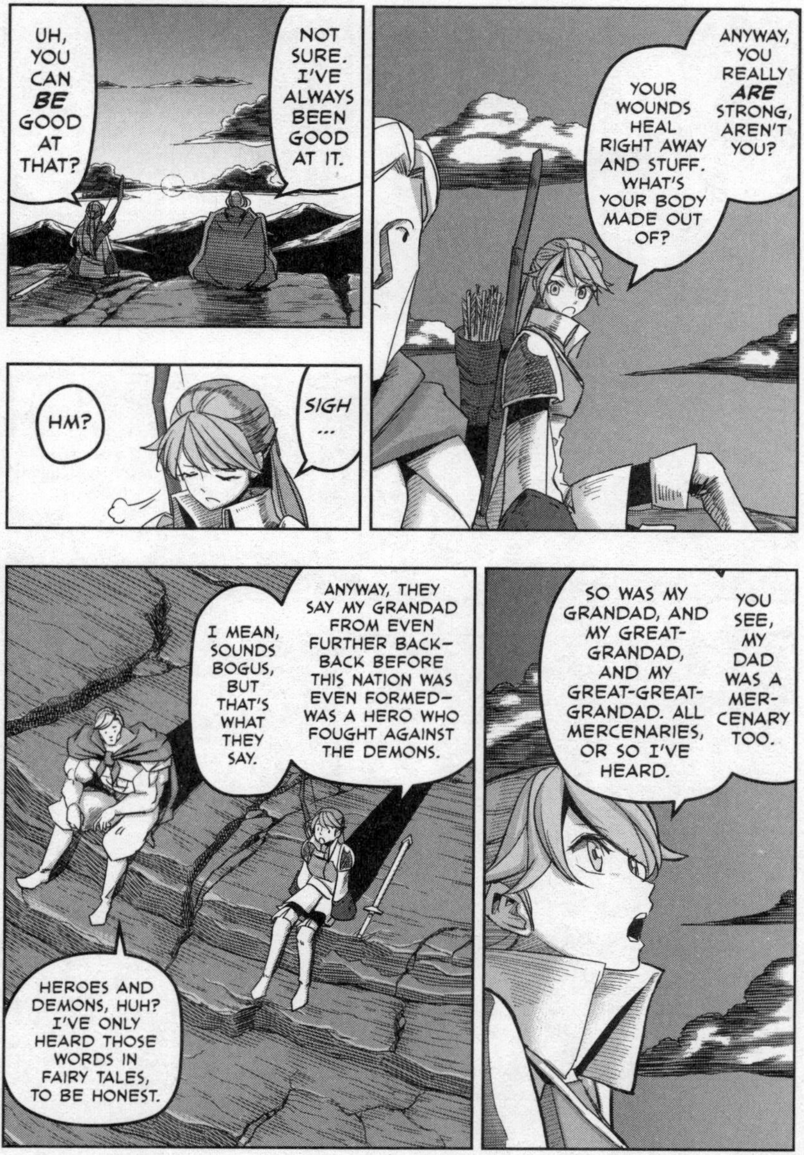
ANYWAY, YOU REALLY *ARE* STRONG, AREN'T YOU?
YOUR WOUNDS HEAL RIGHT AWAY AND STUFF. WHAT'S YOUR BODY MADE OUT OF?
NOT SURE. I'VE ALWAYS BEEN GOOD AT IT.
UH, YOU CAN *BE* GOOD AT THAT?
SIGH ...
HM?
YOU SEE, MY DAD WAS A MERCENARY TOO.
SO WAS MY GRANDAD, AND MY GREAT-GRANDAD, AND MY GREAT-GREAT-GRANDAD. ALL MERCENARIES, OR SO I'VE HEARD.
ANYWAY, THEY SAY MY GRANDAD FROM EVEN FURTHER BACK—BACK BEFORE THIS NATION WAS EVEN FORMED—WAS A HERO WHO FOUGHT AGAINST THE DEMONS.
I MEAN, SOUNDS BOGUS, BUT THAT'S WHAT THEY SAY.
HEROES AND DEMONS, HUH? I'VE ONLY HEARD THOSE WORDS IN FAIRY TALES, TO BE HONEST.

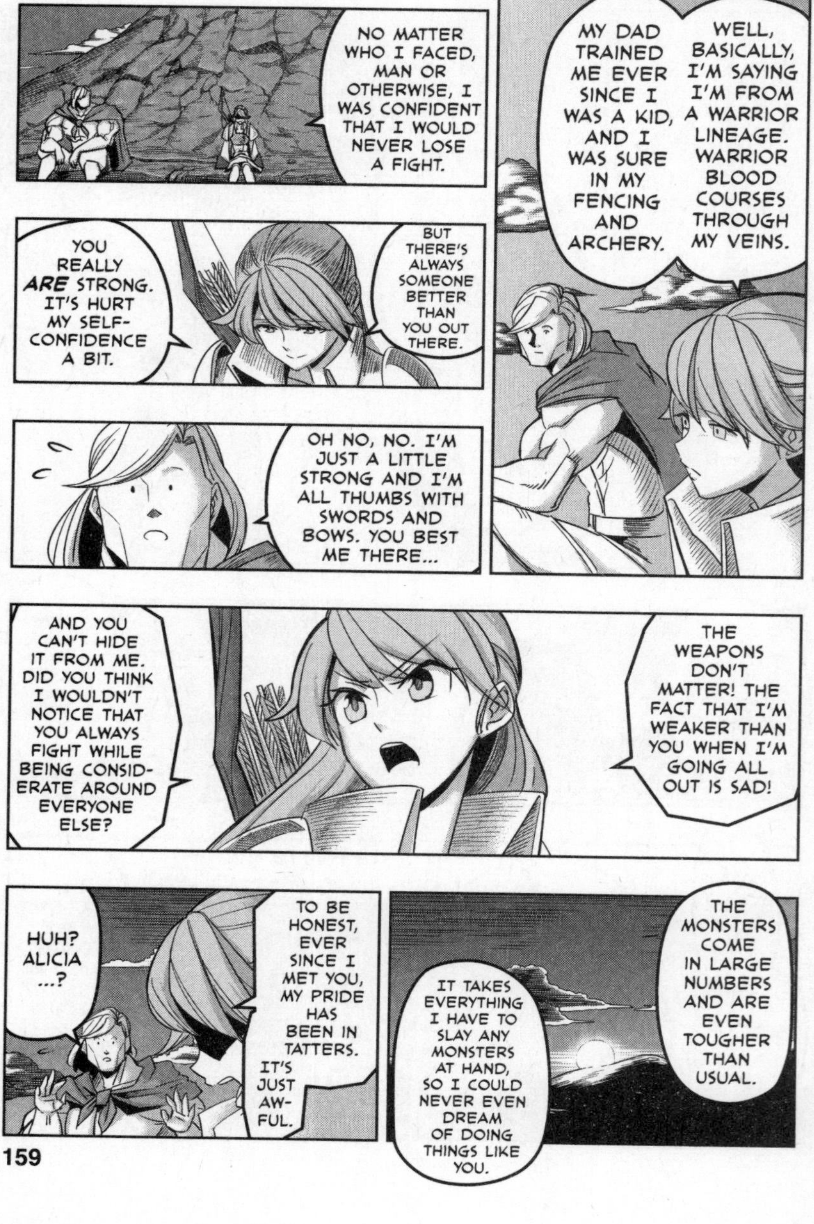
WELL, BASICALLY, I'M SAYING I'M FROM A WARRIOR LINEAGE. WARRIOR BLOOD COURSES THROUGH MY VEINS.
MY DAD TRAINED ME EVER SINCE I WAS A KID, AND I WAS SURE IN MY FENCING AND ARCHERY.
NO MATTER WHO I FACED, MAN OR OTHERWISE, I WAS CONFIDENT THAT I WOULD NEVER LOSE A FIGHT.
BUT THERE'S ALWAYS SOMEONE BETTER THAN YOU OUT THERE.
YOU REALLY *ARE* STRONG. IT'S HURT MY SELF-CONFIDENCE A BIT.
OH NO, NO. I'M JUST A LITTLE STRONG AND I'M ALL THUMBS WITH SWORDS AND BOWS. YOU BEST ME THERE...
THE WEAPONS DON'T MATTER! THE FACT THAT I'M WEAKER THAN YOU WHEN I'M GOING ALL OUT IS SAD!
AND YOU CAN'T HIDE IT FROM ME. DID YOU THINK I WOULDN'T NOTICE THAT YOU ALWAYS FIGHT WHILE BEING CONSIDERATE AROUND EVERYONE ELSE?
THE MONSTERS COME IN LARGE NUMBERS AND ARE EVEN TOUGHER THAN USUAL.
IT TAKES EVERYTHING I HAVE TO SLAY ANY MONSTERS AT HAND, SO I COULD NEVER EVEN DREAM OF DOING THINGS LIKE YOU.
TO BE HONEST, EVER SINCE I MET YOU, MY PRIDE HAS BEEN IN TATTERS.
IT'S JUST AWFUL.
HUH? ALICIA ...?

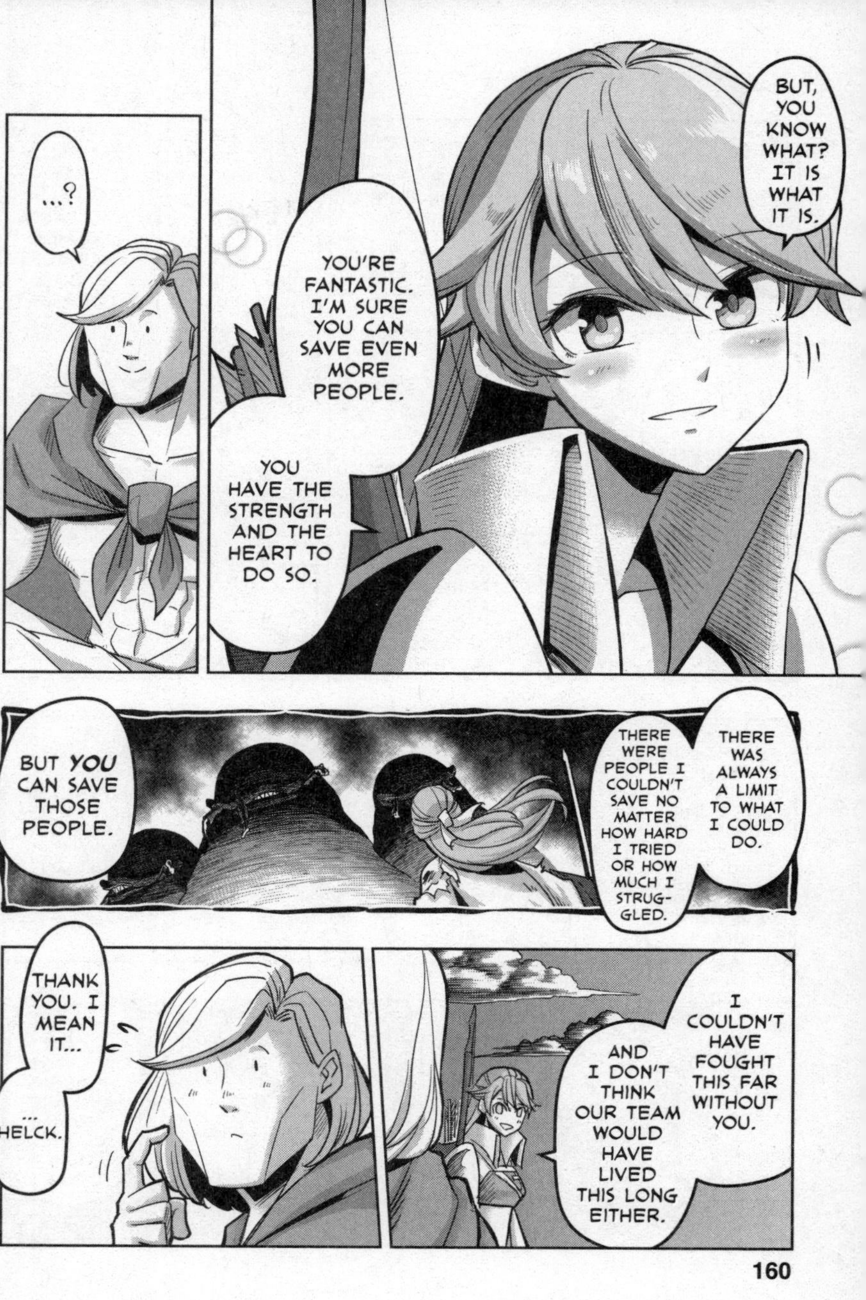

BUT, YOU KNOW WHAT? IT IS WHAT IT IS.
YOU'RE FANTASTIC. I'M SURE YOU CAN SAVE EVEN MORE PEOPLE.
YOU HAVE THE STRENGTH AND THE HEART TO DO SO.
...?
THERE WAS ALWAYS A LIMIT TO WHAT I COULD DO.
THERE WERE PEOPLE I COULDN'T SAVE NO MATTER HOW HARD I TRIED OR HOW MUCH I STRUG-GLED.
BUT YOU CAN SAVE THOSE PEOPLE.
I COULDN'T HAVE FOUGHT THIS FAR WITHOUT YOU.
AND I DON'T THINK OUR TEAM WOULD HAVE LIVED THIS LONG EITHER.
THANK YOU. I MEAN IT...
...HELCK.

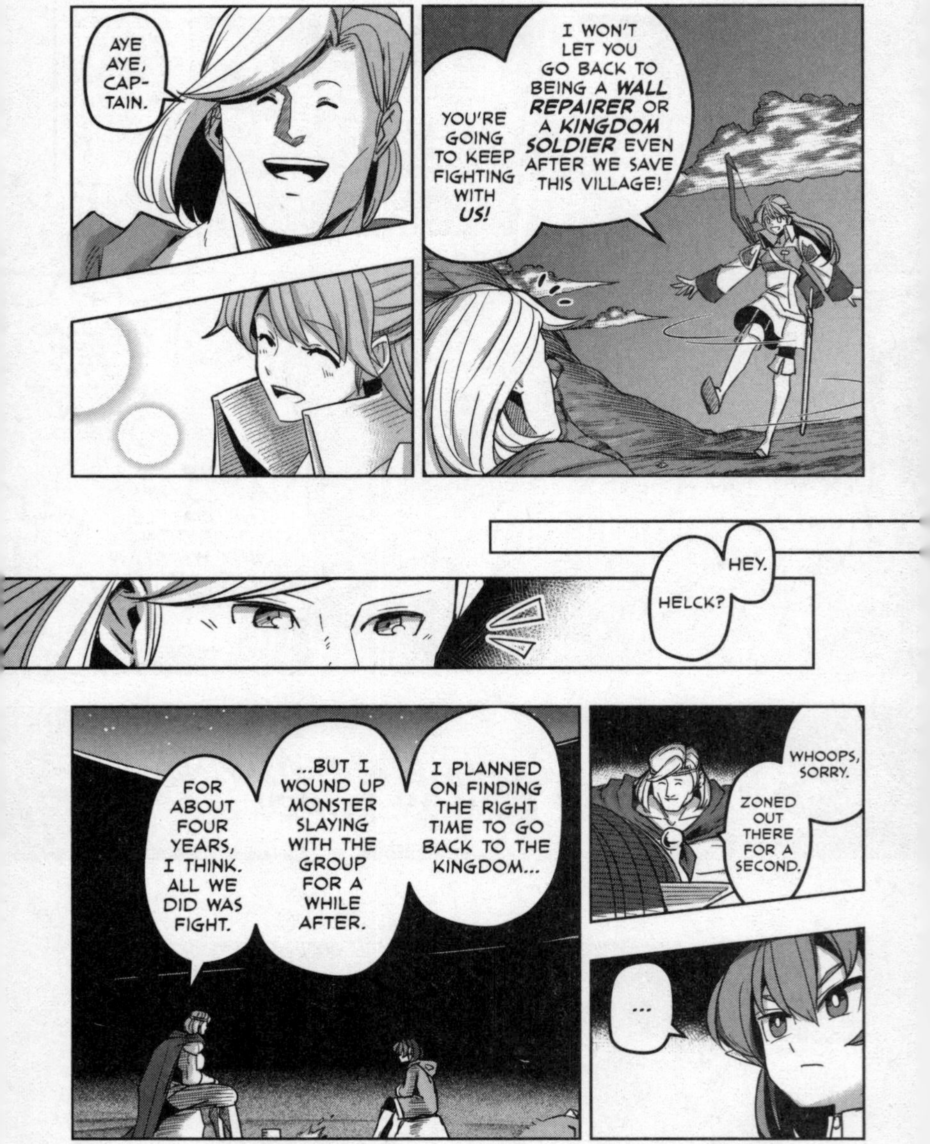
I WON'T LET YOU GO BACK TO BEING A **WALL REPAIRER** OR A **KINGDOM SOLDIER** EVEN AFTER WE SAVE THIS VILLAGE!
YOU'RE GOING TO KEEP FIGHTING WITH ***US!***
AYE AYE, CAP-TAIN.
HEY.
HELCK?
WHOOPS, SORRY.
ZONED OUT THERE FOR A SECOND.
...
I PLANNED ON FINDING THE RIGHT TIME TO GO BACK TO THE KINGDOM...
...BUT I WOUND UP MONSTER SLAYING WITH THE GROUP FOR A WHILE AFTER.
FOR ABOUT FOUR YEARS, I THINK. ALL WE DID WAS FIGHT.

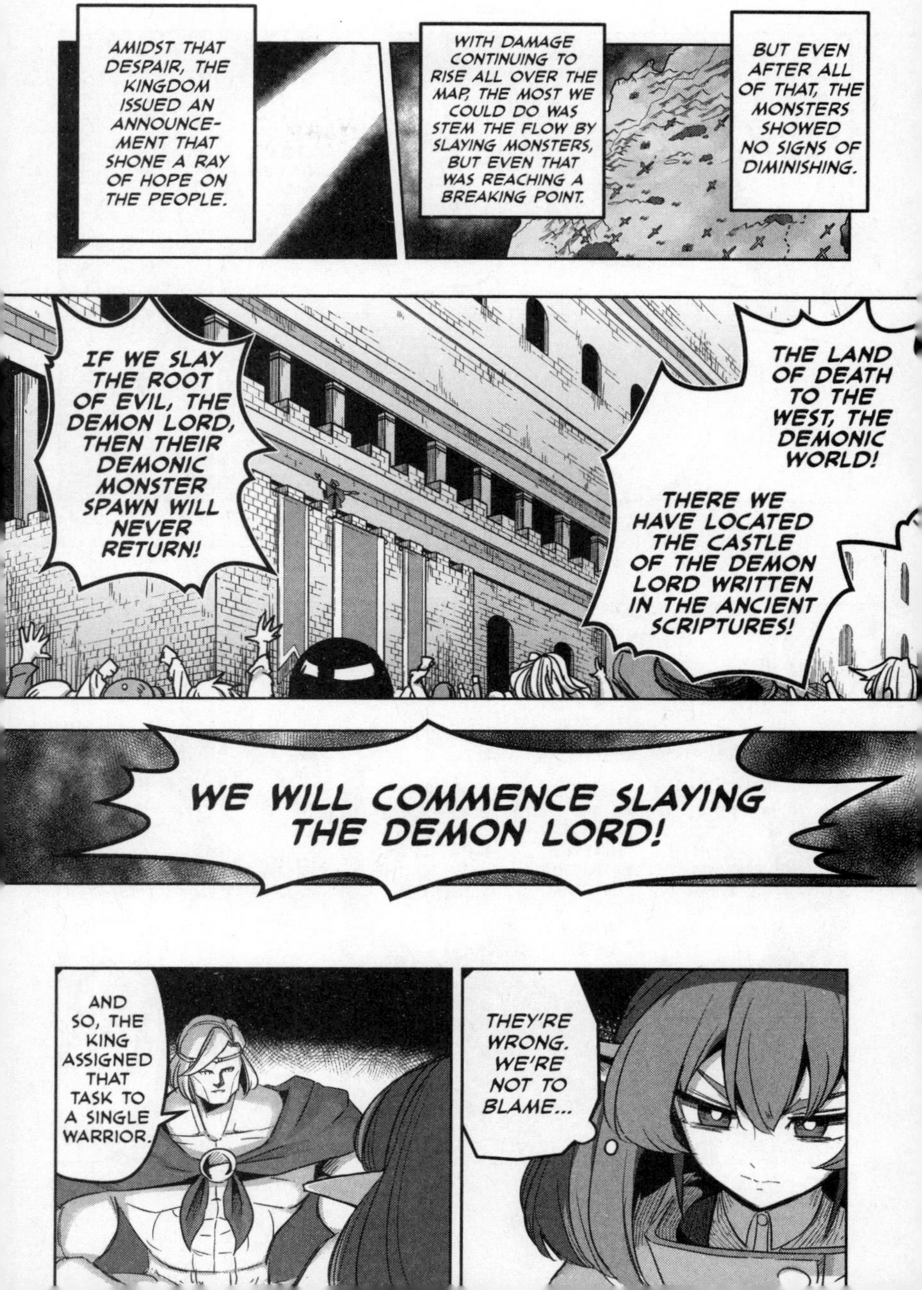
BUT EVEN AFTER ALL OF THAT, THE MONSTERS SHOWED NO SIGNS OF DIMINISHING.
WITH DAMAGE CONTINUING TO RISE ALL OVER THE MAP, THE MOST WE COULD DO WAS STEM THE FLOW BY SLAYING MONSTERS, BUT EVEN THAT WAS REACHING A BREAKING POINT.
AMIDST THAT DESPAIR, THE KINGDOM ISSUED AN ANNOUNCEMENT THAT SHONE A RAY OF HOPE ON THE PEOPLE.
THE LAND OF DEATH TO THE WEST, THE DEMONIC WORLD!
THERE WE HAVE LOCATED THE CASTLE OF THE DEMON LORD WRITTEN IN THE ANCIENT SCRIPTURES!
IF WE SLAY THE ROOT OF EVIL, THE DEMON LORD, THEN THEIR DEMONIC MONSTER SPAWN WILL NEVER RETURN!
WE WILL COMMENCE SLAYING THE DEMON LORD!
THEY'RE WRONG. WE'RE NOT TO BLAME...
AND SO, THE KING ASSIGNED THAT TASK TO A SINGLE WARRIOR.

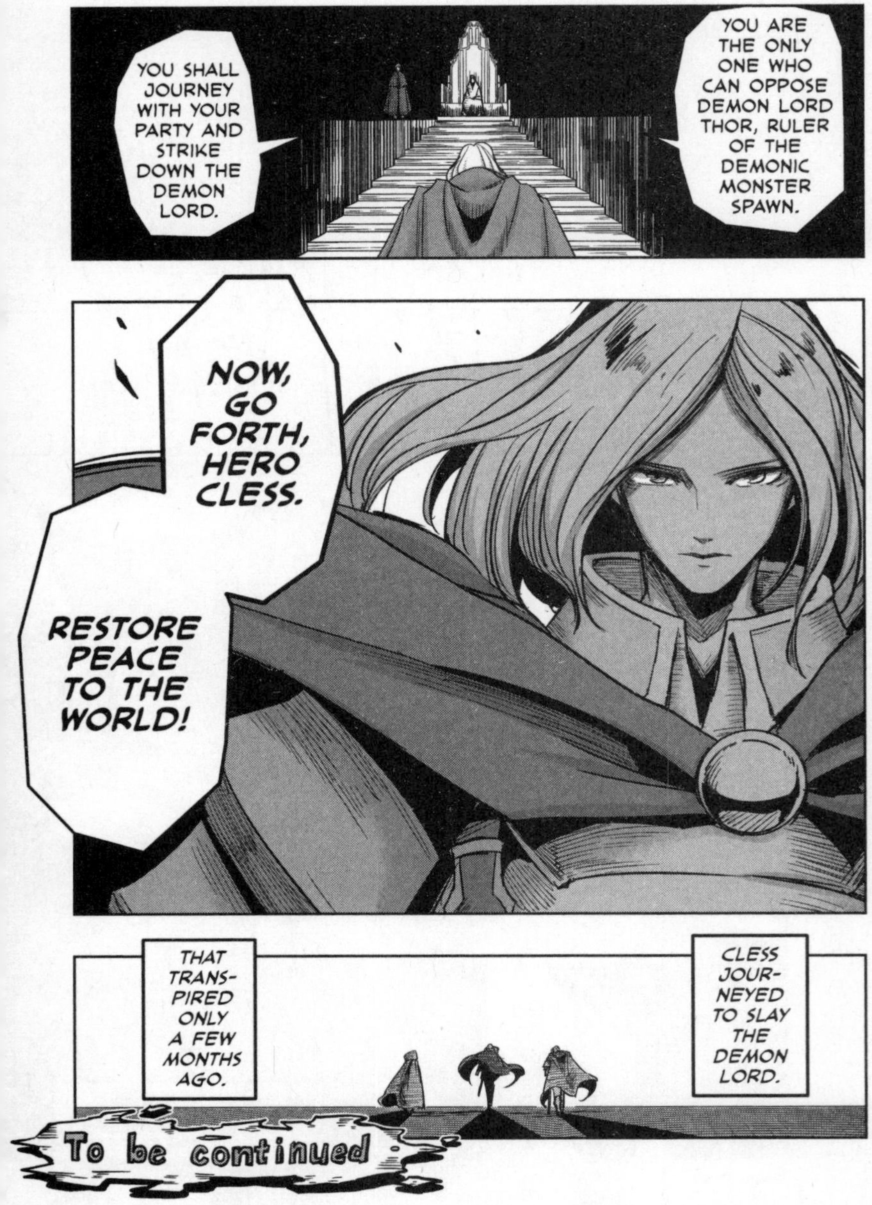
YOU ARE THE ONLY ONE WHO CAN OPPOSE DEMON LORD THOR, RULER OF THE DEMONIC MONSTER SPAWN.
YOU SHALL JOURNEY WITH YOUR PARTY AND STRIKE DOWN THE DEMON LORD.
NOW, GO FORTH, HERO CLESS.
RESTORE PEACE TO THE WORLD!
CLESS JOURNEYED TO SLAY THE DEMON LORD.
THAT TRANSPIRED ONLY A FEW MONTHS AGO.
To be continued

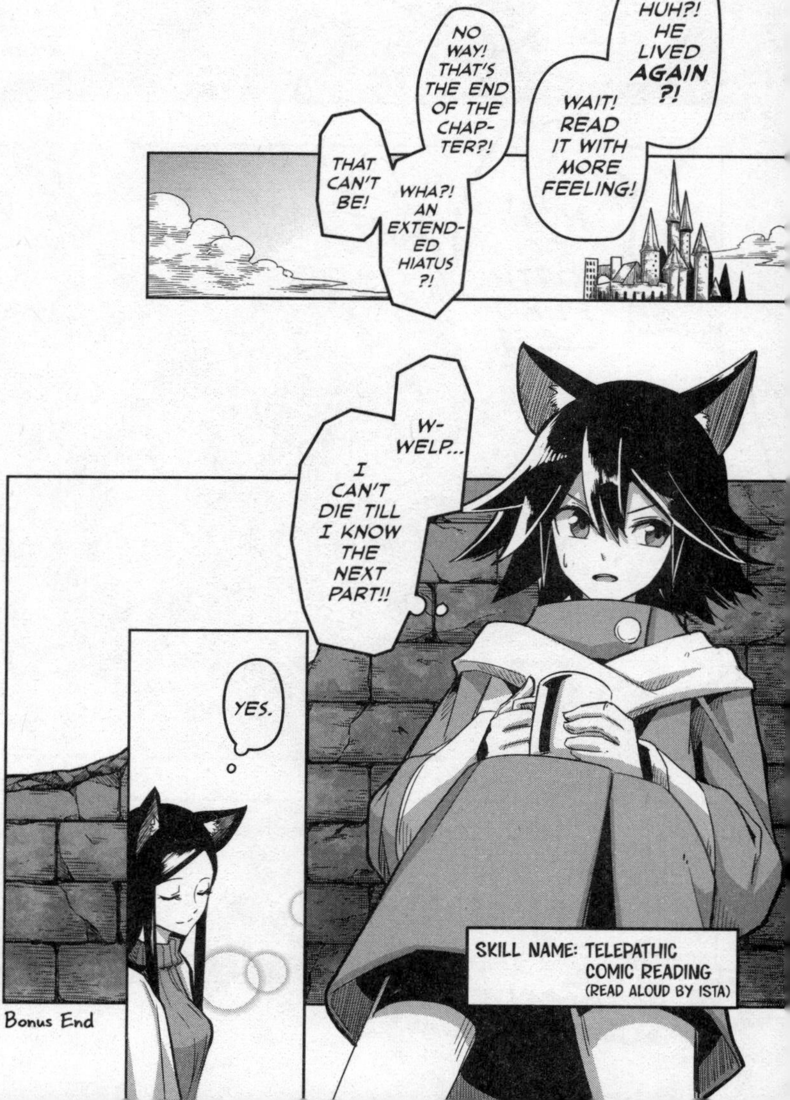
HUH?! HE LIVED AGAIN?!
WAIT! READ IT WITH MORE FEELING!
NO WAY! THAT'S THE END OF THE CHAPTER?!
WHA?! AN EXTENDED HIATUS?!
THAT CAN'T BE!
W-WELP... I CAN'T DIE TILL I KNOW THE NEXT PART!!
SKILL NAME: TELEPATHIC COMIC READING (READ ALOUD BY ISTA)
YES.

Bonus End

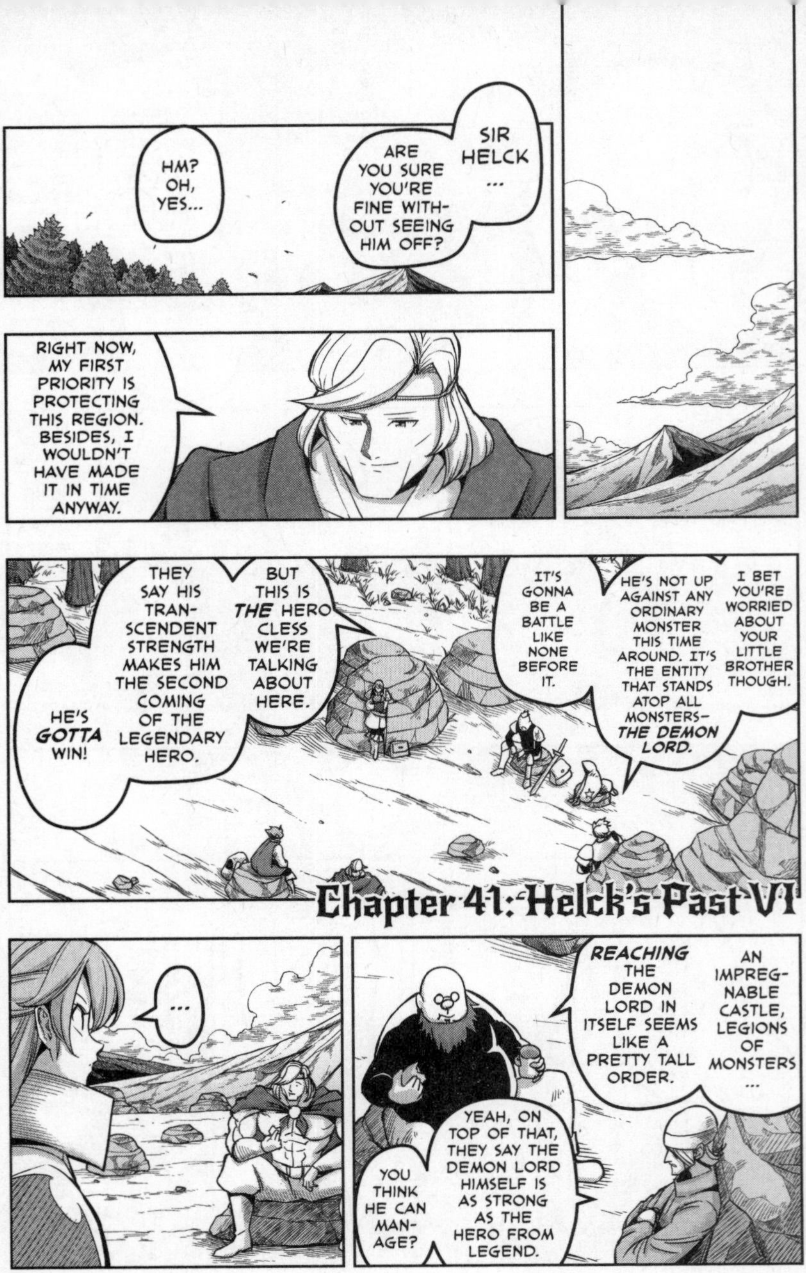
SIR HELCK ...
ARE YOU SURE YOU'RE FINE WITHOUT SEEING HIM OFF?
HM? OH, YES...
RIGHT NOW, MY FIRST PRIORITY IS PROTECTING THIS REGION. BESIDES, I WOULDN'T HAVE MADE IT IN TIME ANYWAY.
I BET YOU'RE WORRIED ABOUT YOUR LITTLE BROTHER THOUGH.
HE'S NOT UP AGAINST ANY ORDINARY MONSTER THIS TIME AROUND. IT'S THE ENTITY THAT STANDS ATOP ALL MONSTERS– *THE DEMON LORD.*
IT'S GONNA BE A BATTLE LIKE NONE BEFORE IT.
BUT THIS IS *THE* HERO CLESS WE'RE TALKING ABOUT HERE.
THEY SAY HIS TRANSCENDENT STRENGTH MAKES HIM THE SECOND COMING OF THE LEGENDARY HERO.
HE'S *GOTTA* WIN!
Chapter 41: Helck's Past VI
AN IMPREGNABLE CASTLE, LEGIONS OF MONSTERS ...
REACHING THE DEMON LORD IN ITSELF SEEMS LIKE A PRETTY TALL ORDER.
YEAH, ON TOP OF THAT, THEY SAY THE DEMON LORD HIMSELF IS AS STRONG AS THE HERO FROM LEGEND.
YOU THINK HE CAN MANAGE?
...

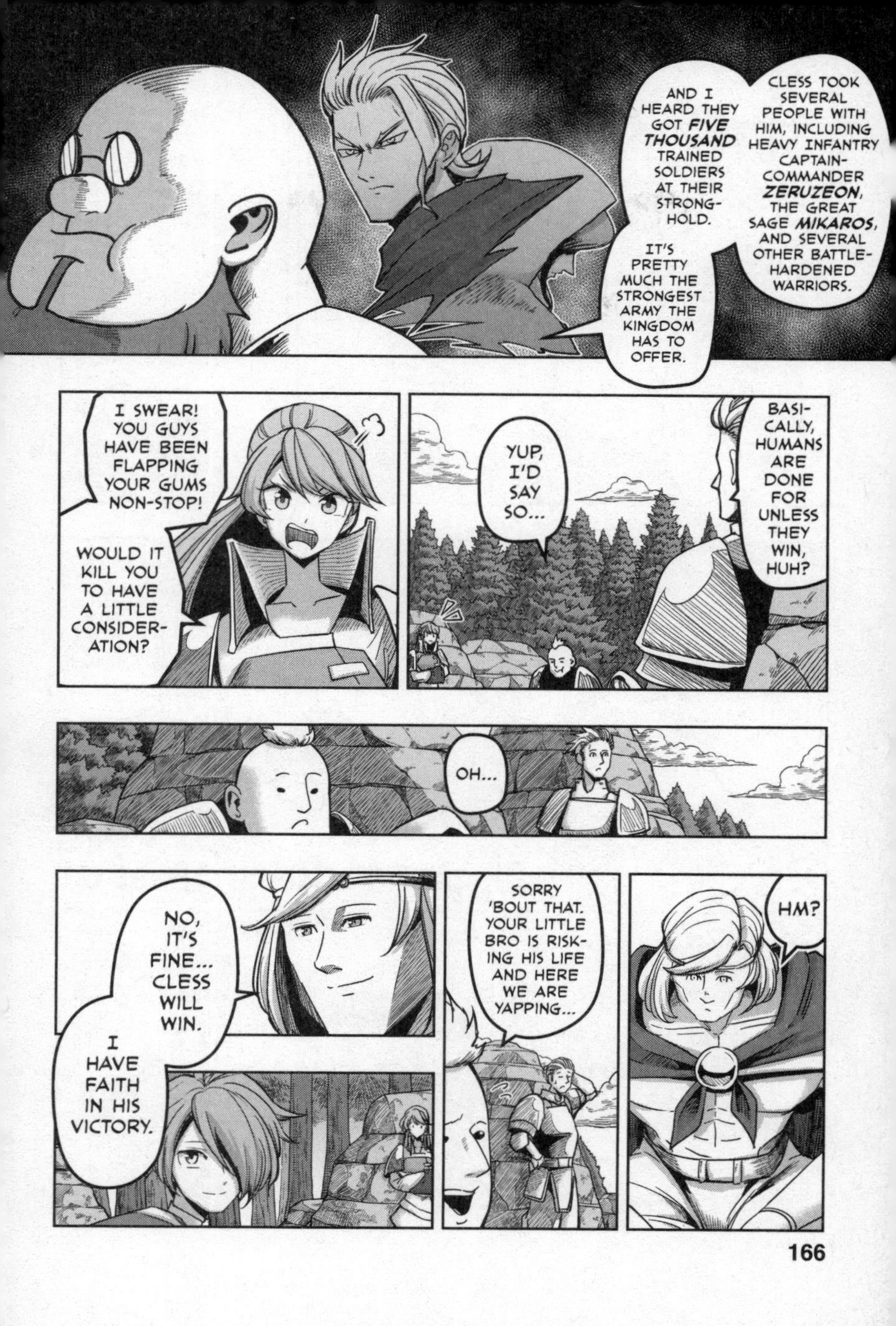
CLESS TOOK SEVERAL PEOPLE WITH HIM, INCLUDING HEAVY INFANTRY CAPTAIN-COMMANDER **ZERUZEON**, THE GREAT SAGE **MIKAROS**, AND SEVERAL OTHER BATTLE-HARDENED WARRIORS.
AND I HEARD THEY GOT ***FIVE THOUSAND*** TRAINED SOLDIERS AT THEIR STRONG-HOLD.
IT'S PRETTY MUCH THE STRONGEST ARMY THE KINGDOM HAS TO OFFER.
BASI-CALLY, HUMANS ARE DONE FOR UNLESS THEY WIN, HUH?
YUP, I'D SAY SO...
I SWEAR! YOU GUYS HAVE BEEN FLAPPING YOUR GUMS NON-STOP!
WOULD IT KILL YOU TO HAVE A LITTLE CONSIDER-ATION?
OH...
HM?
SORRY 'BOUT THAT. YOUR LITTLE BRO IS RISK-ING HIS LIFE AND HERE WE ARE YAPPING...
NO, IT'S FINE... CLESS WILL WIN.
I HAVE FAITH IN HIS VICTORY.

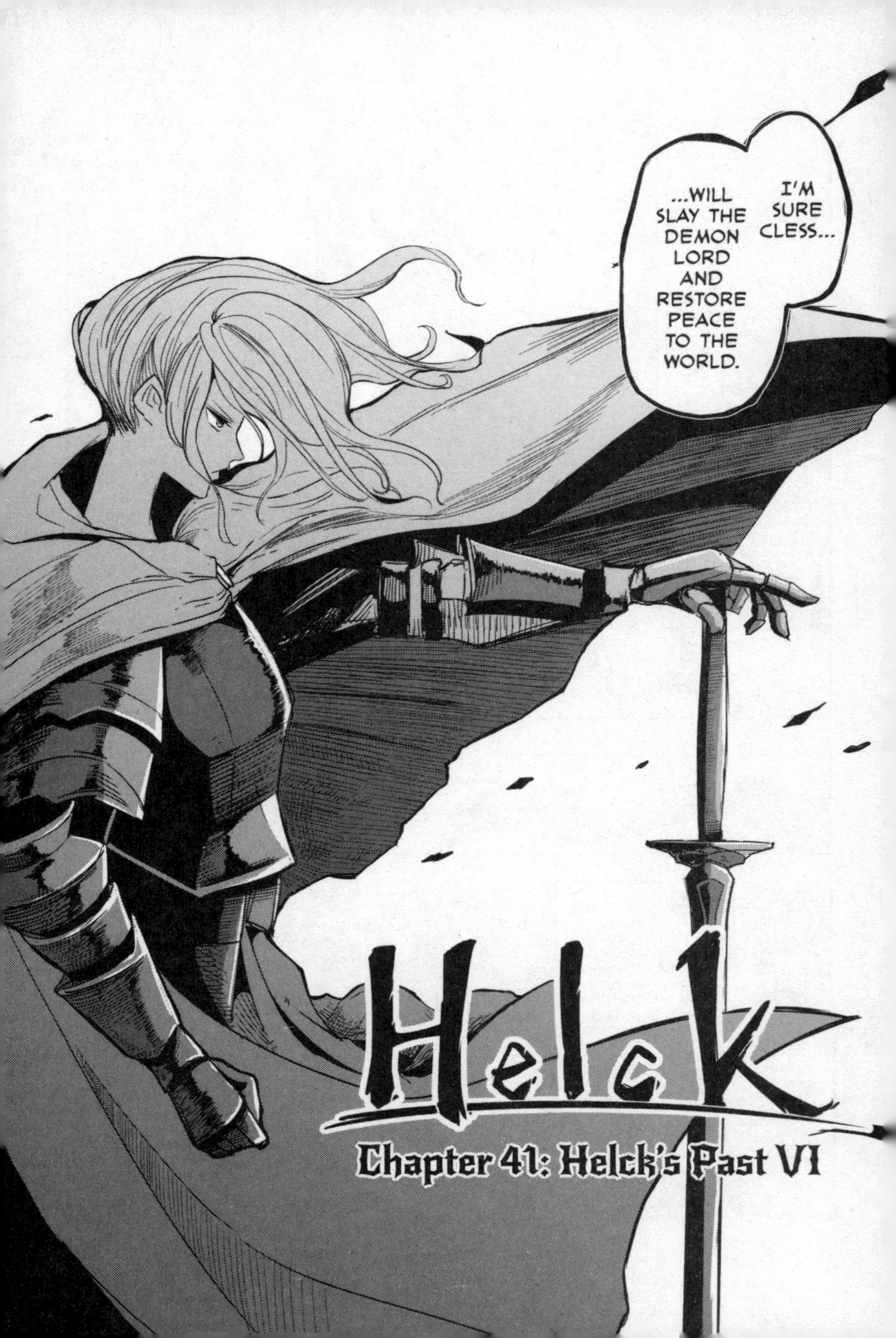
I'M SURE CLESS...
...WILL SLAY THE DEMON LORD AND RESTORE PEACE TO THE WORLD.
Helck
Chapter 41: Helck's Past VI

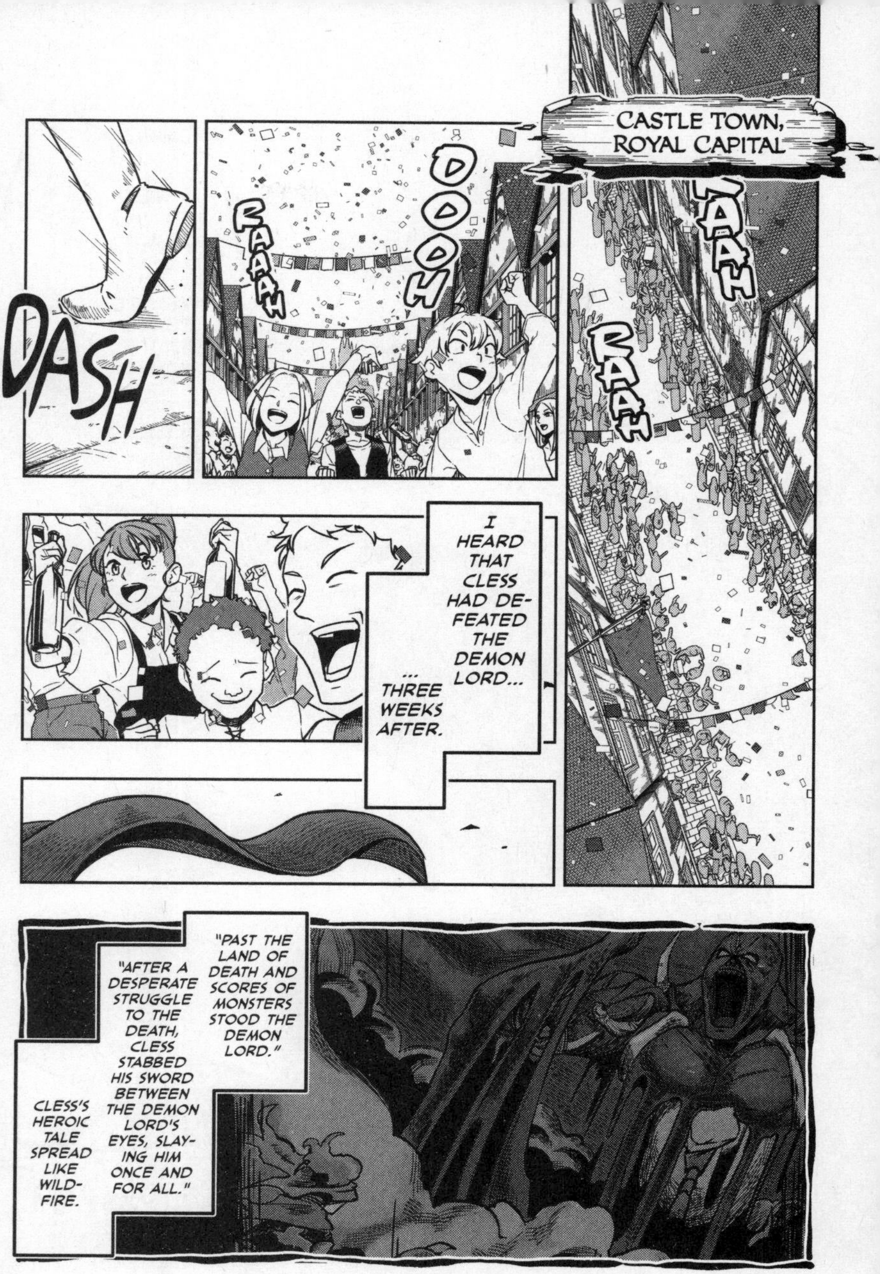
CASTLE TOWN, ROYAL CAPITAL
AAAH
RAAH
DOOOH
RAAAH
DASH
I HEARD THAT CLESS HAD DE-FEATED THE DEMON LORD...
...THREE WEEKS AFTER.
"PAST THE LAND OF DEATH AND SCORES OF MONSTERS STOOD THE DEMON LORD."
"AFTER A DESPERATE STRUGGLE TO THE DEATH, CLESS STABBED HIS SWORD BETWEEN THE DEMON LORD'S EYES, SLAY-ING HIM ONCE AND FOR ALL."
CLESS'S HEROIC TALE SPREAD LIKE WILD-FIRE.

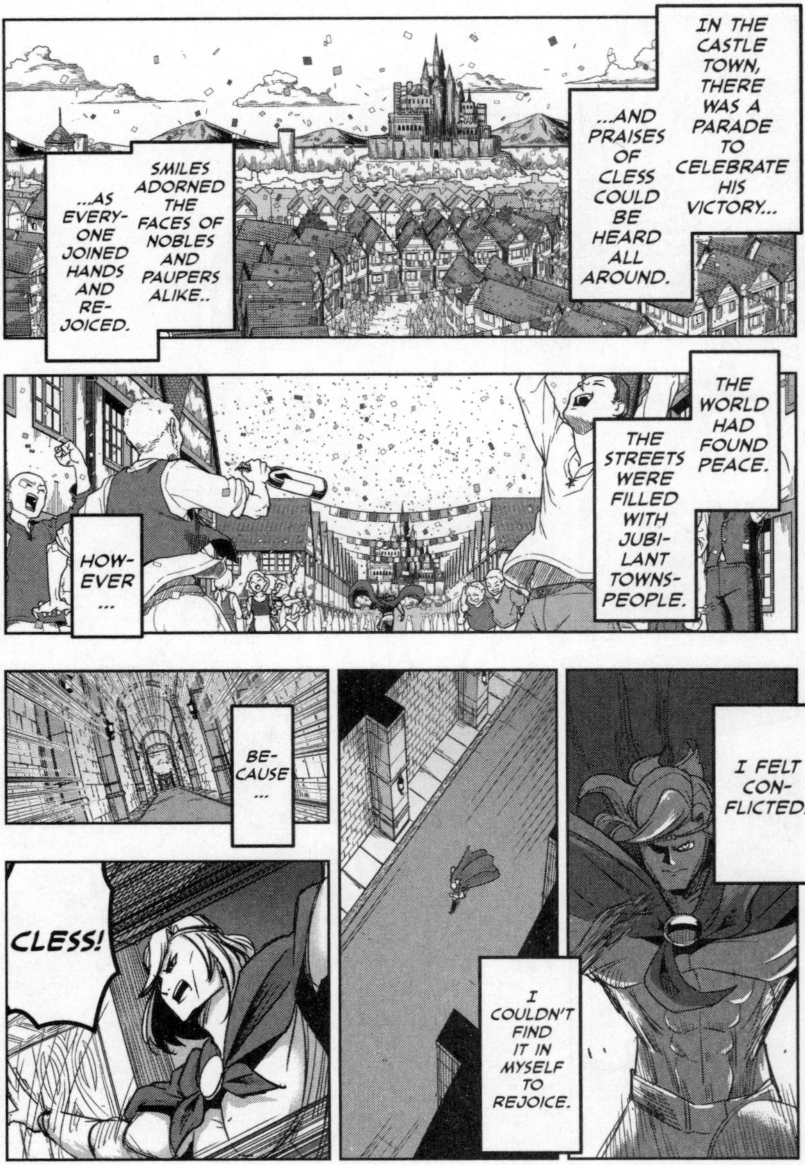
IN THE CASTLE TOWN, THERE WAS A PARADE TO CELEBRATE HIS VICTORY...
...AND PRAISES OF CLESS COULD BE HEARD ALL AROUND.
SMILES ADORNED THE FACES OF NOBLES AND PAUPERS ALIKE..
...AS EVERYONE JOINED HANDS AND REJOICED.
THE WORLD HAD FOUND PEACE.
THE STREETS WERE FILLED WITH JUBILANT TOWNSPEOPLE.
HOWEVER...
I FELT CONFLICTED.
I COULDN'T FIND IT IN MYSELF TO REJOICE.
BECAUSE...
CLESS!

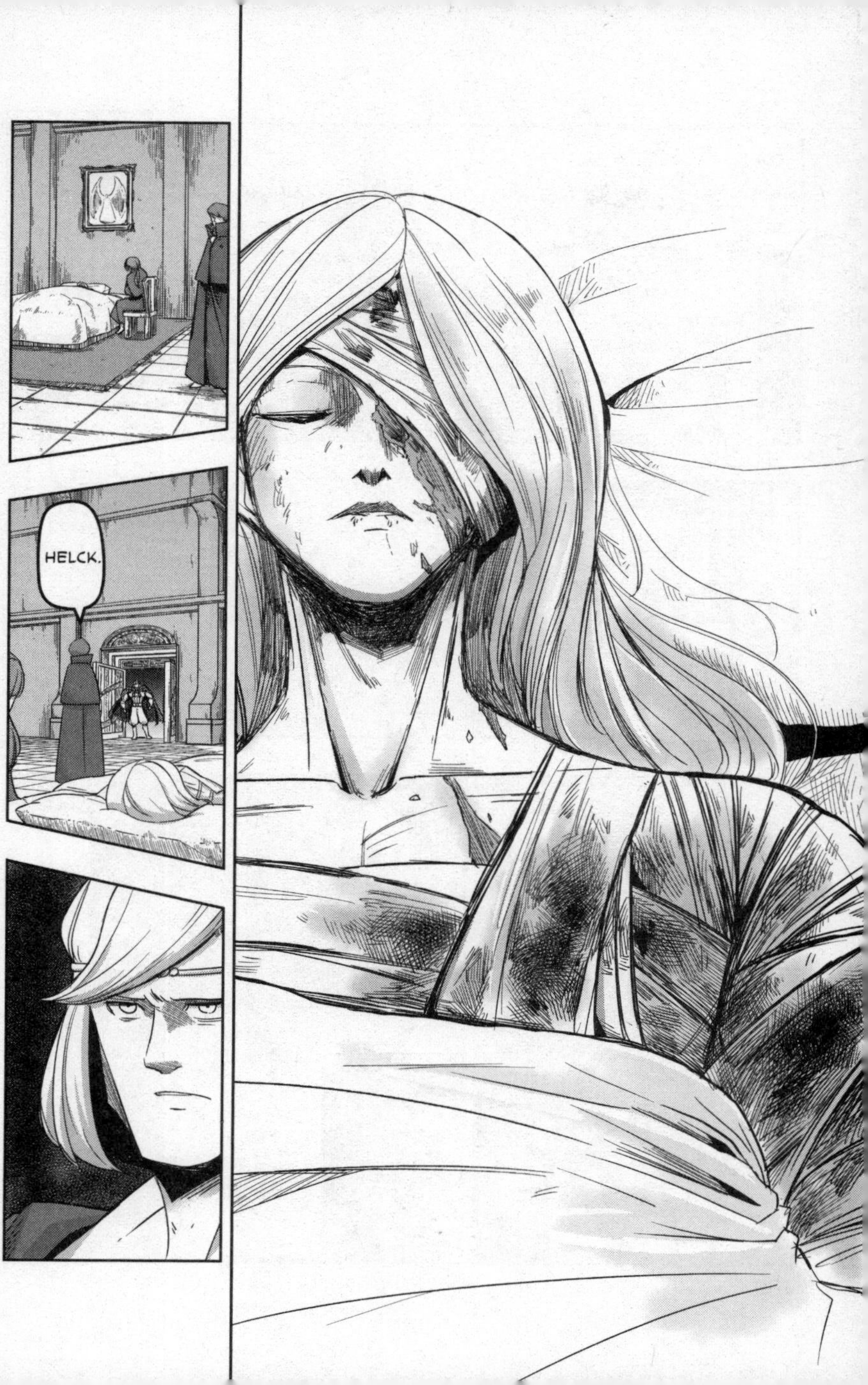
HELCK.

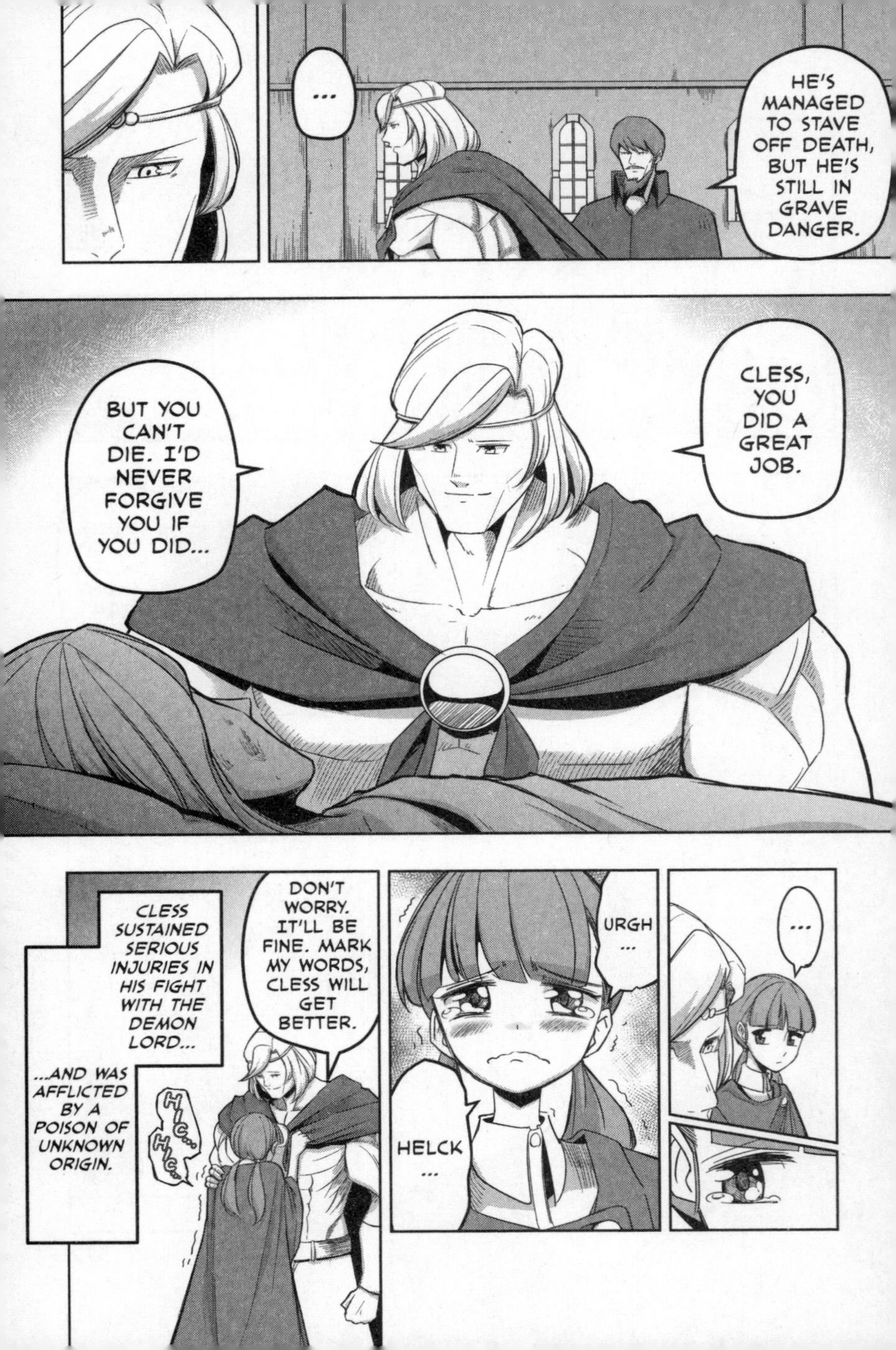
HE'S MANAGED TO STAVE OFF DEATH, BUT HE'S STILL IN GRAVE DANGER.
...
CLESS, YOU DID A GREAT JOB.
BUT YOU CAN'T DIE. I'D NEVER FORGIVE YOU IF YOU DID...
...
URGH ...
HELCK ...
DON'T WORRY. IT'LL BE FINE. MARK MY WORDS, CLESS WILL GET BETTER.
CLESS SUSTAINED SERIOUS INJURIES IN HIS FIGHT WITH THE DEMON LORD...
...AND WAS AFFLICTED BY A POISON OF UNKNOWN ORIGIN.
HIC... HIC...

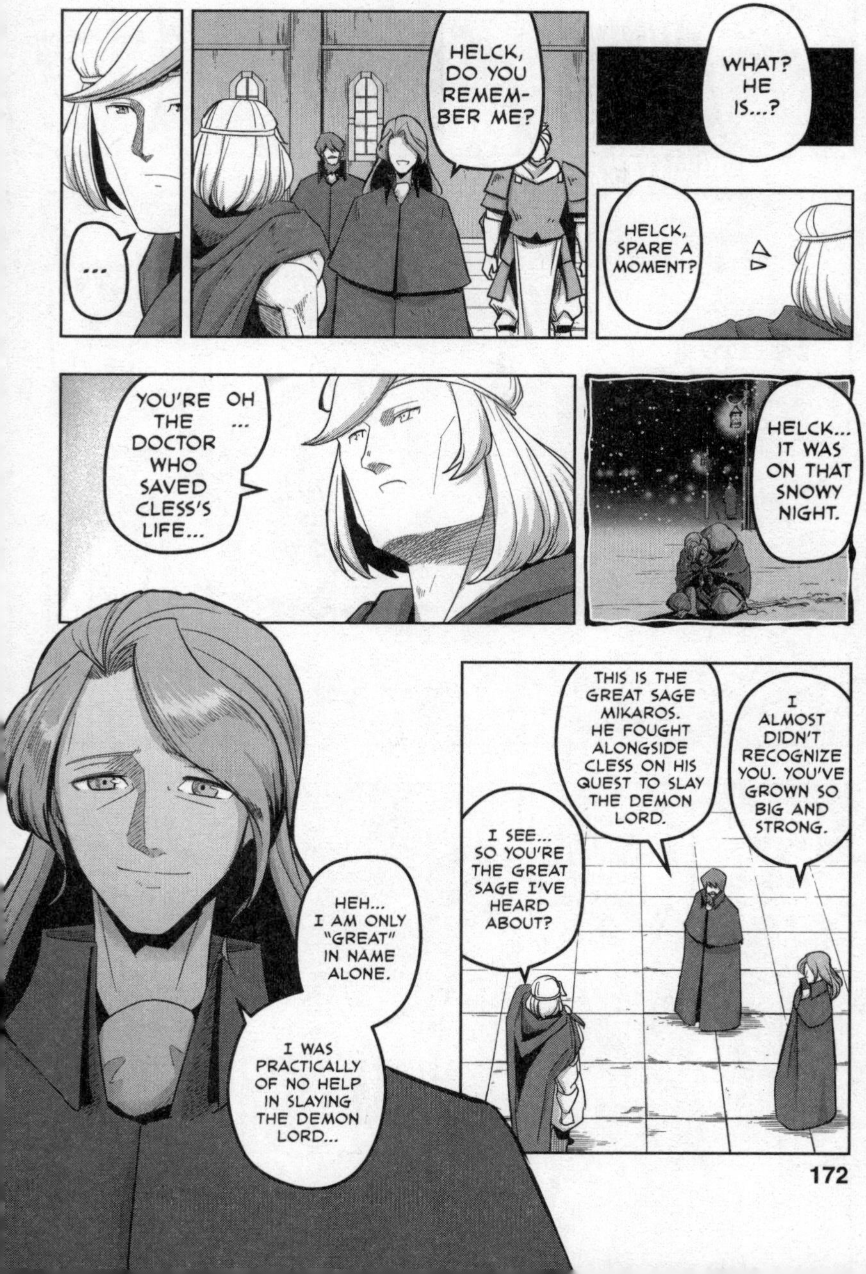
WHAT? HE IS...?
HELCK, SPARE A MOMENT?
HELCK, DO YOU REMEMBER ME?
...
HELCK... IT WAS ON THAT SNOWY NIGHT.
OH...
YOU'RE THE DOCTOR WHO SAVED CLESS'S LIFE...
I ALMOST DIDN'T RECOGNIZE YOU. YOU'VE GROWN SO BIG AND STRONG.
THIS IS THE GREAT SAGE MIKAROS. HE FOUGHT ALONGSIDE CLESS ON HIS QUEST TO SLAY THE DEMON LORD.
I SEE... SO YOU'RE THE GREAT SAGE I'VE HEARD ABOUT?
HEH... I AM ONLY "GREAT" IN NAME ALONE.
I WAS PRACTICALLY OF NO HELP IN SLAYING THE DEMON LORD...

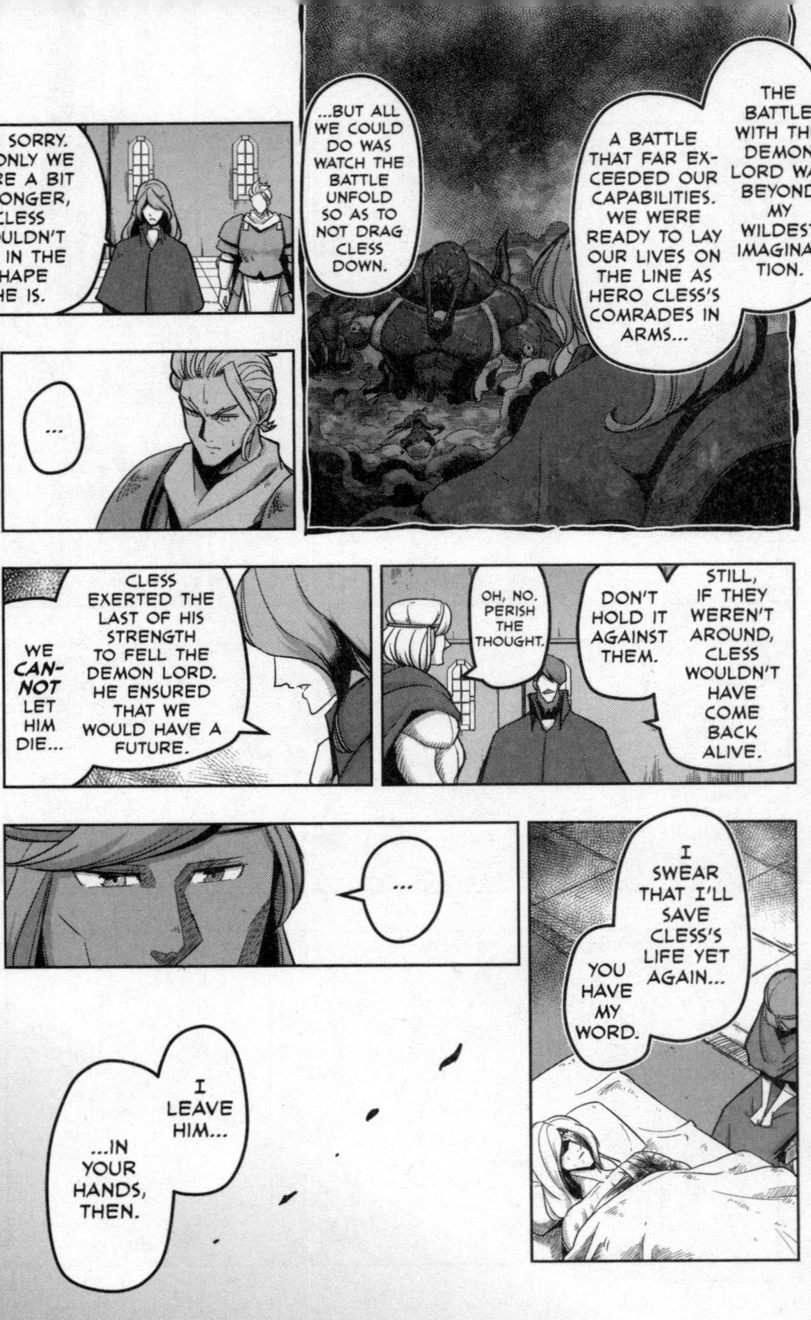
THE BATTLE WITH THE DEMON LORD WAS BEYOND MY WILDEST IMAGINATION.
A BATTLE THAT FAR EXCEEDED OUR CAPABILITIES. WE WERE READY TO LAY OUR LIVES ON THE LINE AS HERO CLESS'S COMRADES IN ARMS...
...BUT ALL WE COULD DO WAS WATCH THE BATTLE UNFOLD SO AS TO NOT DRAG CLESS DOWN.
I'M SORRY. IF ONLY WE WERE A BIT STRONGER, CLESS WOULDN'T BE IN THE SHAPE HE IS.
...
STILL, IF THEY WEREN'T AROUND, CLESS WOULDN'T HAVE COME BACK ALIVE.
DON'T HOLD IT AGAINST THEM.
OH, NO. PERISH THE THOUGHT.
CLESS EXERTED THE LAST OF HIS STRENGTH TO FELL THE DEMON LORD. HE ENSURED THAT WE WOULD HAVE A FUTURE.
WE *CANNOT* LET HIM DIE...
I SWEAR THAT I'LL SAVE CLESS'S LIFE YET AGAIN...
YOU HAVE MY WORD.
...
I LEAVE HIM...
...IN YOUR HANDS, THEN.

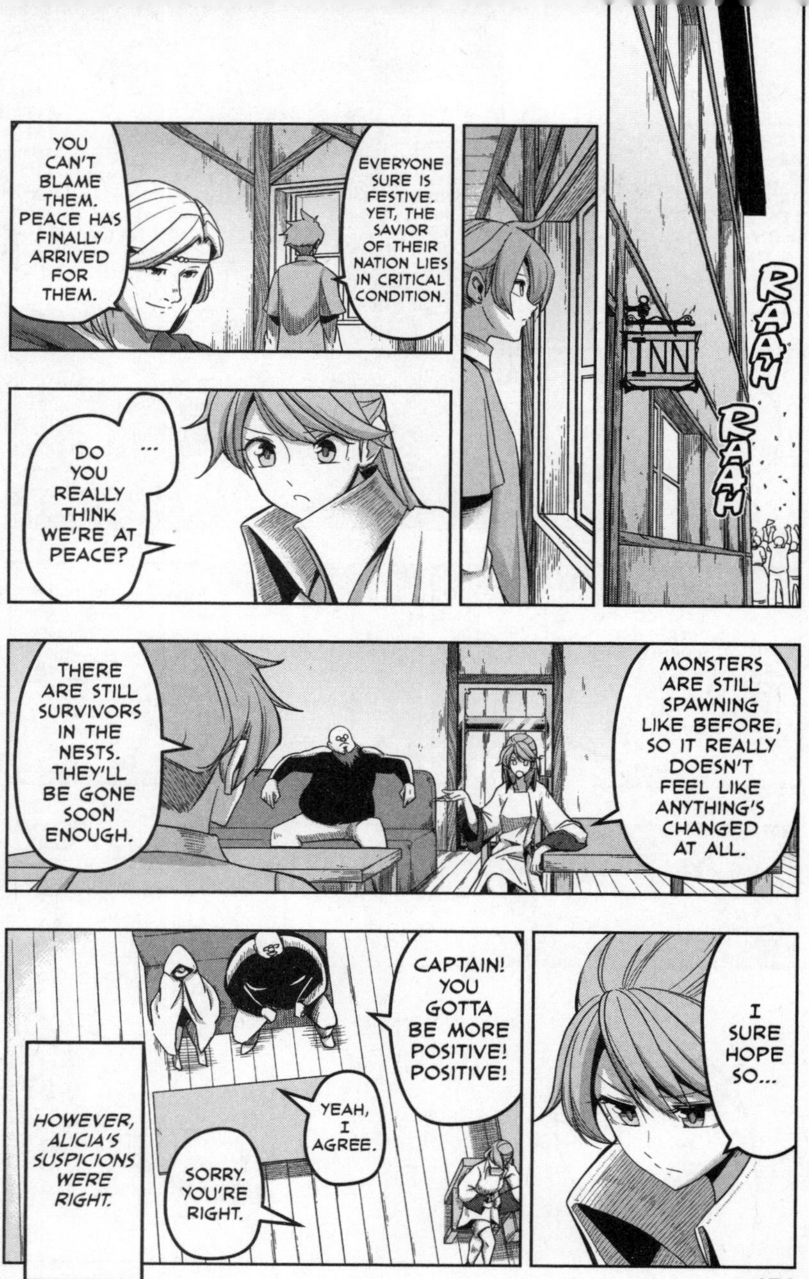
RAAH
RAAH
INN
EVERYONE SURE IS FESTIVE. YET, THE SAVIOR OF THEIR NATION LIES IN CRITICAL CONDITION.
YOU CAN'T BLAME THEM. PEACE HAS FINALLY ARRIVED FOR THEM.
... DO YOU REALLY THINK WE'RE AT PEACE?
MONSTERS ARE STILL SPAWNING LIKE BEFORE, SO IT REALLY DOESN'T FEEL LIKE ANYTHING'S CHANGED AT ALL.
THERE ARE STILL SURVIVORS IN THE NESTS. THEY'LL BE GONE SOON ENOUGH.
I SURE HOPE SO...
CAPTAIN! YOU GOTTA BE MORE POSITIVE! POSITIVE!
YEAH, I AGREE.
SORRY. YOU'RE RIGHT.
HOWEVER, ALICIA'S SUSPICIONS WERE RIGHT.

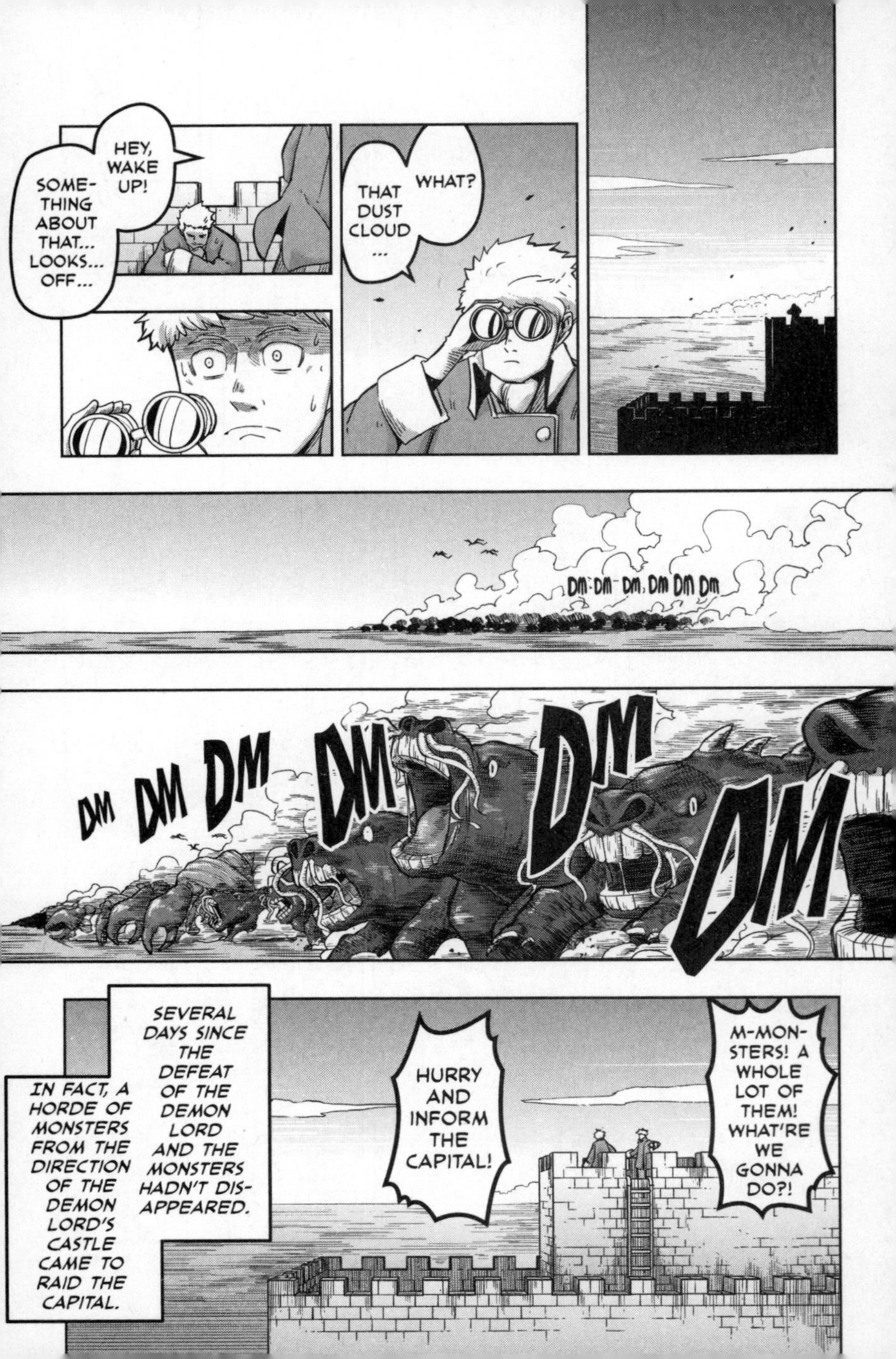
WHAT?
THAT DUST CLOUD ...
HEY, WAKE UP!
SOME-THING ABOUT THAT... LOOKS... OFF...
DM DM DM DM DM DM
DM DM DM DM DM DM
M-MONSTERS! A WHOLE LOT OF THEM! WHAT'RE WE GONNA DO?!
HURRY AND INFORM THE CAPITAL!
SEVERAL DAYS SINCE THE DEFEAT OF THE DEMON LORD AND THE MONSTERS HADN'T DIS-APPEARED.
IN FACT, A HORDE OF MONSTERS FROM THE DIRECTION OF THE DEMON LORD'S CASTLE CAME TO RAID THE CAPITAL.

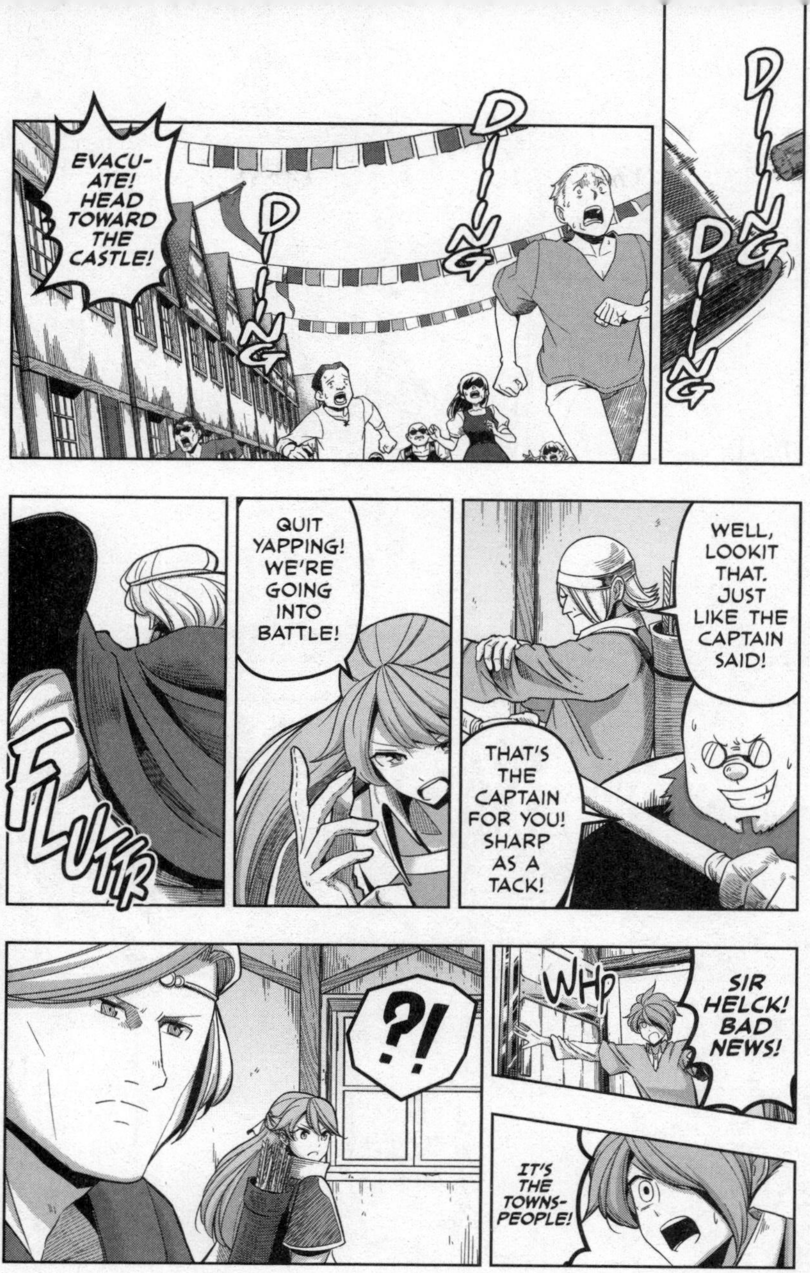
DIIING
DIIING
DIIING
EVACUATE! HEAD TOWARD THE CASTLE!
DIIING
WELL, LOOKIT THAT. JUST LIKE THE CAPTAIN SAID!
THAT'S THE CAPTAIN FOR YOU! SHARP AS A TACK!
QUIT YAPPING! WE'RE GOING INTO BATTLE!
FLUTTR
WHP
SIR HELCK! BAD NEWS!
IT'S THE TOWNSPEOPLE!
?!

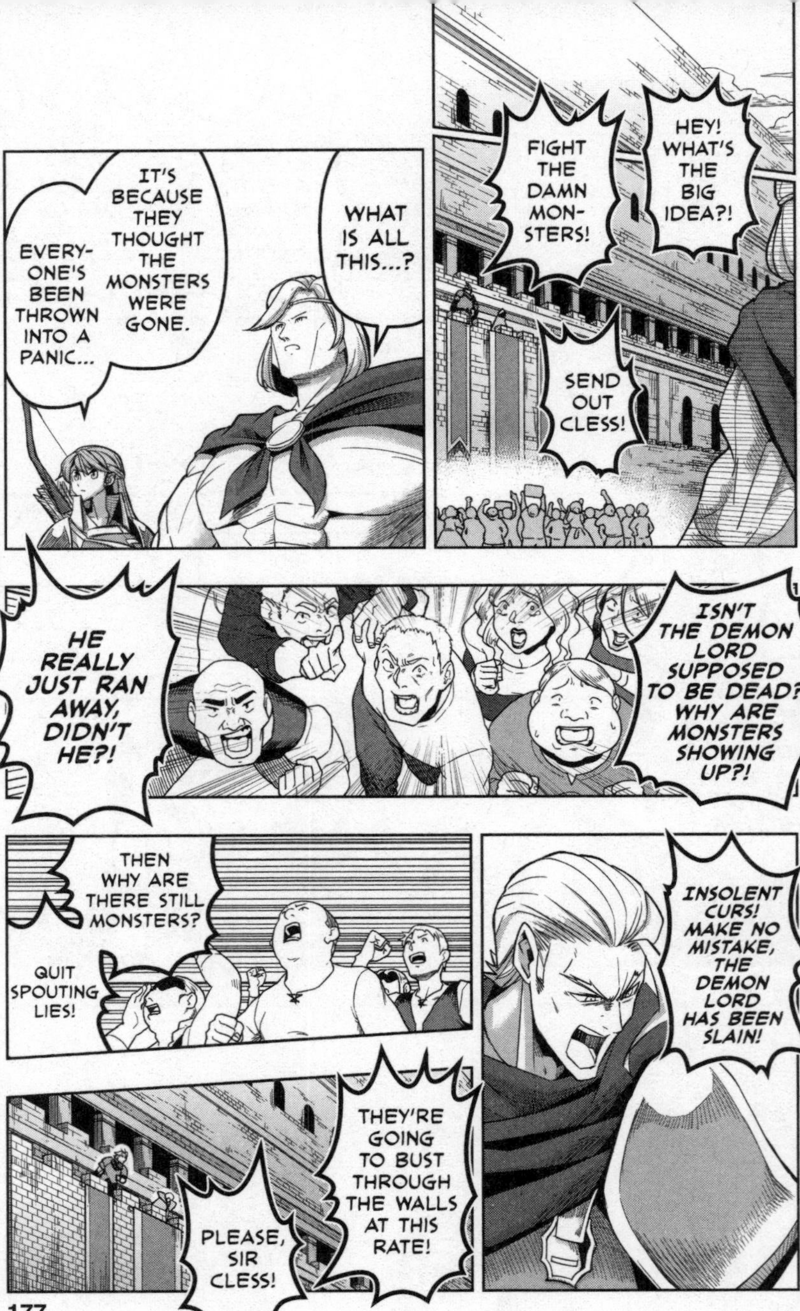

HEY! WHAT'S THE BIG IDEA?!
FIGHT THE DAMN MON-STERS!
SEND OUT CLESS!
WHAT IS ALL THIS...?
IT'S BECAUSE THEY THOUGHT THE MONSTERS WERE GONE.
EVERY-ONE'S BEEN THROWN INTO A PANIC...
ISN'T THE DEMON LORD SUPPOSED TO BE DEAD? WHY ARE MONSTERS SHOWING UP?!
HE REALLY JUST RAN AWAY, DIDN'T HE?!
INSOLENT CURS! MAKE NO MISTAKE, THE DEMON LORD HAS BEEN SLAIN!
THEN WHY ARE THERE STILL MONSTERS?
QUIT SPOUTING LIES!
THEY'RE GOING TO BUST THROUGH THE WALLS AT THIS RATE!
PLEASE, SIR CLESS!

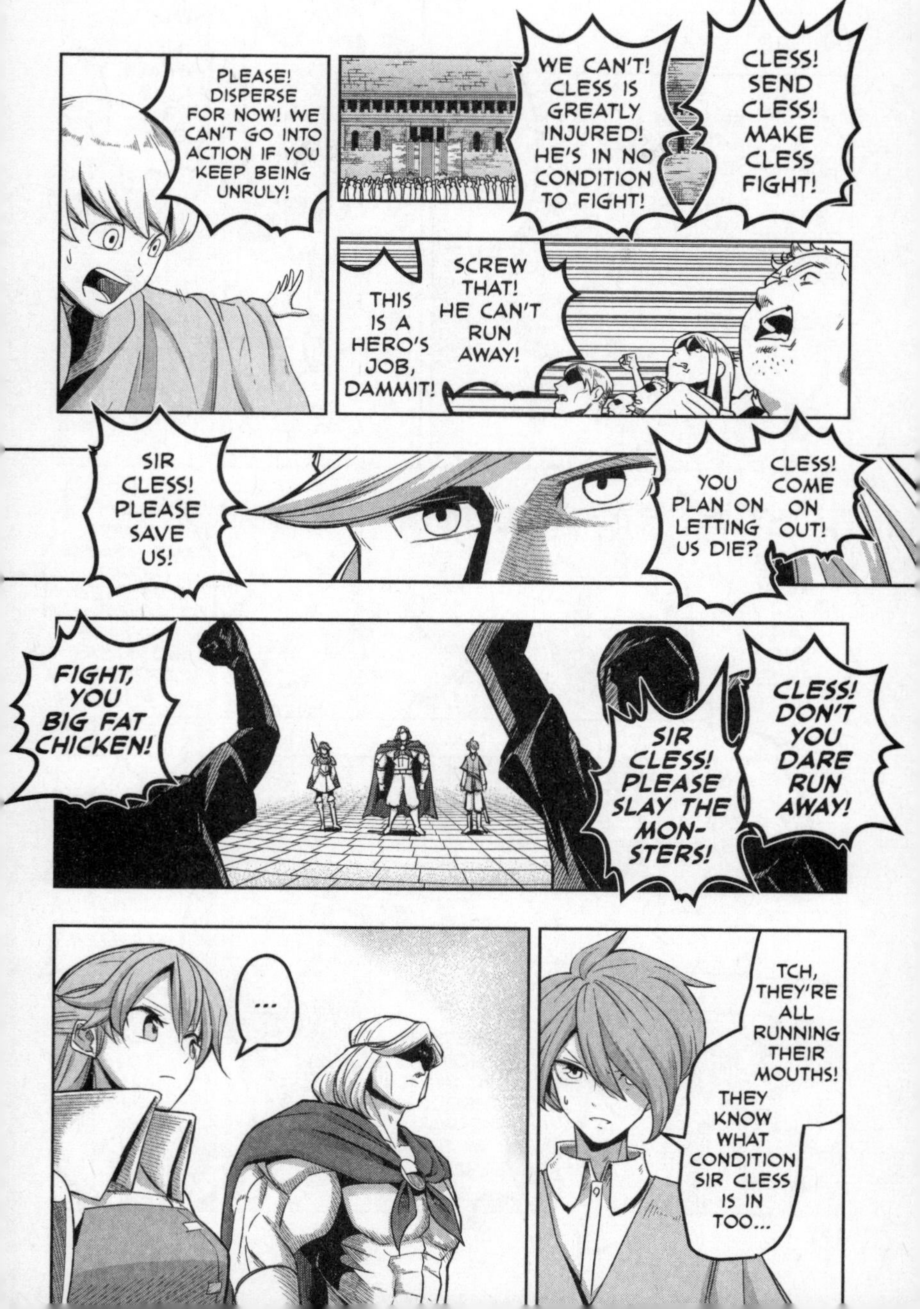
CLESS! SEND CLESS! MAKE CLESS FIGHT!
WE CAN'T! CLESS IS GREATLY INJURED! HE'S IN NO CONDITION TO FIGHT!
SCREW THAT! HE CAN'T RUN AWAY!
THIS IS A HERO'S JOB, DAMMIT!
PLEASE! DISPERSE FOR NOW! WE CAN'T GO INTO ACTION IF YOU KEEP BEING UNRULY!
CLESS! COME ON OUT!
YOU PLAN ON LETTING US DIE?
SIR CLESS! PLEASE SAVE US!
CLESS! DON'T YOU DARE RUN AWAY!
SIR CLESS! PLEASE SLAY THE MON-STERS!
FIGHT, YOU BIG FAT CHICKEN!
TCH, THEY'RE ALL RUNNING THEIR MOUTHS!
THEY KNOW WHAT CONDITION SIR CLESS IS IN TOO...
...

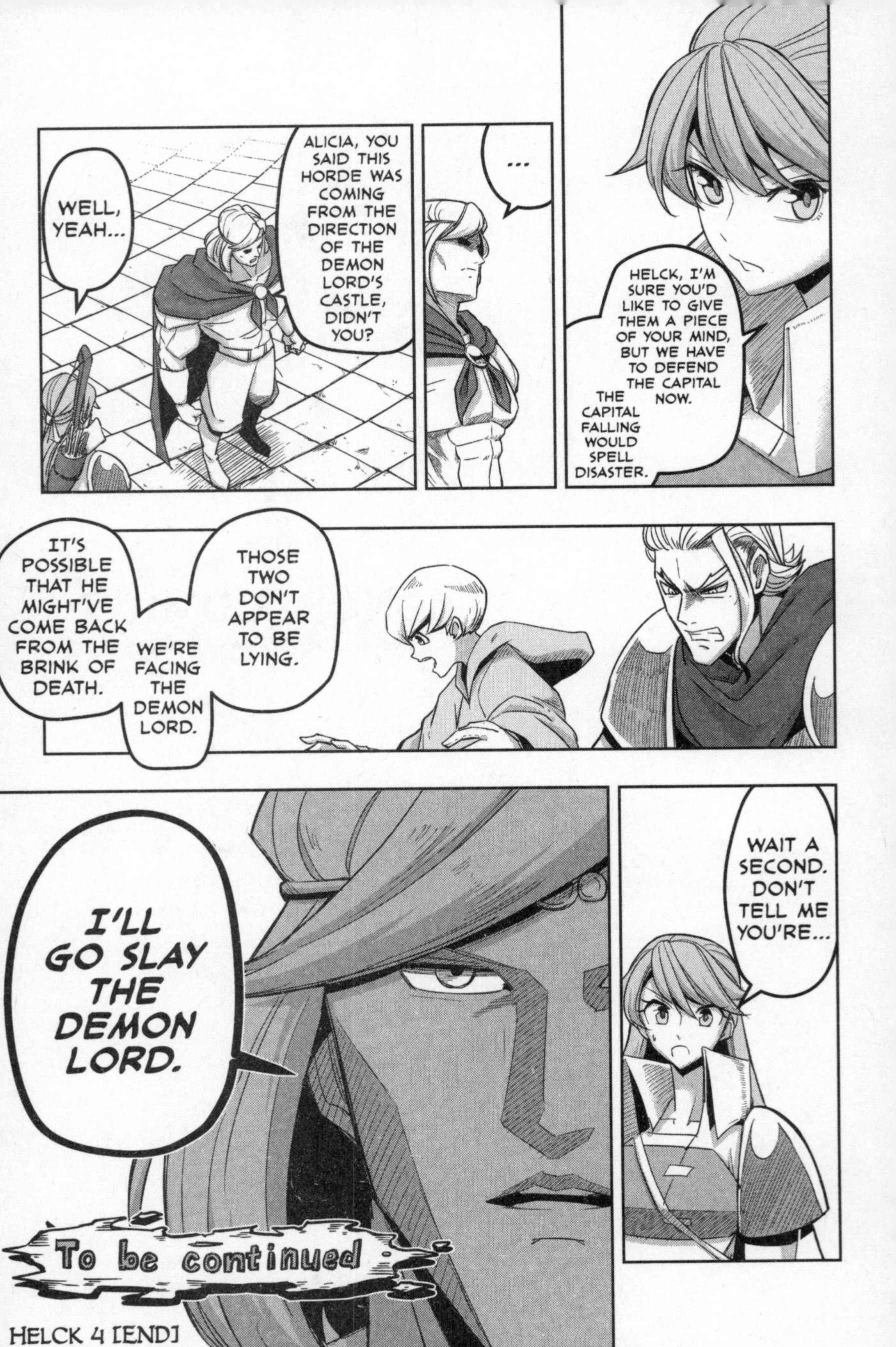
HELCK, I'M SURE YOU'D LIKE TO GIVE THEM A PIECE OF YOUR MIND, BUT WE HAVE TO DEFEND THE CAPITAL NOW.
THE CAPITAL FALLING WOULD SPELL DISASTER.
...
ALICIA, YOU SAID THIS HORDE WAS COMING FROM THE DIRECTION OF THE DEMON LORD'S CASTLE, DIDN'T YOU?
WELL, YEAH...
THOSE TWO DON'T APPEAR TO BE LYING.
WE'RE FACING THE DEMON LORD.
IT'S POSSIBLE THAT HE MIGHT'VE COME BACK FROM THE BRINK OF DEATH.
WAIT A SECOND. DON'T TELL ME YOU'RE...
I'LL GO SLAY THE DEMON LORD.
To be continued

HELCK 4 [END]

BONUS COMIC

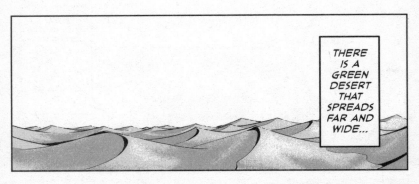

THERE IS A GREEN DESERT THAT SPREADS FAR AND WIDE...

AT ITS ENTRANCE LIES A PLACE WHERE MANY PEDDLERS COME AND GO—THE DESERT CITY OF **PAROUSE.**

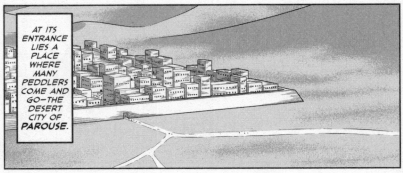

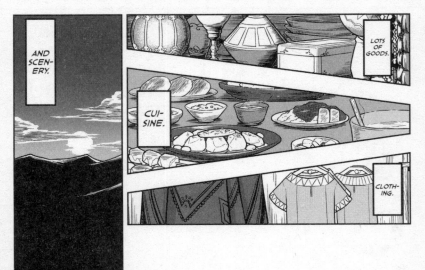

AND SCEN-ERY.

LOTS OF GOODS.

CUI-SINE.

CLOTH-ING.

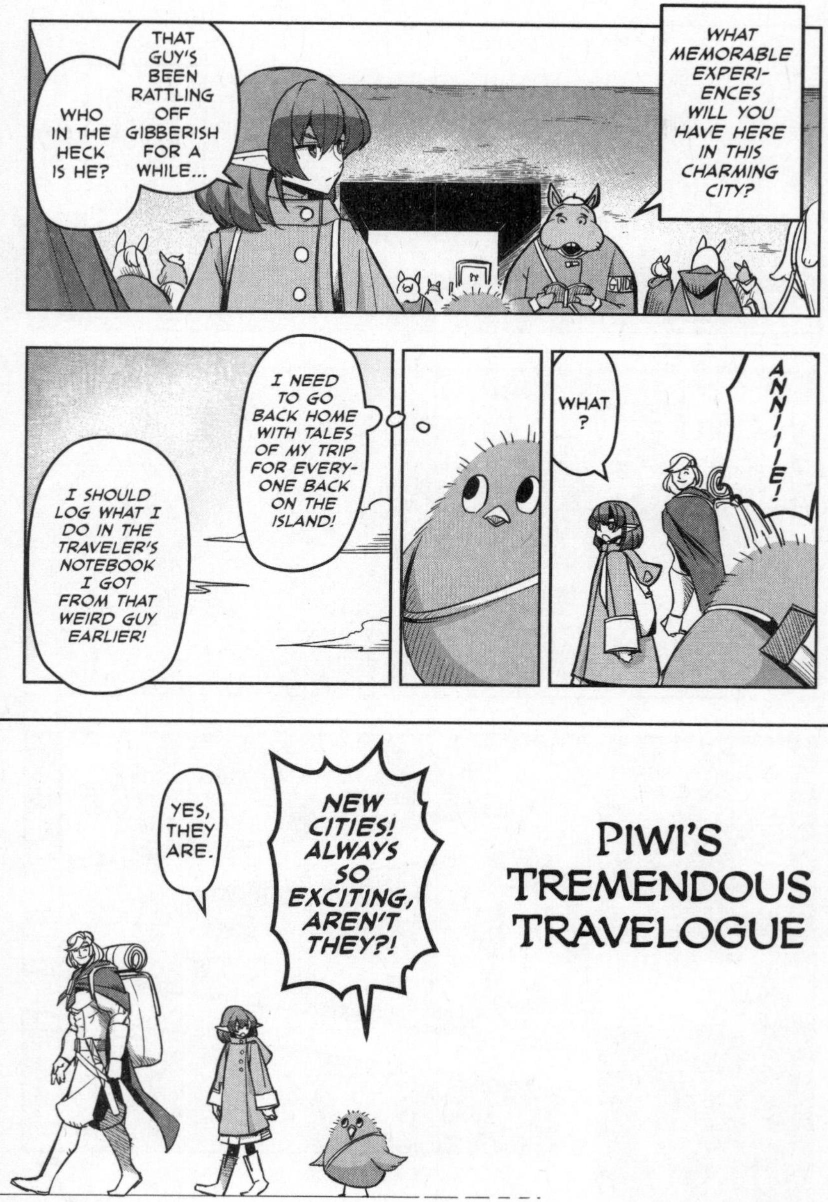
WHAT MEMORABLE EXPERI-ENCES WILL YOU HAVE HERE IN THIS CHARMING CITY?
THAT GUY'S BEEN RATTLING OFF GIBBERISH FOR A WHILE...
WHO IN THE HECK IS HE?
ANNIIIE!
WHAT?
I NEED TO GO BACK HOME WITH TALES OF MY TRIP FOR EVERY-ONE BACK ON THE ISLAND!
I SHOULD LOG WHAT I DO IN THE TRAVELER'S NOTEBOOK I GOT FROM THAT WEIRD GUY EARLIER!
PIWI'S TREMENDOUS TRAVELOGUE
NEW CITIES! ALWAYS SO EXCITING, AREN'T THEY?!
YES, THEY ARE.

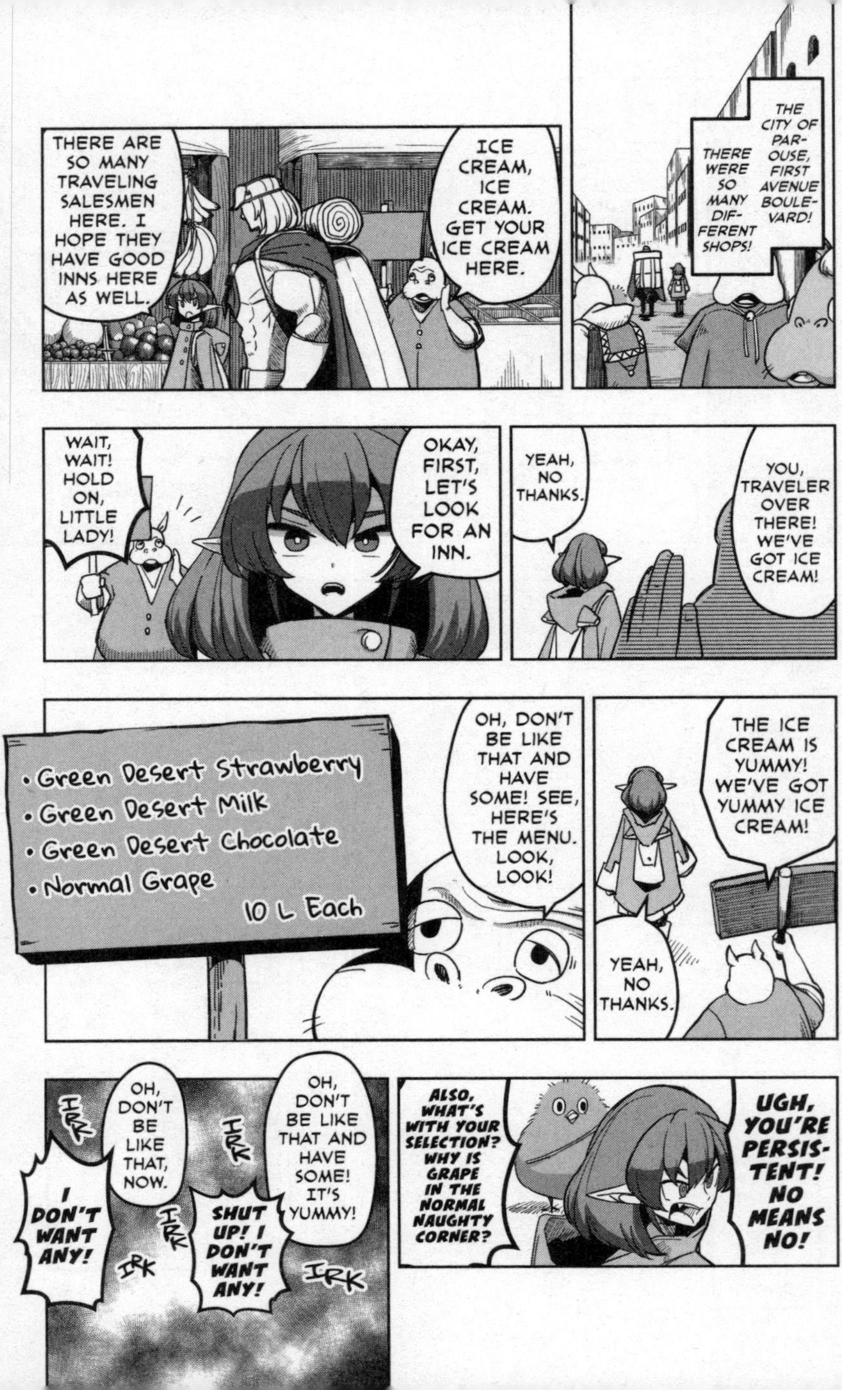
THE CITY OF PAROUSE, FIRST AVENUE BOULEVARD!
THERE WERE SO MANY DIFFERENT SHOPS!
ICE CREAM, ICE CREAM. GET YOUR ICE CREAM HERE.
THERE ARE SO MANY TRAVELING SALESMEN HERE. I HOPE THEY HAVE GOOD INNS HERE AS WELL.
YOU, TRAVELER OVER THERE! WE'VE GOT ICE CREAM!
YEAH, NO THANKS.
OKAY, FIRST, LET'S LOOK FOR AN INN.
WAIT, WAIT! HOLD ON, LITTLE LADY!
THE ICE CREAM IS YUMMY! WE'VE GOT YUMMY ICE CREAM!
YEAH, NO THANKS.
OH, DON'T BE LIKE THAT AND HAVE SOME! SEE, HERE'S THE MENU. LOOK, LOOK!
• Green Desert Strawberry
• Green Desert Milk
• Green Desert Chocolate
• Normal Grape
10 L Each
UGH, YOU'RE PERSISTENT! NO MEANS NO!
ALSO, WHAT'S WITH YOUR SELECTION? WHY IS GRAPE IN THE NORMAL NAUGHTY CORNER?
OH, DON'T BE LIKE THAT AND HAVE SOME! IT'S YUMMY!
IRK
OH, DON'T BE LIKE THAT, NOW.
IRK
SHUT UP! I DON'T WANT ANY!
IRK
IRK
IRK
I DON'T WANT ANY!

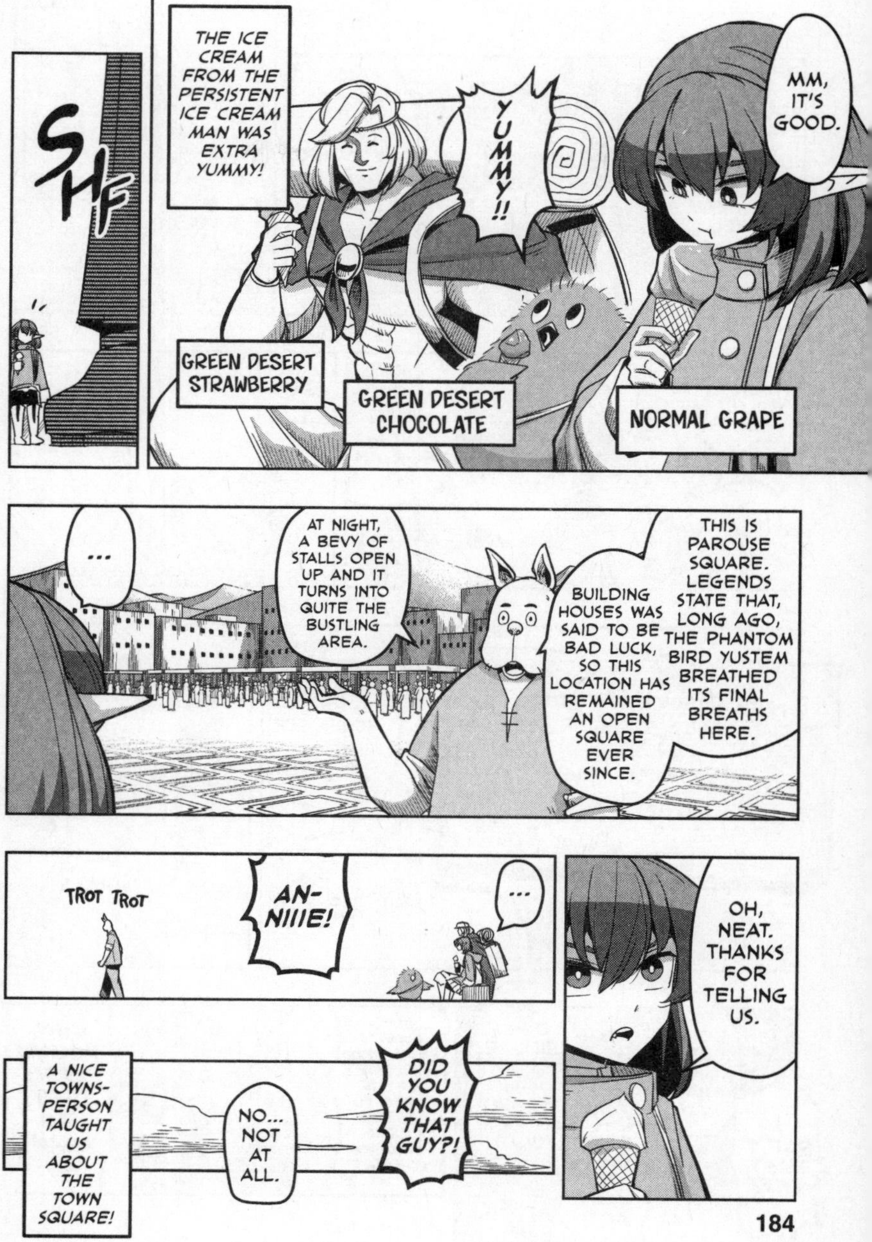
MM, IT'S GOOD.
YUMMY!!
THE ICE CREAM FROM THE PERSISTENT ICE CREAM MAN WAS EXTRA YUMMY!
NORMAL GRAPE
GREEN DESERT CHOCOLATE
GREEN DESERT STRAWBERRY
SHF
THIS IS PAROUSE SQUARE. LEGENDS STATE THAT, LONG AGO, THE PHANTOM BIRD YUSTEM BREATHED ITS FINAL BREATHS HERE.
BUILDING HOUSES WAS SAID TO BE BAD LUCK, SO THIS LOCATION HAS REMAINED AN OPEN SQUARE EVER SINCE.
AT NIGHT, A BEVY OF STALLS OPEN UP AND IT TURNS INTO QUITE THE BUSTLING AREA.
...
OH, NEAT. THANKS FOR TELLING US.
...
AN-NIIIE!
TROT TROT
DID YOU KNOW THAT GUY?!
NO... NOT AT ALL.
A NICE TOWNS-PERSON TAUGHT US ABOUT THE TOWN SQUARE!

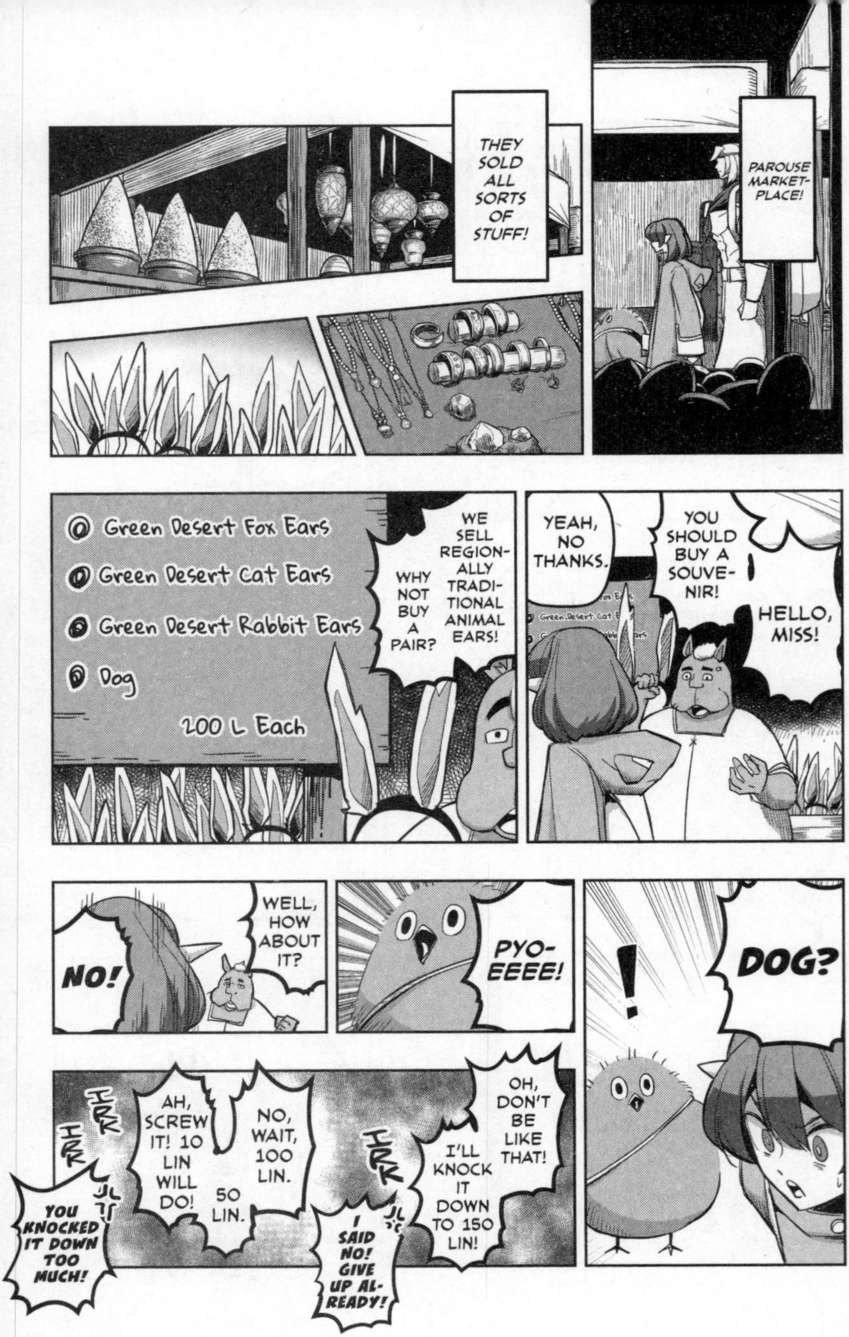
PAROUSE MARKETPLACE!
THEY SOLD ALL SORTS OF STUFF!
HELLO, MISS!
YOU SHOULD BUY A SOUVENIR!
YEAH, NO THANKS.
WE SELL REGIONALLY TRADITIONAL ANIMAL EARS!
WHY NOT BUY A PAIR?
Green Desert Fox Ears
Green Desert Cat Ears
Green Desert Rabbit Ears
Dog
200 L Each
DOG?
!
PYO-EEEE!
WELL, HOW ABOUT IT?
NO!
OH, DON'T BE LIKE THAT!
I'LL KNOCK IT DOWN TO 150 LIN!
I SAID NO! GIVE UP ALREADY!
IRK
NO, WAIT, 100 LIN.
50 LIN.
AH, SCREW IT! 10 LIN WILL DO!
IRK
IRK
YOU KNOCKED IT DOWN TOO MUCH!

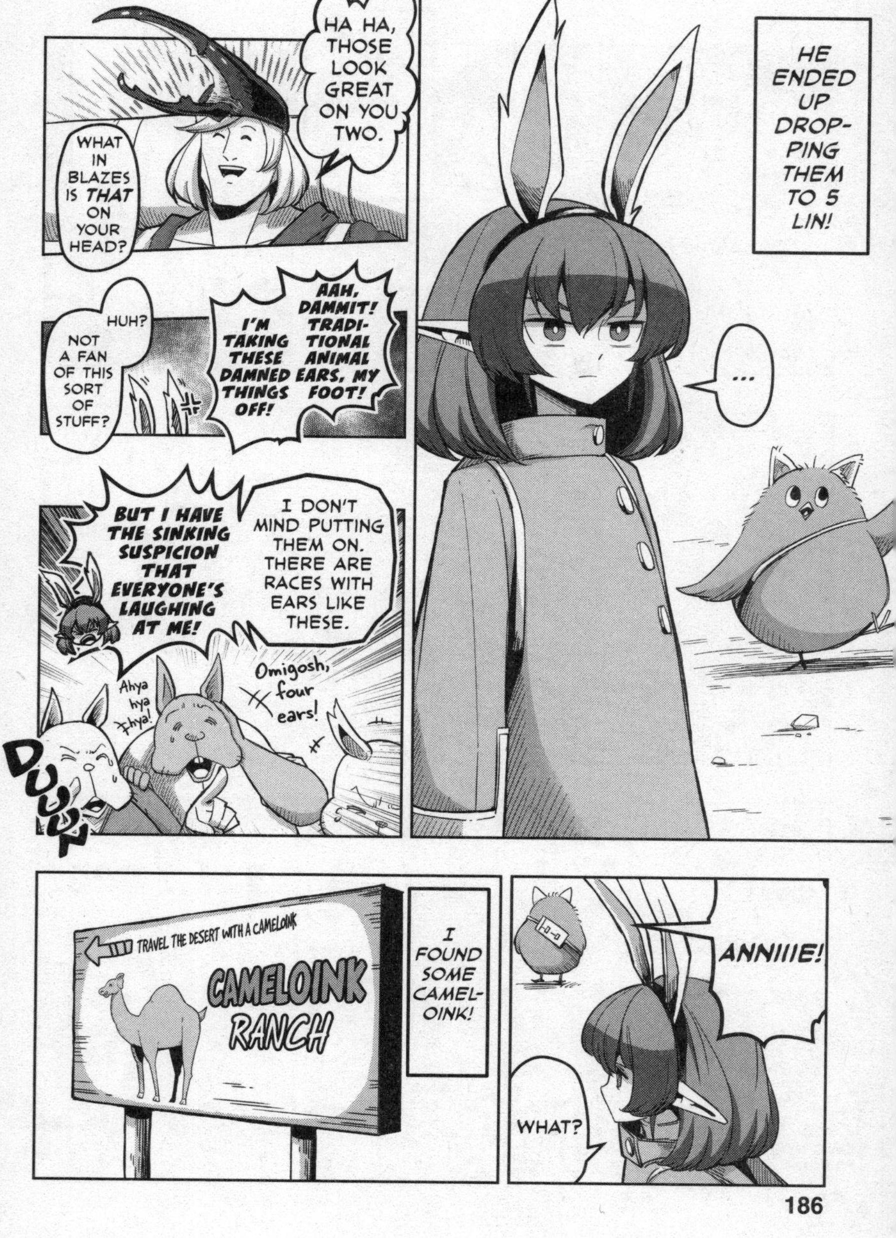
HE ENDED UP DROP-PING THEM TO 5 LIN!
...
HA HA, THOSE LOOK GREAT ON YOU TWO.
WHAT IN BLAZES IS THAT ON YOUR HEAD?
AAH, DAMMIT! TRADI-TIONAL ANIMAL EARS, MY FOOT!
I'M TAKING THESE DAMNED THINGS OFF!
HUH? NOT A FAN OF THIS SORT OF STUFF?
I DON'T MIND PUTTING THEM ON. THERE ARE RACES WITH EARS LIKE THESE.
BUT I HAVE THE SINKING SUSPICION THAT EVERYONE'S LAUGHING AT ME!
Omigosh, four ears!
Ahya hya hya!
DUUUN
ANNIIIE!
WHAT?
I FOUND SOME CAMEL-OINK!
TRAVEL THE DESERT WITH A CAMELOINK
CAMELOINK RANCH

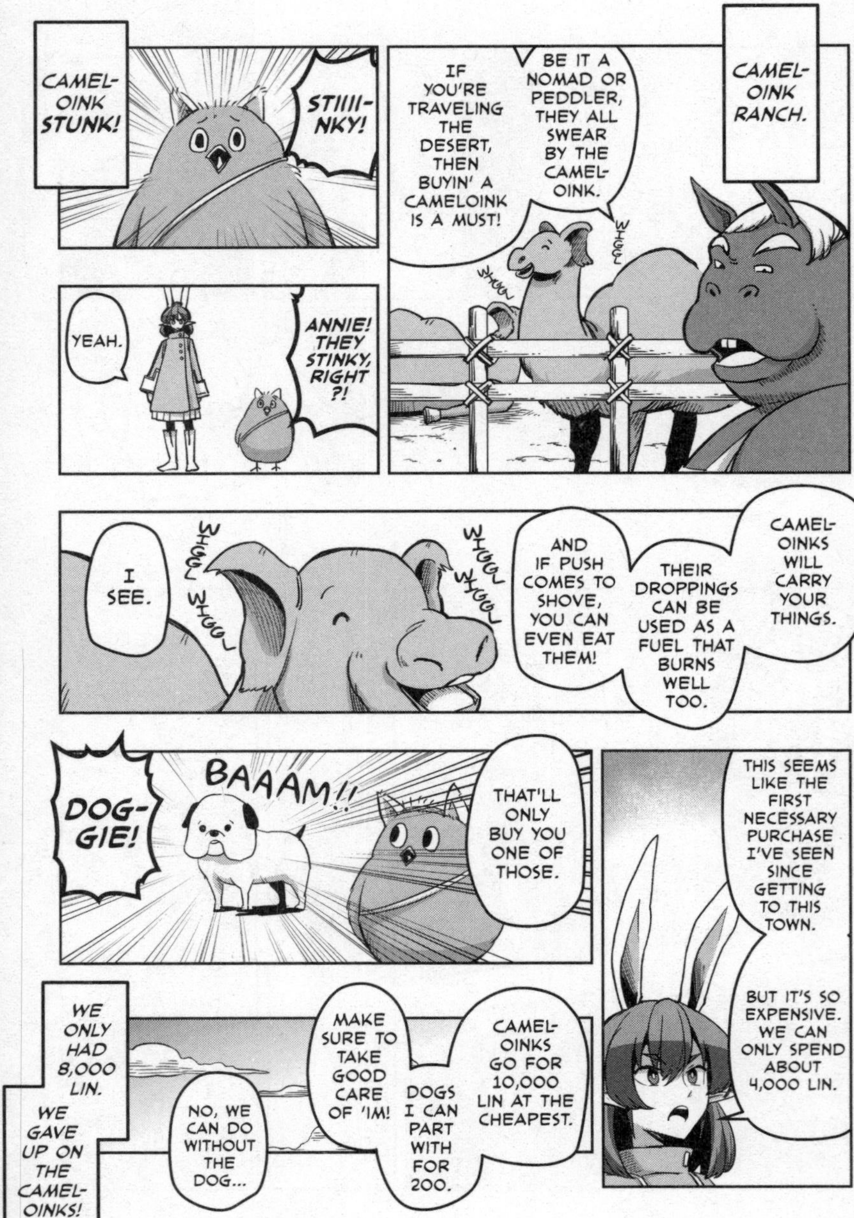
CAMEL-OINK RANCH.
BE IT A NOMAD OR PEDDLER, THEY ALL SWEAR BY THE CAMEL-OINK.
IF YOU'RE TRAVELING THE DESERT, THEN BUYIN' A CAMELOINK IS A MUST!
WIGGL
WIGGL
STIIIII-NKY!
CAMEL-OINK STUNK!
ANNIE! THEY STINKY, RIGHT?!
YEAH.
CAMEL-OINKS WILL CARRY YOUR THINGS.
THEIR DROPPINGS CAN BE USED AS A FUEL THAT BURNS WELL TOO.
AND IF PUSH COMES TO SHOVE, YOU CAN EVEN EAT THEM!
WIGGL WIGGL
WIGGL WIGGL
I SEE.
THIS SEEMS LIKE THE FIRST NECESSARY PURCHASE I'VE SEEN SINCE GETTING TO THIS TOWN.
BUT IT'S SO EXPENSIVE. WE CAN ONLY SPEND ABOUT 4,000 LIN.
THAT'LL ONLY BUY YOU ONE OF THOSE.
BAAAM!!
DOG-GIE!
CAMEL-OINKS GO FOR 10,000 LIN AT THE CHEAPEST.
DOGS I CAN PART WITH FOR 200.
MAKE SURE TO TAKE GOOD CARE OF 'IM!
NO, WE CAN DO WITHOUT THE DOG...
WE ONLY HAD 8,000 LIN.
WE GAVE UP ON THE CAMEL-OINKS!

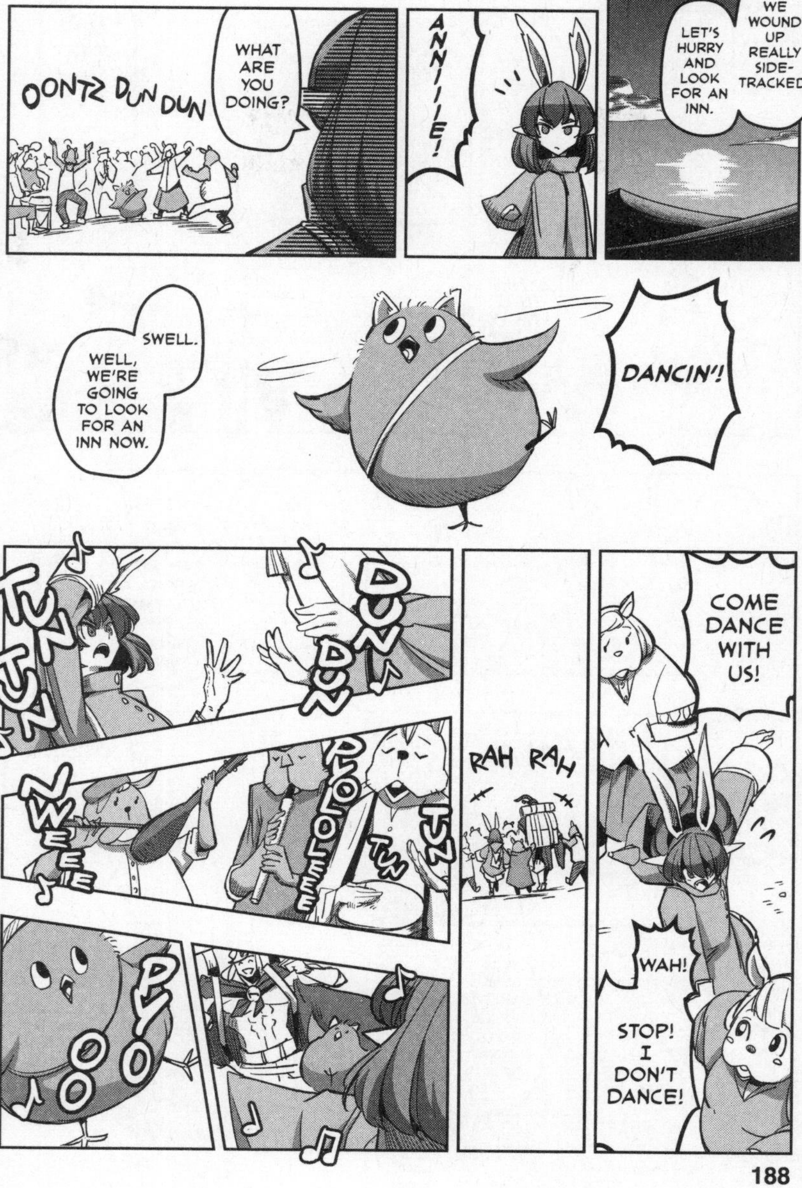
WE WOUND UP REALLY SIDE-TRACKED.
LET'S HURRY AND LOOK FOR AN INN.
ANNIIIE!
WHAT ARE YOU DOING?
OONTZ DUN DUN
DANCIN'!
SWELL.
WELL, WE'RE GOING TO LOOK FOR AN INN NOW.
COME DANCE WITH US!
WAH!
STOP! I DON'T DANCE!
RAH RAH
DUN DUN DUN
TUN TUN
TUN TUN
PYOLOLOLEEE
NWEEEE
PYOOOO

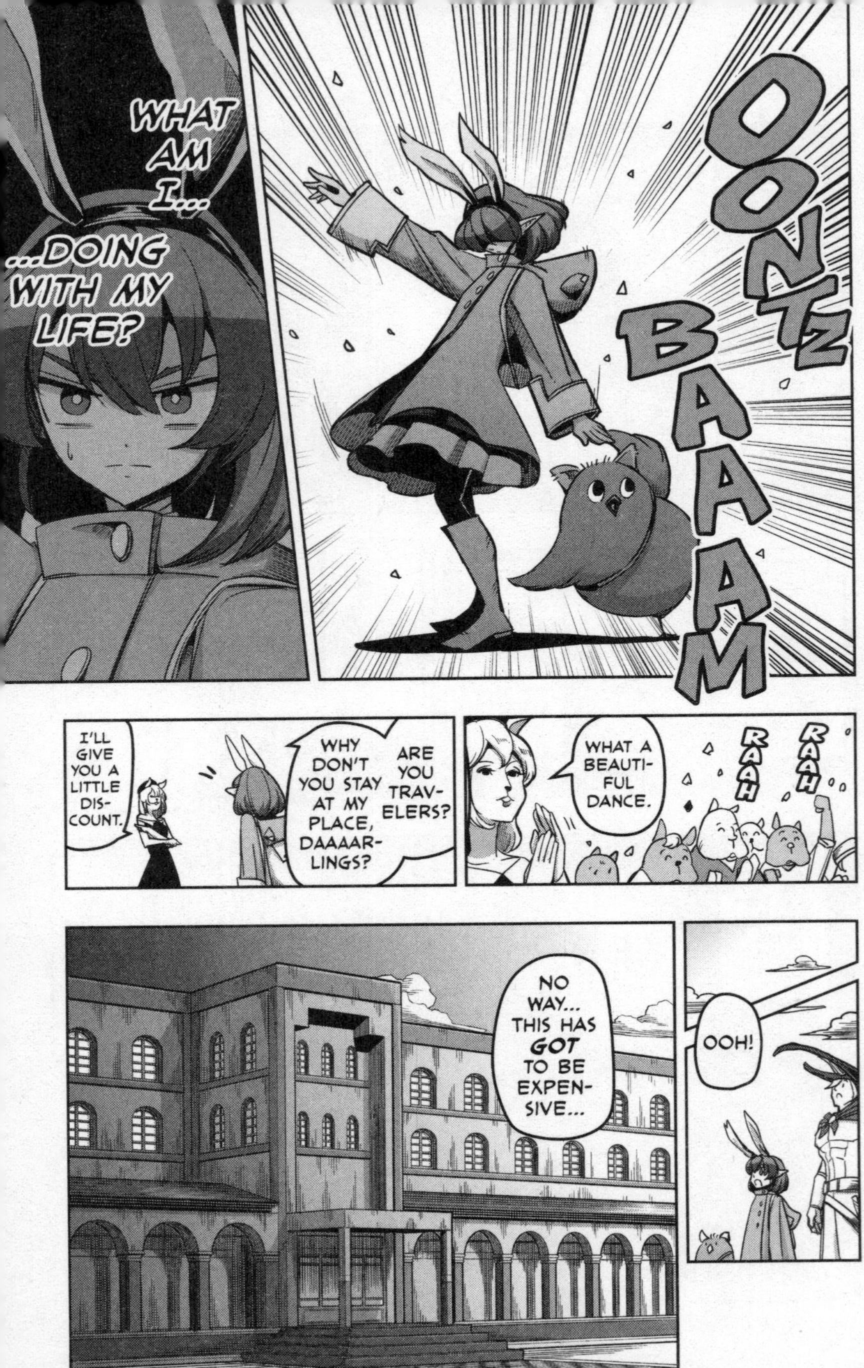
OONTZ
BAAAAM
WHAT AM I...
...DOING WITH MY LIFE?
RAAH
RAAH
WHAT A BEAUTIFUL DANCE.
ARE YOU TRAVELERS?
WHY DON'T YOU STAY AT MY PLACE, DAAAARLINGS?
I'LL GIVE YOU A LITTLE DISCOUNT.
OOH!
NO WAY... THIS HAS *GOT* TO BE EXPENSIVE...

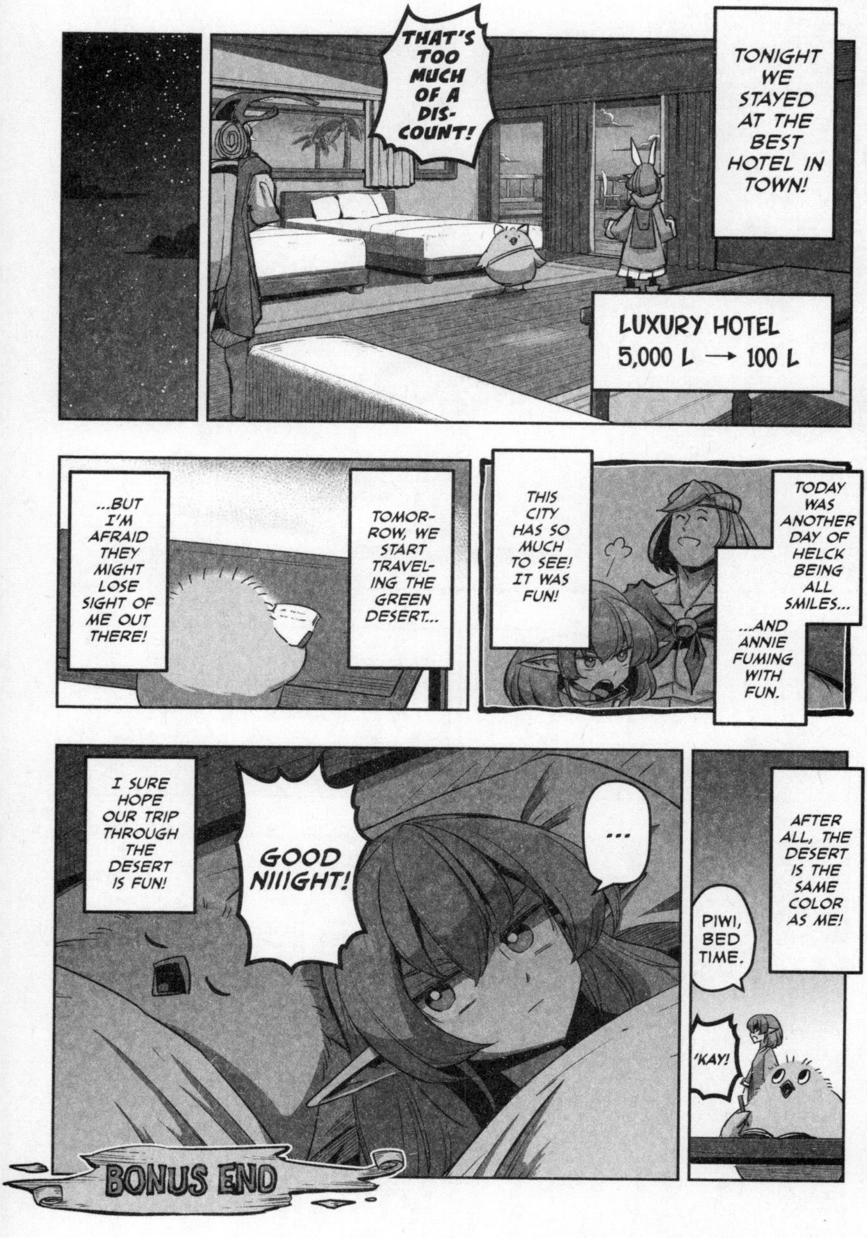
TONIGHT WE STAYED AT THE BEST HOTEL IN TOWN!
THAT'S TOO MUCH OF A DIS-COUNT!
LUXURY HOTEL
5,000 L → 100 L
TODAY WAS ANOTHER DAY OF HELCK BEING ALL SMILES...
THIS CITY HAS SO MUCH TO SEE! IT WAS FUN!
...AND ANNIE FUMING WITH FUN.
TOMOR-ROW, WE START TRAVEL-ING THE GREEN DESERT...
...BUT I'M AFRAID THEY MIGHT LOSE SIGHT OF ME OUT THERE!
AFTER ALL, THE DESERT IS THE SAME COLOR AS ME!
PIWI, BED TIME.
'KAY!
...
GOOD NIIIGHT!
I SURE HOPE OUR TRIP THROUGH THE DESERT IS FUN!
BONUS END

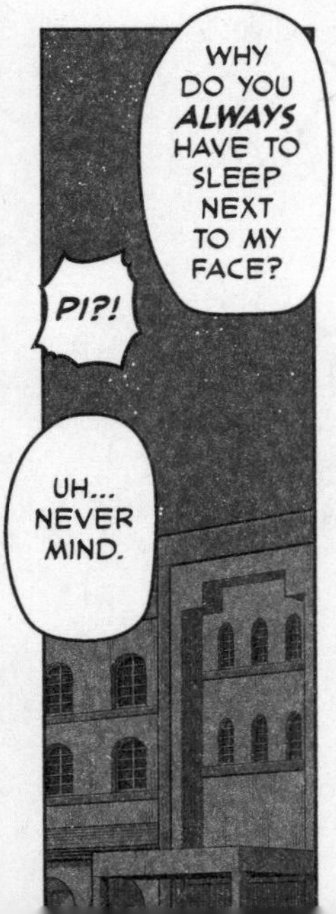
WHY DO YOU *ALWAYS* HAVE TO SLEEP NEXT TO MY FACE?
PI?!
UH... NEVER MIND.

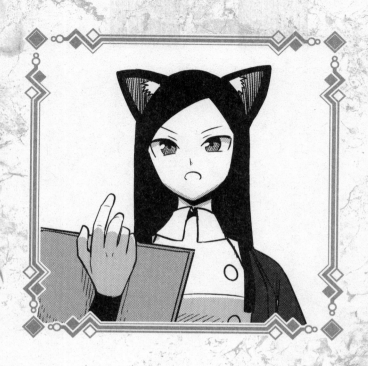

About the Author

Nanaki Nanao is best known for the manga
Helck, originally published in 2014 and re-
released in 2022. Nanao's other works include
Piwi and *Völundo: Divergent Sword Saga*, both
set in the world of *Helck*, as well as *Acaria*.

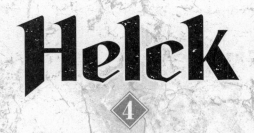

Helck

4

Story and Art by NANAKI NANAO

Translation: DAVID EVELYN
Touch-Up Art & Lettering: ANNALIESE "ACE" CHRISTMAN
Design: KAM LI
Editor: JACK CARRILLO CONCORDIA

HELCK SHINSOBAN Vol. 4
by Nanaki NANAO

Original Japanese edition published by SHOGAKUKAN.
English translation rights in the United States of America, Canada, the United Kingdom, Ireland, Australia and New Zealand arranged with SHOGAKUKAN.

Original Cover Design: Masato ISHIZAWA + Bay Bridge Studio

Printed in the U.S.A.

Published by VIZ Media, LLC
P.O. Box 77010
San Francisco, CA 94107

10 9 8 7 6 5 4 3 2 1
First printing, July 2023

VIZ MEDIA
viz.com

SHONEN SUNDAY
shonensunday.com

ratings.viz.com
RATED T TEEN

PARENTAL ADVISORY
HELCK is rated T for Teen and is recommended for ages 13 and up. This volume contains fantasy violence.

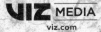

Kidnapped by the Demon King and imprisoned in his castle, Princess Syalis is...bored.

SLEEPY PRINCESS IN THE DEMON CASTLE

Story & Art by
KAGIJI KUMANOMATA

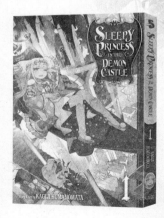

Captured princess Syalis decides to while away her hours in the Demon Castle by sleeping, but getting a good night's rest turns out to be a lot of work! She begins by fashioning a DIY pillow out of the fur of her Teddy Demon guards and an "air mattress" from the magical Shield of the Wind. Things go from bad to worse—for her captors—when some of Princess Syalis's schemes end in her untimely—if temporary—demise and she chooses the Forbidden Grimoire for her bedtime reading...

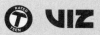

The adventure is over but life goes on for an elf mage
just beginning to learn what living is all about.

Frieren

Beyond Journey's End

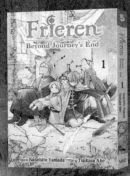

Decades after their victory, the funeral of one
her friends confronts Frieren with her own
near immortality. Frieren sets out to fulfill the
last wishes of her comrades and finds herself
beginning a new adventure...

Story by **Kanehito Yamada**
Art by **Tsukasa Abe**

A new feudal fairytale begins!

YASHAHIME
—PRINCESS HALF-DEMON—

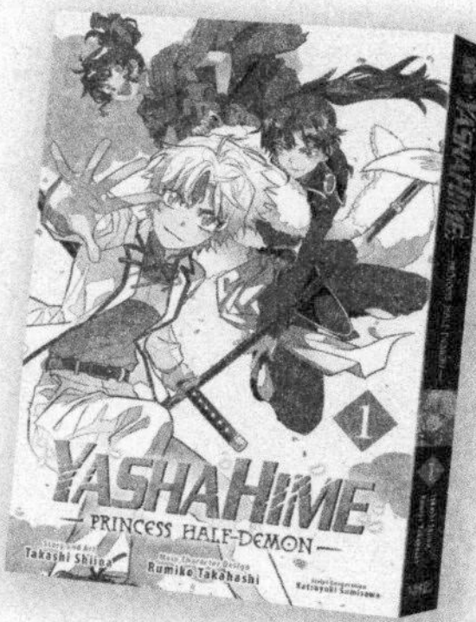
1
YASHAHIME
PRINCESS HALF-DEMON
Takashi Shiina
Rumiko Takahashi

Story and Art
Takashi Shiina

Main Character Design
Rumiko Takahashi

Script Cooperation Katsuyuki Sumisawa

Can the three teenage daughters of demon dog half-brothers Inuyasha and Sesshomaru save their parents, themselves, and both realms from the menace of the seven mystical Rainbow Pearls?

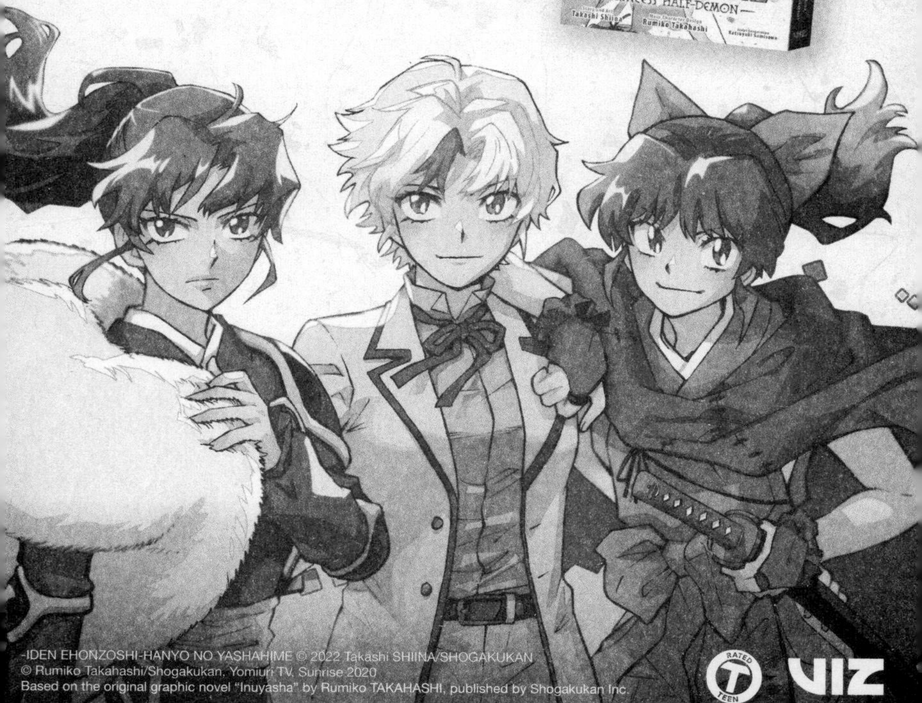

RATED T TEEN

VIZ

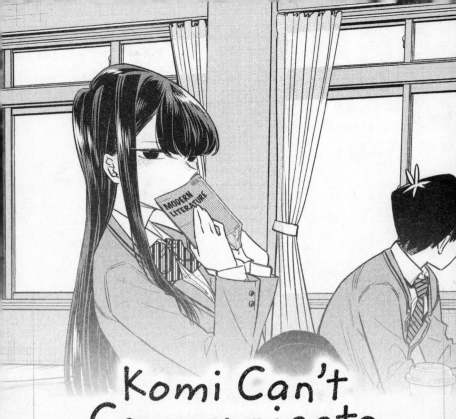

Komi Can't Communicate

Story & Art by Tomohito Oda

The journey to a hundred friends begins with a single conversation.

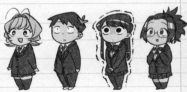

Socially anxious high school student Shoko Komi's greatest dream is to make some friends, but everyone at school mistakes her crippling social anxiety for cool reserve. With the whole student body keeping its distance and Komi unable to utter a single word, friendship might be forever beyond her reach.

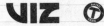

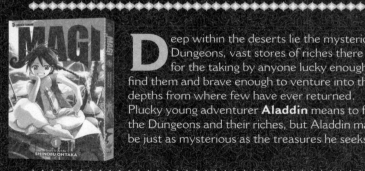
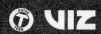

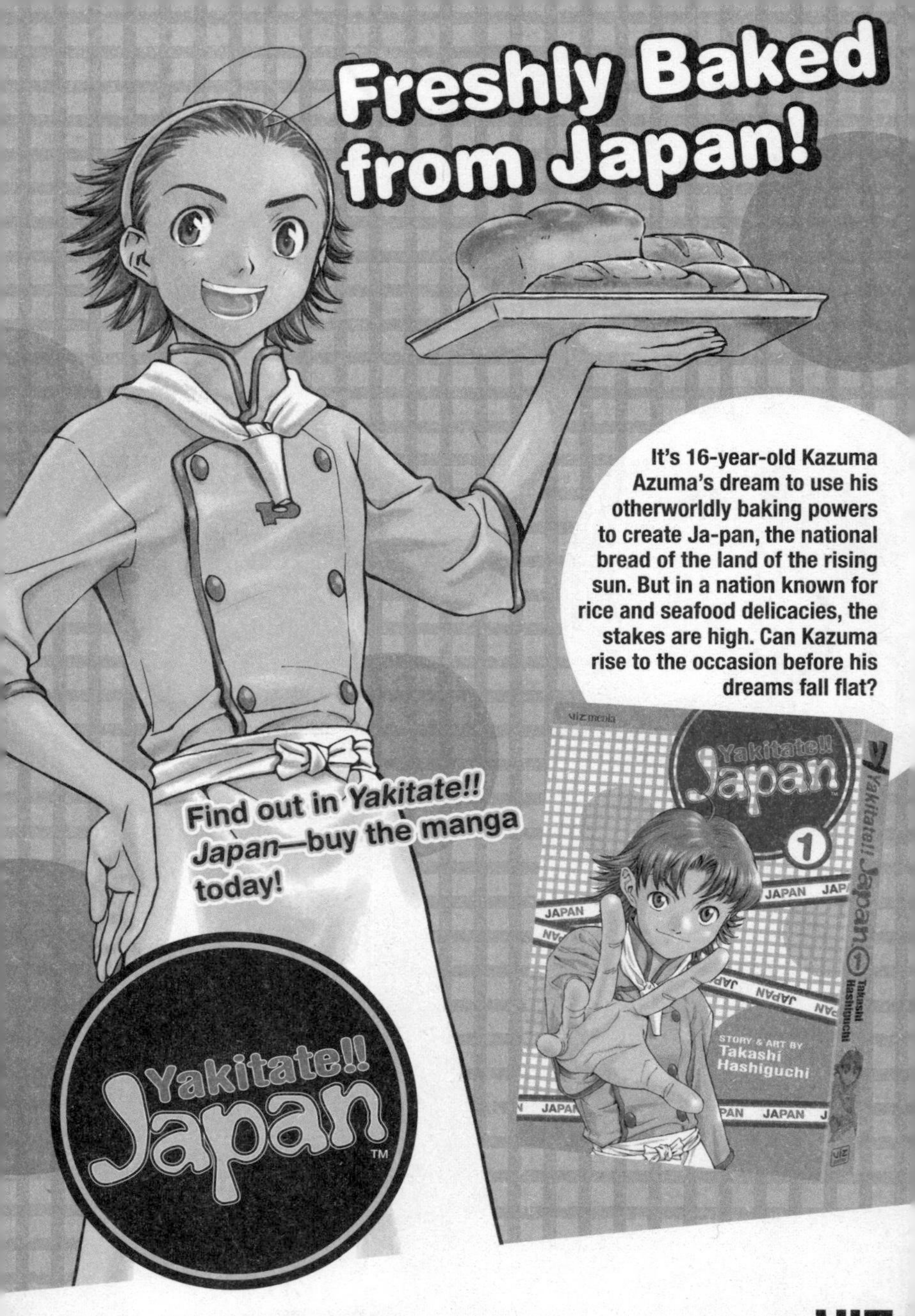
Freshly Baked from Japan!
It's 16-year-old Kazuma Azuma's dream to use his otherworldly baking powers to create Ja-pan, the national bread of the land of the rising sun. But in a nation known for rice and seafood delicacies, the stakes are high. Can Kazuma rise to the occasion before his dreams fall flat?
Find out in Yakitate!! Japan—buy the manga today!
Yakitate!! Japan™
viz media
Yakitate!! Japan 1
STORY & ART BY Takashi Hashiguchi

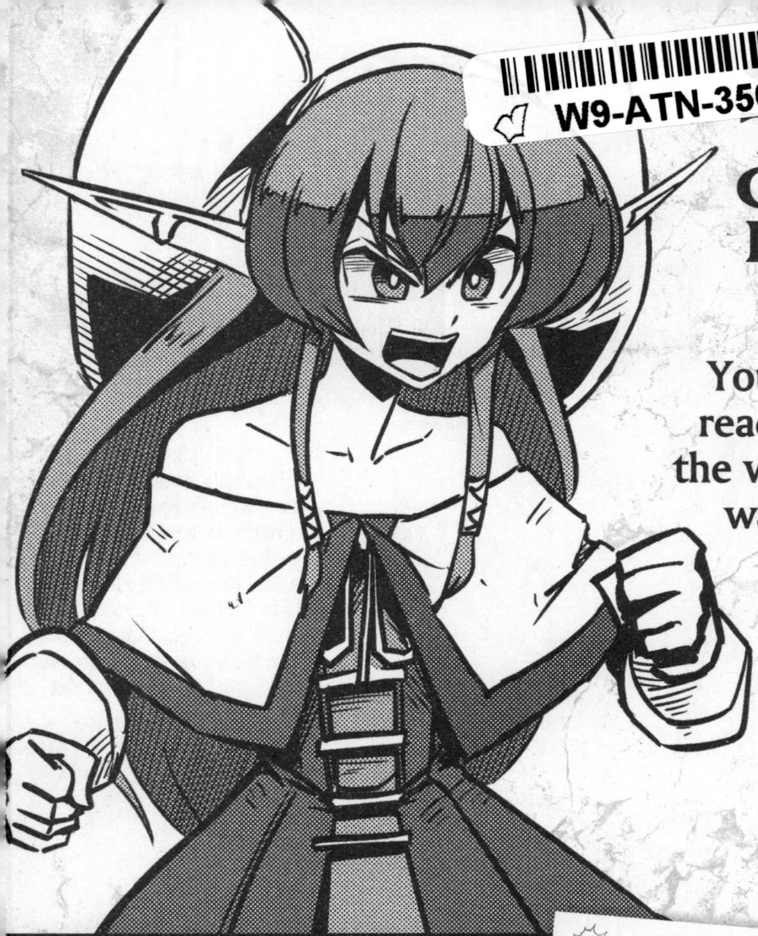

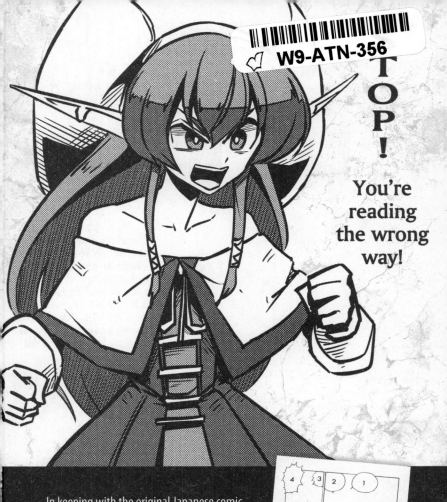

TOP!

You're reading the wrong way!

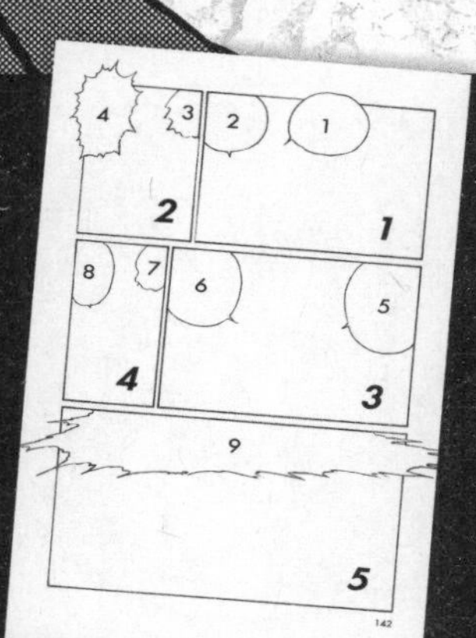
1
2
3
4
1
2
5
6
7
8
3
4
9
5
142

In keeping with the original Japanese comic format, this book reads from right to left—so action, sound effects, and word balloons are completely reversed to preserve the orientation of the original artwork.

Check out the diagram shown here to get the hang of things, and then turn to the other side of the book to get started!